Andrew Ewbank Burn

An Introduction to the Creeds and to the Te Deum

Andrew Ewbank Burn

An Introduction to the Creeds and to the Te Deum

ISBN/EAN: 9783743335813

Manufactured in Europe, USA, Canada, Australia, Japa

Cover: Foto ©ninafisch / pixelio.de

Manufactured and distributed by brebook publishing software (www.brebook.com)

Andrew Ewbank Burn

An Introduction to the Creeds and to the Te Deum

AN INTRODUCTION TO THE CREEDS

AND TO

THE TE DEUM

BY

A. E. BURN, B.D.

TRINITY COLLEGE, CAMBRIDGE
RECTOR OF KYNNERSLEY, WELLINGTON, SALOP
EXAMINING CHAPLAIN TO THE LORD BISHOP OF LICHFIELD

METHUEN & CO.
36 ESSEX STREET, W.C.
LONDON
1899

IN PIAM MEMORIAM
PATRIS IN DEO
IOSEPHI BARBER LIGHTFOOT
EPISCOPI DUNELMENSIS
OPUSCULUM DEDICAUIT
DOMUS ALUMNUS

In Fest. S. Petri mdcccxcviii.

PREFACE

THE following Introduction to the Creeds and to the Early History of the *Te Deum* has been designed, in the first instance, for the use of students reading for the Cambridge Theological Tripos. I have edited all the Creed-forms set for that examination, with the exception of three lengthy formularies, which belong rather to a history of doctrine than to my present subject. These are—the letter of Cyril to Nestorius, the letter of Leo to Flavian, and the Definition of the Council of Chalcedon.

At the same time, I hope that the book may be useful to a wider circle of readers—to clergy and candidates for Holy Orders. The subject is of supreme importance to all teachers of Church doctrine; and the only excuse for adding to the number of books which already deal with it, is the desire to enable others to gather the first-fruits of many writers and of recent researches in England and abroad.

During the past three years I have had the privilege, with the aid of the Managers of the Hort Memorial Fund at Cambridge, of visiting many libraries to collate MSS., and have endeavoured to make good use of the opportunities so kindly offered. In 1896 I visited Leiden, Cologne, Würzburg, Munich, S. Gallen, Karlsruhe, Heidelberg, Wolfenbüttel; in

1897, Amiens, Rouen, Chartres, Orléans, Paris (Bibliothèque Nationale), Troyes (the Town Library and the Treasury of the Cathedral), Rheims; in 1898, Rome (the Vatican Library and the Library of Prince Chigi), the Ambrosian Library at Milan, and the Chapter Library at Vercelli. I desire to express my gratitude for the unfailing courtesy and frequent personal kindness of the Librarians in all these towns.

I have published some of my collations in *The Guardian*, and I beg to thank the proprietors for permission to use articles contributed to their paper on the Athanasian Creed and the *Te Deum*. I have published some "Sermons on the Apostles' Creed" and other notes on creed-forms in the *Zeitschrift für Kirchengeschichte*, xix. Band, 2 Heft, July 1898. I desire to thank Prof. F. Kattenbusch of Giessen for his kind help in translating my English notes into German, as for much information at various times.

The net results of such journeys are not to be measured by the mere storage of new collations in notebooks. So many new avenues of thought are opened out, the imagination is stimulated by the sight of historic buildings and the everlasting hills, knowledge is increased by opportunities of conversation with distinguished scholars.

I must also express my indebtedness to Prof. J. A. Robinson as editor of the *Texts and Studies*, and to the Syndics of the Cambridge University Press for leave to reprint certain pages from my book, *The Athanasian Creed and its Early Commentaries*, on pp. 191 *seq.*, 298–307. My thanks are also due to the Rev. Dr. Robertson, editor of this series; to the Revs. R. Burn, S. C. Freer, J. A. Kempthorne, and J. R. Pyle, for help with the MS. or proofs; and in particular to the Rev. W. G. Clark Maxwell, who has read the proofs throughout. My Chapter on the *Te Deum* is mainly founded on the learned articles of Dom. G. Morin, O.S.B., to whom I am indebted for much information and some valuable collations. I have also acknowledged some interesting suggestions from the Revs. Dr. Gibson and F. E. Brightman.

A kindly French critic [1] of my former book took me to task for "somewhat rash hypotheses." I must plead guilty to the charge of repeating some of those hypotheses, and even of adding to them. Surely it is not possible to make any progress without new hypotheses. The one thing needful is to state the evidence fully enough to serve the critic, who has a better hypothesis to suggest. Such criticism may succeed in altering the historical point of view from which we regard a particular creed; it may change our opinion as to its date or authorship. But it cannot claim to control our conviction as to the truth of the teaching recorded in the Creed, which must rest upon the better foundation of faith. "Eadem tamen quæ didicisti ita doce ut cum dicas noue non dicas noua." [2]

[1] *Revue Critique*, 18th Oct. 1897.
[2] Vincentius, *Commonitorium*, xxvii.

CONTENTS

CHAPTER I
INTRODUCTORY

SEC.   PAGE
- I. Of Method .   1
- II. Of Faith   3

CHAPTER II
"THE FAITH" IN APOSTOLIC TIMES

- I. What we look for in the Epistles of the New Testament . . 8
- II. Four Admitted Epistles of S. Paul 10
- III. The Epistles of his Captivity 13
- IV. The Acts and Pastoral Epistles 14
- V. S. John's Epistles 17
- VI. The Baptismal Formula 20
- VII. Types of Preaching 25
- VIII. The Apostolic Fathers 26
- IX. Conclusions 31

CHAPTER III
THE HISTORIC FAITH IN THE SECOND AND THIRD CENTURIES

- I. A Theory of Growth 33
- II. The Apologists 35
- III. Witnesses to the Old Roman Creed . . . 45
- IV. Was the Old Roman Creed ever Revised ? . . 57
- V. The Date of the Old Roman Creed . . 64
- VI. The Old Creed of Jerusalem . . . 66
- VII. Conclusions 70

CHAPTER IV

THE THEOLOGICAL FAITH OF THE FOURTH CENTURY

SEC.	PAGE
I. Of Theological Creeds	72
II. Arius and Arianism	74
III. The Council of Nicæa in 325	76
IV. "The Fight in the Dark"	81
V. The Council of the Dedication (Second and Fourth Creeds of Antioch)	83
VI. Arianism Supreme	91
VII. Victory in sight	95
VIII. Conclusion	96

CHAPTER V

OUR NICENE CREED

I. The Council of Alexandria	98
II. The Revised Creed of Jerusalem	101
III. The Council of Constantinople	106
IV. The Council of Chalcedon	110
V. Later History: the *Filioque* Clause	114
VI. Conclusions	120

CHAPTER VI

THE ATHANASIAN CREED I

I. Athanasian Faith in the Fifth Century	124
II. Contemporary Professions of Faith	129
III. The Brotherhood of Lerins	134
IV. The Internal Evidence of the *Quicunque*	137
V. Priscillianism	142
VI. Date and Authorship	145

CHAPTER VII

THE ATHANASIAN CREED II

I. The Sermons of Avitus, Cæsarius, and others	150
II. The Canons of Toledo and Autun	153
III. The Trèves Fragment	157
IV. Of Eighth and Ninth Century Quotations	160

CONTENTS

SEC.	PAGE
V. The Early Commentaries	162
VI. Rival Theories of Origin	172
VII. The Later History of the Creed	182
VIII. The Text and a Translation of the *Quicunque*	185

CHAPTER VIII

THE APOSTLES' CREED IN THE FOURTH CENTURY

I. The Old Roman Creed	198
II. Aquileia	201
III. Milan	205
IV. Africa	209
V. Spain	214
VI. Gaul	214

CHAPTER IX

OUR APOSTLES' CREED

I. Gallican Creeds in the Fifth, Sixth, and Seventh Centuries: Salvianus, Faustus, Cæsarius, Cyprian of Toulon, Gregory of Tours, Eligius	221
II. Creeds of the British Church: Pelagius, *Bangor Antiphonary*	228
III. Roman and Italian Creeds: Turin, Ravenna, Rome	230
IV. The Origin of the *Textus receptus* (T)	233

CHAPTER X

UNSOLVED PROBLEMS

I. Bratke's Berne MS.	241
II. The Sermon *Auscultate expositionem*	243
III. The Creed of Damasus	244
IV. The Rhythm of the *Te Deum* and the *Quicunque*	248
V. The Creed of Niceta of Remesiana	252

CHAPTER XI

THE "TE DEUM"

I. MSS. and Quotations	257
II. The Authorship	258
III. The Sources upon which the Author may have drawn	265
IV. The Text	272

CHAPTER XII

OF THE USE OF CREEDS

SEC.		PAGE
I.	Of the Early Use of a Baptismal Creed	280
II.	The History of the term *Symbolum*	282
III.	Our Use of our Apostles' and Nicene Creeds	286
IV.	Our Use of the Athanasian Creed	289

CHAPTER I

INTRODUCTORY

§ I. Of Method.
§ II. Of Faith.

§ I. OF METHOD

IT is a question whether the time has yet come when a complete history of the Apostles' Creed can be written. A standard work on the subject is much needed by our generation. But, in the opinion of some thoughtful writers, the time is not yet ripe. There is much conflicting evidence with respect to the early years of its eventful existence which has to be weighed in the balance. During the past few years great progress has been made. A mass of new material has been collected, and to some extent sifted. We may hope that there is more to come. The third edition of Hahn's *Bibliothek der Symbole*,[1] to name one book only, is a standing monument to the fruitfulness of the labours of Caspari, Heurtley, Kattenbusch, and Swainson. The notes include references to the work of Bäumer and Zahn, while Harnack contributes a valuable appendix in the shape of a revised edition of his treatise on the materials for the history and exposition of the Old Roman Creed from the literature of the two first centuries. Thus this single volume is in itself a vast storehouse of information, tabulated and ready to the hand of the future historian. The task will not be easy, for the mere physical labour of reading the literature on the subject will be appalling. In this respect future students will owe a debt of gratitude to Kattenbusch, whose history of the creed will

[1] Breslau, 1897.

be, when completed, a full introduction to the literature, in addition to its merits as the most elaborate and learned work on the subject. While the main propositions of that book are still *sub iudice*, there is room left for work of a lighter kind. In the following history of the creeds I propose to take a brief survey of the subject. I hope it may be useful to theological students both as a companion to larger works and as a supplement in regard of some sections in which I am able to publish new materials.

Hitherto writers on the Apostles' Creed may have been well advised to begin from the period of its final development, and trace its history backwards from a clearly defined outline to a shadowy image. This method is eminently scientific. We do not want to imagine our facts. But since facts are sometimes stranger than fiction, we ought not to distrust facts merely because they are strange. It is to be feared that some students have an almost unconscious bias against the acknowledging of anything strange which verges on the supernatural. Either miracles are possible or they are not. If not, all vain imaginings to the contrary must be explained away as fast as we find them, picking our way back through the tangled web of Church history. In that case, is it worth while to pursue the study of any creed which contains mention of the resurrection of our Lord? It is well to be candid in these matters. As soon as one begins to thread the mazes of speculation on this subject, it becomes evident that all investigations into the origins of Christian doctrine are motived either by a secret hope or a secret despair.

Neutrality on a matter of such moment to all human souls seems to be impossible. One cannot help being thankful for this. Stormy seas under a darkened sky are better to face than the uncertain perils of calmer waters in a fog. Only in the thick haze of uncertainty is it possible to call darkness light and light darkness, when out of simple confusion of mind we may be led to call all men liars, and find our hope of a credible history vanish like an empty dream. Let us at all costs, if we cannot determine our course, disclose our destination.

As professed scholars of the Eternal Word, incarnate, risen, ascended, it will not be less our duty to present evidence plainly and honestly, nor will it be less obvious if that duty is shirked. While we are collecting our facts, the more scientific method is, doubtless, to proceed from the known to the unknown. But when we come to explain them a theory is necessary, and with any theory an element of uncertainty is introduced. Why then should we not, in presenting our theory, retrace our steps, from the obscure to the obvious, from the days when the currents of Christian life and thought lay unseen beneath the surface of social life, to the days when the persecuted Church of the Catacombs, preserved through that mighty upheaval of ideas which has made our religion dominant in the world's history, found kings to be her nursing fathers and their queens her nursing mothers? I will therefore venture to begin from the beginning, passing from the evidence of the New Testament down to the final and polished forms of our Apostles' and Nicene Creeds, hoping by resolved restraint of language and imagination to commend my theory of their growth. To borrow an illustration from photography. In a clear light the exposure of a plate need only last a moment. In a dull light exposure must be prolonged, and we must be content with less definite outlines. Yet with patience we may hope to reproduce both distance and foreground. By patience we may hope to obtain in our study of "the faith" in apostolic times what above all we need, a sense of perspective, a standard of the relatively great and little thoughts which stirred in the minds of the first Christians. What was the secret of their persistency? What enabled an apostle to write: "This is the victory that overcometh the world, even our faith"?

§ II. OF FAITH

Faith, according to a modern definition, is "thought illuminated by emotion and concentrated by will."[1] It is pre-eminently a personal act, and its proper object is a person.

[1] Bishop Westcott, *The Historic Faith*, p. 7.

Heroes of faith " endure as seeing Him who is invisible." It is an amazing paradox, but it may be illustrated from many records of human friendships. " Seeing is believing" in the sense that to see a friend arrive to our rescue in the moment of peril is the fulfilment of our hope and the justification of our trust in him. But " not seeing is believing " too, if that friend is deemed worthy of our affection. We are ready to say with the Hebrew poet, " Though he slay me, yet will I trust in him." Unforeseen delays, inexperience, overwhelming opposition may combine to frustrate his efforts to bring succour and comfort, yet will we carry our confidence, our love—in one word, our faith in him—down into the grave.

This may seem an extreme test of faith, yet common sense will tell us that it is not unreasonable. And we are concerned to make reasoning an element in the whole act of faith. Without reason, faith degenerates into superstition or credulity; nor are we constrained to contend for it except in its purest type.

The Christian religion differs from all others in this characteristic, that it stands or falls solely according to the measure of faith in its Founder. Buddhism, Confucianism, Mohammedanism, derive their initial influence from the teaching of a man whose whole energy was concentrated upon a form of teaching which he wished to impress on the minds of others. Principles of self-discipline, a code of laws, a burden of prophecy, were the legacies left by the founders of these other religions to their followers. In the religion of Christ all these elements of teaching are indeed combined, but as superstructure, not as the foundation, which is faith in His person.

To support this statement it is not necessary to refer to documents which may be considered of doubtful authenticity. In the admitted epistles of S. Paul, faith in the Christ of the gospel is the starting-point of all his teaching. " Other foundation can no man lay than that is laid, which is Jesus Christ."[1]

The argument may be confirmed by study of the Gospels,

[1] 1 Cor. iii. 11.

but is independent of them, as it is independent of changes in criticism of their dates and authorship. Yet the following expression of opinion is welcome, in witness to the substantial accuracy of the history which their authors relate. " There was a time—the great mass of the public is still living in such a time—in which people felt obliged to regard the oldest Christian literature, including the New Testament, as a tissue of deceptions and falsifications. That time is passed." Again: " A time will come, and it is already drawing near, in which men will not trouble themselves much more about the working out of problems of literary history in the region of primitive Christianity, because whatever can be made out about them will have acquired general assent, namely, the essential accuracy of tradition, with but few important exceptions." [1]

It will be readily admitted that our Lord is represented in the Gospel history as concentrating His attention upon a method not, as we might have expected, of reaching the many, but of training the few. Conversations, sermons, parables, the working of signs, the very journeys which they undertook for Him and with Him, were all made use of for the training of the apostles, till at last they could make the supreme venture of faith and confess Him as the Christ. From the lower level of human friendship they were raised to the plane of worship. Thus it may be truly said that Christ came not so much to preach the gospel, as that there might be a gospel to preach, a gospel of faith in Him.

From these reflections follows an important conclusion. Faith founded on experience must always precede faith formulated. We live first and think afterwards. Christian life must be organised before Christian theology can be thought out. This alone can save theology from becoming a barren system of dogmatic teaching, which, appealing only to the intellectual faculties, would increase knowledge at the expense of faith and love.

This is not a mere axiom of an antiquated type of historical student. We may follow the method of those anthro-

[1] Harnack, *Die Chronologie der altchristlichen Litteratur bis Eusebius*, i. p. viii.

pologists who study the implements of the Stone Age, and when they find themselves baffled by the question how some of these shaped stones were used, seek until in some obscure corner of the globe they find a tribe using such implements to this day, preserving the last relics of a living tradition. We have the records of Christian tradition gathering fulness as the centuries pass; we have the experience of living Christians at our doors. It has been well said that "the Christian religion is one phenomenon—a totality, a whole, of which the New Testament is only a part. We of to-day are in actual contact with a living Christianity, which has persisted through nineteen centuries of human chance and change; and though hindered, now as ever, by schism, treachery, hate, flattery, contempt, presents the same essential features which it presented nineteen centuries ago,—miracles of penitence, miracles of purity, miracles of spiritual power; weakness strengthened, fierceness chastened, passion calmed and pride subdued; plain men and philosophers, cottagers and courtiers, living a new life through the faith that Jesus Christ is God."[1]

From this point of view the position of creeds in the scheme of Christian teaching is easily defined. Some sort of an historic faith, a summary of the Lord's life and teaching, must be included in the training of every catechumen. The ripened believer will ask more — questions must be raised about the relation of the Lord Jesus to the Father and the Holy Spirit. This is the province of reverent theology using metaphysical or psychological terms to aid accurate thinking. Its definitions are useful as a means to detect mistakes, to distinguish, as it were, artificial from natural flowers of Christian thought. That any heresy is an artificial product is only proved by analysis, by argument, not by mere assertion. Christian metaphysic is no more an end in itself than the analysis of good drinking-water. It supports our conviction, that if we drink of the stream when it reaches us, we shall find it not less pure than at the fountainhead. By itself it leaves us thirsty.

[1] Illingworth, *Personality Human and Divine*, pp. 196 f.

It is a mistake to contrast the Sermon on the Mount with the Nicene Creed, to say that the pure Christianity of the one has been overlaid with human inventions in the other. They ought rather to be compared as the description and analysis of the same river of the water of life, flowing on from age to age, an inexhaustible, refreshing stream, freely offered to the thirsty souls of men.

My aim, therefore, is to trace the progress in Christian thought from the simple confession of Jesus as the Lord in the New Testament, to its necessary expansion in the Apostles' Creed and its justification in creeds of the fourth and fifth centuries.

There is great truth in these words of Kattenbusch: "He who brings no questions to the subject will often scarcely mark how fertile it is; he who asks too much easily believes that he receives an answer where in reality silence reigns."[1] I venture to apply them with a somewhat different reference, because I do not believe that we can approach this question from a purely literary standpoint. And what is true of the discussion of a literary question taken alone is equally true of a question in which literary and theological interests are combined. There is some danger lest we should invent explanations of events in past history to correspond to the facts of modern life. But there is far more danger in an attempt to reconstruct the beliefs of the early Christian Church without reference to the fact that the Church exists to-day, and believes that the life of her ascended Lord is still brought near to her in creeds and communicated in sacraments.

[1] *Das ap. Symbol.* ii. p. 25.

CHAPTER II

"THE FAITH" IN APOSTOLIC TIMES

§ I. What we look for in the Epistles of the New Testament.
§ II. Four admitted Epistles of S. Paul.
§ III. The Epistles of his Captivity.
§ IV. The Acts, the Pastoral Epistles.
§ V. S. John's Epistles.
§ VI. The Baptismal Formula.
§ VII. Types of Preaching.
§ VIII. The Apostolic Fathers: Clement, Ignatius, Polycarp (the *Didaché*).
§ IX. Conclusion.

§ I. What we look for in the Epistles of the New Testament

MANY attempts have been made to extract a formal Apostles' Creed from the New Testament by comparison and combination of various passages. However ingenious, they always fail to prove more than this—that there was an outline of teaching ($\tau\acute{\upsilon}\pi o\varsigma\ \delta\iota\delta\alpha\chi\hat{\eta}\varsigma$, Rom. vi. 17) upon which apostolic preachers and writers were agreed. Their message was of Jesus crucified and risen from the dead, of repentance, of baptism for the remission of sins, of faith in His name as the motive power of moral conduct, of confession of that faith as the condition of spiritual health. "For with the heart man believeth unto righteousness, and with the mouth confession is made unto salvation."[1] This was their gospel for the man in the street. Those who followed them, and desired to know more of the mystery of Christ, found that all future

[1] Rom. x. 10.

instruction was based upon this foundation. All that could be told of the life of Jesus of Nazareth, who went about doing good, led up to the supreme act of self-sacrifice on the cross as the highest revelation of Divine love. In this sense it is true that "the cross is the best compendium of the gospel history."[1] It is the keynote of the sermons of S. Peter and S. Paul. When S. Luke wrote for Theophilus "of the things most surely believed among us," he could appeal to his friend's remembrance of catechetical instruction as carrying on echoes of the same deep tone. Through the centuries to come this must be the vantage ground of faith—

"And thou must love me who have died for thee!"

There is no lack of historical illustrations outside the beaten track. The rude caricature of a figure with an ass's head crucified, which was discovered some years ago on the Palatine Hill at Rome, with the rudely traced inscription, "Alexamenos worships his God," witnesses more eloquently than many words to the faith which to the world seemed foolishness, but has outlived the memory of its persecutors.

To Christians the cross was not the symbol of defeat but of victory. They believed that the power of Christ's resurrection gave them courage to seek the fellowship of His sufferings.

I will endeavour to prove that this teaching was summed up in an act of confession of faith which was required from all the baptized, and possessed the character of an historic faith even in its most primitive and simple form, "Jesus is the Lord." Faith in the person of Christ alone leads to belief of His words in the Baptismal Formula: "Go ye therefore, and make disciples of all the nations, baptizing them into the name of the Father, and of the Son, and of the Holy Ghost" (Matt. xxviii. 19). These simplest elements of apostolic preaching are the seed-thoughts out of which grew the later creeds.

[1] Zahn, *Das ap. Symbol.*, 1893, p. 101.

§ II. The Evidence of Admitted Pauline Epistles

Our task is in some ways made easier by the intense glare of criticism which, like a brilliant searchlight, has been cast over every line in early Christian documents. But it is also made more responsible. No chain is stronger than its weakest link. It is therefore advisable to discuss first the evidence of documents of recognised authenticity.

In the four admitted epistles of S. Paul we find stated the whole series of doctrines to which we have referred as the groundwork of apostolic preaching. They would suffice as the basis of all future discussion in this chapter. Their dates are known. They link the generation of Paul of Tarsus to the generation of Ignatius of Antioch. They link the thoughts of men who were contemporaries of the Lord Jesus, with the new thoughts of men who had grown up since the destruction of Jerusalem; when "the sect everywhere spoken against" had made converts even in Cæsar's palace, and planned the evangelisation of the world. These are the Epistles to the Corinthians and Galatians, written, as is generally held, in the year A.D. 57, and the Epistle to the Romans, written in the spring of the following year.

In the words, "No man can say that Jesus is the Lord, save in the Holy Ghost" (1 Cor. xii. 3), faith is traced to its source, and its proper object is stated as a personal act of trust in a Divine person. Yet more clearly is the high aim of faith stated in the earnest exhortation: "If thou shalt confess with thy mouth the Lord Jesus, and shalt believe in thine heart that God hath raised Him from the dead, thou shalt be saved" (Rom. x. 9). There is no limitation here to the fulness of the apostle's Messianic hope. He traces back the prediction of "this word of faith,"[1] which is the staple of his preaching, to the lips of the prophet Joel (chap. ii. 32). He implies that the Lord Jesus is one with the Lord Jehovah, on whose name the prophet bade men call. We may compare the teaching in 1 Cor. i. 2, where he tries to stop

---

[1] Dr. Robertson, *Athanasius*, p. xxii., shows that in this remarkable passage Κύριον Ἰησοῦν = αὐτὸν = Κύριον = יהוה (Joel ii. 32).

THE EARLIEST CONFESSION

1 Cor. xii. 3.	Rom. x. 9.	1 John iv. 15.
A.D. 57.	A.D. 58.	A.D. 80–90.
οὐδεὶς δύναται	ἐὰν ὁμολογήσῃς	ὃς ἐὰν ὁμολογήσῃ
εἰπεῖν	ὅτι	ὅτι
II. 3 [1] Κύριος Ἰησοῦς	II. 3 Κύριος Ἰησοῦς καὶ	Ἰησοῦς [Χριστός] ἐστιν
	πιστεύσῃς ἐν τῇ	ὁ υἱὸς τοῦ Θεοῦ ὁ Θεὸς
	καρδίᾳ σου ὅτι	ἐν αὐτῷ μένει καὶ αὐτὸς
	5 ὁ Θεὸς αὐτὸν ἤγει-	ἐν τῷ Θεῷ.
	ρεν ἐκ νεκρῶν.	
εἰ μ		
III. 9 ἐν πνεύματι		
ἁγίῳ.		

[1] The numerals refer to the numbering of the divisions and clauses of the Apostles' Creed adopted throughout.

factious disputes by reminding the Corinthians of the larger life of Christendom among those who "call upon the name of our Lord Jesus Christ in every place."

Well might he turn upon his foes, found even in "the household of faith," Judaisers among his Galatian converts, with the declaration that his one theme of boasting is "the cross of our Lord Jesus Christ" (Gal. vi. 14). "The rule" by which he exhorted the Galatians to walk (*ibid.* 16) was the confession of faith in Christ crucified, in whom there is neither circumcision nor uncircumcision.

The only formal statement in these passages is the simple confession that "Jesus is the Lord." But the teaching about the life of holiness which He had lived, the institution of the Holy Communion "the same night that He was betrayed," His death and resurrection, leaves out no essential element in the story of the Gospels' evidence, and as such is more valuable, because it assumes that these Churches in Galatia and Corinth and Rome were in possession of the traditional story of the life of Christ. Inferences are drawn which would be utterly unintelligible to us were we not in possession of the key to their explanation.[1]

From these foreshadowings of an historic faith, which give a summary of the teaching about the Lord Jesus, we turn to the theological arguments which the apostle connects with them.

"To us there is one God, the Father, of whom are all things, . . . and one Lord Jesus Christ, by whom are all things" (1 Cor. viii. 6). Our thoughts are led by "the same Spirit," who teaches us to confess "the same Lord," up to faith in "the same God," who worketh all in all (1 Cor. xii. 4–6). The final benediction expresses a similar train of thought: "The grace of our Lord Jesus Christ, and the love of God, and the fellowship of the Holy Ghost, be with you all" (2 Cor. xiii. 13).

Thus we find blended in the teaching of S. Paul the thoughts, which are unfolded in the later Apostles' Creed, of the mystery of Divine life, and of the life which Jesus,

---

[1] Thus Zahn, *op. cit.* p. 64, suggests that Gal. iv. 4, ("born of a woman," in that context implies a reference to the miraculous birth.

the Son of God, lived under human conditions. If all the rest of the New Testament had perished, we might still have pointed to these Epistles to explain alike its Trinitarian framework and its Christological tradition.

§ III. The Epistles of his Captivity

The Epistles to the Philippians, Colossians, and Ephesians, which were written during S. Paul's imprisonment at Rome, cannot be said to add much to our information as to a form of creed which the apostle can be said to have used. There is the constant repetition of the title Lord Jesus Christ to confirm the supposition that this was his one formula. There is the evidence of several Trinitarian sentences, which may be compared with the benediction (2 Cor. xiii. 13), and as clearly point to the words of the Lord in the Baptismal Formula for their origin. As before, he leads the thoughts of his readers up from the "one Spirit," in whom they are united, to the "one Lord" and "one God" and Father of all (Eph. iv. 4–6). Conversely, he gives thanks to "God, the Father of our Lord Jesus Christ," having heard of the "faith" of the Colossians "in Christ Jesus," and their "love in the Spirit" (Col. i. 3, 4, 8). The importance of these epistles consists in the development of S. Paul's Christological teaching, but this belongs to the sphere of dogmatic theology, and we cannot discuss it. Our profound interest is aroused by his teaching of the Gospel of Creation, as we might call it, the eternal purpose of the incarnation, in Col. i. 15–18. That teaching is developed when he writes to the Philippians of the humiliation to which the Son of God must stoop in taking our nature upon Him, his Gospel of the Incarnation (Phil. ii. 5–11). And it is completed in His Gospel of the Ascension, when he writes to the Ephesians (i. 20–23) that He who was nailed to the cross had raised our manhood to the throne of heaven.

"Stone walls do not a prison make, nor iron bars a cage."

The active mind of the apostle had not been warped by

imprisonment, and the justification of the great thoughts which crowded upon him may be found in the moral influence which his epistles exert to this day.

§ IV. The Acts and the Pastoral Epistles

The same keynote is struck in the sermons of S. Peter in the Acts. On the day of Pentecost he assumes that the gift of the Holy Spirit is the fulfilment of the word of the Lord by the same prophet Joel, whose words S. Paul used to emphasise the mystery of Divine life in Christ. He asserts in the same way that Jesus is the Lord, the Christ, whom the Jews crucified, of whose resurrection the apostles are witnesses, who has ascended (Acts ii. 33). On these historical facts he bases an appeal that his hearers should repent and be baptized for the remission of sins. In chapter iii., having laid stress on the same points, the crucifixion and resurrection of Jesus, God's Son, he adds that He will come again. In chapter xiii., S. Paul's sermon at Antioch in Pisidia covers the same ground. A Saviour, Jesus, the Son of God, was crucified, raised, through whom is preached forgiveness of sins. It is interesting to note here the reference to Pilate (ver. 28: "Though they found no cause of death in Him, yet desired they Pilate that He should be slain"), which occurs in one of the four sermons of S. Peter. Apart from the question of the formula used in baptism, which can be discussed separately on its own merits, there can be no doubt as to the Trinitarian belief of the author of the Acts. The whole book has been called "the Gospel of the Holy Spirit."

The Pastoral Epistles add personal touches to this general exhortation of large crowds. S. Paul reminds Timothy (1 Tim. vi. 12) of the confession before many witnesses which he had made, presumably at his baptism. He calls it the beautiful confession ($\kappa\alpha\lambda\dot{\eta}\nu$ $\dot{o}\mu o\lambda o\gamma\acute{\iota}\alpha\nu$) to which Christ Jesus has borne witness before Pontius Pilate, and charges him before God, who quickeneth all things, to keep this commandment undefiled, irreproachable, until the appearing of our Lord Jesus Christ.

This is one of the most important passages in the New Testament, certainly the one most often commented on. Perhaps the simplest explanation of the confession (ὁμολογία) which the Lord witnessed, is to say that it consisted in the avowal that He was a King (John xviii. 36). It may be contrasted with the Baptist's declaration that he himself was not the Christ. The word confession here, as elsewhere, points attention to the fact that He confessed rather than any form of words. The root-idea is that of a transaction.[1]

It is connected by Justin Martyr with the idea of worship (προσκύνησις). This is exactly parallel to the use of S. Paul in Rom. x. 9, when the prophecy quoted leads on to the thought of prayer. In the *Martyrium S. Ignatii*, which is dependent on 1 Tim. vi. 12, ἡ καλὴ ὁμολογία is referred not to the creed, but to the martyrdom of one who witnesses by bloodshedding. It does not seem possible to extract more from the words than that Timothy was to make a similar confession of Christ as King and Lord. Mention of Pilate was included in S. Paul's teaching, not necessarily in his creed.

Again, in the Second Epistle he reminds Timothy (i. 13) of "the form of sound words" which he had taught him. His thoughts seem to pass back from the time of Timothy's ordination to be a herald and teacher of the gospel, and from the perils of present warfare (ii. 3), to the equally troublous times when he himself had been driven from Antioch and Iconium and had come to Lystra (iii. 11), to find this apt pupil so ready to receive instruction. "Hold the pattern of healthful words, which thou hast heard from me, in faith and love which is in Christ Jesus" (i. 13). "Remember (μνημόνευε) Jesus Christ, risen from the dead, of the seed of David, according to my gospel" (ii. 8). He bids him pass on this teaching heard among many witnesses (ii. 2) to faithful men, whom he is to put in remembrance (ὑπομίμνησκε) in his turn (ii. 14). These are explicit references to an outline of teaching which (as we have gathered from the context) had been taught by S. Paul from the beginning of his first missionary journey. It included faith in God, who

[1] Kattenbusch, ii. p. 343, n. 12.

| 1 Tim. vi. 13. | 2 Tim. ii. 8. | 2 Tim. iv. 1. |
| A.D. 67. | A.D. 68. | A.D. 68. |

Παραγγέλλω σοι ἐνώπιον		Διαμαρτύρομαι ἐνώπιον τοῦ Θεοῦ
I. 1. τοῦ Θεοῦ τοῦ ζωοποιοῦντος τὰ πάντα	Μνημόνευε	
II. 2. καὶ Χριστοῦ Ἰησοῦ	Ἰησοῦν Χριστὸν	καὶ Χριστοῦ Ἰησοῦ
4. τοῦ μαρτυρήσαντος ἐπὶ Ποντίου Πιλάτου τὴν καλὴν ὁμολογίαν...	5. ἐγηγερμένον ἐκ νεκρῶν ἐκ σπέρματος Δαυείδ.	
7. μέχρι τῆς ἐπιφανείας τοῦ Κυρίου ἡμῶν Ἰησοῦ Χριστοῦ [1]		8. τοῦ μέλλοντος κρίνειν ζῶντας καὶ νεκρούς, καὶ τὴν ἐπιφάνειαν αὐτοῦ καὶ τὴν βασιλείαν αὐτοῦ.

[1] Cf. vi. 3: Εἴ τις ἑτεροδιδασκαλεῖ, καὶ μὴ προσέρχεται ὑγιαίνουσι λόγοις τοῖς τοῦ Κυρίου ἡμῶν Ἰησοῦ Χριστοῦ.

quickeneth all things, in Christ Jesus, of the seed of David, who suffered under Pontius Pilate, and is coming again to judge the quick and dead.[1]

It is indeed natural that these hints of a form of teaching should be more explicit in letters which refer to Timothy's personal history.

The Epistle to Titus has more general references to "God the Father and the Lord Jesus Christ our Saviour" (i. 4), the glorious appearing of the great God, and our Saviour Jesus Christ, who gave Himself for us (ii. 13, 14). The Holy Spirit is mentioned in connection with baptism (iii. 5), but this passage does not lead to any conclusion as to a Trinitarian form of creed, because the characteristic contrast of the Persons "of God . . . and of Christ Jesus," found in 1 Tim. vi. 13, is lacking.[2]

From these passages it may be gathered that S. Paul's teaching always followed certain lines, but the only trace of a fixed form of confession is the bare "Jesus is the Lord."

§ V. S. John's Epistles

To this primitive form, however, we have testimony from an unexpected quarter, the Eunuch's Confession: "I believe that Jesus is the Son of God," which has been interpolated in the text of Acts viii. 37. It was known to Irenæus in this form.[3] Apparently it represents the form of Baptismal Confession in the Church of Asia Minor, whence Irenæus drew his tradition. And this suggestion is confirmed by the evidence of the Johannine Epistles: "Whosoever confesses that Jesus is the Son of God, God dwelleth in him, and he in God"

---

[1] Zahn, *op. cit.*, p. 40, begging to be excused for the anachronism, calls the former passage *traditio*, the latter *redditio*, of the faith. Undeniably we see here the germ of the later practice, but we must guard against including in S. Paul's Creed all that he desired to teach by way of explanation.

[2] Haussleiter, *Zur Vorgeschichte des ap. Glaubensbekenntnisses*, p. 35, n. 65.

[3] Iren. iii. 12. 8 (p. 485, *ed.* Stieren): "Credo Filium Dei esse Jesum." The Cod. Laudianus (*sæc.* vii.) has "Credo in Christum, Filium Dei" = πιστεύω εἰς τὸν Χριστὸν τὸν υἱὸν τοῦ Θεοῦ, a catena of the twelfth century: πιστεύω τὸν υἱὸν τοῦ Θεοῦ εἶναι Ἰησοῦν Χριστόν.

(1 John iv. 15). "Who is he that overcometh the world, but he that believeth that Jesus is the Son of God?" (1 John v. 5). Haussleiter[1] points out that in the first of these quotations the expression ὃς ἂν ὁμολογήσῃ is to be distinguished from the much more common expression ὃς ὁμολογεῖ (cf. 1 John iv. 2). The aorist tense points to a single definite act, to the confession from which the divine indwelling is dated.

In the second case the context shows the drift of thought. Jesus has been proved to be the Christ historically by (διά) water and blood, His baptism and crucifixion. He now works in the Church, not only in (ἐν) the water of baptism, but also by cleansing in His blood. Thus the writer leads up to the thought of the Baptismal Confession: "This is the victory that overcame (ἡ νικήσασα) the world, even our faith. Who is he that overcometh (νικῶν) the world, but he that believeth that Jesus is the Son of God?" The aorist again points to the single moment of baptism.[2]

The evidence of the Epistle to the Hebrews is of a similar kind. "Having therefore a great high priest, who is passed into the heavens, Jesus the Son of God, let us hold fast our confession" (iv. 14). The other passages in which the author speaks of a confession (ὁμολογία) are less definite. Jesus is called "the Apostle and High Priest of our confession" (iii. 1). This at all events implies confession of Him by this name. And in another passage, where the main thought is still the lifting up of their thoughts to Jesus "within the veil," he bids his hearers hold fast "the confession of their hope" (x. 23).

It seems strange that Kattenbusch[3] should quote these verses to illustrate the use of ὁμολογία in cases where no form was implied. He seems to have in his mind only the form of teaching given to Timothy, which, of course, differs from that before us. It is the parallelism to the Johannine Epistles which redeems it from vagueness.

This simple creed: "I believe that Jesus is the Lord (*or*

---

[1] P. 20.   [2] Cf. Westcott, *Epistles of S. John, ad loc.*
[3] ii. p. 343, n. 12

1 John iv. 15. | 1 John v. 5. | Heb. iv. 14.

ὃς ἐὰν ὁμολογήσῃ ὅτι Ἰησοῦς [Χριστός] ἐστιν ὁ υἱὸς τοῦ Θεοῦ, ὁ Θεὸς ἐν αὐτῷ μένει, καὶ αὐτὸς ἐν τῷ Θεῷ.

τίς ἐστιν [δὲ] ὁ νικῶν τὸν κόσμον, εἰ μὴ ὁ πιστεύων ὅτι Ἰησοῦς ἐστὶν ὁ υἱὸς τοῦ Θεοῦ;

Ἔχοντες οὖν ἀρχιερέα μέγαν, διεληλυθότα τοὺς οὐρανούς, Ἰησοῦν τὸν υἱὸν τοῦ Θεοῦ, κρατῶμεν τῆς ὁμολογίας.

the Son of God)" is the first historic faith of the Church, but it does not stand alone. It leads on our thoughts to the Baptismal Formula.

§ VI. THE BAPTISMAL FORMULA (S. Matt. xxviii. 19)

The early history of the Baptismal Formula is obscure and needs fuller investigation. Some critics have dealt with it capriciously, asserting offhand that it is not a word of the Lord, and that the primitive formula was Christological rather than Trinitarian—"in the name of Jesus (or the Lord Jesus)." They appeal to the following passages: Acts ii. 38, viii. 16, x. 48, xix. 5; Rom. vi. 3; Gal. iii. 27. Further, they maintain that this more primitive formula lasted on till the days of Cyprian (*Ep.* 73), though it was eventually superseded.

We are free to discuss this as a question of literary history without dogmatic bias, because theologians of unimpeachable repute, from S. Ambrose to Thomas Aquinas, have maintained that the two formulæ were equally orthodox. Irenæus himself has said: "In Christi enim nomine subauditur qui unxit et ipse qui unctus est et ipsa unctio in qua unctus est."[1] And Ambrose[2] follows on the same lines. On the other hand, critics writing from a Unitarian standpoint have interpreted the Trinitarian formula as expressing faith in God, in Jesus, and the gift of an impersonal Spirit.

It seems strange that the text of S. Matthew does not show any unsettlement in MSS. or Versions if xxviii. 19 did not form part of primitive oral teaching. It has been suggested[3] that "into the name of the Son" stood at first alone, and has been added to in the same way as the form of the Lord's prayer given in its shortest form in S. Luke has been enlarged. As regards some of the added words in the Lord's prayer, there is no difficulty in supposing that the Lord Himself gave it in a longer and shorter form, the outline remaining unchanged. As regards the doxology, which is traced to the liturgical use of the prayer, and was added to

---

[1] *Adv. hæres.* iii. 18. 3 (p. 519, *ed.* Stieren). [2] *De Spu. Sco.* i. 4. 43.
[3] Haussleiter, *op. cit.*

be as it were the Church's thanksgiving for the prayer, there is marked unsettlement in the texts of both Gospels. Perhaps the earliest witness to it outside the New Testament is the Old Roman Creed itself, which, as we shall see, may be dated with some confidence from the year A.D. 100.

The *Didaché* shows dependence on the Gospel of S. Matthew at other points, so that it is not worth while in this connection to contend for an earlier date than A.D. 120. It has in c. 7 : " Now concerning baptism, baptize thus : Having first taught all these things, baptize ye into the name of the Father, and of the Son, and of the Holy Ghost, in living water. And if thou hast not living water, baptize into other water ; and if thou canst not in cold, then in warm (water). But if thou hast neither, pour (water) thrice upon the head into the name of the Father, and of the Son, and of the Holy Ghost." In c. 9 we find the direction : " Let none eat or drink of your Eucharist, except those baptized into the name of the Lord." Here the writer seems to think rather of the new relationship into which the baptized is brought than of any form of words used.

The evidence of Justin Martyr (*Apol.* i. 61) is no less definite, to the effect that the act of baptism was done " in the name of the Father of all things and our Lord God, and our Saviour Jesus Christ, and the Holy Spirit."

On the other hand, all the references to baptism in (or into) the name of the Lord Jesus might refer either to the confession made by the baptized or to the new relationship to Christ into which they were brought on becoming His members.

There are two prepositions used. " In " ($\dot{\epsilon}\nu$) refers to the sphere of remission of sins wrought by the power of the name of Christ, as the sick were healed by His name. This is S. Peter's word in Acts ii. 38 and x. 48. " Into " ($\epsilon\dot{\iota}\varsigma$) denotes purpose, the desire to bring the baptized within the range of that power. The disciples of John, whom S. Paul met at Ephesus (Acts xix. 3), told him that they had been baptized " into ($\epsilon\dot{\iota}\varsigma$) the baptism of John." This does not mean that John used the formula,

"I baptize into the name of John." We gather from S. Paul's reply that he said "for repentance." The disciples of John seem to have confessed themselves such, just as Corinthian partisans labelled themselves disciples of Cephas or another. We do not need to suppose that S. Paul's words to them (1 Cor. i. 12–15) imply that they baptized into the name of Cephas or Apollos, or Christ or Paul. Why should not the words which follow, "they were baptized into the name of the Lord Jesus," refer to their confession that they would now be Jesus's disciples? The fact that S. Paul took pains to instruct them about the Holy Spirit seems to imply some mention of His work in the form used (*i.e.* the Trinitarian formula?).

The other passages generally quoted in this connexion refer obviously to the benefit of baptism, the death unto sin in Rom. vi. 3: "Know ye not, that as many of us as were baptized into Christ [Jesus] were baptized into His death?" and the life into righteousness in Gal. iii. 27: "As many of you as were baptized into Christ put on Christ."

Such arguments by themselves would appear inconclusive, if we could not appeal to an unbroken traditional use of the Trinitarian formula, witnessed to by Justin Martyr, Irenæus, and Tertullian.

Attention has been called to the sevenfold vow of renunciation of various kinds of sin which a conservative sect, the Elchasaites, made the candidate promise.[1] It does not follow that they did not, like ourselves, add a vow of faith. We know so little about them that we may well be cautious in arguing from their practice as to the practice of the Catholic Church, which it might resemble as little as the peculiar ceremonies of the Salvation Army.

This brings us to the letter of Cyprian to Jubaianus (*Ep.* 73) on the rebaptism of heretics in the year A.D. 256. This is made the court of final appeal in this question, because it is argued that we have here proof that the practice of baptizing "in the name of the Lord" still lasted on in the Church. The question has been discussed most thoroughly by the late

---

[1] *Ap.* Hippolytus, ix. 15. Hatch, *Hibbert Lectures*, p. 337.

Archbishop Benson in his book on Cyprian. He writes: "There seem to have been in Africa some who understood baptism 'in the name of Christ' to be sufficient without the Trinal Invocation. This was evidently very rare, if ever it was more than an exception."[1]

There is an important document to be read with Cyprian's letter, the anonymous tract "On Rebaptism,"[2] an able statement of the Catholic case against Cyprian. This was possibly the actual enclosure sent by Jubaianus to which Cyprian replies. The author does not say a word about any section of the Church as using any but the Trinal Invocation, which is not only "true and right, and by all means to be observed in the Church," but is "also wont to be observed." It is for heretical, not orthodox, baptism "in the name of Jesus" that he pleads that "it might have a sort of initial virtue capable of subsequent completion."

The same view was maintained by Stephen, Bishop of Rome, in the "one harped-on quotation," which we find in the letter of Cyprian to Jubaianus (*Ep.* 73), and in the letter of Firmilian (*Ep.* 75). "Those who are wheresoever and howsoever baptized in the name of Jesus Christ obtain grace of baptism." "Stephen uses 'baptized *in the Name of Christ*' in the New Testament sense as equivalent to Christian baptism." He illustrates the use from the passage of Origen quoted above, and asserts that Firmilian expressly assumes (*Ep.* 75. 11) that Stephen would require the *Symbolum Trinitatis*, even though his principles would (as he supposes) allow, if it were correct in that point and in the interrogations, a baptism by a demoniac or a demon.

It is quite clear that the question at issue between Stephen and Cyprian was not one of comparing the value of two forms, but rather whether a schismatic person can baptize. The less is included in the greater. Since Cyprian denied the validity of heretical baptism under any circumstances, it was useless to discuss any question of forms. But

[1] P. 405.
[2] Printed by Routh, *Rel. Sacr.* v. 291. The only MS. known, formerly at Rheims, has now disappeared. I spent some time looking for it in May 1897.

the latter appears as a subordinate question of exegesis. Cyprian admits that the apostles baptized "in the name of Christ" only. But he assumes that this was only practised in the case of Jews who already confessed the Father. For the Gentiles, the Lord ordained that they should be baptized *in plena et adunata Trinitate* (*Ep.* 73. 18). Therefore it is too much to say that, "had he conceived 'baptism in Christ's name' to imply the disregard of Christ's 'form,' he would have been armed with an argument against Stephen which he could not have failed to use."[1]

Who, then, were the heretics whom the author of the tract "On Rebaptism," and possibly Stephen also, had in mind as baptizing "in the name of Christ," whose baptism Cyprian would reject (to use a modern term) on the ground of "intention" rather than of form? Obviously the Marcionites. Cyprian (*Ep.* 73. 4) says that the epistle sent him by Jubaianus made mention of Marcion, "saying that not even such as came from him were to be baptized, as appearing to have been already baptized in the name of Jesus Christ." Indignantly he denies that the faith with Marcion is the same as with the Church. If Marcion baptized with the Lord's own words, he would not hold the same Trinity as we (c. 6). The case of those baptized in Samaria is quite different, since they were baptized within the Church (c. 8). It appears from these words that Marcion and his followers used the form "in the name of Christ." This was quite in accord with the special variations which Marcion thought fit to introduce into his system. Above all, in his interpretation of Scripture was he a literalist, and in such parts of S. Paul's writings as he accepted he would find support of texts, like Rom. vi. 3, for his new form. Neither Cyprian nor the Roman theologians had a better exegesis to offer. They could only point to the common practice of the Church, and explain the apostles' divergent practice as due to special circumstances.

It is not claimed that this explanation solves all difficulties, and it is not likely that much fresh light will ever be

[1] Benson, p. 407.

thrown upon the question. The "charity which hopeth all things" leads theologians to accept baptism "in the name of Christ," but they do not thereby commit themselves to the position that it must be considered the primitive form, or that its use must be supposed to have been of more than sporadic growth, beginning and ending with the Marcionites at this period, as with the Bulgarians in the ninth century.

In the Acts of Barnabas—a Gnostic document of the second century—occurs the phrase, $\beta a \pi \tau i \zeta o \mu a \iota$ $\epsilon i \varsigma$ $\tau \grave{o}$ $\ddot{o} \nu o \mu a$ $\tau o \hat{v}$ $\kappa v \rho i o v$. This seems to be the earliest witness to the Gnostic practice. It derives some confirmation from the elaborate description of the ceremonies of initiation among the Gnostics, which is given by Irenæus.

§ VII. Types of Preaching

Before leaving the New Testament, it may be well to turn for a moment to some set types of teaching and preaching which may be distinguished from those quoted above. We may conveniently follow Harnack's methodical classification.[1] Thus we find teaching cast (*a*) in the form of a chronicle (Mark xvi. 9 ff.), or (*b*) in the form of a chronicle with short proofs (1 Cor. xv.). (*c*) Sometimes the writer represents his teaching as the fulfilment of prophecy (2 Pet. i. 19). Again, we find the scheme moulded (*d*) on the antithesis $\kappa a \tau \grave{a}$ $\sigma \acute{a} \rho \kappa a$—$\kappa a \tau \grave{a}$ $\pi \nu \epsilon \hat{v} \mu a$ (1 Pet. iii. 18), where the apostle has instruction of candidates for baptism in his mind. After speaking of Christ's suffering for sins, the Just for the unjust, thus founding his message on the cross, he contrasts the death in the flesh with the quickening in the spirit, speaks of the preaching to the spirits in prison and of the salvation of Noah's family in the ark as a type of baptism, leading up to the mention of "the question and answer ($\dot{\epsilon} \pi \epsilon \rho \acute{\omega} \tau \eta \mu a$) of a good conscience toward God through the resurrection of Jesus Christ, who is on the right hand of God, having gone into heaven." (*e*) Another setting is

[1] Hahn,[3] p. 364; and PRE,[3] Art. "ap. Symbolum."

moulded on the thoughts of the First and the Second Coming (2 Tim. iv. 1), when the apostle charges Timothy thus: "I testify in the sight of God, and of Jesus Christ, who shall judge the quick and dead, both of His appearing and His kingdom." (*f*) Lastly, a passage like Eph. iv. 9 is moulded on the scheme καταβάς—ἀναβάς: "Now this, He ascended, what is it but that He also descended (first ?) into the lower parts of the earth ? He that descended is the same also that ascended far above all the heavens, that He might fill all things."

With these quotations we may fairly be said to have exhausted the list of New Testament passages which are in any way parallel to a formal creed. Looked at all round, they show how unsafe it is to classify scriptural names for creeds, which are purely general—"the form of teaching," "the faith," "the deposit." They might be applied to any of these schemes. There are two in the Epistle to the Hebrews, which we have not noted. Heb. vi. 1, "the word of the beginning of Christ," explains the fulfilment of the Messianic prophecies in Jesus of Nazareth. It is to be compared with the phrase in Heb. v. 12, "the beginning of the oracles of God," which refers to the records in which the Messiah is foreshown.[1] These might serve as titles for a Christian apology, but not for a creed.

§ VIII. The Apostolic Fathers

We turn now to the writings of the so-called Apostolic Fathers, pupils and successors of the apostles.

Clement, Bishop of Rome, wrote an Epistle to the Corinthians, which gives a charming impression of the writer's character, his sweet reasonableness (ἐπιείκεια), but does not throw much light on our subject. There is no reference to a confession or creed, but there are two explicit statements of faith in the Trinity which express his consciousness of the distinctions between the Divine Persons. "Have we not one God and one Christ and one Spirit of grace,

[1] Westcott, *ad loc.*

which was poured out upon us?" (1 Cor. xlvi. 6). "As God lives, and the Lord Jesus Christ lives, and the Holy Spirit, the faith and hope of the elect" (*ib.* lviii. 2). "Is it not fair to say that he claims for the Son and the Spirit a personal life, which is not absolutely identified with the life of the Father, and yet is understood to be Divine?"[1]

A more important witness is Ignatius, the martyr-bishop of Antioch, whose letters, while they breathe a fiery enthusiasm, a passion to dare and suffer, teach "a theology wonderfully mature in spite of its immaturity," and an outline of historic faith exactly parallel to the teaching of S. Paul, who started from this same Antioch on his first missionary journey sixty years before.

To the Ephesians, c. 18 : "For our God, Jesus the Christ, was conceived in the womb by Mary, according to a dispensation, of the seed of David, but also of the Holy Ghost; and He was born and was baptized, that by His passion He might cleanse water."

To the Trallians, c. 9 : " Be ye deaf therefore, when any man speaketh to you apart from Jesus Christ, who was of the race of David, who was the Son of Mary, who was truly born and ate and drank, was truly persecuted under Pontius Pilate, was truly crucified and died in the sight of those in heaven and those on earth and those under the earth ; who, moreover, was truly raised from the dead, His Father having raised Him, who in the like fashion will so raise us also who believe on Him—His Father, I say, will raise us—in Christ Jesus, apart from whom we have not true life."

To the Smyrnæans, c. 1 : " I have perceived that ye are established in faith immovable, being as it were nailed on the cross of the Lord Jesus Christ, in flesh and in spirit, and firmly grounded in love in the blood of Christ, fully persuaded as touching our Lord that He is truly of the race of David according to the flesh, but Son of God by the Divine will and power, truly born of a virgin and baptized by John, that *all righteousness might be fulfilled* by Him, truly nailed up in the flesh for our sakes under Pontius Pilate and Herod the

[1] Swete, *The Apostles' Creed,* pp. 31 f.

tetrarch (of which fruit are we—that is, of His most blessed passion); that *He might set up an ensign* unto all the ages through His resurrection, for His saints and faithful people, whether among Jews or among Gentiles, in one body of His Church."

An interesting point is his use of the Pauline phrase " of the seed of David." It would be a necessary element in the first preaching to the Jews, but in the next generation dropped out of the creed of the Church, which was predominatingly Gentile.

I have not attempted to piece together a complete creed on the model of the later historic faith from all the passages in the Ignatian Epistles.[1] There is no need to strain the evidence. It concerns us only to know that Ignatius expressed his faith in the Trinity, in the Son and in the Father and in the Spirit (*ad Magn.* 13), in the same order as S. Paul uses 2 Cor. xiii. 13, which is, as Lightfoot shows, "a natural sequence. Through the *Son* is the way to the *Father* (John xiv. 6): this union with the Father through the Son is a communion in the *Spirit*."[2]

For the same reason we will not linger over the Christological teaching, in which Ignatius seems almost to anticipate Athanasius by his clear-cut antitheses (*ad Eph.* 7) : " There is one only physician, of flesh and of spirit, begotten and unbegotten, God in man, true Life in death, Son of Mary and Son of God, first passible and then impassible, Jesus Christ our Lord."

These are ante-Nicene phrases, and there is no advantage in trying to read into them the precise meanings of post-Nicene statements. It is, after all, natural to leave room for growth and development.

From Ignatius we turn to his friend and pupil, Polycarp, the pupil also in earlier days of the Apostle John. Polycarp

---

[1] Kattenbusch has expressed his conclusion clearly (ii. p. 318), where he says that Ignatius is formally dependent on himself alone, and that the parallels to the Old Roman Creed are accidental, except so far as they are in content unavoidable. See the note 81.

[2] *Apost. Fathers*, II. ii. 137 n.

IGNATIUS OF ANTIOCH (c. 110)

To the Ephesians, c. xviii.

ὁ γὰρ Θεὸς ἡμῶν Ἰησοῦς ὁ Χριστὸς ἐκυοφορήθη ὑπὸ Μαρίας κατ' οἰκονομίαν, ἐκ σπέρματος μὲν Δαυεὶδ πνεύματος δὲ ἁγίου· ὃς ἐγεννήθη καὶ ἐβαπτίσθη ἵνα τῷ πάθει τὸ ὕδωρ καθαρίσῃ.

To the Trallians, c. ix.

Κωφώθητε οὖν, ὅταν ὑμῖν χωρὶς Ἰησοῦ Χριστοῦ λαλῇ τις, τοῦ ἐκ γένους Δαυείδ, τοῦ ἐκ Μαρίας, ὃς ἀληθῶς ἐγεννήθη, ἔφαγέν τε καὶ ἔπιεν, ἀληθῶς ἐδιώχθη ἐπὶ Ποντίου Πιλάτου, ἀληθῶς ἐσταυρώθη καὶ ἀπέθανεν βλεπόντων[τῶν] ἐπουρανίων καὶ ἐπιγείων καὶ ὑποχθονίων, ὃς καὶ ἀληθῶς ἠγέρθη ἀπὸ νεκρῶν, ἐγείραντος αὐτὸν τοῦ πατρὸς αὐτοῦ, κατὰ τὸ ὁμοίωμα ὃς καὶ ἡμᾶς τοὺς πιστεύοντας αὐτῷ οὕτως ἐγερεῖ ὁ πατὴρ αὐτοῦ ἐν Χριστῷ Ἰησοῦ, οὗ χωρὶς τὸ ἀληθινὸν ζῆν οὐκ ἔχομεν.

To the Smyrnæans, c. i.

ἐνόησα γὰρ ὑμᾶς κατηρτισμένους ἐν ἀκινήτῳ πίστει, ὥσπερ καθηλωμένους ἐν τῷ σταυρῷ τοῦ Κυρίου Ἰησοῦ Χριστοῦ, σαρκί τε καὶ πνεύματι, καὶ ἡδρασμένους ἐν ἀγάπῃ ἐν τῷ αἵματι Χριστοῦ, πεπληροφορημένους εἰς τὸν Κύριον ἡμῶν ἀληθῶς ὄντα ἐκ γένους Δαυεὶδ κατὰ σάρκα, υἱὸν Θεοῦ κατὰ θέλημα καὶ δύναμιν, γεγεννημένον ἀληθῶς ἐκ παρθένου, βεβαπτισμένον ὑπὸ Ἰωάννου ἵνα ΠΛΗΡΩΘῌ ΠᾶϹΑ ΔΙΚΑΙΟϹΎΝΗ ὑπ' αὐτοῦ, ἀληθῶς ἐπὶ Ποντίου Πιλάτου καὶ Ἡρώδου τετράρχου καθηλωμένον ὑπὲρ ἡμῶν ἐν σαρκί· ἀφ' οὗ καρποῦ ἡμεῖς ἀπὸ τοῦ θεομακαρίστου αὐτοῦ πάθους· ἵνα ἄΡΗ ϹΎϹ-CΗΜΟΝ εἰς τοὺς αἰῶνας διὰ τῆς ἀναστάσεως εἰς τοὺς ἁγίους καὶ πιστοὺς αὐτοῦ, εἴτε ἐν Ἰουδαίοις εἴτε ἐν ἔθνεσιν, ἐν ἑνὶ σώματι τῆς ἐκκλησίας αὐτοῦ.

was a man of very different mould, unoriginal in the extreme, but on that very account a better witness to the tradition, which it was his to pass on from the first generation of Christian hearers to the third. He is the link between S. John and the young generation of Christian apologists, Justin Martyr, Melito, Aristides, who were coming to the front when he paid his historic visit to Rome and celebrated the Holy Communion for Bishop Anicetus. At that time Irenæus, his old pupil in Asia Minor, was beginning to attract attention by his lectures on heresies in this capital of the Old World, the centre of its commerce and of its speculations. Writing to the Philippians, Polycarp lays stress (c. 2) on the resurrection of Jesus Christ from the dead, in words taken from the First Epistle of S. Peter. This was part of his teaching, but there is no proof that his confession included more than we have gleaned from the First Epistle of S. John. In c. 7 he urges confession of Jesus Christ come in the flesh, and the witness of the cross, in words which are an echo of 1 John iv. 2-4.

Polycarp's death in A.D. 155 marks the close of the apostolic age. He had lived on past the day of small things, to see the Catholic Church exerting a world-wide influence, and to testify that this influence stands or falls with loyalty to the faith of Christ.

Something remains to be said about the Didaché, to which reference has been made more than once. Without attempting to review the reviews of the many theories as to its origin and history, I will only claim for it the date defended by Lightfoot[1] and Zahn[2]—A.D. 80-130. It seems to be a Jewish manual of advice on conduct worked up by a Christian writer, who records details of value as to the administration of Holy Baptism. It belongs to a period of undeveloped Church organisation, and the only trace of a formal creed contained in the reference to those baptized into the name of the Lord (c. 9) agrees with the early Pauline confession.

The prayer (c. x. 2): "We thank thee, Holy Father, . . . for the knowledge and faith and immortality which

[1] *S. Ignatius*, i. 739.   [2] *Forschungen*, iii. 278.

Thou hast made known to us through Jesus Thy servant," seems to contain a reminiscence of S. Peter's sermon (Acts iii. 13, 26) or the prayer (Acts iv. 27, 30).

§ IX. CONCLUSIONS

We arrive at the conclusion that the so-called Apostles' Creed did not exist in apostolic times. At the same time, we are free to admit that the substance of its teaching was primitive. The Ignatian Epistles, which form the connecting-link between the Pastoral Epistles and the apologists of the second century, prove that instruction was given in Antioch on all the points characteristic of the teaching of the developed creed, the miraculous birth, the crucifixion, the resurrection. The following reconstruction of an Apostolic Creed,[1] while it represents the general teaching of the first decade of the second century, is obtained by arbitrary selection of phrases:—

FOR JEWISH CHRISTIANS.

I. Πιστεύω εἰς (πρὸς) Θεὸν (πατέρα) παντοκράτορα.
II. Καὶ εἰς τὸν υἱὸν Θεοῦ Ἰησοῦν Χριστὸν τὸν κύριον ἡμῶν, κατὰ σάρκα ἐκ γένους (σπέρματος) Δαβίδ, κατ' οἰκονομίαν (or θέλημα or δύναμιν) Θεοῦ γεννηθέντα (or γεγεννημένον) ἐκ (ὑπὸ) Μαρίας τῆς παρθένου, βεβαπτισμένον ὑπὸ Ἰωάννου, ἀληθῶς ἐπὶ Ποντίου Πιλάτου (παθόντα) σταυρωθέντα καὶ ἀποθανόντα· Ὃς ἀληθῶς ἠγέρθη ἀπὸ νεκρῶν, ἀνέβη (ἀνελήφθη) εἰς οὐρανούς, ἐκάθισεν ἐν δεξιᾷ τοῦ Θεοῦ, ὃς ἔρχεται κρῖναι (or κριτής) ζῶντας καὶ νεκροὺς (ζώντων καὶ νεκρῶν).

FOR GENTILE CHRISTIANS.

I. Πιστεύω εἰς ἕνα Θεὸν παντοκράτορα
II. Καὶ (or πιστεύω) εἰς ἕνα υἱὸν Θεοῦ Ἰησοῦν Χριστὸν, κύριον ἡμῶν,

γεννητὸν ἐκ (or διὰ) παρθένου καὶ Θεοῦ (or ἁγίου πνεύματος)

τὸν ἐπὶ Ποντίου Πιλάτου σταυρωθέντα, κ.τ.λ.

---

[1] Bäumer, p. 156.

AN INTRODUCTION TO THE CREEDS

For Jewish Christians—*contd.*   For Gentile Christians—*contd.*

III. Καὶ (πιστεύω) εἰς τὸ (or ἐν)   III.
πνεῦμα ἅγιον, ἁγίαν ἐκκλησίαν
(καθολικὴν) ἄφεσιν (λύτρωσιν)
ἁμαρτιῶν, σαρκὸς ἀνάστασιν
(ζωὴν αἰώνιον).

It is interesting to contrast Harnack's reconstruction of "an oldest creed," which he is careful to explain "is not a creed that was ever used or ever likely to be used."[1]

Πιστεύω εἰς (ἕνα) Θεὸν παντοκράτορα, καὶ εἰς Χριστὸν Ἰησοῦν, τὸν υἱὸν αὐτοῦ, τὸν κύριον ἡμῶν, τὸν γεννηθέντα διὰ (ἐκ) παρθένου, τὸν ἐπὶ Ποντίου Πιλάτου παθόντα (σταυρωθέντα) καὶ ἀναστάντα (ἐκ νεκρῶν), καθήμενον ἐν δεξιᾷ τοῦ Θεοῦ, ὅθεν (ἐν δόξῃ) ἔρχεται κρῖναι ζῶντας καὶ νεκρούς, καὶ εἰς τὸ πνεῦμα ἅγιον [*sic*].

The utter uncertainty of all such speculations may leave us content with the moderate anticipations with which we approached the evidence, expecting only to find seed-thoughts, and finding them in the Baptismal Formula and the simple confession, "Jesus is the Lord." At first hearing, such conclusions may sound thin and poor, but we may well ask seriously whether we have any right to expect more. If the growth of the kingdom is compared by Christ to the growth of a seed growing secretly, we must expect to find the early history of creeds obscure. The seed of a garden plant contains in it the promise of bud and flower, but it is only through the hidden working and secret chemistry of nature that it is transformed. To look, then, for the twelve articles of the Apostles' Creed in the New Testament, is like looking for the sprouting of a seed while we keep it in a paper packet.

[1] Hahn,[3] p. 390.

CHAPTER III

THE HISTORIC FAITH IN THE SECOND AND THIRD CENTURIES

§ I. A Theory of Growth.
§ II. The Apologists:
    1. Justin Martyr.
    2. Aristides.
    3. Irenæus.
§ III. Witnesses to the Old Roman Creed:
    1. Marcellus and Rufinus.
    2. Novatian, Dionysius, Cyprian.
    3. Tertullian.
§ IV. Was the Old Roman Creed ever revised?
§ V. The Date of the Old Roman Creed.
§ VI. The Old Creed of Jerusalem.
§ VII. Conclusions.

§ I. A Theory of Growth

Thus far we have watched only what we might call the planting of the creed. The faith of the gospel was preached by the apostles in outlines of teaching, which were like seeds, buried that they might spring up and bear fruit.

The preaching of S. Paul to the Churches of Corinth and Rome was echoed by Clement. The solemn charge in the Epistles to Timothy rang also in the ears of Ignatius. We shall trace the influence of this Pauline form of sound words in the history of the venerable Old Roman Creed (R).

This creed of the future was of composite structure. The Baptismal Formula was its framework, but it gained from the added confession of Jesus as the Lord, born, suffering, dying—thoughts which from the first craved for utterance and fired enthusiasm. By a natural sequence of thought, mention was also added of the work of the Holy Spirit alike in the Holy Church and for the individual believer.

Side by side with it must be set the most ancient short Creed of Jerusalem, the origin of which may possibly be sought in the preaching of S. Peter on the day of Pentecost. To the Baptismal Formula were added only the words, "one baptism for the remission of sins." At a later period it too was enlarged on similar lines, either from current teaching or from the Roman Creed.

Thus we shall trace the growth of its usefulness, first as an historic faith, the rule of a catechist's teaching; then as a theological faith, the watchword of a Church militant against error. The chief difficulty in tracing out a history of development after this kind is to avoid an *a priori* and mechanical theory of two parallel types in East and West, or of one archetype from which all forms are to be derived, as if it was a mould into which they could be pressed. We expect to find frequent variations in the creeds of Churches successively organised, and we have no right to suppose that they can all be explained in one way. When we come to the most difficult stage of our inquiry, the transition from the testimony of individual writers to the acknowledged creed of a Church, it is so easy to strain the evidence, and compile, by a too arbitrary critical process, a Creed of Antioch gleaned from Ignatius, or a Creed of Ephesus from Justin Martyr, or a Creed of Gaul from Irenæus.

I have endeavoured to approach the testimony of the writers of the second century with an open mind. The period is obscure, because so many documents have perished. This is the result of devastating wars and of persecutions in which Christian books were destroyed.

Hence arose the fear of committing precious beliefs to writing, which lasted on, as we shall see, to the fourth century. So it comes to pass that the earliest forms of complete Church creeds which we can identify with certainty are only found in writings of the fourth century, when Christianity became a permitted religion, and Christian books were brought out freely to the light of day. It may be questioned whether the reserve which, in the course of the era of persecution, Christian teachers were constrained to maintain, was felt to be as important in the second century. Justin Martyr does not seem to speak so cautiously as Cyril of Jerusalem. Yet he wrote at a time when the coarse hatred of the world had already raised fierce persecutions against the new religion, with its unbending morality and unflinching protest against wickedness in all places. Even a tolerant philosopher like Marcus Aurelius might fear social dangers from the rapid increase of close guilds of Christians, acting as a solvent upon a corrupt civilisation which despised itself and suspected others.

§ II. The Apologists: 1. Justin Martyr

Justin Martyr, a native of Palestine, was the son of heathen parents, and in his early manhood an ardent student of the Platonic philosophy. When "the gates of light," to use his own beautiful phrase, "were opened to him," and he became a scholar of Christ, he devoted himself to the work of presenting, in a form which might attract thoughtful men, the truth which had brought him peace and joy. He taught in Ephesus, where he was probably baptized, and also in Rome, where he suffered martyrdom (c. 165).

The evidence of his writings is suggestive. It cannot be called complete. In fact, it is very puzzling to any who try to make too much of it. We may classify the passages quoted under two heads: (a) Expansions of the Baptismal Formula; (β) Specimens of Christological teaching.

When Justin speaks of baptism, he states definitely that instruction was given to the candidates, and that a promise was required from them (*Apol.* i. 61): "As many as are persuaded and believe that these things are true which are taught and said by us, and promise that they can live thus, are taught both to pray, and to ask from God with fasting forgiveness of their former sins." The teaching may have varied, as in Justin's varying expansions of the Baptismal Formula. But the substance of the teaching plainly included two points which it is well to emphasise. The Lord Jesus was worshipped (*Dial.* 38): εἶτα ἄνθρωπον γενόμενον, σταυρωθῆναι, καὶ ἀναβεβηκέναι εἰς τὸν οὐρανὸν, καὶ πάλιν παραγίνεσθαι ἐπὶ τῆς γῆς, καὶ προσκυνητὸν εἶναι. This is a charge put into the mouth of Trypho, but it is at once accepted by the apologist. And the Holy Spirit was asserted to possess a distinct individuality (*Dial.* 36): καὶ ἀποκρίνεται αὐτοῖς τὸ πνεῦμα τὸ ἅγιον ἢ ἀπὸ προσώπου τοῦ πατρὸς ἢ ἀπὸ τοῦ ἰδίου.

JUSTIN MARTYR
(a) *Expansions of the Baptismal Formula*

Apol. i. 61.   *ib. ad fin.*

Ὅσοι ἂν πεισθῶσι καὶ πιστεύωσιν ἀληθῆ ταῦτα τὰ ὑφ' ἡμῶν διδασκόμενα καὶ λεγόμενα εἶναι, καὶ βιοῦν οὕτως δύνασθαι ὑπισχνῶνται, εὔχεσθαί τε καὶ αἰτεῖν νηστεύοντες παρὰ τοῦ Θεοῦ τῶν προημαρτημένων ἄφεσιν διδάσκονται, ἡμῶν συνευχομένων καὶ συννηστευόντων αὐτοῖς...

Ἐπ' ὀνόματος γὰρ τοῦ Πατρὸς τῶν ὅλων καὶ Δεσπότου Θεοῦ, καὶ τοῦ Σωτῆρος ἡμῶν Ἰησοῦ Χριστοῦ, καὶ Πνεύματος ἁγίου, τὸ ἐν τῷ ὕδατι τότε λουτρὸν ποιοῦνται.

Τὸ τοῦ Πατρὸς τῶν ὅλων καὶ Δεσπότου Θεοῦ ὄνομα.... Καὶ ἐπ' ὀνόματος δὲ Ἰησοῦ Χριστοῦ τοῦ σταυρωθέντος ἐπὶ Ποντίου Πιλάτου, καὶ ἐπ' ὀνόματος Πνεύματος ἁγίου... ὁ φωτιζόμενος λούεται.

Justin's Christological teaching is found in some five different references to (*a*) general teaching on the Incarnation, (*b*) the fulfilment of prophecy, (*c*) (*d*) the history of the Lord Jesus, (*e*) a prayer of exorcism, (*f*) an Old Testament type. These passages show marked variations from the text of R. The order "Jesus Christ" might be explained as the accidental alteration of a copyist, were it not for the fact that in (*b*) the order is approved by the addition of the word "our"—"Jesus our Christ." And in (*f*) emphatic prominence is given to the name "Jesus, whom we also knew fully as Christ, God's Son."

Again, in five out of these six passages some reference is found to the Lord's death.[1] This had been an element in the

[1] Zahn quotes four others, *Apol.* i. 63; *Dial.* 63, 74, 95.

JUSTIN MARTYR. (β) Christological Teaching

(a) Apol. i. 21.	(b) ib. 31.	(c) ib. 42.	(d) ib. 46.	(e) Dial. 85.	(f) ib. 132.
Τῷ δὲ καὶ τὸν Λόγον, ὅ ἐστι πρῶτον γέννημα τοῦ Θεοῦ, ἄνευ ἐπιμιξίας φάσκειν ἡμᾶς γεγενῆσθαι Ἰησοῦν Χριστὸν τὸν Διδάσκαλον ἡμῶν, καὶ τοῦτον σταυρωθέντα καὶ ἀποθανόντα καὶ ἀναστάντα ἀνεληλυθέναι εἰς τὸν οὐρανόν....	Ἐν δὴ ταῖς τῶν προφητῶν βίβλοις εὕρομεν προκηρυσσόμενον, παραγινόμενον, γεννώμενον διὰ παρθένου, καὶ ἀνδρούμενον, καὶ θεραπεύοντα πᾶσαν νόσον καὶ πᾶσαν μαλακίαν, καὶ νεκροὺς ἀνεγείροντα, καὶ φθονούμενον καὶ ἀγνοούμενον καὶ σταυρούμενον Ἰησοῦν τὸν ἡμέτερον Χριστόν, καὶ ἀποθνῄσκοντα, καὶ ἀνεγειρόμενον, καὶ εἰς οὐρανοὺς ἀνερχόμενον, καὶ Υἱὸν Θεοῦ ὄντα καὶ κεκλημένον....	Ὁ καθ' ἡμᾶς δὲ Ἰησοῦς Χριστὸς σταυρωθεὶς καὶ ἀποθανών, ἀνέστη, καὶ ἐβασίλευσεν ἀνελθὼν εἰς οὐρανόν.	Our opponents acknowledge that we teach that Christ was born ἐπὶ Κυρηνίου, and taught ἐπὶ Ποντίου Πιλάτου...	Κατὰ γὰρ τοῦ ὀνόματος αὐτοῦ τούτου τοῦ Υἱοῦ τοῦ Θεοῦ καὶ πρωτοτόκου πάσης κτίσεως, καὶ διὰ Παρθένου γεννηθέντος καὶ παθητοῦ γενομένου ἀνθρώπου, καὶ σταυρωθέντος ἐπὶ Ποντίου Πιλάτου ὑπὸ τοῦ λαοῦ ὑμῶν, καὶ ἀποθανόντος, καὶ ἀναστάντος ἐκ νεκρῶν, καὶ ἀναβάντος εἰς τὸν οὐρανὸν πᾶν δαιμόνιον ἐξορκιζόμενον νικᾶται καὶ ὑποτάσσεται.	Συναίρεται γὰρ πρὸς τὸ καὶ ἐξ αὐτῆς συνιέναι ὑμᾶς τὸν Ἰησοῦν, ὃν καὶ ἡμεῖς ἐπέγνωμεν Χριστὸν Υἱὸν Θεοῦ σταυρωθέντα καὶ ἀναστάντα καὶ ἀνεληλυθότα εἰς τοὺς οὐρανούς, καὶ πάλιν παραγενησόμενον κριτήν....

| κατὰ τὴν τοῦ Πατρὸς πάντων καὶ Δεσπότου Θεοῦ βουλήν, διὰ Παρθένου ἄνθρωπος ἀπεκυήθη καὶ Ἰησοῦς ἐπωνομάσθη, καὶ σταυρωθεὶς ἀποθανὼν ἀνέστη, καὶ ἀνελήλυθεν εἰς οὐρανόν.... |

teaching of Ignatius to the Trallians (c. 9). At a later time it was stated in the declaration of the elders of Smyrna against Noetus, and Tertullian found reason to insist on it, in connection with 1 Cor. xv. 4, writing against the error of Praxeas. But it is never found in R.

The variety of context in which these parallels to the Apostles' Creed are found is an argument against the supposition that Justin professed one such form in a Baptismal Creed. It is interesting to note that the most complete specimen (e) is a formula of exorcism, and that Irenæus at the end of the century spoke of the power of "the name of Jesus Christ crucified under Pontius Pilate" in a similar connection.[1] But the wording might just as easily have been borrowed from a fixed formal creed as from current modes of teaching.

There is no proof that Justin's personal creed contained more than "Jesus is the Christ the Son of God." His use of the words ὁμολογία and ὁμολογεῖν is varied. In the first Apology they are naturally referred to confession before a ruler. In *Dial.* 64, the Jew Trypho is represented as connecting the thought with prayer to Christ: οὐ δεόμεθα τῆς ὁμολογίας αὐτοῦ οὐδὲ τῆς προσκυνήσεως. Justin's own use implies that the preaching of Jesus crucified is to lead up to confession of Him as Lord and Christ (*Dial.* 35): ὁμολογοῦντας ἑαυτοὺς εἶναι Χριστιανοὺς καὶ τὸν σταυρωθέντα Ἰησοῦν ὁμολογεῖν καὶ Κύριον καὶ Χριστόν. Again, he writes of guarding such a confession (*Dial.* 47): μετὰ τοῦ φυλάσσειν τὴν εἰς τὸν Χριστὸν τοῦ Θεοῦ ὁμολογίαν. In the second Apology the word is used in the sense of teaching.[2] Apparently he laid stress on the act of confessing, rather than any special elaboration of the form.

By an elaborate argument, Kattenbusch[3] seeks to prove Justin's acquaintance with R. Since he had taught in Rome, this is quite possible, and even probable, if R was composed c. 100. The most interesting coincidences of language are:

---

[1] We find traces of such a form in Egypt in the third century. Palladius, *Hist. Lausiaca*, c. 29. Cf. Kattenbusch, ii. p. 291 n.

[2] Kattenbusch, ii. p. 289 n.   [3] *Ib.* 279-293.

(i.) Justin's use of σταυρωθῆναι (*Dial.* 51, 76, 100) in his quotation of Matt. xvi. 21 = Mark viii. 31 = Luke ix. 22, in place of the word ἀποκτανθῆναι of our *Textus receptus*. This is followed by τῇ τρίτῃ ἡμέρᾳ ἀναστῆναι, where Mark (Tischendorf, Westcott and Hort) has καὶ μετὰ τρεῖς ἡμέρας ἀναστῆναι; Matthew, Luke, καὶ τῇ τρίτῃ ἡμέρᾳ ἐγερθῆναι (some MSS. of Luke, ἀναστῆναι).

(ii.) He speaks confidently of the resurrection of the flesh (*Dial.* 80): ἐγὼ δὲ καὶ εἴ τινές εἰσιν ὀρθογνώμονες κατὰ πάντα Χριστιανοί, καὶ σαρκὸς ἀνάστασιν γενήσεσθαι ἐπιστάμεθα. We may give such coincidences their full value, and yet remain unconvinced that the creed was then used in Ephesus.[1]

In any case, the testimony of Justin is valuable for the interpretation of the language of R. He believed in the pre-existence of Christ before the incarnation. Thus he writes (*Dial.* 105): "He was the Only-begotten of the Father of the universe, inasmuch as He was, after a peculiar manner, produced from the Father as His Word and Power." If the word "only-begotten" had come into R, we may fairly explain it in the sense which Justin vindicates. If not (p. 62, *infra*), there still remains the question how to interpret the Divine Sonship taught in R. And from Justin we learn that it is not to be limited to the human life of Jesus in which it was manifested, though Justin connected it specially with that life.[2] The Church as yet thought vaguely[3] about Christ's pre-existent life, but the main point is the fact that it was believed.

The elaborate inquiry contributed to the *Zeitschrift für Kirchengeschichte*[4] by Bornemann offers an interesting summary of his teaching, formed by extracting all the creed-phrases which are most frequently used.

Πιστεύομεν εἰς (ἐπὶ) τὸν πατέρα τῶν ὅλων καὶ δεσπότην

---

[1] On the other hand, the only test of an Eastern type besides the words "Jesus Christ" and "dead," mentioned above, is the word πάλιν with reference to the Return. Apart from μετὰ δόξης this cannot be said to be conclusive.

[2] *Dial.* 88.

[3] Cf. Ps. Clem., 2 Cor. 9: Χριστὸς ὁ Κύριος . . . ὢν μὲν τὸ πρῶτον πνεῦμα ἐγένετο σάρξ.

[4] III. 1879.

Θεόν· καὶ εἰς (ἐπὶ) τὸν κύριον ἡμῶν Ἰησοῦν Χριστὸν, τὸν πρωτότοκον αὐτοῦ υἱὸν, τὸν (κατὰ τὴν τοῦ πατρὸς βουλὴν) διὰ παρθένου γεννηθέντα καὶ παθητὸν γενόμενον ἄνθρωπον καὶ σταυρωθέντα ἐπὶ Ποντίου Πιλάτου καὶ ἀποθανόντα καὶ ἀναστάντα ἐκ νεκρῶν καὶ ἀναβάντα εἰς τὸν οὐρανὸν καὶ μετὰ δόξης πάλιν παραγενησόμενον (κριτὴν πάντων ἀνθρώπων). Καὶ εἰς (ἐπὶ) τὸ ἅγιον προφητικὸν πνεῦμα.

This arithmetical method is too mechanical. It puts before us an artificial form which was certainly never used either in Ephesus or Rome. Creeds are not made by such processes, nor are they to be rediscovered. As a mere digest, like modern gleanings from the sermons of a distinguished preacher, the result is instructive, but withal dull.

2. ARISTIDES, A.D. 140–148

The Apology of Aristides, a philosopher of Athens, was formerly known to us only by the notices in Eusebius and Jerome. In 1878 the Mechitarists of San Lazzaro published a portion of an Armenian version. In 1889, Professor Rendel Harris found a fragment of the Syriac text in the library of the monastery of S. Catherine at Sinai. This enabled Professor Robinson to discover part of the Greek original in the Life of Barlaam and Joasaph.

The following passage suggests the inference that Aristides, like Justin, confessed Jesus Christ as the Son of God, that he also taught that He was pre-existent and manifested by the Holy Spirit, born of a Hebrew virgin. All the words which are doubly attested are printed in spaced type or italics. It would be easy to prove that he also believed in one God, Creator of heaven and earth, but this was not part of his confession.

ARISTIDES[1]

GREEK.	SYRIAC.	ARMENIAN.
οἱ δὲ χριστιανοὶ γε γενεαλογοῦνται ἀπὸ τοῦ Κυρίου Ἰησοῦ	The Christians then reckon the beginning of their religion from Jesus	But the Christians are race-reckoned from the Lord Jesus Christ. He

---
[1] *Texts and Studies*, i. 1. 78 (2nd ed.).

GREEK—contd.	SYRIAC—contd.	ARMENIAN—contd.
Χριστοῦ. οὗτος δὲ ὁ υἱὸς τοῦ Θεοῦ τοῦ ὑψίστου ὁμολογεῖται ἐν πνεύματι ἁγίῳ ἀπ' οὐρανοῦ καταβὰς διὰ τὴν σωτηρίαν τῶν ἀνθρώπων· καὶ ἐκ παρθένου ἁγιᾶς γεννηθείς, ἀσπόρως τε καὶ ἀφθόρως, σάρκα ἀνέλαβε, καὶ ἀνεφάνη ἀνθρώποις.	Christ, Who is named the Son of God Most High; and it is said that God came down from heaven, and from a Hebrew virgin took and clad Himself with flesh; and there dwelt in a daughter of man the Son of God.	is Son of God on high, Who was manifested by the Holy Spirit: from heaven having come down; and from a Hebrew virgin having been born: having taken His flesh from the virgin, and having been manifested by the nature of this humanity [as] the Son of God.

3. IRENÆUS

Irenæus was a native of Asia Minor. In his youth he had been a pupil of Polycarp, and of others who had been disciples of S. John. While he was still a young man he migrated to Gaul, and was ordained priest at Lyons. The first missionaries who came to Gaul seem to have come from Asia Minor, following a great trade route. The sympathy which existed between the Churches was fostered by the letter in which the Christians of Lyons and Vienna described their sufferings during the persecution of A.D. 177 to their brethren in Asia. Before this Irenæus had been sent on an important mission to Rome, and had lectured against heresies. On his return he was chosen as bishop.

IRENÆUS

c. Hær. i. 10.	ib. ii. 4.	ib. ii. 16.
ἡ μὲν γὰρ ἐκκλησία ... παραλαβοῦσα τὴν εἰς ἕνα Θεὸν πατέρα παντοκράτορα, τὸν πεποιηκότα τὸν οὐρανὸν καὶ τὴν γῆν καὶ τὰς θαλάσσας καὶ πάντα τὰ ἐν αὐτοῖς, πίστιν. καὶ εἰς ἕνα Χριστὸν Ἰησοῦν, τὸν υἱὸν τοῦ	in unum Deum credentes per Christum Jesum Dei Filium	Non ergo alterum Filium hominis nouit euangelium nisi hunc, qui ex Maria,

c. Hær. i. 10—contd.	ib. ii. 4—contd.	ib. ii. 16—contd.
Θεοῦ, τὸν σαρκωθέντα ὑπὲρ τῆς ἡμετέρας σωτηρίας· καὶ εἰς πνεῦμα ἅγιον, ... καὶ τὴν ἐκ παρθένου γέννησιν, καὶ τὸ πάθος, καὶ τὴν ἔγερσιν ἐκ νεκρῶν καὶ τὴν ἔνσαρκον εἰς τοὺς οὐρανοὺς ἀνάληψιν τοῦ ἠγαπημένου Χριστοῦ Ἰησοῦ τοῦ κυρίου ἡμῶν καὶ τὴν ἐκ τῶν οὐρανῶν ἐν τῇ δόξῃ τοῦ πατρὸς παρουσίαν αὐτοῦ ἐπὶ τὸ ἀνακεφαλαιώσασθαι τὰ πάντα καὶ ἀναστῆσαι πᾶσαν σάρκα πάσης ἀνθρωπότητος ... καὶ κρίσιν δικαίαν ἐν τοῖς πᾶσι ποιήσηται· ... τοῖς δὲ ἐκ μετανοίας, ζωὴν χαρισάμενος ἀφθαρσίαν δωρήσεται ...	ex uirgine generationem sustinuit et passus sub Pontio Pilato et resurgens et in claritate receptus, in gloria uenturus iudex eorum qui iudicantur	qui et passus est; sed hunc qui natus est Iesum Christum nouit Dei Filium et eundem hunc passum resurrexisse. ... Ipse est Iesus Christus Dominus noster qui et passus est pro nobis et surrexit propter nos et rursus uenturus est in gloria Patris
cp. i. 1. 6.	cp. ii. 49. 3.	cp. iii. 17. 3.
εἰς ἕνα Θεὸν πατέρα παντοκράτορα.	Where the context suggests reference to a form of solemn oath.	sedentem ad dexteram Patris.
iv. 43. 1.		iv. 37. 2.
εἰς ἕνα Θεὸν παντοκράτορα ... καὶ εἰς τὸν υἱὸν τοῦ Θεοῦ Ἰησοῦν Χριστὸν (Lat. Christum Iesum) τὸν κύριον ἡμῶν.	ἐν ὀνόματι Ἰησοῦ Χριστοῦ τοῦ σταυροθέντος ἐπὶ Ποντίου Πιλάτου. ap. Euseb. H.E. v. 20. 2. ἔρχεται κρῖναι ζῶντας καὶ νεκρούς. ...	Christum Iesum, qui sub Pontio Pilato crucifixus est et passus est.

IRENÆUS

The testimony of Irenæus is the more valuable because, as we have seen, it was not moulded by one strain of Christian influence only. The Rule of Faith which he teaches is not unlike that of Justin Martyr. But it is more complete, since it starts from teaching about the Father, which Justin gave only in connection with the Baptismal Formula.

In the Christological part we note the phrase "Son of God," which was found in Ignatius and Justin. Seeing that Irenæus is the earliest witness for the Eunuch's Creed in Acts ix., there is some ground here for the hypothesis that the only ὁμολογία or formal confession, which he had been taught from his youth, was of the same simple kind, "I believe that Jesus is the Son of God." The fact that the Holy Ghost is not mentioned in his Rule of Faith makes it appear improbable that he is reproducing the creed of his Church in Gaul in a stage of development parallel to that of the Old Roman Creed. At the same time, there are many phrases which seem to point to acquaintance with the latter, e.g. the exact wording, "One God the Father Almighty," the order of the names "Christ Jesus," e.g. iv. 37. 2: "Christum Jesum qui sub Pontio Pilato crucifixus est," and the use of "ex" with "Maria uirgine," as in R.

The note of suffering, which is common in Justin, is connected with the name of Pontius Pilate two or three times. This represents, in the later Western Creeds of Milan and Gaul, a distinct variation from the Roman type, under the influence, no doubt, of the teaching of the apologists.

Irenæus lived and wrote during a most critical period. The spread of Gnosticism threatened to effect what has been called in a clever phrase "the acute Hellenising of Christendom."[1] It was an anti-Judaistic movement, which took shape among Gentile Christians. In its origin it was not Christian but heathen. Its fundamental problem, the origin of evil, was solved, not on Christian lines, by the suggestion of a Demiurge. The founders of Gnostic systems have been classed among "the first Christian theologians."[2]

[1] Harnack, D.G.² i. p. 186.
[2] Ib. p. 191. For the other view, see Seeberg, D.G. p. 62.

But this is a mistake, though the first beginnings of formal theology are found to date from that period. Opposition had a stimulating effect upon the minds of Christian teachers. They picked their words more carefully; they were led in time to question more thoroughly the validity of their arguments and of their conclusions. This is the good side of all controversy seen in its human aspect. The historian of the creeds, if he still believes in the Holy Ghost, finds here evidence of His working. In proportion as a Christian theologian in any age does not enter upon controversy with a light heart, seeking less to win advantage over his adversaries than to witness to the truths which are for him "the master light of all his seeing," he will in all humility gain for himself guidance in dark paths of perilous speculation, and that growth in grace which enables him to win moral influence to stir wills as to move minds.

These considerations explain the method while they suggest the wisdom of the appeal of Irenæus to the Scriptures as the ultimate rule of faith, the touchstone of the teaching of the living Church.

With Irenæus we leave behind the age of the apologists, and look forward to the fruit of their labours. The Church was strongly organised, and increasing everywhere. Irenæus speaks of many countries — Germany, Iberia, the Celts, Egypt, Libya—as receiving one faith. This is not mere exaggeration in view of the multiplicity of faiths in current use at the beginning of the fourth century. While they were many in outward expression, they were one in their common outline and the substance of their teaching. We hear of no difficulties raised by travelling Christians, like Marcion or Marcellus, as to differences which they found in the Old Roman Creed compared with other summaries of the faith. Augustine, as we shall see, used indifferently the Creeds of Milan and Africa. The fires of controversy were already kindled, and would blaze for many years to come, but the last of the apologists, when he passed to his rest, might thank God and take courage, because he had not laboured in vain nor spent his toil for nought.

§ III. The Old Roman Creed

At this point, where we pass from the indirect testimony of possible quotations to the definite evidence of an established form of Church creed, it seems wise to reverse our method and pass on to the period when the whole of the Old Roman Creed was quoted openly. There is no doubt that Tertullian and Cyprian quoted from fixed forms. But it will be easier to combine such quotations with the less determinate testimony of Novatian, and to work back to a decision as to the parallels or quotations found in Irenæus and Justin, if we start from an undisputed position. Kattenbusch has done this on a large scale, and it is open to anyone to reap the benefit of his researches.

The Old Roman Creed is quoted in full by two writers of the fourth century, Marcellus and Rufinus.

1. *Marcellus and Rufinus*

Marcellus, Bishop of Ancyra, in Galatia, having been exiled from his diocese through Arian intriguers, spent the greater part of the years A.D. 340, 341 in Rome. On his departure he left with Bishop Julius a statement of his belief on the main outline of the faith and on some disputed points, to be used by his friends in his defence.

It is to the credit of an English theologian, Archbishop Ussher, that he was the first to discover that this document, which has been preserved by the historian Epiphanius (*Hær.* lxxii.), did not contain the Creed of Ancyra, but the Creed of the Church in Rome, which Marcellus adopted and made his own. There are two small variations, the omission of the word "Father" in the first article and the addition of the words "eternal life" in the last. Probably these were not intentional. They do not seem to bear any relation to the private speculations of Marcellus, which will occupy our attention presently. The three MSS. in which this part of the text of Epiphanius is preserved come from the same source,

THE OLD ROMAN CREED

RUFINUS, c. A.D. 400.	MARCELLUS, c. A.D. 341 (Epiph. Hær. lxxii. 3).	NOVATIAN, c. A.D. 260. *Regula exigit veritatis ut primo omnium.*	DIONYSIUS, c. A.D. 259.
I. 1. Credo in Deum Patrem omnipotentem ;	Πιστεύω εἰς Θεὸν παντοκράτορα,	Credamus in Deum Patrem et *Dominum* omnipotentem ;	εἰς Θεὸν πάτερα παντοκράτορα,
II. 2. Et in Christum Jesum, unicum Filium eius, Dominum nostrum,	καὶ εἰς Χριστὸν Ἰησοῦν, τὸν υἱὸν αὐτοῦ τὸν μονογενῆ, τὸν κύριον ἡμῶν,	credere etiam in Filium Dei, Christum Jesum Dominum *Deum* nostrum, sed Dei Filium	καὶ εἰς Χριστὸν Ἰησοῦν τὸν υἱὸν αὐτοῦ,
3. Qui natus est de Spiritu Sancto ex Maria virgine,	τὸν γεννηθέντα ἐκ πνεύματος ἁγίου καὶ Μαρίας τῆς παρθένου,	ex Maria,	
4. crucifixus sub Pontio Pilato et sepultus ;	τὸν ἐπὶ Ποντίου Πιλάτου σταυρωθέντα καὶ ταφέντα,		
5. tertia die resurrexit a mortuis,	καὶ τῇ τρίτῃ ἡμέρᾳ ἀναστάντα ἐκ τῶν νεκρῶν,	resurrecturus a mortuis,	
6. ascendit in cœlos	ἀναβάντα εἰς τοὺς οὐρανοὺς		
7. sedet ad dexteram Patris:	καὶ καθήμενον ἐν δεξιᾷ τοῦ Πατρός,	sessurus ad dexteram Patris	
8. inde uenturus est iudicare uiuos et mortuos.	ὅθεν ἔρχεται κρίνειν ζῶντας καὶ νεκρούς.	iudex omnium ;	
III. 9. Et in Spiritum Sanctum,	καὶ εἰς τὸ ἅγιον πνεῦμα,	credere etiam in Spiritum Sanctum, ecclesiam . . . ueritatis sanctitate,	καὶ εἰς τὸ ἅγιον πνεῦμα.
10. sanctam ecclesiam,	ἁγίαν ἐκκλησίαν,		
11. remissionem peccatorum,	ἄφεσιν ἁμαρτιῶν,		
12. carnis resurrectionem.	σαρκὸς ἀνάστασιν, [ζωὴν αἰώνιον.]	ad resurrectionem . . . corpora nostra producat.	

and are full of errors.[1] It seems likely enough that these variations are due to a copyist.

Sixty years later (A.D. 400), Rufinus, a priest of Aquileia, wrote a commentary on the creed of his native city, and to our advantage compared with it the Old Roman Creed. He was a man who had travelled much, and had lived for some time in or near Jerusalem, besides visiting Alexandria and Rome. He had read sermons preached in other Churches by famous men, and, as we should expect from a man of such wide culture, wrote an interesting book.

Rufinus believed that the Old Roman Creed was the Apostles' Creed, composed as a rule of faith by the Twelve in solemn conclave before departing from Jerusalem. In other Churches additions had been made to meet certain heresies, but the Church of Rome had remained free from heresy, and had kept up the ancient custom that candidates for baptism should repeat the creed publicly, so that no additions could be permitted.

An interesting question may be at once raised. Which is the original form, the Greek of Marcellus or the Latin of Rufinus? Probably the former. S. Paul wrote to his Roman converts in Greek, and there is abundant evidence to prove that the early Church in Rome used Greek in her Liturgy. Yet she must always have been bilingual, and the Latin version is probably almost as old. Some of the later MSS. show a more slavish rendering of the Greek, using participles, *natum*, *crucifixum*, etc., in place of the free relative sentence, but it is possible that these might point to later translations from a standard Greek text. We can reserve them for consideration when we compare the Old Roman Creed with its derivative African and Italian forms.

2. *Novatian, Dionysius, and Cyprian*

We must now follow back the history of the creed, and we may take as our first witness Novatian (*c.* 260). He was a priest of the Church of Rome, who held strict views

[1] Caspari, iii. 105 f.

against the restoration of the lapsed to Church privileges. In consequence he obtained schismatical consecration in opposition to Bishop Cornelius. His book, *de Trinitate*, is founded on the teaching of Tertullian, whose phrase *regula veritatis*, rule of truth, he uses with obvious reference to the creed. I have quoted the closer parallels on p. 46, *supra*.[1] Since the creed was transmitted orally, it is less important to mark the exact words used than to note how exactly Novatian teaches the substance of the creed on Creation, Redemption, Sanctification.

The order Christ Jesus, which appears regularly in nearly all forms of the Roman Creed, was used both by Novatian and by a contemporary, Bishop Dionysius, who wrote a treatise against the Sabellians, from which Athanasius[2] quotes an extract in his "Defence of the Nicene Definition."

In the letters of S. Cyprian, Bishop of Carthage, *c.* A.D. 255, we find the following quotations:—

Ep. 69: "Credis in remissionem peccatorum et uitam æternam per sanctam ecclesiam?"

Ep. 70: "Credis in uitam æternam et remissionem peccatorum per sanctam ecclesiam?"

3. *Tertullian*

In the writings of Tertullian[3] we find a bridge which spans the gulf between the formal quotations of R in the fourth century and the parallels in the writings of Irenæus and Justin Martyr. The quotation made by Cyprian, and the less definite testimony of Novatian and Dionysius, offer independent support.

Though a native of Carthage, Tertullian, before his lapse into Montanism, had been ordained priest in Rome. His varied training, both in the school of Stoic philosophy and at

---

[1] Caspari, iii. 462 n.   [2] Ath. *de Decretis*, 26.
[3] Kattenbusch, ii. pp. 53-101, has made a careful study of all the passages in his writings which have any reference to the creed, and has left little or nothing for other students to do.

the bar, enabled him to plead for Christian thought and life in the spirit of a true apologist.

In plain words, Tertullian expresses the agreement of the African Church with the Church of Rome in matters of faith. All who believe have the testimony of truth, which rests on apostolic tradition. He represents all Churches as turning for guidance to apostolic sees—Achaia to Corinth, Macedonia to Philippi and Thessalonica, Asia to Ephesus, the neighbourhood of Italy to Rome (*de Præscr.* 36): "Si autem Italiæ adiaces, habes Romam, unde nobis quoque auctoritas præsto est. Quam felix ecclesia cui totam doctrinam apostoli cum sanguine suo profuderunt, ubi Petrus passioni dominicæ adæquatur, ubi Paulus Ioannis exitu coronatur, ubi apostolus Ioannes, posteaquam in oleum igneum demersus nihil passus est, in insulam relegatur. Videamus, quid didicerit, quid docuerit, quid cum Africanis quoque ecclesiis *contesserauit*. Unum Deum nouit creatorem uniuersitatis et Christum Iesum ex uirgine Maria Filium Dei creatoris et carnis resurrectionem."

It is clear from this passage that the creed of the African Church, here called watchword (Tessera), agreed with that of Rome, from which he quotes the first and last words, and the exact order Christum Iesum. He regarded it as a summary of apostolic teaching, and in the general Church tradition recognised the influence of S. John with S. Peter and S. Paul.

His use of words for the creed is very varied. "Rule of Faith" is a common term, as in later writers. He explains that it contains what the Lord ordained (instituit), so that speculation is concerned only with thoughts which lie outside it (*de Præscr.* 12): "Quod salua regula fidei potest in quæstionem uenire." He traces its origin in the teaching of Christ, without showing any acquaintance with the later legend of its composition by the apostles (*ib.* c. 37): "In ea regula quam ecclesia ab apostolis, apostoli a Christo, Christus a Deo tradidit." Again, he calls it the oath of allegiance (sacramentum) imposed on the Christian soldier at the font.

Ad Mart. 3: "Vocati sumus ad militiam Dei uiui iam tunc, cum in sacramenti uerba respondemus."

THE OLD ROMAN CREED QUOTED BY TERTULLIAN (c. 200)

De Uirg. Uel. c. 1.	De Prescr. c. 13.	Ib. c. 36.	Adv. Praxean, c. 2.
Regula quidem fidei una omnino est...	Regula est fidei... qua	Quid ecclesia (Romana)... cum Africanis quoque ecclesiis contesserauit:	
I. 1. credendi in unicum Deum omnipotentem, mundi conditorem,	creditur unum Deum esse nec alium preter mundi conditorem, qui[1]...	unum Deum nouit, creatorem uniuersitatis,	unicum Deum credimus...
II. 2. et Filium eius Iesum Christum,	Filium eius...	et Christum Iesum	Filium Dei... Iesum Christum
3. natum ex Maria uirgine,	delatum ex Spiritu Patris Dei et uirtute in uirginem Mariam ... ex ea natum (I.C.),	ex uirgine Maria Filium Dei creatoris,	ex ea (uirginem) natum,
4. crucifixum sub Pontio Pilato;	fixum cruci;		passum hunc mortuum et sepultum...
5. tertia die resuscitatum a mortuis,	tertia die resurrexisse		et resuscitatum...
6. receptum in cœlis,	in cœlos ereptum		et in cœlo resumptum

TERTULLIAN

7. sedentem nunc ad dexteram Patris,	sedere ad dexteram Patris, ...		sedere ad dexteram Patris,
8. uenturum iudicare uiuos et mortuos,	uenturum ... ad profanos iudicandos		uenturum iudicare uiuos et mortuos ...
III. 9.			Spiritum Sanctum,
10.			
11.			
12. per carnis etiam resurrectionem.	cum carnis restitutione.	et carnis resurrectionem.	sanctificatorem fidei eorum, qui credunt in Patrem et Filium et Spiritum Sanctum. Hanc regulam ab initio euangelii decucurrisse.
	[1] (qui) uniuersa de nihilo produxerit per uerbum suum ... id uerbum Filium eius appellatum. = Hermas, *Mand.* i. + John i. l.		

De Spect. 4 : " Cum aquam ingressi christianam fidem in legis suae uerba profitemur, renuntiasse nos diabolo et pompae et angelis eius ore nostro contestamur."

De Cor. Mil. 3 : " Dehinc ter mergitamur, amplius aliquid respondentes quam Dominus in euangelio determinauit."

De Bapt. 13 : " Fuerit salus retro per fidem nudam ante Domini passionem et resurrectionem. At ubi fides aucta est credendi in natiuitatem, passionem resurrectionemque eius, addita est ampliatio sacramento, obsignatio baptismi uestimentum quodam modo fidei, quae retro erat nuda, nec potentiam habuit sine sua lege. Lex enim tinguendi imposita est, et forma praescripta. 'Ite,' inquit, 'docete nationes, tinguentes eas in nomine Patris et Filii et Spiritus Sancti.' "

It would be useless to discuss at this point the many shades of meaning which have been observed in Tertullian's use of the word "sacramentum." In the last passage quoted it seems to me to correspond closely with the meaning given to it in our Catechism, "an outward sign of an inward grace." The creed is the sign; faith enlarged by knowledge of the whole scheme of redemption is the grace which clothes the soul. The Baptismal Formula supplies the framework, and the birth, passion, and resurrection of the Lord are included in it.

The construction " in sacramenti uerba " (not " uerbis "), " in legis uerba " (not " uerbis "), seems to imply, further, that the baptizer recited the whole creed, to which the baptized only replied with " credo." Last, and not least important, is this use of the term " symbolum " in his treatise against Marcion (*adv. Marc.* v. 1) : " Quamobrem, Pontice nauclere, nunquam furtiuas merces uel illicitas in acatos tuos recepisti, si nullum omnino onus auertisti uel adulterasti, cautior utique et fidelior in Dei rebus, edas uelim nobis, quo *symbolo* susceperis apostolum Paulum, quis illum tituli charactere percusserit, quis transmiserit tibi, quis imposuerit, ut possis cum constanter exponere." Kattenbusch points out that Tertullian is using metaphors from trade, referring to Marcion's former occupation, and that one meaning of the word symbolum was "an agreement." A passage in Harpocrates (*vid.* Pape's Lexicon) proves that the Greek word in the plural (τὰ σύμβολα) was used in commercial language for the pleadings which were laid before a court of law in any suit. Such an explanation might be given in this case. The creed was the Church's agreement by which her children were bound to faith in one God. Marcion's teaching of two Gods, for which he claimed the sanction of S. Paul, must be derived from some other source, so Tertullian asks him to show the agreement.

In general, Tertullian thinks of the creed as a great act of worship which every Christian knows and uses. His teaching represents a great advance from the position of Irenæus, who regarded Holy Scripture as the rule of faith side by side with the rule of Church doctrine, to whom the creed was the sum of Scripture and the minimum of what is worth knowing. Tertullian never calls Holy Scripture "the rule." He has new difficulties to contend with. Heretics had by this time their own canon of Scripture. So he is the first to explain why the creed stands above Scripture. He is a thorough lawyer, and couples his apologetic explanations with the law of faith, in which he finds what is most safe, most positive, and highest, appealing to the Roman Creed as raised into a rule to meet Gnostic error.

What made reply to the Gnostics so difficult, was the fact that they still held to the Roman Creed. Irenæus seems to imply this when he writes that Valentinus imitated "nostrum tractatum" (iii. 15. 2). It is more distinctly stated by Tertullian (*adv. Valent.* 1): "Si subtiliter temptes (eos) per ambiguitates bilingues communem fidem adfirmant." This embittered his opposition to Marcion (*adv. Marc.* i. 20): "Marcionem non tam innouasse regulam separatione legis et euangelii, quam retro adulteratam recurasse; . . . (*ib.* 21): post apostolorum tempera adulterium ueritas passa est circa Dei regulam."

In the latter passage he refers in the context to the teaching of God as Creator, from which Kattenbusch concludes: (i.) that his creed contained no definite statement as to the creation; (ii.) that it contained some expression which Marcion could interpret of his good God; and (iii.) that he was in no way hindered by the creed from believing in two Gods. This argument deserves careful consideration. It raises the two most debatable questions about the creed of Tertullian: Did it contain *unum* and *patrem* in the first article?

(i.) It is quite true that Tertullian lays stress on the work of God in creation with a variety of phrases, which seems to imply that this thought had no fixed form in the creed. In all four of the passages which I have quoted in parallel columns there is some such reference. It is interesting to note that, in writing against Praxeas, he quoted S. John's words of the office of the Word of God "*through* whom all things were made," whereas in his controversy with Gnostics it was always the Father to whom he referred. No one would argue from these passages that the creation was mentioned in the Old Roman Creed, but they offer the obvious explanation of the clause in the later African Creed:[1] *universorum creatorem* (Aug. Ps.-Aug. Fulg.), though it is not certain how soon after Tertullian's time it was introduced.

(ii.) The next question is much more important. Kattenbusch infers, and I think rightly, that Marcion found in the first article of the creed, which he deceitfully held, some word which he could interpret of his good God. This must have been "Father." There is sufficient corroborative evidence to prove that Tertullian possessed this word in the first article of his creed. Zahn, indeed, suggests that Tertullian would have been glad to use it against Praxeas, but was obliged to infer it from the second article before he could distinguish God the Father from the Son. As Harnack points out, there was no need of a lengthy argument; the word stood already in the clause relating to the ascension. An insuperable objection to Zahn's theory is the fact that Tertullian regarded the creed as based on the Baptismal Formula. In the passage quoted from his work against Praxeas he leads up to that formula. Is it then conceivable that Father did not stand in the front of his creed?

[1] Kattenbusch, i. p. 144, n. 3.

In the second passage the phrase *delatum ex Spiritu Patris Dei* points back to the first article. Again, in his treatise "On Baptism" he writes of a confession in which the Church is mentioned, and the three heavenly witnesses are involved (*de Bapt.* 6): "Cum autem sub tribus et testatio fidei et sponsio salutis pignerentur, necessario adicitur ecclesiæ mentio, quoniam ubi tres, id est Pater et Filius et Spiritus Sanctus, ibi ecclesia, quia trium corpus est." We may compare a sentence in his treatise "On Prayer," where he passes from the thought of "our Father" in the Lord's Prayer to the creed (*de Orat.* 2): "Dicendo autem 'Patrem' 'Deum' quoque cognominamus item in Patre Filius inuocatur . . . ne mater quidem ecclesia præteritur, siquidem in Filio et Patre mater recognoscitur, de qua constat et Patris et Filii nomen." The combination "Patrem Deum" looks like a reminiscence.[1]

(iii.) The third question is the most difficult to answer. Did Marcion find anything in the creed which would forbid his doctrine of two Gods? Kattenbusch argues that he did not, and that the creed cannot have contained the word "one," though "unicum" and "unum" appear in all Tertullian's reproductions of the Rule of Faith. It must be remembered, however, that some Gnostics, to a certain extent Marcion, and more plainly his pupil Apelles, taught the unity of God, their good God. The phrase "one God" would not come into conflict with their teaching, and this argument falls to the ground.

Again, it has been suggested that in the second passage given Tertullian is quoting a sentence from Hermas (*Mand.* i.) combined with S. John i. 1 f., as Irenaeus before him had done. There is no doubt that the earliest compound phrase, so to speak, about the Being of God was "one God Almighty," which is found in the Apocalypse of S. John, Clement, Hermas, etc., and that the introduction of the word "Father" into it involved the abandonment of merely Jewish Monotheism. But there is no intelligible reason why Christian writers should not continue to use this biblical expression

---

[1] I owe these references to Harnack's article, *Zeit. für Theol. u. Kirche*, 1894, pp. 155 f.

side by side with their confession of the Father; why Tertullian, in the case before us, should not be supposed to use the words of his own accord. There is no proof that he quoted Hermas, and there is no need for it. We shall return to this question again, when we have to make our final decision as to the original wording of the Old Roman Creed; but in the meantime, so far as Tertullian is concerned, we must consider it probable that "one" stood in the first article of his creed.

Zahn asks whether "only" was found in the second article. It is true that it is nowhere found as a predicate of Son. And there is little doubt that it failed in some later provincial creeds. We shall return to this question also from a larger point of view. All that can be said at present is simply this, that it would be very dangerous to apply the principle that words apparently omitted by Tertullian were omitted in his creed. This would lead us to exclude "our Lord" as well as "only" from the second article.

The participial construction so marked in the passages quoted, e.g. in the first-quoted *natum, crucifixum, resuscitatum*, makes it probable that Tertullian was most familiar with the Greek form of the Roman Creed. But when we compare his text with that of Marcellus, it seems as if *resuscitatum* would answer to ἐγερθέντα rather than to ἀναστάντα, *receptum* to ἀναληφθέντα rather than to ἀναβάντα.[1] Perhaps Tertullian deliberately veiled his allusions to the creed, and this is another proof of the early and deep-rooted fear of writing the creed, which contributed to the awe and reverence in which it was held.

These results may sound somewhat tentative, and so they are. But the three words of the creed about which all this discussion is raised form a very small fraction of the total number. We may readily satisfy ourselves that Tertullian is a trustworthy witness to the great bulk of an Old Roman Creed substantially the same in form as that which was quoted in full by Marcellus. And in his argument against Marcion he brings us back in thought to a very early date,

[1] Caspari, iii. pp. 458 ff. Cf. Kattenbusch, i. p. 144.

WAS THE OLD ROMAN CREED REVISED? 57

the first half of the second century, since Marcion's breach with the Roman Church took place c. A.D. 145.

We may conclude with a most interesting conjecture made by Zahn, which belongs rather to the literary history of Marcion than of Tertullian. In one passage of the New Testament, as revised by Marcion, we find the mysterious passage, Gal. iv. 24, remodelled by the addition of words from Eph. i. 21 and others. We read there about the two covenants: "The one, from Mount Sinai, which is the synagogue of the Jews after the law, begotten into bondage; the other, which is exalted above all might, majesty, and power, and over every name that is named not only in this world, but also in that which is to come; which (covenant) is the mother of us all, which begets us in the holy Church, which we have acknowledged (or to which we have vowed allegiance). Marcion does not say, or rather does not allow the apostle to say, 'which we acknowledge,' but he looks back to the confession and the oath taken once for all with reference to the 'holy Church.' The word used here, 'repromittere,' 'ἐπαγγέλλεσθαι,' describes such an oath, and had been used earlier by Ignatius of the oath taken on the confession of the Christian faith. . . . Marcion thought much of the Church as he understood her, and considered the Christian relation to her a very close one. . . . As far as I can see, it follows from the passage quoted from his Epistle to the Galatians that the words 'a holy Church' were contained in Marcion's Baptismal Confession, and therefore in the Roman Creed of A.D. 145."[1]

§ IV. WAS THE OLD ROMAN CREED EVER REVISED?

An important question must be considered in the light of this evidence. Was the Old Roman Creed revised during the third century? There is no special reason why we should believe that what Rufinus says about its immutability was true at every stage of its history. When he compared it with other forms of Baptismal Confession, with the Aquileian and Eastern Creeds, some of which bore the marks of recent

[1] Zahn, pp. 32 f.

alteration, it was natural to come to this conclusion. The comparative freedom from the assaults of heresy which the Roman Church enjoyed during the fourth century, when Rome was the refuge of Athanasius and Marcellus, tended to obscure the fact that during the second and third centuries the city was the favoured resort of false teachers. Naturally enough, they sought to win adherents in what was then the capital of the empire. Thus one reason which he gives to explain his assertion falls to the ground, and with it the probability that he had any better proof of the fact. He also praises the Church of Rome for carefulness about the exact repetition of the creed by catechumens in the presence of the congregation, but this does not prove that similar care had been taken throughout the centuries past. Christian common sense looks for continuity of thought rather than of words. Otherwise, as Zahn shrewdly remarks, there would have been no history of the development of the creed.

The problem may be stated briefly. From the evidence of Tertullian and Irenæus, we have concluded that the earliest form of the Old Roman Creed was, "I believe in one God the Father Almighty." How is the omission of "one" from the time of Novatian to be explained?

The treatise of Tertullian against Praxeas introduces us to the central controversy which at that time disturbed the peace of the Church. The simple-minded Christians of the second century had been, so to speak, "naïvely Monarchian."[1] They had professed their belief in the divinity of Christ and the unity of God. They had been taught by the apologists that the Father and the Son were distinct, but they had not attempted to reconcile the necessary inference that the Son was in some sense subordinate to the Father, with their true Monarchian conviction of the unity of God. Reflection led to varying attempts to solve the problem. Some teachers identified the one God with the Christ of the Gospels. They assumed that the Father became incarnate in Christ, whom they therefore regarded as personally Divine. The inevitable inference from such teaching, as their opponents at once

[1] Robertson, *Athanasius*, p. xxiv.

pointed out, was that the Father suffered, a doctrine abhorrent to Christian common sense. Praxeas was the first of these modalist Monarchians. He arrived in Rome early in the century. Tertullian says of him : " unicum Dominum uindicat, omnipotentem mundi creatorem." He combined with such teaching strong opposition to Montanism, which was itself the exaggerated expression of another current of Christian thought.

Belief in the Holy Spirit as the Guide of individual souls, was torn from its place in the teaching of Christ to explain and approve the enthusiasm of fanatics who regarded themselves as specially possessed and inspired. Tertullian, as a Montanist, thus tersely describes the teaching of Praxeas : " He expelled prophecy and brought in heresy; he routed the Paraclete, and crucified the Father."

There was, however, another set of opinions which prevailed in some circles at Rome. Men who believed in the continual personal distinction of the Son from the Father, were led to explain Christ's divinity by the assumption that it was communicated, that the influence or energy of Divine life was given to Him as a chosen man, personally human but by adoption deified. Hence they have been called dynamic Monarchians or Adoptionists. This heresy was introduced by Theodotus, a tanner from Byzantium, who was excommunicated by Bishop Victor. His namesake, another Theodotus, some time a peripatetic philosopher, continued to teach under Bishop Zephyrinus.

From Tertullian we learn that the leaders of thought in Rome were strongly influenced by the former of these trains of thought. Zephyrinus is reported to have used the formula : " I believe in one God, Jesus Christ." His successor, Callistus, attempted some form of compromise : " Christ the Divine was distinguished from Jesus the human." He was thereupon deserted by the teacher Sabellius, who reproached him as inconsistent, and defined further the position of modalist Monarchians, asserting that the Trinity represented successive aspects ($\pi\rho\acute{o}\sigma\omega\pi\alpha$) of the one God. Tertullian's statements are confirmed by Hippolytus, a learned Roman theologian, who probably became a rival bishop to Callistus.

This being the position of parties at the beginning of the second century, we are prepared to discuss Zahn's acute suggestion that the word "one" was omitted from the Roman Creed to counteract Monarchian teaching. He quotes a passage from Eusebius [1] in which heretics are said to have accused the Roman Church of recoining (παραχαράττειν) the truth like forgers. What is meant by the word is shown by a countercharge that the heretics had tampered with the text of the Scriptures.[2]

Harnack in reply [3] suggests that the change complained of was only the addition to the rule of some words like Θεὸν or λόγον τοῦ Θεοῦ as a predicate of Christ. By the time of Cyprian and Novatian the formula *Deus et Dominus noster* had passed into the iron mould of Latin ecclesiastical language.[4] At a later time it is found in Spanish symbols (Martin of Bracara), and the creed at the end of the Gallican Sacramentary. The creed of the Bangor Antiphonary has the strong form, *Dominus noster, Deus omnipotens*. Yet no one would argue that these words ever found a place in the Old Roman Creed. We should therefore conclude that the accusation which was brought by the dynamic Monarchians did not apply to the corruption of a creed-text, but to the corruption of the preaching, which was regarded as an exposition of the Baptismal Confession. Such teaching as that of Hippolytus in a favourite phrase (*c. Noet.* 8), "Son of God and God," seemed to them a forsaking of the old tradition, the thought (φρόνημα) of the earliest times. And the error was made worse by the still more precise form of Novatian's teaching in his "Rule of Faith" (c. 9): "Credo in Filium Dei Christum Jesum, Dominum Deum nostrum, sed Dei Filium."

This would be a valid objection if Zahn's theory referred to the opinions of these dynamic Monarchians only or chiefly. So far as the omission of ἕνα is concerned, they would be neutral in their teaching, because they were secure in their belief in the Divine unity, whereas they called the representatives of the Logos Christology (Hipp., Tert.), Ditheists.

[1] *H.E.* v. 28. 3, 13.   [2] *Ib.* v. 28. 19.
[3] *Zeit. für Theol. u. Kirche*, iv. 2. 135 f.   [4] *Ib.* p. 137.

From this point of view it would seem to be against the interests of the latter to object to the assertion "one God."

But it was one thing for the orthodox party to assert this in their own teaching, and quite another to submit to it when forced upon them by Zephyrinus, or by Callistus when he was in that mood. Harnack himself suggests [1] that the minority may have proposed to strike out ἕνα, and that they eventually gained the day, though the history of their movement remains utterly obscure. Such an attempt, in opposition to modalist Monarchianism, would not be regarded as an alteration so much as a simplification of the sense to guard against error. No new doctrine was to be propagated thereby, but the old faith preserved.

We have yet to consider whether this change further included the addition of πατέρα, or whether that word was already found in the creed. Though the word does not come into the formal quotations made by Tertullian, we have seen reason to suppose that it was implied. In the one definite passage found in Irenæus it is unmistakably included.

Zahn raises the objection that if πατέρα had stood in the creed, Hippolytus and Tertullian would have been glad enough to quote it. As a matter of fact, they might have quoted it just as well from the later article, "at the right hand of the Father." But the following passage from Hippolytus reads like a quotation of R (c. Noet. 8): ὁμολογεῖν πατέρα Θεὸν παντοκράτορα καὶ Χριστὸν Ἰησοῦν υἱὸν Θεοῦ Θεὸν ἄνθρωπον γενόμενον.

A far more important point is raised by Zahn when he proves that "God Almighty" without "Father" is a biblical and natural phrase, which is found frequently in the oldest literature in the Apocalypse of S. John, 1 Ep. Clement, Hermas, and Polycarp. We may even admit that it would come more readily to the lips of the earliest preachers of Christianity than any mention of the Divine Fatherhood when they spoke of His Being. Harnack points out four passages in which Irenæus, desiring to state the doctrine of God the Creator (and the Logos) by itself, e.g. iv. 20. 2, combines the phrase of Hermas (Mand. 1) with S. John i. 1 f.

[1] P. 137, n. 1.

Similar dependence on Hermas is said to be found in Tertullian, *de Præscr.* 13 (see p. 51, *supra*), but is very uncertain. Irenæus, however, often quotes πάτηρ with Θεός (*e.g.* iii. 6. 5): "Distinxit enim et separauit eos qui dicuntur quidem, non sunt autem dii, ab uno Deo Patre, ex quo omnia, et unum Dominum Jesum Christum ex sua persona firmissime confessus est."

All such evidence is inconclusive. The final decision as to the insertion of the word "Father" in the creed must turn upon the question whether or not it was based upon the Baptismal Formula. This is generally admitted with respect to the Old Roman Creed. Can we doubt, then, that the word Father was from the first taken into the creed? The evidence of Justin Martyr in his expansions of the Formula gives support to the theory, though it is doubtful whether his "Father of all and Lord God" can be considered a synonym of "Almighty." The following is definite enough (*Dial.* 139): ὁ Χριστὸς κατὰ τὴν τοῦ παντοκράτορος πατρὸς δύναμιν δοθεῖσαν αὐτῷ παρεγένετο.

There is yet another question to be raised about the earliest form of the Old Roman Creed. Did it contain μονογενῆ (*unicum*)? There is no positive proof on either side. There is no trace of it in the Rules of Faith in Irenæus, Tertullian, or Novatian. It is wanting in some later African Creeds (Ps. Aug. *Serm.* 238; Ps. Ambrose), as in the Creeds of Niceta and Faustus. Yet it cannot be said that this means much. These African Creeds are not so important as the African form used by Augustine himself, which contained the word. The Creeds of Niceta and Faustus are isolated specimens in this respect, in neither of which is the form quite certain. Nor is there any special reason why the word should have been introduced into the Roman Creed at this period. It was used in the Septuagint (Ps. xxii. 21, xxxv. 17) and by S. John, from whose Gospel it probably came into the creed at its making.

Kattenbusch offers an interesting suggestion, that it was connected in the earliest form of the creed with "our Lord" —τὸν υἱὸν αὐτοῦ [τὸν] μονογενῆ κύριον ἡμῶν. In this case

WAS THE OLD ROMAN CREED REVISED? 63

it might have been brought into the creed independently of S. John's Gospel, though he does not think it improbable that that book was received in Rome by the year 100. At a later period the phrase was connected with the teaching of S. John, and the article was added before κύριον.

This theory has the support of three texts of R in which *unicum* is plainly to be construed with *Dominum*, *i.e.* in Bratke's Berne MS., a Munich MS. *Cod. lat.* 14,508, and in *Cod. Sessorianus* 52, as in the texts of the *Textus receptus* found in the Book of Deer and some old English Creeds. But there is not a single instance in which the Greek text supports it, and the cases quoted from the Latin text might be derived from independent mistakes so easy in the Latin form, where no article guards us from connecting the word *unicum* with *Dominum*.

It is true that the sub-apostolic writers did not use the term, whereas the Valentinians appropriated the name *Monogenes* for the Aeon *Nous*. "The Catholic writers," says Swete,[1] "began, although slowly, to reclaim it; Justin uses it sparingly; it occurs once in the Smyrnean circular on the martyrdom of Polycarp; in Irenæus at length it becomes frequent. Thus it is not unlikely that the word took its place in the vocabulary of the Church by way of protest against the Valentinian misuse of St. John; and the same cause may have gained for it admission to the creed." Such an explanation would not account for its insertion during the Monarchian controversy, but may suggest the reason why it was not referred to in the Rules of Faith quoted by Irenæus, Tertullian, and Novatian. Gnostic errors survived, and they would be afraid to refer to it openly, lest they should give some handle to their opponents.

We conclude, therefore, that ἕνα, πατέρα, and μονογενῆ were found in the original text of the Old Roman Creed, and that ἕνα was dropped out during the controversy with the modalist Monarchians. This conclusion is supported by the evidence of an inscription on a tombstone[2] which is supposed to belong to the second or beginning of the third century

[1] *The Apostles' Creed*, p. 25.   [2] Bäumer, p. 122.

"Cassius Vitalio qui in unu Deu credidit." It corresponds to the teaching in the *Shepherd of Hermas*, which was written in Rome at all events before A.D. 150: "First of all, believe that God is one." So Clement of Rome wrote in his first Epistle, c. A.D. 100: "Have we not one God?" It would be absurd to lay much stress on such testimony, but one may fairly say that it confirms the argument.

V. THE DATE OF THE OLD ROMAN CREED

Though the evidence is scanty, it is generally agreed that a very early date may be assigned to the Old Roman Creed. We have traced it back through Tertullian to the date of Marcion's arrival in Rome, A.D. 145. This fact, that it was in use as a Rule of Faith, enables us to argue with some confidence that the parallels in the writings of Irenæus and Justin Martyr show acquaintance with it. We may not be able to prove how far actual quotations of its words extend, but this matters little. It may be taken for granted that the form came into existence from A.D. 100–120. Beyond this date it is not safe to go, because of the silence of the *Shepherd of Hermas*, and of Clement's first Epistle. Caspari,[1] indeed, quotes the oath found in that epistle (c. 58. 2): ζῇ γὰρ ὁ Θεὸς καὶ ζῇ ὁ κύριος Ἰησοῦς Χριστὸς καὶ τὸ πνεῦμα τὸ ἅγιον ἥ τε πίστις καὶ ἡ ἐλπὶς τῶν ἐκλεκτῶν, where the words ἡ πίστις stand in apposition to the preceding sentence. He compares with it Jerome against John of Jerusalem (c. 28): "in symbolo fidei et spei nostræ . . . omne dogmatis christiani sacramentum carnis resurrectione concluditur." Then he asks whether these words do not point to the neighbourhood where the Old Roman Creed was composed. This is quite probable. The words prove that theological thought in Rome had been focussed, so to speak, on an expansion of the Baptismal Formula through the addition of words confessing Jesus Christ as Lord, who in the words of S. Paul, 1 Tim. i., "is our hope." But there is no need to search for the name-

---

[1] *Der Glaube an die Trinität Gottes, sein Vorhandensein im ersten christl. Jahrhundert*, 1894.

less author among the immediate successors of Clement, there is no need to inquire whether he had any colleagues in the task or a model upon which to plan his work.[1]

The internal evidence may be relied on to confirm such a view. The simplicity and the monumental terseness of the style, if I may attempt a free rendering of Caspari's phrase "Lapidarstyl," points to the sub-apostolic age. There is no mention of God's work in creation, which became an inseparable part of outlines of Christian doctrine after the rise of Gnostic heresies. On the other hand, the words "resurrection of the flesh" are not to be considered anti-Gnostic, as some writers have supposed. Justin Martyr quotes the words (*Dial.* 80) with a reference to the chiliastic hope,[2] which still lasted on as a part of orthodox belief though the bright dreams of early Christians, of which 1 Thessalonians is so vivid an example, were fast fading away. Clement, too, in his first Epistle, c. 26, quotes the words of Job xix. 26 : καὶ ἀναστήσεις τὴν σάρκα μου ταύτην, where the MSS. of the LXX. give τὸ δέρμα or τὸ σῶμα. This, at all events, shows that the phrase was in current use.

We learn from these inquiries that the creed was composed during a time of peace, and became a rule of faith without dispute. From Tertullian's description we are led to call it simply "the Faith," a short and intelligible summary of the teaching which Christianity offered. Its terse and rhythmical sentences were not unworthy of the great apostles, S. Peter and S. Paul, who had laboured and suffered in the imperial city. We may even conjecture that they helped not a little to mould the noble traditions of faith and learning which through centuries to come enhanced the reputation of the holy Roman Church. It may fitly be called an Apostolic Creed, because it contains the substance of apostolic teaching, and is the work of a mind separated only by one generation from the apostles.

It may seem tempting to try to set the date further back still. Zahn conjectures the existence of an apostolic archetype, distinguished from the sister forms found *c.* A.D. 120 at

[1] Kattenbusch, ii. pp. 329 f.   [2] *Ib.* ii. p. 335 ; cf. p. 297.

Rome and Ephesus by the addition[1] of the phrase of "the seed of David," which we noted in the teaching of Ignatius. He brings together all the evidence which can be obtained from the Epistles to Timothy to support the conjecture that an Apostolic Creed was actually drawn up before S. Paul started on his famous missionary journey. But the difficulties in the way of such a theory are very great. We saw that the New Testament evidence, considered apart from any question of later formulated creeds, led us to conclude that the Baptismal Formula and the simple Christological Confession existed side by side, but were not fused into a creed in apostolic times. The inference that the teaching about the Lord's confession before Pilate, and His return to judge, did not stand in a Trinitarian scheme, is very strongly confirmed by the teaching of S. John's First Epistle. If the thought of the Only-begotten is S. John's contribution under the Holy Spirit's guiding to the creed, which was to be the root of all reverent speculation in the future, we must allow time for the development of such reflection, and for the transport of Johannine books to Rome. We are therefore confined to the date A.D. ± 100, and in this way freed from the obligation of facing the final and most formidable objection. If the creed was literally written by the apostles, how could the next generation have presumed to alter its wording? In every Church, not excepting the Church of Rome, later generations still permitted further alterations, consistently if they need only desire to maintain a continuity of sense, impiously if they were really bound by the letter of their law of believing.

§ VI. The Old Creed of Jerusalem

Two early Creeds of Jerusalem are found in the catechetical lectures of Cyril of Jerusalem. As a young man he was priest in charge of the catechumens in the great church which Constantine had built on Golgotha. When he speaks of the cross, he reminds his hearers that they stand on holy ground. His addresses are very earnest and practical. He

[1] Ignatius, possibly also of some reference to the baptism by John.

keeps constantly in view the moral training of his hearers, exposed to many temptations. He scarcely glances at the great dogmatic controversy of the day within the Church. But he recognises fully the influence of faith on conduct, and is careful to instruct them according to the proportion of faith preserved in their Baptismal Creeds. At the same time, he warns them against the strange doctrines of Gnostics, Jews, and Samaritans, which would cut away their historic faith by the roots.

THE OLD CREED OF JERUSALEM

CYRIL, *Cat.* xix.

I. 1. Πιστεύω εἰς . . . πατέρα

II. 2. Καὶ εἰς
τὸν υἱὸν

III. 9. Καὶ εἰς τὸ πνεῦμα
τὸ ἅγιον

11. καὶ εἰς ἓν βάπτισμα μετανοίας
εἰς ἄφεσιν ἁμαρτιῶν

ib. vi.–xviii.

I. 1. Πιστεύομεν εἰς ἕνα Θεὸν πατέρα παντοκράτορα, ποιητὴν οὐρανοῦ καὶ γῆς ὁρατῶν τε πάντων καὶ ἀοράτων

II. 2. Καὶ εἰς ἕνα κύριον Ἰησοῦν Χριστὸν τὸν υἱὸν τοῦ Θεοῦ τὸν μονογενῆ, τὸν ἐκ τοῦ πατρὸς γεννηθέντα Θεὸν ἀληθινὸν πρὸ πάντων τῶν αἰώνων δι' οὗ τὰ πάντα ἐγένετο,

3. σαρκωθέντα καὶ ἐνανθρωπήσαντα

4. σταυρωθέντα καὶ ταφέντα

5. ἀναστάντα τῇ τρίτῃ ἡμέρᾳ

6. καὶ ἀνελθόντα εἰς τοὺς οὐρανοὺς

7. καὶ καθίσαντα ἐκ δεξιῶν τοῦ πατρός

8. καὶ ἐρχόμενον ἐν δόξῃ κρῖναι ζῶντας καὶ νεκροὺς οὗ τῆς βασιλείας οὐκ ἔσται τέλος.

III. 9. Καὶ εἰς ἓν ἅγιον πνεῦμα τὸν παράκλητον τὸ λαλῆσαν ἐν τοῖς προφήταις

11. καὶ εἰς ἓν βάπτισμα μετανοίας εἰς ἄφεσιν ἁμαρτιῶν

10. καὶ εἰς μίαν ἁγίαν καθολικὴν ἐκκλησίαν

12. καὶ εἰς σαρκὸς ἀνάστασιν καὶ εἰς ζωὴν αἰώνιον.

The first form is very short. It was used apparently at the very moment of baptism. It is found in a lecture addressed to the newly baptized (*Cat.* xix.). He reminds them how they renounced Satan and all his works, turning to the West, the land of darkness. Then turning to the East, as the land of light, they said : " I believe in the Father and in the Son and in the Holy Spirit, and in one baptism of repentance for the remission of sins." They were then baptized and anointed.

But it is not difficult to trace in these lectures the outline of a longer confession. Its relation to the shorter form is made obvious by the order of the clauses 10, 11, in which the words " one baptism of repentance for remission of sins " precede the words " and in one holy Catholic Church."

The first form takes us back, we might almost imagine, to the days when S. Peter preached his first sermon at Jerusalem. The other, like a map of geological strata, shows the history of its gradual formation. The term " Only-begotten Son of God," and the title Paraclete given to the Holy Spirit, point to the teaching of S. John, the word " catholic " to the times of Ignatius ; whereas the words " whose kingdom shall have no end " seem to be a recent addition against Marcellus.

The chief characteristic of this longer form, thus restored by Hort, is the absence of any precise reference to the miraculous birth or to Pontius Pilate. Kattenbusch, who thinks that it was derived from the Old Roman Creed, proposes to restore to it the readings ἐκ πνεύματος ἁγίου καὶ Μαρίας τῆς παρθένου and ἐπὶ Ποντίου Πιλάτου. These are found in the later revised Jerusalem Creed, better known as the Constantinopolitan Creed, which (as we shall see in Chap. V.) is to be regarded as Cyril's own revision. This is a most ingenious theory, and there can be no doubt that Cyril taught these facts. But there is no parallel in his writings to the exact form of the sentence on the incarnation, and when he mentions Pilate in his lecture on the crucifixion there is no emphasis on the name which would give us a hint that he found it in the creed. Beside inserting Nicene terms, he altered the form by transposing the order of clauses 10, 11, and by substituting " resurrection of the dead " for " resurrection of the flesh." There is therefore no reason to

THE OLD CREED OF JERUSALEM 69

think that he would scruple to add these words under the influence of another creed, or simply because they were found in the common tradition of other Churches.

Cyril did not speak of the creed as a watchword (σύμβολον). His name for it was "the Faith." He regarded it as a summary of doctrine, but did not suggest that it was unalterable.

We are led to the conclusion that the Old Jerusalem Creed, which in its short form may be older than R, has had an independent history. Originally founded on the Baptismal Formula, apart from the Christological Confession, it needed expansion, and received it from current Church teaching. But we are utterly ignorant of the process of development.

With this short Creed of Jerusalem it is interesting to compare a short creed found in the last book of the work "On the Trinity," ascribed to Vigilius of Thapsus. Montfaucon,[1] followed by Caspari,[2] claimed that the whole passage was a translation[3] from Athanasius. The writer distinguishes between the Baptismal Formula (Fidei sacramentum) and the Baptismal Confession (Confessio fidei): "Confessio fidei immo ipsa fides sanctorum et testamentum quod disposuimus ad Patrem et Filium et Spiritum Sanctum, ad sacrum laværum regenerationis uenientes, confessi sic: Credo in Deum Patrem omnipotentem et in Iesum Christum Filium eius unigenitum et Spiritum Sanctum."

A similar form is found in the Egyptian Church Order, which may be translated from the Coptic as follows: "I believe in the true God alone, the Father, the Almighty; and His Only-begotten Son Jesus Christ our Lord and Saviour; and in His Holy Spirit the all-lifegiving."

All that can be said about them is that they show a similar process of development at work.

[1] *Opp. Athanasii*, ii. 601. [2] iii. 51.
[3] Possibly by Vigilius ; Kattenbusch, ii. 259.

§ VII. Conclusions

To sum up. Eastern creeds are generally supposed to deal with ideas, and Western creeds with facts. This is true rather of the history of their development than of the simple skeleton form with which they began. The distinction will be obvious enough when we come to the controversies of the fourth century, and find the Western Churches maintaining their simple historic faith side by side with the elaborate theological confessions of Councils. Augustine in his sermons to catechumens uses the baptismal faith which he had learnt from Ambrose at Milan at the very time when our Nicene Creed, the revised Creed of Jerusalem, having obtained some sort of recognition at the Council of Constantinople, was starting on that path of progress which has made it the common heritage of Eucharistic worship in East and West. Again at Chalcedon it represented the triumph of Athanasian principles to a Council which were yet willing to receive the Old Roman Creed of Leo as quoted in his letter to Flavian.

Throughout the second century the Church of Rome was assailed by all manner of speculative heresies. It is a marvel that her creed came out of the ordeal so simple and so little changed. And it is an inspiring thought that, within two generations from the apostles, the doctrines of the incarnation, the resurrection, and the ascension were taught in the words of that creed, the very words which rise to our lips as the faith of our baptism. Not less distinctly than the Old Creed of Jerusalem, it points us back to the Baptismal Formula as the earliest creed of the Christian Church.

This is the stock from which have grown, following the same general laws of development, many and diverse flowers, whose hardy growth bears strong testimony to the vitality of the thought from which they sprang. The historian of the creeds is like a botanist among flowers. To other eyes they look a bewildering medley of varying shapes and colours. To his trained eye this heap of specimens is no medley. He can sort and classify, and then, taking one by one, he can dissect. Let the historian only remember that the deadness of the dried botanical specimen is to the grace and beauty of the living flower as a specimen creed analysed in a book to a creed in daily use as the watchword of a living Church. The creed is not for the student tempted to pedantry, but for the soldier of the Cross whose faith fires him on the battlefield of life with a noble resolve, as if his ears had heard his Master's voice, "In this sign thou shalt conquer."

CHAPTER IV

THE THEOLOGICAL FAITH OF THE FOURTH CENTURY

§ I. Of Theological Creeds.
§ II. Arius and Arianism.
§ III. The Council of Nicæa in 325.
§ IV. "The Fight in the Dark."
§ V. The Council of the Dedication (the second and fourth Creeds of Antioch).
§ VI. Arianism supreme.
§ VII. Victory in sight.
§ VIII. Conclusion.

§ I. Of Theological Creeds

A THEOLOGICAL creed is the strong meat of Christian teaching, not the milk of the word. This is its primary use, and it is easy to see how the need for such instruction would arise in the ordinary course of catechising, particularly when the candidates for baptism were men of culture and ability. The Creed of Gregory Thaumaturgus [1] may be cited as showing a type which does not merely state the facts of Christian experience, but also attempts to supply the interpretation. Thus Gregory uses the word "Trinity," which is not found in Scripture. And some Churches had by this time introduced into their creeds the word "catholic." The explanations given of such terms were hardly as yet scientific. Theological science, like any other, has to make its way slowly and forge its definitions as best it can, hindered by the limited resources of human language. We can trace development in the

---

[1] Hahn,[2] iii. p. 253. Since Caspari has investigated the question, the authenticity of this creed has been generally accepted.

dogmatic standards taught by individual teachers in their rules of faith from Ignatius to Irenæus, and from Irenæus to Origen. All subsequent Latin writers owe a debt to Tertullian, who gave a great impetus to the moulding of theological terms in a language far less delicate than Greek as an instrument of human thought. We must therefore remember that theological debates did not begin with the fourth century, and that the Creed of the Council of Nicæa was not the first theological creed used as the watchword of a Church militant against error. In Christ a new type of character had appeared in the world, and must be explained in relation to God and men. The very failures of speculation in regard to the Divine nature in Christ prepared men's minds to appreciate more fully the mystery of human nature in themselves, the mystery of personality, which is the gateway of all knowledge.[1]

The Council of Nicæa, indeed, marks the beginning of a new era. Christianity had become a permitted religion. So far the Church had triumphed over the world, only to find that in success temptations must be faced more subtle than those which she had encountered in her recent humble and despised station. It was not heresy alone, but heresy arrayed in all the pomp of place and power, which she had now to combat. Foes in her own household tried to introduce heathen speculations under the cloak of Christian philosophy, or by a vehement reaction to stiffen distinctive Christian teaching into a series of barren dogmas, properly so called, rigid formularies, which would cramp the mind and leave no room for the exercise of loving faith. It is true to say that many formularies of this creed-making epoch added to the contents of the historic faith mere negations, closing misleading avenues of thought without aiding faith's advance. The first Nicene Creed, with its anathemas, is a typical instance. But this is not the form which has been finally adopted for liturgical use. There was a silver lining to the cloud of controversy which loomed so darkly over the horizon of Church life. In our Nicene Creed is set forth the positive

[1] Illingworth, *Personality*, p. 13.

result reached; we are shown how dogmatic definition was made subordinate to worship of Christ as the "Light of Light."

§ II. Arius and Arianism

Arius was a clever and influential priest in a district of Alexandria called Baucalis. He was also a teacher of exegesis, and sure enough of his opinions to criticise loudly a sermon preached by his bishop as favouring the Sabellian heresy. He had studied at Antioch in the school of Lucian the Martyr, and had brought away a theological method which, to say the least, minimised the Divine glory of Christ. He found in Alexandria a circle of admirers who dreaded Sabellianism, and were easily persuaded by a parade of argument that the idea of an eternal Sonship is unthinkable. "Arius started from the *idea* of God and the *predicate* 'Son.' God is above all things uncreated, or unoriginate, ἀγέν[ν]ητος. . . . Everything else is created, γενητόν. The name 'Son' implies an *act* of procreation. Therefore before such act there was no Son, nor was God, properly speaking, a Father. The Son is not co-eternal with Him. He was originated by the Father's will, as indeed were all things. He is, then, τῶν γενητῶν, He came into being from non-existence (ἐξ οὐκ ὄντων), and before that did not exist (οὐκ ἦν πρὶν γένηται). But His relation to God differs from that of the universe generally. Created nature cannot bear the awful touch of bare Deity. God therefore created the Son that He in turn might be the agent in the creation of the universe—'created Him as the beginning of His ways' (Prov. viii. 22, LXX.). This being so, the nature of the Son was in the essential point of ἀγεννησία unlike that of the Father; (ξένος τοῦ υἱοῦ κατ' οὐσίαν ὁ Πατὴρ ὅτι ἄναρχος): their substances (ὑποστάσεις) are ἀνεπίμικτοι—have nothing in common. The Son therefore does not possess the fundamental property of Sonship, identity of nature with the Father. He is a Son by adoption, not by nature; He has advanced by moral probation to be Son, even to be μονογενὴς Θεός (John i. 14). He is not the eternal Λόγος, reason, of God, but *a* Word (and God has spoken many): but yet He is *the* Word by grace; is *no longer* what He is *by nature*, subject to change. He cannot know the Father, much less make Him known to others. Lastly, He dwells in flesh, not in full human nature. The doctrine of Arius as to the Holy Spirit is not recorded; but probably He was placed between the Son and the other κτίσματα."[1] The worst of it was, that in his shortsightedness he insisted on translating his theories into verses, which were sung to the tunes of licentious and comic songs, "jesting on such matters as on a stage."[2] A tree is known by its fruits. It was this want of humility and reverence in dealing with sacred things which throughout the subsequent controversy betrayed the defect of Arian theology. Gregory of Nyssa thus describes the pass to which idle gossip on deep subjects had brought men in his time: "Men of yesterday and the day before, mere mechanics, off-hand dogmatists in theology, servants, too, and slaves that have been flogged, runaways from servile work, are solemn with us, and philosophise about things incomprehensible. Ask about pence, and the tradesman will discuss the generate and the ingenerate; inquire the price of bread, and he will say, 'Greater is the Father, and the Son is subject'; say that a bath would suit you, and he defines that 'the Son is out of nothing.'"

A Synod was held of the bishops of Egypt and Libya. Arius and his allies were deposed. But he entered into correspondence with bishops abroad, Eusebius of Cæsarea and Eusebius of Nicomedia. The latter, a fellow-Lucianist, consulted other bishops on his behalf. In Egypt the new movement spread rapidly, and news of the disturbance of religious peace reached the emperor's ears. He sent Hosius, Bishop of Cordova, with a letter to Alexandria, and, after receiving his report, determined to summon a Council of Bishops from the whole world to settle the doctrinal questions raised.

[1] Robertson, *Athanasius*, p. xxviii. [2] Athanasius, *c. Ar.* i. 2.

§ III. THE COUNCIL OF NICÆA IN 325

The place which Constantine selected for the Council was admirably adapted for such a gathering. It could be easily approached by sea or land. The posting arrangements of the empire were excellent, and the emperor ordered that the bishops and their attendants should travel at public expense. The magnificent gathering of some three hundred bishops, which met thus at the invitation of the first Christian emperor, has been often described. The imagination of their contemporaries was chiefly stirred by the marks of suffering which so many bore on their faces and limbs, endured during the time of persecution recently ended. It was this which gave their decision so much weight. As a matter of fact, they were almost unanimous in condemning the new heresy, but wide divergences of opinion prevailed as to the reasons for their judgment.

It seems to have been understood from the first that some formula should be drawn up to express the teaching of the Church. But the scriptural arguments which were brought up in the preliminary discussions were all received with suspicious readiness by the Arians, who suggested to each other methods of evasion. Athanasius describes the scene vividly (*de Decretis*, 20): "They were caught whispering to each other, and winking with their eyes, that 'like' and 'always' and 'power' and 'in Him' were, as before, common to us and the Son, and that it was no difficulty to agree to these. As to 'like,' they said, it is written of us, 'Man is the image and glory of God'; 'always,' that it was written, 'For we which live are alway'; 'in Him,' 'In Him we live and move and have our being'; . . . as to 'power,' that the caterpillar and the locust are called 'power' and 'great power.'" The bishops were therefore "compelled, on their part, to collect the sense of the Scriptures, and to re-say and re-write what they had said before more distinctly still, namely, that the Son is 'one in essence' with the Father."

The term ὁμοούσιος, "one in essence," had probably been

CREED OF EUSEBIUS

suggested by Hosius on his visit to Alexandria, for it was a word which had been used by teachers of repute, especially in the West. But it had been disclaimed by Arius and by Eusebius of Nicomedia. S. Ambrose (*de Fid.* iii. n. 125) quotes a letter in which Eusebius wrote: "If we call Him true Son of the Father and uncreate, then are we granting that He is 'one in essence.'" Thus it was a phrase, so to speak, held in reserve.

The Arian party boldly presented a creed which stated their theories concisely. It was received with indignation and torn to pieces.

Then Eusebius of Cæsarea, venerable for age and learning, came forward with a creed as follows:—

"As we have received from the bishops who preceded us, and in our first catechisings, and when we received the Holy Laver, and as we have learned from the Divine Scriptures, and as we have believed and taught in the presbytery and in the episcopate itself, so believing also at the time present, we report to you our faith, and it is this:—

'We believe in one God, the Father Almighty, the Maker of all things visible and invisible. And in one Lord Jesus Christ, the Word of God, God from God, Light from Light, Life from Life, Son Only-begotten, firstborn of every creature, before all the ages, begotten from the Father, by whom also all things were made; who for our salvation was made flesh, and lived among men, and suffered, and rose again the third day, and ascended to the Father, and will come again in glory to judge the quick and dead. And we believe also in one Holy Ghost: believing each of these to be and to exist, the Father truly Father, and the Son truly Son, and the Holy Ghost truly Holy Ghost, as also our Lord, sending forth His disciples for the preaching, said, 'Go teach all nations, baptizing them in the name of the Father, and of the Son, and of the Holy Ghost.' Concerning whom we confidently affirm that so we hold, and so we think, and so we have held aforetime, and we maintain this faith unto the death, anathematising every godless heresy. That this we have ever thought from our heart and soul, from the time we recollect ourselves, and now think and say in truth, before God Almighty and our Lord Jesus Christ do we witness, being able by proofs to show and to convince you, that, even in times past, such has been our belief and our preaching."

Opinions are divided on the question whether Eusebius composed this document for the occasion,[1] or whether his second paragraph was a verbatim quotation of the creed of his native Church.[2] His words imply that it was a summary of teaching, of the kind usually given to catechumens, constructed on the lines of the creed, and explaining it. It is not likely that a baptismal creed of this date would have ended with mere mention of the Holy Spirit, and no reference to His work. The Creeds of Jerusalem and Antioch alone prove this. Nor is it likely that Eusebius, if he intended to quote the creed exactly, would stop short in it. We must conclude that he added to a free quotation of suitable phrases the warning against Sabellianism with which he leads up to the Baptismal Formula, thus ending the document which he wished the council to accept and endorse.

The Creed of Eusebius was read. So far as it went it was above criticism. But it did not contain the term ὁμοούσιος, which was felt to guard against all evasions of scriptural words. The emperor himself, prompted by Hosius, proposed its insertion. Finally, this was agreed on, and the creed was thoroughly revised under the direction of Hosius, Marcellus, Eustathius of Antioch, and perhaps Macarius of Jerusalem, for in its final shape it contains phrases which remind us of the Creed of Jerusalem as well as that of Antioch.[3] For the anti-Sabellian phrases of Eusebius were substituted anti-Arian anathemas.

The principal changes were as follows:—(i) The term "Word" (λόγος) was cut out, and "Son" (υἱός) was moved up into its place. This was an improvement on the vague Christology of the Creed of Eusebius. The central problem of Divine Sonship was set before the consideration of the Son's work in our creation and redemption. (ii) "Only-

[1] Harnack, art. "Apostolisches Symbolum," *R.E.*³
[2] Robertson, *Athanasius*, p. xix., following Hort.   [3] Hort.

CREEDS OF EUSEBIUS AND NICENE COUNCIL

begotten" (μονογενής) was explained by the words "of the essence of the Father" (ἐκ τῆς οὐσίας τοῦ πατρός). Thus the argument used by Eusebius of Nicomedia in his letter to Paulinus of Tyre was contradicted.[1] (iii) Further, it was guarded by the emphatic assertion begotten, not made (γεννηθέντα οὐ ποιηθέντα), in reply to Arius and Asterius, leading up to "of one essence with the Father" (ὁμοούσιος τῷ πατρί). (iv) The word "incarnate" (σαρκωθέντα) was explained by the addition "was made man" (ἐνανθρωπήσαντα),

CREED OF EUSEBIUS (Ep. ad Cæs. ap. Ath. de Decretis)	CREED OF NICENE COUNCIL (ib.)
Πιστεύομεν εἰς ἕνα Θεὸν πατέρα παντοκράτορα τὸν τῶν ἁπάντων ὁρατῶν τε καὶ ἀοράτων ποιητήν Καὶ εἰς ἕνα κύριον Ἰησοῦν Χριστόν, τὸν τοῦ Θεοῦ λόγον, Θεὸν ἐκ Θεοῦ, φῶς ἐκ φωτὸς, ζωὴν ἐκ ζωῆς, υἱὸν μονογενῆ, πρωτότοκον πάσης κτίσεως, πρὸ πάντων τῶν αἰώνων ἐκ τοῦ Θεοῦ πατρὸς γεγεννημένον, δι' οὗ καὶ ἐγένετο τὰ πάντα τὸν διὰ τὴν ἡμετέραν σωτηρίαν σαρκωθέντα καὶ ἐν ἀνθρώποις πολιτευσάμενον καὶ παθόντα καὶ ἀναστάντα τῇ τρίτῃ ἡμέρᾳ καὶ ἀνελθόντα πρὸς τὸν πατέρα καὶ ἥξοντα πάλιν ἐν δόξῃ κρῖναι ζῶντας καὶ νεκρούς. Πιστεύομεν καὶ εἰς ἓν πνεῦμα ἅγιον, τούτων ἕκαστον εἶναι καὶ ὑπάρχειν πιστεύοντες, πατέρα ἀληθῶς πατέρα, καὶ υἱὸν ἀληθῶς υἱόν, καὶ πνεῦμα ἅγιον ἀληθῶς ἅγιον πνεῦμα, καθὼς καὶ ὁ κύριος ἡμῶν ἀποστέλλων εἰς τὸ κήρυγμα τοὺς ἑαυτοῦ μαθητὰς εἶπε· πορευθέντες μαθητεύσατε πάντα τὰ ἔθνη, κ.τ.λ.	Πιστεύομεν εἰς ἕνα Θεὸν πατέρα παντοκράτορα πάντων ὁρατῶν τε καὶ ἀοράτων ποιητήν Καὶ εἰς ἕνα κύριον Ἰησοῦν Χριστὸν, τὸν υἱὸν τοῦ Θεοῦ, γεννηθέντα ἐκ τοῦ πατρὸς μονογενῆ, τουτέστιν ἐκ τῆς οὐσίας τοῦ πατρός, Θεὸν ἐκ Θεοῦ, φῶς ἐκ φωτὸς, Θεὸν ἀληθινὸν ἐκ Θεοῦ ἀληθινοῦ, γεννηθέντα οὐ ποιηθέντα, ὁμοούσιον τῷ πατρὶ δι' οὗ τὰ πάντα ἐγένετο, τά τε ἐν τῷ οὐρανῷ καὶ τὰ ἐν τῇ γῇ, τὸν δι' ἡμᾶς τοὺς ἀνθρώπους καὶ διὰ τὴν ἡμετέραν σωτηρίαν κατελθόντα καὶ σαρκωθέντα ἐνανθρωπήσαντα, παθόντα καὶ ἀναστάντα τῇ τρίτῃ ἡμέρᾳ, ἀνελθόντα εἰς τοὺς οὐρανοὺς, ἐρχόμενον κρῖναι ζῶντας καὶ νεκρούς. Καὶ εἰς τὸ πνεῦμα τὸ ἅγιον. Τοὺς δὲ λέγοντας· ἦν ποτε ὅτε οὐκ ἦν, ἢ οὐκ ἦν πρὶν γεννηθῆναι, ἢ ἐξ οὐκ ὄντων ἐγένετο, ἢ ἐξ ἑτέρας ὑποστάσεως ἢ οὐσίας φάσκοντας εἶναι, ἢ κτιστὸν ἢ τρεπτὸν ἢ ἀλλοιωτὸν τὸν υἱὸν τοῦ Θεοῦ, τούτους ἀναθεματίζει ἡ καθολικὴ καὶ ἀποστολικὴ τοῦ Θεοῦ ἐκκλησία.

---

[1] Theodoret, i. 5.

in place of the less definite "lived as a citizen amongst men." That beautiful phrase was found in the Creed of Eusebius,[1] and it is to be regretted that it was dropped. But it did not answer the fundamental question, "How is Christ the ideal citizen?" The fate of all Christian socialism depends on the answer.

We do not know how long the debates lasted, but when the final moment came for decision the defeat of the Arian party was crushing. All signed except two, Eusebius of Nicomedia with a reservation exposing himself to the scorn of the stalwart Secundus and Theonas.

The explanation of his action which Eusebius of Cæsarea thought fit to send to his flock, laid stress on the emperor's influence and denial of false ways in which the term "of one essence" could be interpreted. In the same strain he interpreted "of the essence" negatively, "of the Father, but not as a part," without attempting to say what it does mean.

Thus the original Nicene Creed was the work of a minority, a form proposed and carried through by the sheer force of clearer conviction and foresight. Those who best understood Arianism were most active in opposing it. We do not know what influence Athanasius the deacon actually obtained at the Council. He is said to have spoken,[2] and was already Alexander's trusted adviser. But the identification of ὑπόστασις and οὐσία in the fourth anathema was foreign to the prevailing tone of thought at Alexandria, where men spoke of τρεῖς ὑποστάσεις. Loofs says truly of Athanasius, "He was moulded by the Nicene Creed; did not mould it himself."[3]

The creed thus proposed to the whole Church by the Council, with the emperor's approval, was intended as a standard of doctrine, an authoritative exposition of the "one faith" contained in the varying baptismal creeds and the rules of faith held in reverence by the different Churches, which no one wished to disturb.

[1] Cf. the fourth Creed of Antioch.   [2] *Apol. c. Ar.* 6.
[3] *DG.*² p. 151.

§ IV. "The Fight in the Dark"

Truth conquers only when it stimulates conviction. Men constrained to believe or to act would fain rebel against the logic of their position or the commands laid upon them. Most of the bishops, when they returned from Nicæa to their homes, were agreed that Arius should be condemned, but were doubtful whether the new watchword of orthodoxy was a true interpretation of their faith in Christ. "A reaction was inevitable." Feelings were embittered by the harsh punishment dealt to the Arians by the will of the emperor, with the consent of the Nicene leaders. In this respect time brought revenge. During his exile in Illyria, Arius made good use of his opportunities to spread his opinions. Two of the ablest of the next generation of Arian leaders—Ursacius, Bishop of Singidunum (Belgrade), and Valens, Bishop of Mursa (Mitrowitz)—came under his personal influence.

Within five years, Eusebius of Nicomedia, who soon followed into exile, was recalled. Constantine was loyal to the Council, but had missed his ready adviser, and was easily persuaded to pardon Arius also when assured that they accepted the Council's Creed. Thenceforward the Imperial Court became the headquarters from which a series of intrigues were planned against all orthodox bishops, especially Athanasius. The original strength of the Arian party consisted in the fact that they had a definite plan of dogmatic teaching as fellow-Lucianists. They were now reinforced by politicians, place-hunters, and found it easy to make an alliance with the schismatic Meletians in Egypt. Society also was on their side among the heathen, and the clever sophist Asterius roused much interest on their behalf by his lectures.

In Asia Minor the Nicene party were outnumbered from the first. The traditional theology there was realistic, out of sympathy with Origen. Their hatred of the speculations of Paul of Samosata led them by a true instinct to condemn Arianism, but it was soon balanced by an equal hatred of the teaching of Marcellus. They were jealous of the triumph of

Western theologians, and their discontent was kept alive by the intriguers at court, where the political importance of those provinces was highly esteemed.

In Syria, Eusebius of Cæsarea had a large following. He was "neither a great man nor a clear thinker,"[1] but signed the creed honestly, putting his own interpretation on it, and sympathising with Arius rather than with Arianism. His age and learning made him the leader of the conservatives, whose chief dread was Sabellianism.

In 329 he joined with Arian and reactionary bishops in a Synod at Antioch, which deposed Eustathius on the double charge of Sabellianism and immorality. Other bishops were then attacked, and trouble was fomented in Egypt with the aim of deposing Athanasius and restoring Arius to communion in Alexandria. At Tyre in 335 the Arians met in force, and Athanasius had to escape to Constantinople. The emperor was annoyed by the continuance of strife, and when an entirely new charge of treason was fabricated, banished him to Trèves.

In 336 the storm broke which had been gathering over the head of Marcellus. His treatise against Asterius had laid him open to the charge of Sabellianism, and he was attacked by Eusebius of Cæsarea. He taught that the Divine Unity, for the work of creation and redemption, extended itself into a Trinity ($\pi\lambda\alpha\tau\upsilon\nu\omu\acute{\epsilon}\nu\eta$ $\epsilon\acute{\iota}\varsigma$ $\tau\rho\iota\acute{\alpha}\delta\alpha$). The incarnation was therefore the manifestation of supreme Divine energy ($\acute{\epsilon}\nu\epsilon\rho\gamma\epsilon\acute{\iota}\alpha$ $\delta\rho\alpha\sigma\tau\iota\kappa\acute{\eta}$) under conditions of time and space which would come to an end. Then the Divine Word, proceeding from the eternal silence, having delivered up the Kingdom to the Father "that God may be all in all" (1 Cor. xv. 28), would relapse into repose. Thus he ascribed to the Divine Word only a potential personal existence.

He was defended by the Nicene party. Athanasius, who met him again at Rome after the death of Constantine, to the end of his life refused to condemn him, though compelled to reject some of his speculations.

[1] Gwatkin.

§ V. The Council of the Dedication (Second and Fourth Creeds of Antioch)

When the Council of the Dedication of Constantine's golden church at Antioch met in 341, the controversy passed into a new phase. Its members were mostly conservatives who were prepared to go some way in the direction of reconciliation with the Nicene leaders. Hilary calls it a "Synod of Saints," and its canons have passed into the general body of Church law. But the Arians present formed a compact party under the leadership of the veteran Eusebius, who had been translated from Nicomedia to Constantinople, and the see of Cæsarea was now held by the unprincipled Acacius.

The first business was to frame a reply to a letter received from Julius, Bishop of Rome, a masterly summary of matters in dispute, which rather irritated them. Then the work of creed-making was begun by the Arians. While professing to accept the Nicene Creed, they brought forward a formulary suspiciously like the deceptive profession of Arius, though it began with an absurd protest that they should not be considered his followers, because bishops would not follow a priest. This was rejected, and the second Creed of Antioch, often called the Lucianic Creed, was proposed and passed.

SECOND CREED OF ANTIOCH

Πιστεύομεν ἀκολούθως τῇ εὐαγγελικῇ καὶ ἀποστολικῇ παραδόσει εἰς ἕνα Θεὸν, πατέρα παντοκράτορα, τὸν τῶν ὅλων δημιουργόν τε καὶ ποιητὴν καὶ προνοητήν. Καὶ εἰς ἕνα κύριον Ἰησοῦν Χριστόν, τὸν υἱὸν αὐτοῦ τὸν μονογενῆ, Θεόν, δι' οὗ τὰ πάντα, τὸν
10 γεννηθέντα πρὸ τῶν αἰώνων ἐκ τοῦ πατρός, Θεὸν ἐκ Θεοῦ, ὅλον ἐξ ὅλου, μόνον ἐκ μόνου, τέλειον ἐκ τελείου, βασιλέα ἐκ βασιλέως, κύριον ἀπὸ κυρίου, λόγον
15 ζῶντα, σοφίαν ζῶσαν, φῶς ἀληθινόν, ὁδόν, ἀλήθειαν, ἀνάστασιν,

We believe, conformably to the evangelical and apostolical tradition, in one God, the Father Almighty, the Framer, and Maker, and Provider of the universe, from whom are all things. And in one Lord Jesus Christ, His Son, Only-begotten God (John i. 18), by whom are all things, who was begotten before all ages from the Father, God from God, whole from whole, sole from sole, perfect from perfect, King from King, Lord from Lord, Living Word, Living Wisdom, true Light, Way, Truth, Resurrection, Shepherd, Door, both unalterable and

ποιμένα, θύραν, ἄτρεπτόν τε καὶ
ἀναλλοίωτον, τῆς θεότητος, οὐσίας
τε καὶ βουλῆς καὶ δυνάμεως καὶ
20 δόξης τοῦ πατρὸς ἀπαράλλακτον
εἰκόνα, τὸν πρωτότοκον πάσης
κτίσεως, τὸν ὄντα ἐν ἀρχῇ πρὸς
τὸν Θεόν, Θεὸν λόγον, κατὰ τὸ
εἰρημένον εὐαγγελίῳ· καὶ Θεὸς ἦν
25 ὁ λόγος, δι' οὗ τὰ πάντα ἐγένετο
καὶ ἐν ᾧ τὰ πάντα συνέστηκε· τὸν
ἐπ' ἐσχάτων τῶν ἡμερῶν κατελθόντα ἄνωθεν καὶ γεννηθέντα ἐκ
παρθένου, κατὰ τὰς γραφάς καὶ
30 ἄνθρωπον γενόμενον, μεσίτην
Θεοῦ καὶ ἀνθρώπων, ἀποστολόν
τε τῆς πίστεως ἡμῶν, καὶ ἀρχηγὸν
ζωῆς, ὥς φησι· ὅτι καταβέβηκα
ἐκ τοῦ οὐρανοῦ, οὐχ ἵνα ποιῶ τὸ
35 θέλημα τὸ ἐμόν, ἀλλὰ τὸ θέλημα
τοῦ πέμψαντός με· τὸν παθόντα
καὶ ἀναστάντα ὑπὲρ ἡμῶν τῇ
τρίτῃ ἡμέρᾳ καὶ ἀνελθόντα εἰς
οὐρανοὺς καὶ καθεσθέντα ἐν
40 δεξιᾷ τοῦ πατρός, καὶ πάλιν
ἐρχόμενον μετὰ δόξης καὶ
δυνάμεως κρῖναι ζῶντας καὶ
νεκρούς. Καὶ εἰς τὸ πνεῦμα
τὸ ἅγιον, τὸ εἰς παράκλησιν καὶ
45 ἁγιασμὸν καὶ τελείωσιν τοῖς πισ-
τεύουσι διδόμενον καθὼς καὶ ὁ
κύριος ἡμῶν Ἰησοῦς Χριστὸς διε-
τάξατο τοῖς μαθηταῖς, λέγων·
πορευθέντες μαθητεύσατε πάντα
50 τὰ ἔθνη, βαπτίζοντες αὐτοὺς εἰς
τὸ ὄνομα τοῦ πατρὸς καὶ τοῦ υἱοῦ
καὶ τοῦ ἁγίου πνεύματος· δηλονότι
πατρὸς ἀληθῶς πατρὸς ὄντος, υἱοῦ
δὲ ἀληθῶς υἱοῦ ὄντος, τοῦ δὲ ἁγίου
55 πνεύματος ἀληθῶς ἁγίου πνεύματος
ὄντος, τῶν ὀνομάτων οὐχ ἁπλῶς
οὐδὲ ἀργῶς κειμένων ἀλλὰ σημαιν-
όντων ἀκριβῶς τὴν οἰκείαν ἑκάστου
τῶν ὀνομαζομένων ὑπόστασιν καὶ
60 τάξιν καὶ δόξαν· ὡς εἶναι τῇ μὲν
ὑποστάσει τρία, τῇ δὲ συμφωνίᾳ
ἕν. Ταύτην οὖν ἔχοντες τὴν πίστιν,

unchangeable; exact image of the
Godhead, Essence, Will, Power, and
Glory of the Father; the first-born
of every creature, who was in the
beginning with God, God the Word,
as it is written in the Gospel, "and
the Word was God" (John i. 1);
by whom all things were made,
and in whom all things consist
(Col. i. 17); who in the last days
descended from above, and was
born of a virgin according to the
Scriptures, and was made man,
Mediator between God and man,
and Apostle of our faith, and Prince
of life, as He says, "I came down
from heaven, not to do Mine own
will, but the will of Him that sent
Me" (John vi. 38); who suffered
for us and rose again on the third
day, and ascended into heaven, and
sat down on the right hand of the
Father, and is coming again with
glory and power, to judge quick
and dead. And in the Holy Ghost,
who is given to those who believe
for comfort, and sanctification, and
initiation, as also our Lord Jesus
Christ enjoined His disciples, saying, "Go ye, teach all nations,
baptizing them in the name of the
Father, and the Son, and the Holy
Ghost" (Matt. xxviii. 19); namely,
of a Father who is truly Father,
and a Son who is truly Son, and of
the Holy Ghost who is truly Holy
Ghost, the names not being given
without meaning of effect, but
denoting accurately the peculiar
subsistence, rank, and glory of each
that is named, so that they are
three in subsistence, and in agreement one. Holding then this faith,
and holding it in the presence of
God and Christ, from beginning to
end, we anathematise every heretical

SECOND CREED OF ANTIOCH 85

καὶ ἐξ ἀρχῆς καὶ μέχρι τέλους ἔχοντες ἐνώπιον τοῦ Θεοῦ καὶ τοῦ Χριστοῦ πᾶσαν αἱρετικὴν κακοδοξίαν ἀναθεματίζομεν. καὶ εἴ τις παρὰ τὴν ὑγιῆ τῶν γραφῶν ὀρθὴν πίστιν διδάσκει, λέγων, ἢ χρόνον ἢ καιρὸν ἢ αἰῶνα ἢ εἶναι ἢ γεγονέναι πρὸ τοῦ γεννηθῆναι τὸν υἱόν, ἀνάθεμα ἔστω. Καὶ εἴ τις λέγει τὸν υἱὸν κτίσμα ὡς ἓν τῶν κτισμάτων, ἢ γέννημα ὡς ἓν τῶν γεννημάτων ἢ ποίημα ὡς ἓν τῶν ποιημάτων, καὶ μὴ ὡς αἱ θεῖαι γραφαὶ παραδέδωκαν τῶν προειρημένων ἕκαστον ἀφ' ἑκάστου, ἢ εἴ τις ἄλλο διδάσκει ἢ εὐαγγελίζεται παρ' ὃ παρελάβομεν, ἀνάθεμα ἔστω. ἡμεῖς γὰρ πᾶσι τοῖς ἐκ τῶν θείων γραφῶν παραδεδομένοις ὑπό τε τῶν προφητῶν καὶ ἀποστόλων ἀληθινῶς καὶ ἐμφόβως καὶ πιστεύομεν καὶ ἀκολουθοῦμεν.

heterodoxy. And if any teaches beside the sound and right faith of the Scriptures, that time, or season, or age, either is or has been before the generation of the Son, be he anathema. Or if anyone says that the Son is a creature as one of the creatures, or an offspring as one of the offsprings, or a work as one of the works, and not the aforesaid articles one after another, as the Divine Scriptures have delivered, or if he teaches or preaches beside what we have received, be he anathema. For all that has been delivered in the Divine Scriptures, whether by prophets or apostles, do we truly and reverently both believe and follow.

LINE 5. om. καὶ προνοητήν, S.[1] 9. πάντα] + ἐγένετο, S. 10. προ] + πάντων, S. 14. ἀπὸ] ἐκ, H. 15. om. ζῶντα, H. 15. ζῶσαν] ζωήν, SH. 16. ὁδὸν ἀληθείας, SH. 18. τῆς] pr. τήν, S. 19. om. καὶ βουλῆς, SH. 23. > λόγον Θεοῦ, S. 24. κατὰ τὸ εἰρ. εὐαγγ.] ἐν τῷ εὐαγγελίῳ, S. 30. ἄνθρωπον] agnus, H. 33. ζωῆς] pr. τῆς, S. 36. παθόντα] + ὑπὲρ ἡμῶν, S. 43. καί] + εἰς, S. 48. ordinauit discipulos, H. 52. δηλονότι πατρὸς ἀληθινῶς ὄντος πατρὸς καὶ υἱοῦ ἀληθινῶς υἱοῦ ὄντος καὶ πνεύματος ἁγίου ἀληθῶς ὄντος πνεύματος ἁγίου, S. 57. ἀργῶς] ἀργῶν, S. 58. οἰκείαν] ἰδίαν, S. 60. ὑπόστασίν τε καὶ δόξαν καὶ τάξιν, S. 64. om. καὶ ἐξ ... ἔχοντες, S. 66. > ἀναθεμ. κακοδ. S. 68. om. ἢ χρόνον, S. 69. αἰῶνα εἶναι, S. 71. πρὸ τοῦ γενν. τὸν υἱὸν] πρὸ τοῦ τὸν υἱὸν τοῦ Θεοῦ, S. 75. om. ἢ ποίημα ... ποιημάτων, S. 76. παραδεδώκασι, SH. 77. ἕκαστον] ἕκαστα, SH. 83. ἀληθινῶς τε καὶ ἐμφανῶς, S.

Athanasius[2] says sarcastically that they wanted something newer and fuller, but, after all, it represents some extent of concession on the Arian side. In it are heaped up all the scriptural phrases by which disciples of Origen thought to defend the Lord's divinity. It is catholic in the assertion of "the exact likeness of the Son to the Father's essence." The word "essence" honestly accepted

[1] Socrates (S), Hilary (H). [2] *De Synod.* 23.

would confute any attempt to explain it away by the mental reservation that this had not always been true. Catholic also is the phrase "mediator between God and men." But it marks the beginning of a doctrinal reaction. The term ὁμοούσιος is omitted. The phrases which Eusebius of Cæsarea had proposed against Sabellianism reappear. A further declaration follows against Marcellus, ending with the phrase, τῇ μὲν ὑποστάσει τρία τῇ δὲ συμφωνίᾳ ἕν, which is "an artfully chosen point of contact between Origen on the one hand, and Asterius, Lucian, and Paul of Samosata on the other."[1] In the anathemas the phrases condemned at Nicæa are proscribed, but in a way which might admit of an Arian interpretation. Athanasius points out that they condemn every heretical heterodoxy, not naming the Arian. The mention of Scripture is dubious, because each party fancied themselves the best interpreters.

Thus completed, the creed was not much use against Marcellus, who admitted both the pretemporal generation and the true Sonship. But it was often quoted, and became at a later time a stepping-stone by which semi-Arians were able to climb to a more orthodox standpoint. According to Sozomen,[2] the bishops declared that they had found the entire form in the writing of Lucian. But he adds that he cannot say whether they spoke truly or desired to obtain respect for their own writing. He also says that the Synod which met in Caria in 367 acknowledged it as Lucianic, supposing that it had been so called at Seleucia in 357. Kattenbusch[3] points out that Sozomen is here dependent on Socrates,[4] who says nothing about any such declaration of semi-Arians or Homœans at Seleucia. If anything of the kind was said in 357, we must remember that eighteen years had passed, giving time for such a fable to grow up. Possibly Sozomen confused the second with the fourth Creed of Antioch, which is more probably Lucianic.[5]

There may be in the second a kernel of Lucianic teaching, but if so it is strange that Athanasius and Hilary are silent

---

[1] Robertson, *Athanasius*, p. xliv. [2] *H.E.* iii. 5. [3] i. p. 257.
[4] *Hist.* ii. 39. [5] Kattenbusch, i. pp. 261ff.

about it. Athanasius remarks that the Nicene party have no monopoly of unbiblical phrases: "In the so-called Dedication, Acacius and Eusebius and their fellows used expressions not in Scripture, and said that 'the first-born of the creation' was the exact image of the essence and power and will and glory."[1] From Epiphanius we learn that Acacius, in his book against Marcellus, quoted the sophist Asterius as the author of the whole of this set of phrases in the creed, from ἄλλος μεν . . . εἰκόνα.[2] Now, Asterius, who had died some ten years before, was a pupil of Lucian, and might of course have simply quoted his master. On the other hand, Philostorgius[3] says that Asterius had changed Lucian's teaching, implying that he had come nearer to the Nicene position. Since this was the attitude of the majority at this Council, it seems reasonable to accept Kattenbusch's argument, and assume that they quoted Asterius rather than Lucian.

The third Creed of Antioch was a personal profession of faith presented by Theophronius, Bishop of Tyana. It was rabidly anti-Marcellian.

The fourth Creed was the work of a few bishops who reassembled in Antioch a few months later. Constans had requested Constantius to send him a deputation on the affairs of Athanasius, and this creed was constructed for the deputies to take. It is based on the creed found in the sixth book of the Apostolic Constitutions, which is a revised form of the creed found in the Didascalia. (See Appendix F.)

FOURTH CREED OF ANTIOCH

We believe in one God, the Father Almighty, Creator and Maker of all things; from whom all fatherhood in heaven and earth is named (Eph. iii. 15).

And in His Only-begotten Son, our Lord Jesus Christ, who before all ages was begotten from the Father, God from God, Light from Light, by whom all things were made in the heavens and on the earth, visible and invisible, being Word, and Wisdom, and Power, and Life, and True

---

[1] *De Synod.* 36.   [2] *Hær.* 72. 6.   [3] ii. 14, 15, quoted by Photius.

Light; who in the last days was made man for us, and was born of the Holy Virgin; who was crucified, and dead, and buried, and rose again from the dead the third day, and was taken up into heaven, and sat down on the right hand of the Father; and is coming at the consummation of the age, to judge quick and dead, and to render to everyone according to his works; whose kingdom endures indissolubly into the infinite ages; for He shall be seated on the right hand of the Father, not only in this age but in that which is to come.

And in the Holy Ghost; that is the Paraclete; which having promised to the apostles, He sent forth after His ascension into heaven, to teach them and to remind of all things; through whom also shall be sanctified the souls of those who sincerely believe in Him.

But those who say that the Son was from nothing, or from some other substance and not from God, and there was time when He was not, the Catholic Church regards as aliens.

FOURTH CREED OF ANTIOCH

Apostolic Constitutions, vii. 41.

Πιστεύω καὶ βαπτίζομαι εἰς ἕνα ἀγέννητον, μόνον ἀληθινὸν Θεὸν παντοκράτορα
τὸν πατέρα τοῦ Χριστοῦ
κτιστὴν καὶ δημιουργὸν τῶν ἁπάντων
ἐξ οὗ τὰ πάντα

Καὶ εἰς τὸν κύριον Ἰησοῦν τὸν Χριστόν, τὸν μονογενῆ αὐτοῦ υἱόν,
τὸν πρωτότοκον πάσης κτίσεως
-ὸν πρὸ αἰώνων εὐδοκίᾳ τοῦ πατρὸς γεννηθέντα

δι᾽ οὗ τὰ πάντα ἐγένετο τὰ ἐν οὐρανοῖς καὶ ἐπὶ γῆς
ὁρατά τε καὶ ἀόρατα,

τὸν ἐπ᾽ ἐσχάτων τῶν ἡμερῶν κατελθόντα ἐξ οὐρανῶν
καὶ σάρκα ἀναλαβόντα
καὶ ἐκ τῆς ἁγίας παρθένου Μαρίας γεννηθέντα

ap. Athanasius, *de Synod.* 25.

Πιστεύομεν εἰς ἕνα Θεὸν πατέρα παντοκράτορα

κτιστὴν καὶ ποιητὴν τῶν πάντων
ἐξ οὗ πᾶσα πατριὰ ἐν οὐρανοῖς καὶ ἐπὶ γῆς ὀνομάζεται.

Καὶ εἰς τὸν μονογενῆ αὐτοῦ υἱόν,
τὸν κύριον ἡμῶν Ἰησοῦν Χριστόν,

τὸν πρὸ πάντων τῶν αἰώνων ἐκ τοῦ πατρὸς γεννηθέντα
Θεὸν ἐκ Θεοῦ, φῶς ἐκ φωτός,
δι᾽ οὗ ἐγένετο τὰ πάντα ἐν τοῖς οὐρανοῖς καὶ ἐπὶ τῆς γῆς
τά (τε) ὁρατὰ καὶ τὰ ἀόρατα
λόγον ὄντα καὶ σοφίαν καὶ δύναμιν καὶ ζωὴν καὶ φῶς ἀληθινόν,
τὸν ἐπ᾽ ἐσχάτων τῶν ἡμερῶν

δι᾽ ἡμᾶς ἐνανθρωπήσαντα
καὶ γεννηθέντα ἐκ τῆς ἁγίας παρθένου

FOURTH CREED OF ANTIOCH

Apostolic Constitutions—contd.

καὶ πολιτευσάμενον ὁσίως κατὰ τοὺς νόμους τοῦ Θεοῦ καὶ πατρὸς αὐτοῦ
καὶ σταυρωθέντα ἐπὶ Ποντίου Πιλάτου
καὶ ἀποθανόντα ὑπὲρ ἡμῶν

καὶ ἀναστάντα ἐκ νεκρῶν μετὰ τὸ παθεῖν τῇ τρίτῃ ἡμέρᾳ
καὶ ἀνελθόντα εἰς τοὺς οὐρανοὺς

καὶ καθεσθέντα ἐν δεξιᾷ τοῦ πατρὸς καὶ πάλιν ἐρχόμενον ἐπὶ συντελείᾳ τοῦ αἰῶνος μετὰ δόξης κρῖναι ζῶντας καὶ νεκροὺς

οὗ τῆς βασιλείας οὐκ ἔσται τέλος.

Βαπτίζομαι καὶ εἰς τὸ πνεῦμα τὸ ἅγιον
τουτέστι τὸν παράκλητον

τὸ ἐνεργῆσαν ἐν πᾶσι τοῖς ἀπ' αἰῶνος ἁγίοις, ὕστερον δὲ ἀποσταλὲν καὶ τοῖς ἀποστόλοις παρὰ τοῦ πατρὸς κατὰ τὴν ἐπαγγελίαν τοῦ σωτῆρος ἡμῶν Ἰησοῦ Χριστοῦ καὶ μετὰ τοὺς ἀποστόλους δὲ πᾶσι τοῖς πιστεύουσιν ἐν τῇ ἁγίᾳ καθολικῇ
καὶ ἀποστολικῇ ἐκκλησίᾳ, εἰς σαρκὸς ἀνάστασιν καὶ εἰς ἄφεσιν ἁμαρτιῶν καὶ εἰς βασιλείαν οὐρανῶν καὶ εἰς ζωὴν τοῦ μέλλοντος αἰῶνος.[1]

ap. Athanasius, *de Synod.—contd.*

τὸν σταυρωθέντα

καὶ ἀποθανόντα
καὶ ταφέντα
καὶ ἀναστάντα ἐκ νεκρῶν τῇ τρίτῃ ἡμέρᾳ
καὶ ἀναληφθέντα εἰς οὐρανὸν
(Socr. καὶ ἀνεληλυθότα εἰς τοὺς οὐρανούς)

καὶ καθεσθέντα ἐν δεξιᾷ τοῦ πατρὸς καὶ ἐρχόμενον ἐπὶ συντελείᾳ τοῦ αἰῶνος κρῖναι ζῶντας καὶ νεκροὺς καὶ ἀποδοῦναι ἑκάστῳ κατὰ τὰ ἔργα αὐτοῦ
οὗ ἡ βασιλεία ἀκατάλυτος
(Socr. ἀκατάπαυστος) οὖσα διαμενεῖ εἰς τοὺς ἀπείρους αἰῶνας· ἔσται γὰρ καθεζόμενος ἐν δεξιᾷ τοῦ πατρὸς οὐ μόνον ἐν τῷ αἰῶνι τούτῳ ἀλλὰ καὶ ἐν τῷ μέλλοντι
καὶ εἰς τὸ ἅγιον πνεῦμα
(Socr. το πνεῦμα τὸ ἅγιον)
τουτέστι τὸν παράκλητον
(Socr. τὸ παράκλητον)
ὅπερ ἐπαγγειλάμενος τοῖς ἀποστόλοις μετὰ τὴν εἰς οὐρανοὺς αὐτοῦ ἄνοδον ἀπέστειλε διδάξαι αὐτοὺς καὶ ὑπομνῆσαι πάντα, δι' οὗ καὶ ἁγιασθήσονται αἱ τῶν εἰλικρινῶς εἰς αὐτὸν πεπιστευκότων ψυχαί.
(Add. anathema)

Professor Kattenbusch[2] rounds off his theory that this was the true Lucianic Creed, which Sozomen confused with

---

[1] καὶ μετὰ τὴν ἐπαγγελίαν ταύτην κατ' ἀκολουθίαν ἔρχεται καὶ εἰς τὴν τοῦ ἐλαίου χρίσιν. [2] i. p. 394.

the second Creed, by suggesting that Lucian was possibly the compiler of the Didascalia. But he has not proved it, nor are the Lucianic characteristics which he finds in the Creed of the Apostolic Constitutions very definite. There is no reference to the Logos-teaching which Lucian introduced in his Christology. The creed must therefore belong to the earlier period of his life. The simple biblical phrase " Father of Christ " comes naturally from the lips of an exegetist. The unique phrase " begotten by the goodwill of the Father " (Matt. iii. 17, xvii. 5 ; Eph. i. 5), if Lucianic, shows that he approached Christology from the point of view of redemption. The phrase " took flesh " indeed fits in with the statement of Epiphanius,[1] that Lucian taught that the Son of God had flesh, not a soul. And the expression " lived as a citizen holily " might be taken to express Lucian's teaching of the patience of Christ and progress by moral effort. But all this reasoning is inconclusive.

It only remains to say that the assertion of the eternal kingdom, originally anti-Sabellian, is expanded in the fourth Creed against Marcellus, though he is not named. The Nicene anathemas are skilfully altered to discredit him, and in favour of Arian teaching. The creed thus substituted for the second Creed (the true creed of the Council) by the deputation which went to wait on Constans, became the pattern of later Arian confessions at Philippopolis in 343, at Antioch in 344 (the so-called Machrostich), and Sirmium in 351.

The deputation found that Constans had left Milan. They followed him to Trèves, but he would not receive them. He admired the character of Athanasius, whom he had admitted to an audience, and was determined to call another General Council to end the strife. So a Council was called at Sardica (now Sophia, in Bulgaria) in the year 344. After some preliminaries had been discussed, the Eastern bishops, finding themselves in a minority, decamped by night. At Philippopolis they stopped to draw up a long angry statement. They proposed that all their opponents should be deposed,

[1] *Ancorat.* 33.

and professed the fourth Creed of Antioch, with a new anathema against Marcellus. All hope of a true peace was now lost, but the Western bishops considered at length all the charges brought against the exiled Nicene leaders and acquitted them. Athanasius returned in triumph to his diocese amid public rejoicings, and began what has been called in a picturesque phrase "the golden decade" of his episcopate, his longest period of uninterrupted ministry.

The armed truce preserved by the might of Constans came to an end at his death. When Constantius obtained sole power, he was false to his pledges, and ordered the arrest of Athanasius, who, however, escaped into the desert.

§ VI. ARIANISM SUPREME

At court Arianism was supreme under the new leaders, Valens, a pupil of Arius, and an Arian by conviction, and Acacius, a politician without convictions. They were determined to substitute an Arian Creed for the Nicene, and the emperor was willing to impose it on all his subjects. But "the coalition fell to pieces the moment Arianism ventured to have a policy of its own."[1] We must distinguish three groups, ultra-Arians, political Arians, and conservatives. The political Arians were willing to unite with the conservatives in confession of "the Essential Likeness" (ὁμοιούσια) of the Son. This was a word with a good history, which had been freely used by Athanasius. But the ultra-Arians, arguing from the point of view that likeness is a relative term, and may imply some degree of unlikeness, were ready to twist it into conformity with their tenets, and by their cunning over-reached themselves. Valens, by astute diplomacy, united these Anomœans (*i.e.* those confessing the Essential Unlikeness) with the political Arians. A small Synod met at Sirmium in 357, and drew up a Latin Creed which asserted the unique Godhead of the Father, the subjection of the Son, and proscribed the terms ὁμοούσιος and ὁμοιούσιος, with all discussion of the term "being," οὐσία, as applied to God.

[1] Gwatkin, *Studies of Arianism*, p. 158.

This was a trumpet-blast of defiance which defeated its own end. A new party was formed among the conservatives, who have received through Epiphanius the misleading nickname semi-Arians. They were men who held at heart the Nicene doctrine, though the scandal caused by the speculations of Marcellus and the defection of his pupil Photinus led them to look with suspicion at the term ὁμοούσιος. Basil of Ancyra was their leader, and communications were opened with the orthodox bishops in Gaul through Hilary, who was in exile. The emperor had some regard for Basil, and was willing to listen to him till a deputation in favour of Anomœan tenets arrived from Syria. Valens seized the opportunity to suggest that a double Council should be held. He proposed to preside himself over a meeting of the Western leaders at Ariminum, while Acacius presided over the Eastern leaders at Seleucia. To secure agreement, he began to negotiate with Basil of Ancyra and others. On Whitsun Eve a creed was drawn up by Mark of Arethusa, which is known as the Dated Creed. It is only known to us in a Greek text and a late Latin translation, though originally written in Latin.

THE DATED CREED OF SIRMIUM

Ath. *de Syn.* 8; Socr. ii. 37; Epiph. *Scholast.* p. 264.

Πιστεύομεν εἰς ἕνα τὸν μόνον καὶ ἀληθινὸν Θεόν, πατέρα παντοκράτορα, κτίστην καὶ δημιουργὸν τῶν πάντων. Καὶ εἰς ἕνα μονογενῆ 5 υἱὸν τοῦ Θεοῦ, τὸν πρὸ πάντων τῶν αἰώνων καὶ πρὸ πάσης ἀρχῆς καὶ πρὸ παντὸς ἐπινοουμένου χρόνου καὶ πρὸ πάσης καταληπτῆς οὐσίας γεγεννημένον ἀπαθῶς ἐκ 10 τοῦ Θεοῦ, δι' οὗ οἵ τε αἰῶνες κατηρτίσθησαν καὶ τὰ πάντα ἐγένετο· γεγεννημένον δὲ μονογενῆ μόνον ἐκ μόνου τοῦ πατρός, Θεὸν ἐκ Θεοῦ, ὅμοιον τῷ γεννήσαντι 15 αὐτὸν πατρί, κατὰ τὰς γραφάς· οὗ τὴν γέννησιν οὐδεὶς ἐπίσταται εἰ	We believe in one Only and True God, the Father Almighty, Creator and Framer of all things. And in one Only-begotten Son of God, who, before all ages, and before all origin, and before all conceivable time, and before all comprehensible essence, was begotten impassibly from God: through whom the ages were disposed and all things were made; and Him begotten as the Only-begotten, Only from the Only Father, God from God, like to the Father who begat Him, according to the Scriptures; whose origin no one knoweth save the Father alone who

THE DATED CREED OF SIRMIUM

μὴ μόνος ὁ γεννήσας αὐτὸν πατήρ.
Τοῦτον ἴσμεν τοῦ Θεοῦ μονογενῆ
υἱὸν νεύματι πατρικῷ παραγενό-
20 μενον ἐκ τῶν οὐρανῶν εἰς ἀθέτησιν
τῆς ἁμαρτίας, καὶ γεννηθέντα ἐκ
Μαρίας τῆς παρθένου, καὶ ἀναστραφέντα μετὰ τῶν μαθητῶν, καὶ
πᾶσαν τὴν οἰκονομίαν πληρώ-
25 σαντα κατὰ τὴν πατρικὴν βούλησιν·
σταυρωθέντα καὶ ἀποθανόντα, καὶ
εἰς τὰ καταχθόνια κατελθόντα καὶ
τὰ ἐκεῖσε οἰκονομήσαντα· ὃν πυλωροὶ ἅδου ἰδόντες ἔφριξαν· καὶ
30 ἀναστάντα ἐκ νεκρῶν τῇ τρίτῃ
ἡμέρᾳ καὶ ἀναστραφέντα μετὰ τῶν
μαθητῶν καὶ πᾶσαν τὴν οἰκονομίαν
πληρώσαντα καὶ τεσσαράκοντα
ἡμερῶν ἀναπληρουμένων ἀναληφ-
35 θέντα εἰς τοὺς οὐρανοὺς καὶ καθεζόμενον ἐκ δεξιῶν τοῦ πατρός, καὶ
ἐλευσόμενον ἐν τῇ ἐσχάτῃ ἡμέρᾳ
τῆς ἀναστάσεως τῇ δόξῃ τῇ πατρικῇ
ἀποδιδόντα ἑκάστῳ κατὰ τὰ ἔργα
40 αὐτοῦ. Καὶ εἰς τὸ ἅγιον πνεῦμα,
ὃ αὐτὸς ὁ μονογενὴς τοῦ Θεοῦ
Ἰησοῦς Χριστὸς ἐπήγγειλε πέμ-
ψαι τῷ γένει τῶν ἀνθρώπων, τὸν
παράκλητον κατὰ τὸ γεγραμμένον·
45 ἀπέρχομαι πρὸς τὸν πατέρα
μου καὶ παρακαλέσω τὸν
πατέρα, καὶ ἄλλον παρά-
κλητον πέμψει ὑμῖν, τὸ
πνεῦμα τῆς ἀληθείας, ἐκεῖνος
50 ἐκ τοῦ ἐμοῦ λήψεται καὶ
διδάξει καὶ ὑπομνήσει ὑμᾶς
πάντα. Τὸ δὲ ὄνομα τῆς οὐσίας
διὰ τὸ ἁπλούστερον ὑπὸ τῶν
πατέρων τεθεῖσθαι, ἀγνοούμενον
55 δὲ ὑπὸ τῶν λαῶν σκάνδαλον
φέρειν, διὰ τὸ μήτε τὰς γραφὰς
τοῦτο περιέχειν, ἤρεσε τοῦτο περι-
αιρεθῆναι καὶ παντελῶς μηδεμίαν
μνήμην οὐσίας ἐπὶ Θεοῦ εἶναι τοῦ
60 λοιποῦ, διὰ τὸ τὰς θείας γραφὰς
μηδαμοῦ περὶ τοῦ πατρὸς καὶ υἱοῦ
οὐσίας μεμνῆσθαι. ὅμοιον δὲ λέγο-

begat Him. We know that He, the Only-begotten Son of God, at the Father's bidding came from the heavens for the abolishment of sin, and was born of the Virgin Mary, and conversed with the disciples, and fulfilled all the Economy according to the Father's will, was crucified and died and descended into the parts beneath the earth, and regulated the things there, whom the gate-keepers of hell saw (Job xxxviii. 17, LXX.) and shuddered; and He rose from the dead the third day, and conversed with the disciples, and fulfilled all the Economy, and when the forty days were full, ascended into the heavens, and sitteth on the right hand of the Father, and is coming in the last day of the resurrection in the glory of the Father, to render to everyone according to his works. And in the Holy Ghost, whom the Only-begotten of God Himself, Jesus Christ, had promised to send to the race of men, the Paraclete, as it is written: "I go to My Father, and I will ask the Father, and He shall send you another Paraclete, even the Spirit of Truth, He shall take of Mine and shall teach and bring to your remembrance all things" (John xiv. 16, 17, 26, xvi. 14). But whereas the term "essence" has been adopted by the Fathers in simplicity, and gives offence as being misconceived by the people, because it is not contained in the Scriptures, it has seemed good to remove it, that no mention of "essence" with regard to God should be made at all in the future, because the Divine Scriptures nowhere mention "essence" of the Father and Son. But we say the Son is like the Father in all things,

μεν τὸν υἱὸν τῷ πατρὶ κατὰ as also the Holy Scriptures say and
πάντα, ὡς καὶ αἱ ἅγιαι γραφαὶ teach.
65 λέγουσί τε καὶ διδάσκουσιν.

LINE 9. οὐσίας] ἐπίνοίας, S; et ante omnem comprehensibilem substantiam, E. 16. γέννησιν] γένεσιν, A; generationem, E; μόνος] pr. ἢ, S. 19. τὸν μονογενῆ αὐτοῦ υἱόν, S; unigenitum Dei Filium, E. 26. σταυρωθέντα] + καὶ παθόντα, S. 30. om. ἐκ νεκρῶν, S. 34. om. καὶ πᾶσαν - πληρ. S. τεσσαράκοντα] πεντήκοντα, A; quinquaginta, E. 34. ἀναπλρ.] πλησώσαντα, S. 38. om. τῆς ἀναστάσεως, S. 41. Θεοῦ] + υἱός, S; quem unigenitus promisit, E. 45. John xvi. 7, 13 f., xiv. 16 f., xv. 26. 59. Θεοῦ, pr. τοῦ, S, ed. Walch. 61. τοῦ πατρὸς] πνεύματος, S, ed. Walch. 64. om. καὶ, S E.

Basil must have felt that in signing this he was sacrificing principles, for he added a memorandum in which he defended the use of the term "essence," asserted the "Essential Likeness," and denied that "unoriginate" (ἀγεννησία) is the primary idea of God.

At Ariminum it was rejected with scorn. The feeling of the Synod may be illustrated from a sentence in the treatise of Athanasius "On the Synods" (c. 3): "After putting into writing what it pleased them to believe, they prefix to it the Consulate, and the month and the day of the current year; thereby to show all sensible men that their faith dates, not from of old, but now from the reign of Constantius."

At Seleucia, Acacius proposed an altered form, but was defeated. Getting angry, his friends declared openly against the Nicene formula. It was, however, defended by a majority, though they complained (so Athanasius tells us) of the word "of one essence" as being obscure, and therefore open to suspicion. They then proceeded to confirm the second Creed of Antioch, and rejected a rival formulary drawn up by the Acacians. Having excommunicated the Arians, their delegates proceeded to Constantinople. Then they were persuaded to accept the Arian Creed of Niké, which was also thrust upon the Council at Ariminum. It is not to our purpose to pursue their history further.

§ VII. Victory in Sight

In the year 359, Athanasius wrote his "noble work" *de Synodis*, with a double object—to expose all these pitiable intrigues, and to win the confidence of the semi-Arians. He wrote hopefully, and his hopeful tone was justified by the event. In fact, after the fiasco of "the Dated Creed," the victory was really won. The ill-treatment which the bishops received at Ariminum and Niké widened the breach between the Anomœans and the semi-Arians, who in less than three years were reconciled to the Nicene party. The rise of the Anomœan leaders to supremacy at court, through the accession of another Arian Emperor Valens (A.D. 363), could not break this alliance. A new generation of young theologians was growing up, who were full of a genuine admiration for Athanasius, and responded readily to his appeal. The foremost among them—Basil of Cæsarea, in Cappadocia—had accompanied his bishop, Basil of Ancyra, to Constantinople, and recoiled from the spirit of intrigue which was manifested there. A short time later he adopted the words of Athanasius (*Ep.* viii. 9): "One God we confess—one in nature, not in number, for number belongs to the category of quantity, . . . neither like nor unlike, for these terms belong to the category of quality. . . . He that is essentially God is co-essential with Him, that is, essentially God. . . . If I am to state my own opinion, I accept "like in essence," with the addition of "exactly," as identical in sense with "co-essential," . . . but "exactly like" [without "essence"] I suspect. . . . Accordingly, since "co-essential" is the term less open to abuse on this ground, I too adopt it."

"Basil the Great is not, indeed, the only, but the conspicuous and abundant justification of the insight of Athanasius in the *de Synodis*."[1] This personal triumph of Athanasius was not valued by him as a triumph of policy so much as of principle. When Sulpicius Severus speaks of him as *Episcopus iurisconsultus*, we are not to think of a mere special pleader. He was a statesmen with large ideas, and

[1] Robertson, *Athanasius*, p. 449.

he was persuaded that truth would prevail. Not dismayed, like lesser men, by frequent failures, he held that " we fall to rise, are baffled to fight better." Through the long turmoil he never lost heart, praying, as at the end of the *de Synodis* he begs others to do, that now at length " all strife and rivalry may cease, and the futile questions of the heretics may be condemned, and all logomachy; and the guilty and murderous heresy of the Arians may disappear, and the truth may shine again in the hearts of all."

§ VIII. Conclusion

The Arian heresy represents a mode of thought which will always prove attractive to some minds. Its appeal is to the present, to pressing intellectual difficulties in justification of a compromise, an illogical compromise, between faith and reason. It permits a worship of Christ which on its own showing is little better than idolatry.

Dr. Bright[1] recalls an incident of its revival in the last century. "An Arian teacher, Clarke, was maintaining his case in a royal drawing-room against an orthodox divine, who condensed the whole matter into one tremendous crucial question, 'Can the Father, on your hypothesis, annihilate the Son?' There was silence, and then Clarke helplessly muttered that it was a point which he had never considered. It was a point on which all might be said to turn."

The case breaks down. From the position, we will call Christ *good* though we cannot call him *God*, extremists are led on to deny that He is like the Father, to deny His goodness, to denounce worship of Him as hypocrisy. History repeats itself: the Arian becomes the Anomœan. And the warning which history gives is this—that to cut a knot which he cannot untie is for every man a confession of failure. Worshippers of Christ are not all hypocrites, and the main object of Nicene opposition to Arianism was religious rather than theological, to ensure that prayers

[1] *Waymarks in Church History*, p. 70.

CONCLUSION

might be offered to Christ not with hope only, but with certainty.

In the writings of Athanasius the primary interest is certainly religious. Even Gibbon lays aside, as someone has said, "his solemn sneer" to do honour to the memory of this champion of the faith, who never lost heart, but could make of failure "a triumph's evidence for the fulness of the days." It has been suggested that he left the people out of account, that his appeal is always to theologians and the professionally religious.[1] But a very different impression may be derived from the references to the faith and hope of all Christian people in his Festal Letters. And in the famous letter to Dracontius,[2] on the duty of a bishop, he says plainly: "The laity expect you to bring them food, namely, instruction from the Scriptures. When, then, they expect and suffer hunger, and you are feeding yourself only,[3] and our Lord Jesus Christ comes, and we stand before Him, what defence will you offer when He sees His own sheep hungering?" Such a passage—and many more might be quoted—proves also that theological learning and the demands of controversy did not make the idea of the historical Christ unintelligible to Athanasius. It rather grew more clear before his imagination. About A.D. 371 he wrote to the philosopher Maximus in the simplest scriptural words, teaching worship of the Crucified, and with this aim urges, "Let what was confessed by the Fathers at Nicæa prevail."[4]

[1] Harnack, *D.G.* ii. 275. [2] *Ep.* 49.
[3] *I.e.* by shutting himself up in a monastery, and caring only for his own spiritual life.
[4] *Ep.* 61.

CHAPTER V

OUR NICENE CREED

§ I. The Council of Alexandria.
§ II. The Revised Creed of Jerusalem.
§ III. The Council of Constantinople.
§ IV. The Council of Chalcedon.
§ V. Later History : the *Filioque* clause.
§ VI. Conclusions.

§ I. THE COUNCIL OF ALEXANDRIA

"THE FAITH" of the Nicene Council is related to our Nicene Creed as a bud from a garden rose to the wild-rose stock into which it is grafted. The rose-grower with cunning hand unites the beauty of colour and form which he has cultivated to the hardy nature and vigorous growth of the wild plant. Our Nicene Creed is the old Baptismal Creed of Jerusalem, revised by the insertion of Nicene theological terms. Thus the improved theology was grafted into the stock of the old historic faith. It was not the only attempt that was made in this direction, but it was by far the most successful. It was fitted, alike by its rhythm and by the preservation of proportion in its theological teaching, to become hereafter a liturgical treasure for all Christendom.

The Creed of the Nicene Council was an elaborate dogmatic formulary constructed to meet a particular crisis, to be read with its anathemas. During thirty years it had held its own, and the tenacity and loyalty of its defenders through this long period of doubtful conflict won for it a sanction which no Council of Bishops, however learned, or spiritually minded, or unanimous, could bestow on a new confession. Leaders of Christian thought, who most dreaded this new advance in theological analysis, had come round to the opinion that its phrases, though not scriptural, conveyed the meaning of Scripture. Men who had been reared in a very different climate of thought, whose faculties had been trained to a high level of discernment in the best schools of Greek philosophy, fully recognised its value as a bulwark against the assaults of heathenising theology, a sign-post warning the traveller against the errors of a false logic. Such were Basil and the Gregories. Nor was it only accepted in the interests of the higher theology. A hard-working parish priest like Cyril of Jerusalem, whose mind was set on the teaching of a practical religion, a preacher of the gospel in all simplicity, came to find in it a remedy for the present distress, a clue to escape from the long labyrinth of competing creeds in which he unwillingly found himself turned adrift.

The triumph of Athanasius and his great Western ally Hilary was assured. But in the hour of victory they showed a wise moderation. They did not make of their creed a mere Shibboleth to be thrust upon a new generation anyhow. They cared more for deeds than words. The grace which enabled so-called semi-Arians to suffer for their faith and hope in Christ was precious in their sight. They feared to break the bruised reed or quench the smoking flax. With rare insight into the bearing of differences in theological expression, and tender sympathy for all fellow-seekers after truth, Hilary in Asia Minor, Athanasius from his hiding-places in the Egyptian desert, laboured in the work of conciliation. Is there not pathos, is there not power, in these words of Hilary *de Synodis*? They form the conclusion of his appeal (c. 91) to first principles of theology as an eirenicon: "I have never heard the faith of Nicæa save on the eve of exile. The Gospels and Apostles have instilled into me the meaning of *same in substance* and *like in substance.*" For the former term he had suffered exile, but he was not hardened into a bigot; he was ready to accept *like in substance* as a stepping-stone of faith from men whom he regarded as honest.

The same magnanimity was shown by Athanasius in his treatise *de Synodis*, in which "even Athanasius rises above himself." "No sooner is he cheered by the news of hope than the importunate jealousies of forty years are hushed in a moment, as though the Lord had spoken peace to the tumult of the grey old exile's troubled soul."[1]

He turned to the semi-Arians with a careful defence of the ὁμοούσιον. He was successful in his appeal. "Not only did many of the semi-Arians (*e.g.* the fifty-nine in 365) accept the ὁμοούσιον, but it was from the ranks of the semi-Arians that the men arose who led the cause of Nicæa to its ultimate victory in the East."[2]

The death of Constantius in A.D. 361 became a turning-point in the history of the controversy, because the way had been paved for a new alliance and an immediate advance. Exiled bishops were everywhere recalled to their sees. Athanasius was back at his post in twelve days, and in a few months had summoned, early in 362 at Alexandria, "a Synod of Saints and Confessors," which, though small in numbers, had exceptional influence. Jerome writes enthusiastically that "it recovered the world from the jaws of Satan."[3] An interesting record of their discussions is preserved in the tome, or concise statement, which they sent to the divided Church in Antioch. Guided by Athanasius, they took a wide outlook on ecclesiastical affairs. Thus they advocated acceptance of the Nicene formula as the terms of reunion. They denounced Sabellianism as the trend of thought in some quarters towards the heresy afterwards connected with the name of Apollinaris of Laodicea, whose legates were present at the Council. But they were careful to explain in what way the terms ὑπόστασις and οὐσία might be distinguished, so that those who clung to the term μία ὑπόστασις (= οὐσία) might not be offended when they heard others say τρεῖς ὑποστάσεις, meaning not three substances but three sub-sistences. Their chief concern, however, was the state of affairs in Antioch, where a band of irreconcilable Eustathians under their priest Paulinus, who sent legates to the Council,

[1] Gwatkin, *Studies*, p. 176.   [2] Robertson, *Athanasius*, p. 449.   [3] *Adv. Lucif.* 20.

refused to communicate with the Bishop Meletius. They urged reconciliation. Meletius had been in exile for the true faith, and was returning to take charge of the congregation in the Old Church, which had been infected with heresy, but should now be restored to communion with the faithful remnant under Paulinus.

Their efforts failed. The firebrand Lucifer of Cagliari had in the meantime perpetuated the schism by the consecration of Paulinus as bishop. But their wise counsels had far-reaching influence. The new alliance with the semi-Arians, who were willing to range themselves under the standard of the Homoousians, survived misunderstandings about Paulinus. Athanasius had before this given offence by communicating with Paulinus, whom he now refused to excommunicate. He distressed Basil, but he was willing to make common cause in the higher interests of the faith with its veteran defenders. During the reign of the Arian Valens which followed the brief reign of Julian, Arian leaders regained court influence, but their cause was doomed to fail. From this time on many local creeds were reconstructed by admission of Nicene phrases, or the Nicene Creed was introduced in their place.

Basil, who had been convinced by the words of Athanasius in his *de Synodis* that "co-essential" was the term less open to abuse than others, led the way in Cappadocia, where he seems to have introduced the Nicene Creed. He wrote in A.D. 373 : τοὺς ἢ προληφθέντας ἑτέρᾳ πίστεως ὁμολογίᾳ καὶ μετατίθεσθαι πρὸς τὴν τῶν ὀρθῶν συνάφειαν βουλομένους. ἢ καὶ νῦν πρῶτον ἐν τῇ κατηχήσει τοῦ λόγου τῆς ἀληθείας ἐπιθυμοῦντας γενέσθαι, διδάσκεσθαι χρὴ τὴν ὑπὸ τῶν μακαρίων πατέρων ἐν τῇ κατὰ Νίκαιάν ποτε συγκροτηθείσῃ συνόδῳ γραφεῖσαν πίστιν.[1]

§ II. THE REVISED CREED OF JERUSALEM

By far the most important was the revision of the Creed of Jerusalem, which in a former chapter we gleaned from the

[1] *Ep.* 125. 1 ; cf. 140. 2, quoted by Kattenbusch, i. pp. 346 f.

Catecheses of Cyril. It is found in a treatise called "The Anchored One" (*Ancoratus*), which was written by Epiphanius, Bishop of Salamis, about the year A.D. 374. He wrote for those who had been tossed on a sea of doubts and fears, but had found an anchor of the soul. He was a travelled man, and learned; in pedantry a contrast to Athanasius; in temper violent, but a friend of good men. He introduced into his book two creeds.

The former of these is our Nicene Creed, commonly called the Constantinopolitan Creed, which I will print side by side with the Creed of Jerusalem, all common words being underlined, with a straight line if they are repeated exactly, with a wavy line if they are not. All the words which are found in the original Nicene Creed are pointed out by means of underlying dotted lines, so that it is possible to see at a glance to what extent it has been quoted. I have not thought it worth while to include small variations found in the text of Epiphanius, which are as likely as not due to an interpolator.[1] They are—Art. 1, οὐρανοῦ + τε; Art. 2, αἰώνιων + τουτέστιν ἐκ τῆς οὐσίας τοῦ πατρός; ἐγένετο + τά τε ἐν τοῖς οὐρανοῖς καὶ τὰ ἐν τῇ γῇ.

OUR NICENE CREED.

CREED OF JERUSALEM Cyril, *Catech.* vi.-xviii.	REVISED CREED OF JERUSALEM Epiphanius, *Ancoratus*.
Πιστεύομεν εἰς ἕνα Θεὸν πατέρα παντοκράτορα, ποιητὴν οὐρανοῦ καὶ γῆς ὁρατῶν τε πάντων καὶ ἀοράτων.	1. Πιστεύομεν εἰς ἕνα Θεὸν πατέρα παντοκράτορα ποιητὴν οὐρανοῦ καὶ γῆς ὁρατῶν τε πάντων καὶ ἀοράτων.
Καὶ εἰς ἕνα κύριον Ἰησοῦν Χριστὸν τὸν υἱὸν τοῦ Θεοῦ τὸν μονογενῆ, τὸν ἐκ τοῦ πατρὸς γεννηθέντα Θεὸν ἀληθινὸν πρὸ πάντων τῶν αἰώνων.	2. Καὶ εἰς ἕνα κύριον Ἰησοῦν Χριστὸν τὸν υἱὸν τοῦ Θεοῦ τὸν μονογενῆ, τὸν ἐκ τοῦ πατρὸς γεννηθέντα πρὸ πάντων τῶν αἰώνων. φῶς ἐκ φωτὸς, Θεὸν ἀληθινὸν ἐκ

[1] Kattenbusch, i. p. 235.

OUR NICENE CREED

CREED OF JERUSALEM—cont.	REVISED CREED OF JERUSALEM—cont.
	Θεοῦ ἀληθινοῦ, γεννηθέντα οὐ ποιηθέντα, ὁμοούσιον τῷ πατρί,
δι' οὗ τὰ πάντα ἐγένετο,	δι' οὗ τὰ πάντα ἐγένετο,
	τὸν δι' ἡμᾶς τοὺς ἀνθρώπους καὶ διὰ τὴν ἡμετέραν σωτηρίαν κατελθόντα ἐκ τῶν οὐρανῶν
σαρκωθέντα	3. καὶ σαρκωθέντα ἐκ πνεύματος ἁγίου καὶ Μαρίας τῆς παρθένου
καὶ ἐνανθρωπήσαντα,	καὶ ἐνανθρωπήσαντα,
σταυρωθέντα	4. σταυρωθέντα τε ὑπὲρ ἡμῶν ἐπὶ Ποντίου Πιλάτου καὶ παθόντα
καὶ ταφέντα καὶ ἀναστάντα τῇ τρίτῃ ἡμέρᾳ	5. καὶ ταφέντα καὶ ἀναστάντα τῇ τρίτῃ ἡμέρᾳ κατὰ τὰς γραφὰς
καὶ ἀνελθόντα εἰς τοὺς οὐρανοὺς	6. καὶ ἀνελθόντα εἰς τοὺς οὐρανοὺς
καὶ καθίσαντα ἐκ δεξιῶν τοῦ πατρὸς	7. καὶ καθεζόμενον ἐκ δεξιῶν τοῦ πατρὸς
καὶ ἐρχόμενον ἐν δόξῃ κρῖναι ζῶντας καὶ νεκρούς, οὗ τῆς βασιλείας οὐκ ἔσται τέλος.	8. καὶ πάλιν ἐρχόμενον μετὰ δόξης κρῖναι ζῶντας καὶ νεκρούς, οὗ τῆς βασιλείας οὐκ ἔσται τέλος.
Καὶ εἰς ἓν ἅγιον πνεῦμα τὸν παράκλητον	9. Καὶ εἰς τὸ πνεῦμα τὸ ἅγιον, τὸ κύριον καὶ τὸ ζωοποιὸν, τὸ ἐκ τοῦ πατρὸς ἐκπορευόμενον, τὸ σὺν πατρὶ καὶ υἱῷ συνπροσκυνούμενον καὶ συνδοξαζόμενον,
τὸ λαλῆσαν ἐν τοῖς προφήταις	τὸ λαλῆσαν διὰ τῶν προφητῶν
11. καὶ εἰς ἓν βάπτισμα μετανοίας εἰς ἄφεσιν ἁμαρτιῶν	10. εἰς μίαν ἁγίαν καθολικὴν καὶ ἀποστολικὴν ἐκκλησίαν·
10. καὶ εἰς μίαν ἁγίαν καθολικὴν ἐκκλησίαν	11. ὁμολογοῦμεν ἓν βάπτισμα εἰς ἄφεσιν ἁμαρτιῶν·
καὶ εἰς σαρκὸς ἀνάστασιν καὶ εἰς ζωὴν αἰώνιον.	12. προσδοκῶμεν ἀνάστασιν νεκρῶν καὶ ζωὴν τοῦ μέλλοντος αἰῶνος.
	Ἀμήν.

In this form quoted by Epiphanius, beside the variations, which have been noted as due to interpolation, we find other variations from the text of our Nicene Creed. The words "both which are in the heavens and in the earth" are added after "through whom all things were made"; the words "God of God," and in Art. 8 "and of the Son," are omitted. The first two are unimportant,—the one implied and the other expressed in the text of the original Nicene Creed. The third must be discussed later on.

We gather from Epiphanius that the creed had been introduced into his diocese as a Baptismal Creed before his consecration, and that he recognised in it the Apostolic Creed as explained by the Nicene Council. He adds to it their anathemas with variations; *e.g.*, ἢ κτιστὸν ἢ τρεπτὸν ἢ ἀλλοιωτὸν τὸν υἱὸν τοῦ Θεοῦ ἀναθεματίζει ἡ καθολικὴ ἐκκλησία he reads ῥευστὸν ἢ ἀλλοιωτὸν τὸν τοῦ Θεοῦ υἱὸν τούτους ἀναθεματίζει ἡ καθολικὴ καὶ ἀποστολικὴ ἐκκλησία.

The longer creed which follows is a free paraphrase of the original Nicene Creed. It seems to have been his own composition for the use of catechumens who had held heretical opinions. It is introduced with the words: "We and all orthodox bishops, in a word, the whole holy Catholic Church, offer to candidates for baptism in accordance with the faith quoted of these holy Fathers," etc. It is verbose and wearisome. As it is printed in Hahn,[3] p. 135, it need not be reprinted here, but a word may be added about a form closely related to it, the so-called "Interpretation of the Creed" formerly ascribed to Athanasius. This is probably an adaptation by some followers of Epiphanius.[1] The Armenian scholar Catergian suggests that it was introduced into Armenia in the sixth century, and formed the groundwork of the later Armenian Creed.

It is to the credit of an English scholar, Professor Hort, that he was the first to point out that our Nicene Creed, which was transcribed by Epiphanius in A.D. 374, was not the work of the Council of Constantinople. His theory connecting it with Cyril of Jerusalem has been accepted

[1] Kattenbusch, i. 303 ff.

widely by German and English critics, with some differences as to detail. Kattenbusch writes of it: "The only wonder is that it was not discovered before."

Hort's theory may be summarised as follows. Epiphanius had lived for some time in Palestine, and shows a knowledge of circumstances relating to Jerusalem, Eleutheropolis in Judæa, near to his birthplace, and Cæsarea. He gives a list of Bishops of Jerusalem who lived through the troublous times. In A.D. 377 he corresponded with Basil about dissensions among the brethren on the Mount of Olives. It is therefore easy to understand how the revised Creed came into his hands.

It is also possible to connect it with Cyril, who, on his return to his diocese in A.D. 362–364, would find "a natural occasion for the revision of the public creed by the skilful insertion of some of the conciliar language, including the term which proclaimed the restoration of full communion with the champions of Nicæa, and other phrases and clauses adapted for impressing on the people positive truth."

The change from καθίσαντα to καθεζόμενον agrees with the teaching in his lectures, that the Son was from all eternity sitting on the right hand of the Father, not only from the ascension (*Cat.* xi. 17, xiv. 27–30).

The change from ἐν δόξῃ to μετὰ δόξης is parallel to the teaching in *Cat.* xv. 3, where Cyril uses his own words.

The most remarkable change, however, is the substitution of νεκρῶν for σάρκος, in accordance with his constant practice (xviii. 1–21), and his interpretation εἰς σάρκος ἀνάστασιν τοῦτ' ἐστι τὴν τῶν νεκρῶν.

Other changes may be traced to the following sources: ἐπὶ Ποντίου Πιλάτου, καὶ ἀποστολικήν, ζωὴν τοῦ μέλλοντος αἰῶνος to the Creed of the Apostolic Constitutions, together with ἐκ τῶν οὐρανῶν, ὑπὲρ ἡμῶν, παθόντα, πάλιν (μετὰ δόξης?); the omission of μετανοίας has a parallel in the Mesopotamian Creed; the omission of παράκλητον seems to be "necessitated by the accompanying enlargement."

Kattenbusch's proposal to restore the text of the Old Jerusalem Creed from the text of the revised form has been discussed above (Chap. III. p. 68). It is most ingenious, but does not explain the facts so simply as Hort's theory. This is particularly the case with the phrase σαρκωθέντα ἐκ πνεύματος ἁγίου καὶ Μαρίας τῆς παρθένου. " In extant creeds," according to Hort, " this combination is unique." The revised Mesopotamian Creed has σαρκωθέντα ἐκ πνεύματος ἁγίου. In Cat. iv. 9, Cyril wrote γεννηθέντα ἐξ ἁγίας παρθένου καὶ ἁγίου πνεύματος, followed after two lines by σαρκωθέντα ἐξ αὐτῆς ἀληθῶς. So we see how the thought shaped itself in his mind. The form γεννηθέντα ἐκ . . . καὶ . . . , from which he advanced to the other, is frequently found.[1] He seems to have wished to guard in the new combination either against Docetic teaching, or against the theory, put forward at this time in the name of Apollinaris, that our Lord's body had a heavenly origin. The phrase σαρκωθεὶς (σάρκωσις) ἐξ ἁγ. παρθένου Μαρίας occurs often in epistles bearing the name of Julius of Rome, which show an Apollinarian tendency.

We have yet to discover how Cyril's revised Creed came to be attributed to the Council of Constantinople.

§ III. The Council of Constantinople

The events which led up to the Council are many of them obscure, and the loss of its Acts, with the exception of some Canons of doubtful meaning, is irreparable. It is possible that future research may clear up some points. We are no longer limited to the printed works on the great Councils of Mansi, Labbé, Hardouin, and others. Maassen's researches have made possible for the future historian a closer study of early collections of Canons in many MSS., particularly at the Vatican, which would richly repay labour spent on them. Hort laments that the Canons of Chalcedon have not been critically edited, and until that is done many

---

[1] Hort quotes Origen's Rule of Faith, Marcellus, Athelstan's Psalter, Creed of Niké, 359; Julianus of Eclanum; Paulinus of Antioch, in his assent to the tome of the Council of Alexandria, 362; Athanasius, c. Apol. i. 20, p. 938 E, etc.

THE COUNCIL OF CONSTANTINOPLE 107

points of interest with relation to the Council of Constantinople must remain doubtful.

The revival of Arianism under Valens had not proved serious. It was the work of courtiers, and had no root. Nicene principles spread quietly on all sides. An important series of Synods was held at Rome under Damasus in the course of the years A.D. 369–376. Their discussions did not merely cover old ground, but included the new questions raised by Apollinaris and Macedonius. Their interest in Church affairs was far-reaching. The second Synod addressed a letter to the bishops in Illyria respecting an outbreak of Arianism, of which they had been informed by brethren among the Gauls and Bessi.[1] Zahn[2] suggests that their information may have been derived from Niceta, Bishop of Remesiana, who worked among the Bessi. He also infers that the spreading of Arian principles south of the Danube may have been the result of the devoted labours of Ulphilas. This is likely. In 378 an influential Synod was held at Antioch on the Orontes, which failed to end the schism between the followers of Meletius and Paulinus, but agreed to sign the tome of the Roman Synod of 369. Now, it is an interesting fact that the name Niceta Macedonius is found among the names of the bishops present at that Synod.[3] And it fits in very well with Zahn's theory to suppose that, as he brought information to the Roman Synod in 369, so he supported its Acts at Antioch in 378. It is quite true that such lists are often unreliable, but we have the positive testimony of his writings to prove acquaintance with the discussions of this Roman Synod on the one hand, and with the writings of Cyril of Jerusalem on the other. This gives some confirmation of the suggestion, which is only offered because we so greatly need new light on the negotiations carried on by Damasus with Eastern bishops, and must follow up every possible clue.

[1] The old reading in Mansi, III. 443, made no sense, "the brethren in Gaul and Venice." The Benedictines of Monte Cassino have found the new reading *Spicilegium Casinense.*

[2] *Neue Kirchl. Zeit.* vii. 102.

[3] The full list of names has never been published, but I have found it in *Codd. lat. Paris.* 3836 and 4279.

On the accession of Theodosius in 380, a new impetus was given to the hopes of all who were true to the Nicene faith.

He convened a great Council at Constantinople, to which he invited Damasus with other Western bishops. It has been suggested that Damasus was badly advised as to the course of events in the East. If it were true, it would not be surprising. We hardly know to what extent the emperor was influenced by the political aim of attaching to himself the powerful support of orthodox Eastern bishops.[1] It is certainly remarkable that when the Council met in the autumn of 381 he received Meletius, who was made president, with special favour.

The triumph of Meletius brought with it the signal vindication of Cyril of Jerusalem, whose orthodoxy was formally recognised by the Council. Hort conjectures that charges were laid against him by envoys from Jerusalem, or by Egyptian bishops, and that Gregory of Nyssa[2] defended him, while the Council giving judgment in his favour may have expressed approval of his creed. This would explain how the creed came to be attributed to Gregory,[3] and how it could have been copied into the Acts of the Council, from which it was afterwards extracted by Aëtius at the Council of Chalcedon. We know that the Council of Constantinople, on its own account, only ratified the original Nicene Creed.

We cannot linger over the discussions of the Council prolonged by the death of Meletius. He was succeeded by Gregory Nazianzen, who has left in his famous discourse a vivid picture of the dissensions which led to his resignation. The pride of Eastern prelates, who boasted that the sun rose in the East as the home of light and learning, was rebuked by the reminder that Christ was crucified in the East. This is a commentary on the refusal of Western bishops to attend this Council. There is little doubt that a complete rupture

---

[1] Duchesne, *Autonomies Ecclésiastiques*, Égl. sep. p. 176.

[2] Gregory of Nyssa, in a letter written about this time, dissuaded his brethren in Cappadocia from undertaking a pilgrimage to Jerusalem, where, he said, affairs were in confusion.

[3] Niceph.-Callistus, *Hist. Eccl.* xii. 13.

THE COUNCIL OF CONSTANTINOPLE 109

was threatening between East and West. The Meletian schism was perpetuated by the consecration of Flavianus for the see of Antioch; and the letter which was sent to the Synod of Rome, asking for the recognition of Flavianus, together with Cyril and Nectarius the new Bishop of Constantinople, arrived after the reception of his rival Paulinus.

Paulinus was accompanied to Rome by Epiphanius and Jerome (*Ep.* 68), who had been staying in Constantinople. They travelled by way of Thessalonica, where Paulinus received the famous letter from Damasus, *Dilectissimo fratri Paulino Damasus*, which is often quoted in Collections of Canons, and is also to be found in the history of Theodoret.[1] The greater part consists of a series of anathemas, which express very accurately the dogmatic standpoint reached by the Western Synods, especially in regard to the Incarnation and the Holy Spirit.[2]

During the following spring Synods were again held at Rome and at Constantinople. The Eastern bishops refused to go to Rome, on account of the distance and the shortness of the invitation, so that they were unable to communicate with their brethren.

Rade[3] makes the interesting suggestion that the so-called 5th Canon of the Council of 381 really belongs to this second Synod of Constantinople, and represents some concession to the followers of Paulinus.[3] "The tome of the Westerns" might refer to this letter from Damasus. The Canon is as follows: Περὶ τοῦ τόμου τῶν Δυστικῶν καὶ τοὺς ἐν Ἀντιοχείᾳ ἀπεδεξάμεθα τοὺς μίαν ὁμολογοῦντας πατρὸς καὶ υἱοῦ καὶ ἁγίου πνεύματος Θεότητα.

Hefele thinks that "the tome of the Westerns" refers to the Roman treatise of 369 or 380. He calls attention to the fact that the Synodical letter sent to Damasus by the bishops in 382 is connected in thought with this Canon. This is true, but tends to prove that they were referring rather to a recent document than to the treatise of 369, which had been accepted at Antioch in 378.

[1] v. 11. [2] Cf. Harnack, *D.G.* ii. p. 271, n. 1.
[3] *Damasus*, pp. 107, 116 f., 133.

At least, it is an important fact that Epiphanius travelled to Rome on the morrow of the Council. We are sure that he would carry with him the praises of Cyril's Creed regarded as an uncontroversial document. This fact, which seems to have escaped notice, would account for its subsequent acceptance at Rome.

One thing is clear. Our Nicene Creed does not represent a mere compromise between the new theologians of the East, Basil, the Gregories, and Cyril on the one side, and the Macedonians, representing the latest advance of Arian heresy, on the other. The letter of Damasus urged that the ὁμοουσία of the Holy Spirit should be asserted against them. This was a logical deduction from the confession of the ὁμοουσία of the Son, which had been made by Cyril and his friends. It is true that the Macedonians could sign Cyril's Creed so far as the teaching on the Holy Spirit is concerned. But the fact remains, that their heresy is of a later date than the creed itself, which cannot be expected to condemn them any more than it might be expected to condemn Nestorius. It is therefore a mistake to talk of any surrender of Athanasian principles. The creed cannot have been brought up as a formula for union (Unionsformel) between the orthodox semi-Arians and Pneumatomachi,[1] because the latter were definitely condemned.

§ IV. The Council of Chalcedon

We must pause to consider what was the Baptismal Creed of Constantinople at this time. Kattenbusch[2] has suggested that Gregory Nazianzen introduced the original Nicene Creed. It will be convenient to call this Creed N, reserving the letter C for the so-called Constantinopolitan Creed. This would be natural under the circumstances of Gregory's call to rule the small company of the orthodox in Arian times. And there are some probable quotations, e.g. Orat. xl.: Πιστεύε τὸν υἱὸν τοῦ Θεοῦ, τὸν προαιώνιον λόγον, τὸν γεννηθέντα ἐκ τοῦ πατρὸς ἀχρόνως καὶ ἀσωμάτως, τοῦτον

[1] Harnack, *D.G.* ii. 267.   [2] Kattenbusch, i. p. 366.

ἐπ' ἐσχάτων τῶν ἡμερῶν γεγενῆσθαι διά σε καὶ υἱὸν ἀνθρώπου, ἐκ τῆς παρθένου προελθόντα Μαρίας ἀρρήτως καὶ ἀρυπάρως . . . ὅλον ἄνθρωπον τὸν αὐτὸν καὶ Θεὸν . . . τοσοῦτον ἄνθρωπον διά σε ὅσον σὺ γίνῃ δι' ἐκεῖνον Θεός. Τοῦτον ὑπὲρ τῶν ἀνομιῶν ἡμῶν ἤχθαι εἰς θάνατον, σταυρωθέντα τε καὶ ταφέντα . . . καὶ ἀναστάντα τριήμερον, ἀνεληλυθέναι εἰς τοὺς οὐρανοὺς . . . ἤξειν τε πάλιν μετὰ τῆς ἐνδόξου αὐτοῦ παρουσίας, κρίνοντα ζῶντας καὶ νεκροὺς . . . Δέχου πρὸς τούτοις ἀνάστασιν, κρίσιν, ἀνταπόδοσιν.

It is true that there is a passage in Chrysostom's sixth Homily on the Epistle to the Colossians (c. A.D. 399), in which he seems to quote the words "eternal life" from a creed. But he might quote these from the revised Creed of Antioch.

In A.D. 430, Nestorius, at the Council of Ephesus, quoted the words σαρκωθέντα ἐκ πνεύματος ἁγίου καὶ Μαρίας τῆς παρθένου as from N, to the amazement of Cyril of Alexandria, who quoted the correct form (adv. Nest. i. 8). It does not follow that Nestorius was here quoting C. Variations soon crept into copies of N. Hort points out that the copy of N quoted at the fifth session of the Council of Chalcedon was "encrusted with Constantinopolitan variations, including this."[1] At all events, it is certain that Nestorius intended to quote N, for in his letter to Pope Cælestine he quoted the same sentence "from the words of the holy Fathers of Nicæa."

A new argument has been advanced by Kunze[2] to prove that C had been introduced into Constantinople by Nectarius. He shows that a certain Galatian called Nilus, perhaps from Ancyra, who had held high office in Constantinople, and afterwards went to live as a monk on Mount Sinai, quoted C as his creed. He might just as likely have come across it on his travels.

Kunze[3] also quotes the evidence of Proclus, Bishop of

---

[1] He quotes a MS. in the Cambridge University Library which does not contain this particular phrase, nor four of the other interpolations, but retains as many more.
[2] *Marcus Eremita*, p. 161 ff.   [3] p. 169.

Constantinople 434–446, and of Marcus the hermit, who had lived in Ancyra, and was a pupil of Chrysostom. The facts of the life of Marcus are so uncertain that it is not safe to speculate much about his creed, and one sentence, τὸν ἐκ Μαρίας γεννηθέντα, certainly points to N rather than C. Theodotus of Ancyra (430–440) speaks of N as the current creed.

The historian Socrates (iii. 25) appears to quote N as the Creed of Constantinople. He refers to the letter of the Macedonians to Jovian, which contained N. But he quotes only the first words, καὶ τὰ λοιπὰ τοῦ μαθήματος.

Thus it appears that we have only the doubtful quotation from Chrysostom, and the uncertain evidence of Nilus, Proclus, and Marcus, to weigh against the probable quotations in Gregory's treatise, the negative evidence of Nestorius and the testimony of Socrates. The balance is decidedly in favour of Kattenbusch's theory that N was the Baptismal Creed of Constantinople down to the date of the Council of Chalcedon, when it was received with enthusiasm as the Baptismal Creed of a large majority.

When we reach the Acts of the Council of Chalcedon, the history of C comes out into clearer light. We come upon a reference to it in the minutes of the first meeting. Diogenes, Bishop of Cyzicus, accused Eutyches of falsehood in denying that the faith of the Nicene Council could receive any additions. "It received an addition from the holy Fathers because of the perversities of Apollinarius and Valentinius and Macedonius, and men like them; and there have been added to the symbol of the Fathers the words, 'who came down and was incarnate of the Holy Ghost and the Virgin Mary.' . . . The holy Fathers at Nicæa had only the words, 'He was incarnate,' but those that followed explained it by saying, 'of the Holy Ghost and the Virgin Mary.'"[1]

Diogenes appears to quote C, not a revised text of N, because he says it was enlarged by holy Fathers, and the reference to Macedonius seems to imply that he included in the text further teaching on the Holy Spirit. The Egyptian bishops contradicted him, on the ground that

[1] Mansi, vi. 632.

THE COUNCIL OF CHALCEDON

Eutyches had correctly quoted the creed, which to them meant N, and that no addition could be made.

At the close of the debate, the president desired the bishops each one to set forth his faith in writing, and referred to both the creeds which had been quoted as the expositions of the 318 and the 150.

At the next session, Eunomius, Bishop of Nicomedia, recited N. It was received with much enthusiasm. A chorus of voices exclaimed: "This we all believe, in this we were baptized, in this we baptize, this taught the blessed Cyril, this is the true faith. . . . Pope Leo so believes."

Then Aetius, Archdeacon of Constantinople, read C as "the holy faith which the 150 holy Fathers set forth in harmony with the holy and great Synod at Nicæa." This also was greeted by some voices with: "This is the faith of all, this is the faith of the orthodox, so we all believe." There does not seem to be any special reason why we should expect it to be received with the same enthusiasm as N. Reference had been made to the archives, and it was generally agreed that it was "the exposition of the 150." There is no need to impute dishonest motives to Aetius,[1] as if he had hatched a plot for palming off a new Constantinopolitan Creed upon the Church by forging minutes of the former Council. The facts are plain. Constantinopolitan churchmen had naturally a greater interest in the Council of A.D. 381 than the representatives of other Churches. So they pressed for recognition of the creed which they had somehow come to regard as its work. In their definition the two creeds were not identified, but C was treated as an instruction, while the faith of the 318 Fathers was to remain inviolate. Thus the way was prepared for subsequent confusion of the two creeds, but the approval stamped upon C was not the result of mere ignorance or political chicanery. Aetius knew what he was about, and most probably the Pope's legates had some reason for their consent. Either the Council of A.D. 381 had sent it to Damasus with their vindication of Cyril of Jerusalem, or he had learnt to value it through Epiphanius.

[1] Swainson, p. 121.

Some eighty-five years pass before we hear of C again, at the Council of Constantinople in A.D. 535, when it was said that the 150 Fathers confirmed the symbol of the 318. After another eighteen years, at the Council of 553, it was finally identified with N, and regarded, to quote Hort's words, "as an improved recension of it."

Two centuries had passed since it was first compiled. The times had changed, but the truth for which Athanasius and Cyril both suffered had endured. The true divinity of our Lord was confessed both in N and C; but while in N the thought was connected with special circumstances and stern anathemas, in C it was connected with the continuous life of the mother Church of Christendom enduring from generation to generation.

§ V. Later History: the "Filioque" Clause

The liturgical use of the Nicene Creed can be traced back to the fifth century. Peter Fullo, Bishop of Antioch, introduced it at every service.[1] Some years later the custom spread to Alexandria. In A.D. 511, Timothy, Bishop of Constantinople, introduced a more frequent use in his diocese, where it was the custom only to recite it on the Thursday in Holy Week. In this case it was certainly N which was meant under the title "the faith of the 318," but the text might have been corrupted by those additions which made the subsequent identification of N and C so easy.

In A.D. 568 the Emperor Justinian directed that in every Catholic church the faith should be sung by the people before the Lord's Prayer, though in subsequent practice it preceded the consecration.

The first mention of its introduction into the liturgy of a Western Church is found in the records of the famous Third Council of Toledo, A.D. 589, when the Visigothic King Reccared, in the name of his nation, renounced Arianism. The Canon is worth quoting in full.

"For the reverence of the faith and to strengthen the

[1] ἐν πάσῃ συνάξει, Theodorus Lector, ii. p. 566, ed. Valerius.

minds of men, it is ordered by the Synod, at the advice of Reccared, that in all the churches of Spain and Galicia, following the form of the Oriental churches, the symbol of the faith of the Council of Constantinople, that is, of the 150 bishops, shall be recited; so that before the Lord's Prayer is said the creed shall be chanted with a clear voice by the people; that testimony may thus be borne to the true faith, and that the hearts of the people may come purified by the faith to taste the body and blood of Christ."

It has been pointed out that John, Abbot of Biclaro,[1] who was highly esteemed by Reccared, and was made Bishop of Gerona shortly after the Council, had recently returned from Constantinople, where he had resided for seventeen years. In his Chronicle John notes that this custom had been introduced into Eastern Churches by the younger Justinian. It seems probable that the Canon was passed under his influence, and a very important question is raised: "Could he have been ignorant of the true text?" It is generally supposed that this Council promulgated the additional words "and the Son" in the clause dealing with the Procession of the Holy Spirit. There can be no doubt that they believed in the doctrine involved, because they stated it plainly in their 3rd Canon, in which they anathematised all who did not believe that the Holy Spirit proceeds from the Father and the Son, or that He is co-eternal with the Father and the Son, and co-equal.

Two early editions of the Councils, however—Cologne (1530) and Paris (1535)—omit the words in the text of the creed quoted by the Council, and D'Aguirre admits that some MSS. do not contain them. In the light of subsequent history, it seems far less probable that they would be intentionally omitted by a copyist than that they would be added. But we must be content to leave the point doubtful until the evidence of the MSS. has been collected and sifted.

Even if the interpolation was not made at that time, it must have been made very soon after, and that in good faith, in direct dependence on the Canon, which asserted the immemorial belief of the Western Church.

[1] Pusey, "On the clause 'and the Son,'" p. 184.

The mysterious question of the relationship of the Holy Spirit to the Father and the Son necessarily followed discussion of His claim to be worshipped.

Eastern theologians expressed it in the phrase, "Who proceedeth from the Father and receiveth from the Son" ('Ἐκ τοῦ Πατρὸς ἐκπορευόμενον, καὶ ἐκ τοῦ Υἱοῦ λαμβανόμενον), which is first found in the longer Creed of Epiphanius. The Cappadocian Fathers expressed it under the metaphor of "successive dependence," ὥσπερ ἐξ ἁλύσεως,[1] using the words of John xiv. 11, but arguing that the Godhead of the Father was the one primary source of the derived Godhead of the Son and the Spirit.

Western theologians approached the problem from another point of view. Hilary, starting from the thought of Divine self-consciousness as the explanation of the co-inherence of the Father in the Son and the Son in the Father, says distinctly that the Spirit receives of both.[2]

Augustine teaches that the Father and the Son are the *one* principle of the Being of the Holy Spirit.[3] Thus he brought men to the threshold of the later controversy. But it was not merely his own private speculation. The same teaching had been given in Gaul years before the publication of his work on the Trinity.

Victricius of Rouen, by birth a Briton, had taught, before A.D. 400, that "the Holy Spirit is truly of the Father and the Son, and thus the Father and the Son are in the Holy Spirit."[4]

The unknown author of the *Quicunque uult*, if he lived in the first half of the fifth century, accurately summed up the teaching of the Western theology in a sentence which was soon found useful by Auitus of Vienne in his controversy with Burgundian Arians: "The Holy Spirit is of the Father and of the Son, not made nor created nor begotten, but proceeding."

A Spanish bishop, Pastor, whose confession was quoted

---

[1] Basil, *Ep.* 38, p. 118 D., quoted by Robertson, *Athanasius*, p. xxxii.
[2] *Op. hist. frag.* 2. [3] *De Trin.* v. 13.
[4] *De Laude Sanctorum*, c. iv., ed. Tougard, Paris, 1895.

by a Spanish Council of Toledo in A.D. 447 against the Priscillianists, seems to have taught the same doctrine.¹

It is quite possible that the Council of 589 were influenced by the teaching of the *Quicunque uult*, since the words of their 3rd Canon suggest a reminiscence of clause 24. In any case the teaching was widespread, and it was inevitable that the additional words should be inserted in the creed. It is possible that this was done by more than one copyist independently, in Gaul as well as in Spain.

A century later the English Synod of Heathfield, in A.D. 680, upheld the doctrine, "glorifying the Holy Ghost proceeding in an inexpressible manner from the Father and the Son, as those holy apostles and prophets and doctors taught whom we have above mentioned."² Thus the English Church has been, as it were, cradled in this faith, though it does not follow that the interpolation had yet been made in the creed. The earliest Anglo-Saxon version of the creed, which is found in an eleventh-century MS. of Ælfric's Homilies, contains it.

Nearly another century had passed before the question was disputed. We are told in the Chronicle of Ado of Vienne that a controversy between the Greeks and the Romans arose at the Synod of Gentilly in A.D. 767. Ambassadors from Constantine Copronymus were present, and reproached the Westerns with adding to the creed. After this the matter was not suffered to rest. At the Council of Friuli, Paulinus, Bishop of Aquileia, drew up a clear statement justifying the insertion of the words. He maintained that the 150 holy Fathers had made additions to the faith, "as if expounding the meaning of their predecessors. . . . But afterwards too, on account, forsooth, of these heretics, who whisper that the Holy Ghost is of the Father alone, and proceeds from the Father alone, there was added, 'who proceedeth from the Father and the Son.' And yet those

---

¹ Hahn,³ p. 209, "a Patre Filioque procedens." Some MSS. omit Filioque. The reading is defended by Florez, *Espana sagrada theatro geogr. hist. de la iglesia de Espana*, vi. 77, against Quesnel, *Opp. Leonis M.* Diss. xiv.
² Bede, *Hist. eccl.* iv. 17.

holy Fathers are not to be blamed, as if they had added anything to or taken anything away from the faith of the 318 Fathers, who had no thought on Divine subjects contrary to their meaning, but in an honest manner studied to complete their sense without spoiling it." He justifies the addition by quoting John xiv. 11, with the explanation: "If, therefore, as He Himself testifies, the Father is inseparably and substantially in the Son, and the Son in the Father, how can it be believed that the Holy Ghost, who is consubstantial with the Father and the Son, does not always proceed essentially and inseparably from the Father and the Son?"

But the view so ably defended by Paulinus, one of the leading theologians of the brilliant circle which Charles the Great had gathered round him, was not yet held in Rome. In fact, some years previously, Pope Hadrian had been taken to task by the king for expressing approval of a confession put forth by Tarasius, Bishop of Constantinople, in which the words occur, "who proceedeth from the Father by the Son." The Pope in reply quoted passages from Athanasius, Eusebius, and Hilary, in defence of Tarasius. It may seem strange that the Pope did not quote the Nicene Creed in his reply, less probably in fear of the king than in despair of explaining the interpolation. His successor, Pope Leo III., was quite consistent in admitting the truth of the doctrine of the Double Procession, which he called "one of the more abstruse mysteries of the faith," while he refused to admit the words into the creed. We can understand why his legatees were authorised, at the Council of Frankfort in A.D. 794, to accept the strong statements of the doctrine put forward both in the *libellus* of the Italian bishops against Elipandus, the Adoptionist, and in the Synodical letter of the bishops of Gaul and Germany.

A more critical discussion followed at the Council of Aachen in A.D. 809. The Latin monks of the monastery on Mount Olivet had been called heretics because they interpolated the words in their creed, and sang it as they had heard it sung in the royal chapel. They sent to Rome for advice, and asked that the emperor might be informed, since they had received from him two works in which the clause was found, a homily of S. Gregory and the rule of S. Benedict. They also quoted, as containing it, the *Quicunque uult*, and a dialogue of S. Benedict which the Pope had given them. The Pope duly informed the emperor, who thereupon summoned the Council, which supported the monks and sent an embassy to the Pope. But Leo took the bold line of urging that the clause should be expunged from the creed, though the doctrine might be taught. His biographer says that he set up two silver shields in the Basilica of S. Peter, on which the creed was inscribed in Greek and Latin.[1] We can readily understand that the object was to perpetuate the pure text.

His successors were less firm. Within sixty years Pope Nicholas I. had been excommunicated by Photius, Bishop of Constantinople, on the ground that he had corrupted the creed by the addition of these words. He wrote to Hincmar of Rheims and other archbishops about the question, and the book of Ratramn of Corbey seems to have been written in response to his appeal.

Two other alterations, which are found in the text of our Nicene Creed, may be passed over with a few words.

These are the addition of the words "God of God" and the omission of the word "Holy" in the clause referring to the Church. They are both found in the text quoted at the Synod of Toledo in A.D. 589. The former was obviously derived from the text of the first Nicene Creed. From the first it had been implied in the words which follow: "Very God of Very God." The latter was certainly an accidental alteration, since the word stood in the original Creed of Jerusalem, and there could be no reason for its omission in the revised Creed.

[1] Anastasius, *in Vita Leonis*; Migne, *Patrol. lat.* 128, 1238. Lumby proves from the testimony of S. Peter Damian that this was the Constantinopolitan Creed.—*Hist. Creeds*, ed. ii. p. 98.

§ VI. Conclusions

This is the history of our Nicene Creed, like a long and tangled skein, only to be unravelled and transformed into a straight length by care and patience. Among many thoughts which the story unfolded suggests for reflection, two may be singled out as most important.

We cannot be too thankful that the creed of our Eucharistic worship owes its final form to the earnest zeal of a great catechist. The *Filioque* clause may be left out of consideration for the moment, because it may be regarded as an interpretation of the doctrine of God taught in the creed rather than an addition. It is true that the theological terms inserted in the old historic faith of Jerusalem are the fruit of controversy. As students we are reminded of the long trials and doubtful conflicts and long-delayed triumph of Athanasius. But they convey a different impression to the mind when removed from their original context, from associations of prolonged controversy and heated debate. As worshippers we are able to let our minds rest in meditation on the positive truths taught, without hindrance from negative warnings against error. In his earlier days Cyril would have thought himself the last person likely to adopt in a profession of faith dogmatic utterances from the Nicene Creed, which he never names, but seems to have in mind when he contrasts the Scriptures as a rule of truth with the teaching of fallible men. Time proves all things. In the evening of life he found that these novel phrases were the only successful method of defending the central truth of the Lord's divinity against subtle misinterpretations of the very Scriptures to which he had taught men to look for guidance. So he adopted them, and his action was no retrograde movement. On the contrary, it was an advance, and it was made, as we have seen, not by Cyril only, but all along the line from Jerusalem to Antioch and Salamis.

Too much has been made of the omission of the words ἐκ τῆς οὐσίας, which Athanasius is supposed to have thought quite as important as ὁμοούσιος. Harnack goes so far as to say that a kind of semi-Arianism, under the title of Homöusianism (= confession of ὁμοιούσιος), has been made orthodox in all Churches.[1] This, if true, would be, as he suggests, a biting satire on the churchman's confidence in the victory of faith formulated. But we have found no reason to suppose that the creed was a concordat between orthodox, semi-Arians, and those who doubted the divinity of the Holy Spirit at the Council of Constantinople or before. We must not confuse the issues. Athanasius accepted the semi-Arian alliance on the basis of the confession of ὁμοούσιος. It stood on record that the Council had added ἐκ τῆς οὐσίας against the original Arians.[2] If the same difficulties arose again, let them be met in the old way. As to the future, which was unknown, the wisdom of Athanasius was justified by the use of the term "consubstantial" to guard the Godhead of the Holy Ghost.

Objections are often raised to the importation of Greek metaphysics into the creed of the Christian religion. There would be some reason to object if the Church had stopped there. This was not the case. Athanasius and his allies had safeguarded belief in the divinity of our Lord. Their use of the metaphysical term "substance" was a means to an end. "The theology of Athanasius and of the West is that of the Nicene formula in its original sense. The inseparable unity of the God of revelation is its pivot. The conception of *personality* in the Godhead is its difficulty. The distinctness of the Father, Son, and Spirit is felt (ἄλλος ὁ Πατήρ, ἄλλος ὁ υἱός), but cannot be formulated so as to satisfy our full idea of personality. *For this Athanasius had no word;* πρόσωπον meant too little (implying, as it did, no more than an aspect possibly worn but for a special period or purpose), ὑπόστασις (implying such personality as separates Peter from Paul) too much."[3] On this mysterious subject there were profound thoughts latent in the writings of Hilary, who had been led to faith in the Blessed Trinity by meditation on the idea of Divine self-consciousness. He had neither time nor means to work them out, hampered as he was by controversy,

[1] *D.G.* ii. 269.   [2] Specially against Eusebius of Nicomedia.
[3] Robertson, *Athanasius*, p. xxxii.

and, to some extent, dependent on Origen. Where Greek metaphysics failed, the strong intellect of Augustine took up the task, and in his great work *On the Trinity* made his contribution to the development of the doctrine of Divine Personality from the new vantage ground of Christian psychology.

The second thought, which needs emphasising, relates to the future use of this creed as a bond between divided Churches. Duchesne [1] has a most interesting passage on the difference between the theologies of East and West, which can be traced back to the fourth century, and even to the third. In the West, consubstantiality is regarded as the essence of the mystery of the Trinity. The idea of Divine Unity is cultivated above all, the idea of Triune Personality being subordinated to it. Western theologians think of the Trinity as a necessity of Divine life,—to use a technical term, as immanent, an abiding reality. On the other hand, Eastern theologians start from the thought of the eternal distinctions (hypostases), reconciling them as best they can with their idea of Divine Unity. They think of the doctrine of the Trinity as an explanation of the creation, as œconomic, manifested in the work of the Father, the Son, and the Holy Spirit. To this day they cling to the point of view attained by the Cappadocian Fathers, and reject the *Filioque*, which, apart from controversy as to its introduction into the creed, is a watchword of Western theology. Duchesne suggests that some taint of semi-Arianism is the cause of their opposition. Surely this is to erect a barrier which Athanasius refused to build. The eloquent words of Duchesne, "Faith unites, theology sometimes separates us," express the whole gist of Athanasius's dealing with the semi-Arians. We must be careful not to read the present into the past. The shadow of the *Filioque* controversy had not yet passed over the Church. We may fully agree as to the importance of the truth which those words teach, and yet shrink from branding with the reproach of semi-Arianism a Church which refuses to use them. Logically, we should have to extend our

[1] *Autonomies Ecclésiastiques, Égl. sep.* p. 83.

suspicion to the whole creed, which we all use, since it originated in a semi-Arian circle. The fact is, however, that in it and through it the semi-Arians became Catholics. From this Catholic standpoint began, it is true, a divergence of views, represented in the teaching of Augustine and John Damascene. These are the really antagonistic theologies which are confronted to-day, and which need closer study than they have received, by contrast as well as by comparison. It is no use to explain away words. The ideas, which they express more or less imperfectly, are imperishable, and will reappear in a new dress. It would be disastrous to cut out the *Filioque*, for in so doing we should be disloyal to the truths which our fathers have been at pains to learn. What is needed is statement, frank explanations on both sides. The report of the Bonn Conference of 1872 showed that agreement of interpretation is at least possible. We do not teach that there are two founts of Deity, confessing with S. Paul, "One God the Father, of whom are all things." In regard to the manifestation of God in creation and revelation, we confess with the Eastern Church, that the Holy Spirit proceeds from the Father through the Son. This is their distinctive line of thought, and the conclusion is valid. Only, we note that, along another line of thought, uplifted to the contemplation of the mystery of Divine life, they should acknowledge the procession of the Spirit from the Son as a true inference from belief in the Divine *Coinherence*. In the words of the great Cyprian let us agree: "Saluo iure communionis diuersa sentire."

CHAPTER VI

THE ATHANASIAN CREED I

§ I. Athanasian Faith in the Fifth Century.
§ II. Contemporary Professions of Faith.
§ III. The Brotherhood of Lerins.
§ IV. The Internal Evidence of the *Quicunque*.
§ V. Priscillianism.
§ VI. The Date and Authorship.

THE history of the Athanasian Creed is one of the most difficult subjects in Patristic literature. It is agreed that it was not written by S. Athanasius, and that it was written in Latin. All the Greek MSS. are plainly translations from a Latin text. Beyond this limit of agreement nothing is settled. Having collected my facts, I propose to follow the method which I have used above, and arrange them, proceeding from the obscure to the obvious; treating first of the modes of thought in the period in which its origin should be sought, of its internal evidence, and of the evidence of some possible quotations in the fifth century, with the light which these throw on the question of authorship. We shall then be prepared to trace the diverging lines of external evidence, broadening out from the sixth to the ninth century, and to discuss the merits of rival theories as to the origin of the creed.

§ I. ATHANASIAN FAITH IN THE FIFTH CENTURY

Between the death of S. Athanasius in 373, and the death of S. Augustine in 430, which marks the close of the great creed-making epoch in early Church history, theological thinking had not come to a standstill. On the one hand, Macedonianism, the following of Macedonius, semi-Arian Bishop of Constantinople, had spread to some extent. His denial of the divinity of the Holy Spirit was a necessary corollary to Arian propositions, and reappeared whenever Arianism took hold of a people. Thus Niceta of Remesiana found it an active heresy at the end of the fourth century along the banks of the Danube, probably through the influence of the Gothic Arian Bishop Ulphilas. But this heresy never attained an independent existence, and with the decline of Arianism its fate was sealed. On the other hand, Apollinarianism, the denial of the Lord's human soul, had found expression in statements more crude than any which the learned Apollinaris, himself an aged confessor, had ventured to formulate. It was with great pain that his old allies in the Arian controversy felt constrained to attack and condemn his error. S. Athanasius never mentions him by name in the treatise which he is said to have written against his teaching. The strong point in the new heresy was its pleading for reverence, what S. Hilary called "an irreligious solicitude about God." Apollinaris thought that the consubstantial Word, taking the place of the human mind in the Incarnate Christ, would alike preserve the unity of His Divine personality, and the truth that He was impeccable, since the human mind, being changeable and moved by impulse, is therefore capable of sinning. A wide propaganda was established, and a large supply of tracts and hymns were put into circulation, which were read and sung by people of devout minds with a tendency to mysticism, who could not detect the drift of such teaching. Later adherents to the theory denied that the Lord had even an animal as distinguished from a reasoning soul. They conjectured the conversion of the Godhead into flesh, even more thoroughly destroying the idea of His true Manhood to preserve His Divinity from taint of fleshly sinfulness. The answer to this phase of error was given unhesitatingly by the teachers who followed S. Athanasius. They affirmed the perfectness of both natures, Manhood and Godhead, in Christ. Thus only can we believe in Him as the Redeemer of our whole nature, though we agree that He was impeccable, for in His Divine personality He could not sin. This thread of argument, taken up in the East by the Cappadocian Fathers, in the West by S. Ambrose and S. Augustine, is stated with precision in the second part of the *Quicunque*. The perfectness of the human nature which Christ assumed consists in the possession of a reasoning soul and human flesh. It was a truly human life which He consecrated in suffering and death. At the same time, in the mystery of His Divine nature He was " God of the substance of His Father, begotten before all worlds." Thus Arianism was for ever excluded from the domain of Christian thought. As a confession in these words of the main truth for which S. Athanasius contended, the *Quicunque* deserves to be dignified by his name, which has been attached to it certainly from the seventh century. The *Quicunque* introduces, however, a new word, " person " (persona), to express the eternal distinction (ὑπόστασις) of the Son from the Father and the Holy Spirit, which represents a definite advance from the position gained for thought by S. Athanasius, confirming rather than contradicting his speculation, and helping to explain it. He had affirmed that the Father and the Son and the Holy Spirit were distinct in working (ἄλλος καὶ ἄλλος καὶ ἄλλος), but how to express this Trinity in Unity as consisting in Triune Personality he knew not, because he had no word for Personality.

The first part of the *Quicunque*, which develops such a theory of Divine Personality, owes nearly as much to S. Augustine as the second part to S. Athanasius. But there is one marked exception, which tends to prove the Gallican rather than African origin of the formulary, the use of the term "substantia." Augustine preferred to use "essentia," and in his book *On the Trinity* actually condemned it. He says (*de Trin.*), vii. 5. 1 : " In Deo substantia proprie non dicitur," but admitted it in some of his later writings, *e.g.*, *c. Max.* ii. 1. He would even use " substantia " as a synonym for " persona " (= ὑπόστασις). This was to revive the old misunderstandings between Eastern and Western theologians, which came to a head at the Council of Alexandria in 362, when, as we have seen,[1] S. Athanasius mediated between them,

[1] P. 100, *supra*.

showing that the Western use, *una substantia* (= μία οὐσία), was not Sabellian, and that the Greek use, τρεῖς ὑποστάσεις (= *tres personæ*), was not Trithcistic.

The acute mind of S. Hilary of Poitiers had also been exercised on the problem. It is not surprising that such difficulties should arise while theological language was in the making. His use of *persona* was indeed occasional and somewhat tentative, but his use of *substantia* = *essentia* = οὐσία was consistently maintained in Gaul, and may be regarded as a Gallican contribution to the *Quicunque*.

S. Hilary's explanation of these terms was an appeal to the philosophy of common sense. "A person" is one who acts.[1] "Substance" is that in which a thing subsists.[2] Readers of the English Psalter cannot fail so to understand the words "a wicked person" (Ps. ci. 4), or "Thine eyes did see my substance, yet being imperfect" (Ps. cxxxix. 16).

This explanation is quite distinct from that suggested by Tertullian in the third century, and by Faustus of Riez in the fifth. Both of them had been trained as lawyers, and not unnaturally carried legal ideas into theology. To a lawyer a "person" is a theoretical owner of rights and property; "substance" is the aggregate of rights and property. In the legal sense, a slave, who has no rights, has no personality, while a corporation has both "personality" and "substance." Thus we understand the words (Luke xv. 13) "he wasted his substance," or the phrase "a substantial farmer."

Thus Tertullian (*adv. Prax.* 7): "Filius ex sua persona profitetur patrem"; (*ib.*): "Non ius eum substantiuum habere in re per substantiæ proprietatem, ut res et persona quædam uidere possit (*scil.* Logos)."

These passages show how his legal training coloured his conception of the term *persona* in his Latin Bible.[3] By them-

---

[1] *De Trin.* iv. 21.

[2] *De Synodis*, 12 : "Essentia est res quæ est, uel ex quibus est et quæ in eo quod maneat subsistit. Dici autem essentia, et natura, et genus, et substantia uniuscuiusque rei poterit. Proprie autem essentia idcirco est dicta, quia semper est. Quæ idcirco etiam substantia est, quia res quæ est, necesse est, subsistat in sese."

[3] *Adv. Prax.* 6 (Prov. viii. 30): "Cottidie oblectabar in persona eius"; *adv.*

selves they might be used to show that Tertullian's method in speaking of distinctions between the Divine Persons was "the method of Juristic fictions."[1] But there are others which might point to a simpler explanation of the terms:[2]— *adv. Hermog.* 3 : " Deus substantiæ ipsius (Christi) nomen est diuinitatis." *Apol.* 21 : " Hunc ex Deo prolatum didicimus et prolatione generatum et idcirco Filium Dei et Deum dictum ex unitate substantiæ."

Faustus, in his book *On the Holy Spirit*, explains that "to persons it belongs to subsist each one properly by himself," though not unnaturally he afterwards reverts to the legal phrase, *persona res iuris*.

This question of definition has a wider range than the mere historical problem, whether the use made of these terms in the *Quicunque* points to a Gallican or African origin. Before we can discuss in the sequel the usefulness of this creed, we must make out what these terms meant at the time of their introduction into Christian formularies. We inherit them also in the Collect and Special Preface for Trinity Sunday, as in the first of the Thirty-nine Articles. Our theology would not be simplified by rejection of this creed. Too much has been made sometimes of S. Augustine's caution that we should use the term "person" to express distinctions in the Godhead, not as a satisfactory explanation, but only that we should not remain altogether silent. It is only of the term that he is shy, and that probably because of the danger of taking it in a bold legal sense. He does not shrink from following out the train of thought to which a philosophical explanation of it leads, from a most elaborate analysis of self-consciousness, or from explaining the doctrine of the Trinity by such analogies. As Mr. Illingworth has so clearly shown in his lectures on the doctrine of Personality, men can only obtain more accurate knowledge of the mysteries of Divine Being by more accurate analysis of the mystery of their own being. S. Augustine followed out a

Prax. 14 (Lam. iv. 20): "Spiritus personæ eius Christus Dominus." In both cases the LXX. has πρόσωπον.

[1] Harnack, *D.G.* ii. p. 307.   [2] Seeberg, *D.G.* i. p. 87.

train of thought already suggested by S. Hilary, and those writers who condemn Augustinian speculation most loudly, ignore the theological preparation made for them, which proves them to be the crown of a long series, and not merely the rash deductions of an isolated thinker.

§ II. Contemporary Professions of Faith

At the beginning of the fifth century there were in existence in Gaul a number of private professions of faith, relics of a time of restless unsettlement when heresies abounded. Some of them were written in self-defence, some of them simply in the ordinary course of teaching. The history of the Church in Gaul at that period is at many points obscure, and it is difficult to estimate how widely they were used or even known. But it is important to take account of them before discussing the history of the *Quicunque*, since some of them are found grouped with it in many collections of canons and expositions. Their relation to its history has never been fully investigated, because until recently they have not been critically edited. Their importance consists in the fact that they show the same trend of thought towards fuller teaching on the Trinity and Incarnation.

The most important is the so-called "Faith of the Romans," which will come again under our notice as containing a quotation from the Apostles' Creed. It is attributed to Phœbadius, Bishop of Agen, during the last half of the fourth century. Its further interest for us consists in its clear teaching that the Father, Son, and Holy Spirit are not three Gods, but one God; that the Son is not created, but begotten; that we venerate the Holy Spirit as God, not unbegotten nor begotten, not created nor made, but of the Father and the Son always in the Father and the Son co-eternal. The Father begetting the Son did not diminish or lose the fulness of His Deity. In dealing with the incarnation, the author states clearly the facts against Apollinarianism. It was incorporated in a book *On the*

Trinity,[1] which became widely popular under the name of Athanasius, and in this way the profession got the name "Libellus Fidei S. Athanasii," by which Hincmar of Rheims called it in the ninth century. Probably it was by association with it in MSS. containing this book that the *Quicunque* also got the name " Faith of S. Athanasius." In collections of creeds the most common name is " The Faith of the Romans, or the Roman Church." This name points to early use in Rome, and the opinion is confirmed by the fact that a long quotation from it is found in the apocryphal Acts of Liberius (p. 215 *infra*). It is worth while to dwell on these points, because they throw light on the history of a kindred form known as the Creed of Damasus, a full account of which I must reserve for Chapter X. At this moment I will only point out that it belongs to this period, and is found in a MS. of the sixth century. It is partly dependent on the *Fides Romanorum*, and deals in the same way with the doctrines of the Trinity and the Incarnation.

Another confession of great interest was presented by Victricius, Bishop of Rouen, to Pope Innocent I. in 403. We know it only from the references in a letter written to him by his intimate friend, Paulinus of Nola. He was accused, it would seem unjustly, of a leaning to Arian or Apollinarian heresy, and wrote to the Pope to defend himself, expressing his faith in a co-eternal Trinity, of one divinity and substance, and in the incarnation as the assuming of full manhood in body and soul.[2] There is a parallel passage in his book, *de Laude Sanctorum*, which I will print with it.

PAULINUS, *Ep.* 37.	VICTRICIUS, *de Laude Sanctorum*, c. iv.
Cum ergo fides et confessio tua, ut credimus atque confidimus coæternam Trinitatem, unius diuinitatis et substantiæ et operis et regni esse testetur ; cumque Patrem Deum et	Confitemur Deum Patrem, confitemur Deum Filium, confitemur Spiritum Sanctum Deum. Confitemur quia tres unum sunt. Unum dixi; quia ex uno, sicut Filius de Patre

---

[1] This work, formerly ascribed to Vigilius of Thapsus, is now ascribed by Morin to an unknown theologian of the fourth century.—*Ben. Rév.* 1898.
[2] Paulinus, *Ep.* 37. 5.

PAULINUS—*contd.*

Filium Deum et Spiritum Sanctum Deum, ut est qui est et erat et uenturus est . . . quod ita ut ipse a Deo doctus es, doces unitatem Trinitatis sine confusione iungens, et Trinitatem ipsius unitatis sine separatione distinguens, ita ut nulla alteri persona conueniat, et in omni persona trium Deus unus eluceat ; et tantus

VICTRICIUS—*contd.*

ita Pater in Filio ; Sanctus Spiritus uero de Patre et Filio : ita et Pater et Filius in Spiritu Sancto. Una Deitas, una substantia . . . . quia ut tres ex uno, ita unitas in tribus. Sic confitemur quia sic credimus indiuiduam Trinitatem, ante quam nihil potest attingi nec mente concipi.

quidem Filius quantus et Pater, quantus et Spiritus Sanctus ; sed semper quisque nominis sui proprietate distinctus, indiuiduam retinet in uirtutis et gloriæ æqualitate concordiam.

Certi autem sumus, quod et Filium Dei ita prædicas, ut eundem et Filium hominis confiteri non erubescas ; tam uere hominem in nostra natura quam uere Deum in sua ; sed Filium Dei ante sæcula, quia ipse est Dei Uerbum Deus, qui erat in principio apud Deum, æque Deus coomnipotens et cooperator Patris. . . . Et hoc Uerbum, pietatis immensæ mysterio, caro factum est et habitauit in nobis. Non autem caro tantum corporis nostri, sed homo totus, et corporis nostri et animæ assumptione, animæ autem rationalis, quæ iuxta naturale opificium Dei habet insitam mentem ; alioquin in tenebris Apollinaris errabimus, si hominem assumptum a Deo animam mentis humanæ uacuam, qualis est pecorum et iumentorum, dicamus habuisse ; et eum hominem, quem suscepit Dei Filius, necesse est ea ueritate, quæ ueritas est et qua creauit hominem, totum susceperit, ut opus suum plena salute renouaret.

The so-called "Creed of Bacchiarius" deals with precisely the same problems, and shows how eagerly they were discussed at the beginning of the fifth century. Bacchiarius was probably a Spanish monk who had come into Gaul while there was widespread suspicion of Priscillianism, and was made to defend himself before some Gallican bishops from complicity in such heresy. He too asserts the eternal distinctions in the Divine relationships of Father, Son, and Holy Spirit, their unity in substance, power, and will. In words which resemble the parallel clauses of the *Quicunque*, he elaborates the teaching of the scriptural terms, "begotten" and "proceeding."

FIDES BACCHIARII, *Cod. Ambros.* O. 212 *sup.*

Pater Deus et Filius Deus, sed non idem Pater, qui Filius, sed idem creditur esse Pater, quod Filius. Et Spiritus Sanctus non Pater ingenitus, sed Spiritus ingeniti Patris. Filius genitus . . . Pater enim unus ingenitus, Filius unus est genitus, Spiritus Sanctus a Patre procedens Patri et Filio coæternus. . . .

Itaque Spiritus Sanctus nec Pater esse ingenitus nec Filius genitus æstimetur, sed Spiritus Sanctus, qui a Patre procedit ; sed non est aliud, quod procedit, quam quod unde procedit. Si persona quæritur, Deus est. Hæc per hoc tripertita coniunctio et coniuncta diuisio et in personis excludit unionem et in personarum distinctione obtinet Unitatem. Sicque credimus beatissimam Trinitatem, quod unius naturæ est, unius deitatis, unius eiusdemque uirtutis atque substantiæ, ne inter Patrem et Filium et Spiritum Sanctum sit ulla diuersitas, nisi quod ille Pater est et hic Filius et ille Spiritus Sanctus, Trinitas in subsistentibus personis, Unitas in natura atque substantia.

He confesses the truth of the incarnation in the taking of human flesh and soul, and the dependent truth of the future resurrection of men in their bodies. He concludes with statements on the origin of the soul, the nature of the devil, marriage, and the canon of Holy Scripture.

To these professions we must also add the creed of the heretic Pelagius, which, with the exception of one passage on free will, is a document of great dogmatic value, and so fully orthodox that it has been ascribed both to Jerome and Augustine.

He explains the Greek terms ὁμοούσιον and ὑπόστασις, asserting the equality of the Divine Persons in the Trinity of one substance and eternity, in which there are no grades, "nihil quod inferius superiusue dici possit."

"Atque ut, confundentes Arium, unam eandemque dicimus Trinitatis esse substantiam et unum in tribus personis fatemur Deum, ita, impietatem Sabellii declinantes, tres personas expressas sub proprietate distinguimus, non ipsum sibi Patrem, ipsum sibi Filium, ipsum sibi Spiritum Sanctum esse dicentes, sed aliam Patris aliam Filii aliam Spiritus Sancti esse personam.

"Sic autem confitemur in Christo unam Filii esse personam, ut dicamus, duas esse perfectas atque integras substantias, id est, deitatis et humanitatis, quæ ex anima continetur et corpore."

Leporius, a native of Trèves,[1] who became a priest at

[1] One MS. of Cassian, *de Incarnatione*, i. 2 (ed. Petschenig), *i.e.*, *Cod. lat. Paris.* 14,860, preserves the reading *ex maxima Belgarum urbe*.

Marseilles, fell at this time into a heresy something like the error of Nestorius regarding the two natures in Christ. He was, however, converted by S. Augustine, with whom he stayed for a time at Hippo. On his return to Gaul he presented a confession to the Bishops of Marseilles and Aix, in which he made full amends for his error by a precise statement.

LEPORII LIBELLUS EMENDATIONIS (ed. Hahn,[3] p. 299)

Confitemur Dominum ac Deum nostrum Iesum Christum, unicum Filium Dei, qui ante sæcula natus ex Patre est, nouissimo tempore de Spiritu Sancto et Maria semper uirgine factum hominem, Deum natum ; et confitentes utramque substantiam, carnis et uerbi, unum eundemque Deum atque hominem inseparabilem pia fidei credulitate suscepimus, et ex tempore susceptæ carnis sic omnia dicimus, quæ erant Dei, transiisse in hominem, ut omnia quæ erant hominis, in Deum uenirent, ut hac intelligentia Uerbum factum sit caro, non ut conuersione aut mutabilitate aliqua coeperit esse, quod non erat, sed ut potentia diuinæ dispensationis Uerbum Patris, nunquam a Patre discedens, homo propre fieri dignaretur, incarnatusque sit unigenitus secreto illo mysterio, quod ipse nouit (nostrum namque est credere, illius nosse), ac sicut ipse Deus Uerbum totum suscipiens, quod est hominis, homo sit, et adsumptus homo totum accipiendo, quod est Dei, aliud quam Deus esse non possit. . . .

Caro igitur proficit in Uerbum, non Uerbum proficit in carnem, et tamen uerissime Uerbum caro factum est ; sed, ut diximus, solum proprie personaliter, non cum Patre aut Spiritu Sancto naturaliter, quia unigenitus Deus, Deus uerus, qui cum Patre et Spiritu Sancto unus est in natura alter est in persona. Non enim ipsum Patrem dicimus esse, quem Filium ; nec iterum eundem Filium dicimus esse, quem Patrem'; aut rursus Spiritum Sanctum Patrem uel Filium nuncupamus ; sed distinguentes personas in suis proprietatibus Patrem Deum Patrem proprie nominamus, et Filium Deum Filium proprie dicimus, et Spiritum Sanctum Deum Spiritum Sanctum proprie confitemur. Et cum ter numero dicimus Deum et Deum et Deum, non tres credimus Deos sed unum omnipotentiæ suæ trinitate perfectum. Nascitur ergo nobis proprie de Spiritu Sancto et Maria, semper uirgine, Deus homo Iesus Christus Filius Dei, ac sic in alterutrum unum fit uerbum et caro, ut manente in sua perfectione naturaliter utraque substantia sine sui præiudicio et humanitati diuina communicent et diuinitati humana participent ; nec alter Deus, alter homo, sed idem ipse Deus, qui et homo, et uicissim idem ipse homo, qui et Deus, Iesus Christus unus Dei Filius et nuncupetur et uere sit. Et ideo agendum nobis semper est et credendum, ut Dominum Iesum Christum Filium Dei, Deum uerum, quem cum Patre semper, et æqualem Patri ante sæcula confitemur, eundem a tempore susceptæ carnis factum Deum hominem non negemus, nec quasi per gradus et tempora proficientem in Deum, alterius status ante resurrectionem, alterius post resurrectionem, eum fuisse credamus, sed eiusdem semper plenitudinis atque uirtutis. . . .

Sed quia Uerbum Deus in hominem dignanter hominem suscipiendo descendit, et per susceptionem Dei homo ascendit in Deum Uerbum, totus Deus Uerbum factus est totus homo. Non enim Deus Pater homo factus est nec Spiritus Sanctus, sed unigenitus Patris; ideoque una persona accipienda est carnis et Uerbi, ut fideliter sine aliqua dubitatione credamus, unum eundemque Dei Filium inseparabilem semper geminæ substantiæ etiam gigantem nominatum. . . .

By the study of these confessions we are brought into contact with fresh and vigorous minds working out for themselves formulæ in which to express new aspects of the central truth guarded by the Nicene Creed. From that vantage ground they discerned new aspects of the doctrine of God, and felt constrained to use them. If it is true to say that we know only in part, and therefore wrongly, it is also true that the very knowledge of our imperfection makes us eager to correct, to improve. We may paraphrase the words of the great Gallican teacher, S. Hilary: "We are compelled to attempt what is unattainable, to climb where we cannot reach, to speak what we cannot utter; instead of the mere adoration of faith, we are compelled to entrust the deep things of religion to the perils of human understanding."[1]

§ III. THE BROTHERHOOD OF LERINS

The opening years of the fifth century were indeed a time of trouble and rebuke to all citizens of the old Roman Empire. That the fair provinces of Gaul should be overrun by barbarian armies almost without resistance, seemed a direct judgment of God upon the deep-seated sores of misgovernment and foul licentiousness, which crushed the spirit and drained the strength of the provincials. The famous treatise *On the Government of God*, written by Salvianus, priest of Marseilles, lays bare the real root of widespread misery in social corruption, and preaches faith in the one living God as the only hope. Together with many other thoughtful and religious men, Salvianus sought rest in retire-

[1] *De Trin.* ii. 2.

ment from the world, and seems to have entered for a time the famous monastery of Lerins.[1]

At the beginning of the fifth century (c. 426), Honoratus, the founder of this monastery, had gathered round him a remarkable band of men; Hilary, who became his successor as abbot, and afterwards as Bishop of Arles; Vincentius, author of the famous *Commonitorium*; Lupus, who became the saintly Bishop of Troyes, and with Germanus of Auxerre, preached so successful a mission against the Pelagian error in Britain; Faustus, who in his turn became abbot, and finally Bishop of Riez, one of the ablest theologians of the day.

On a neighbouring island lived Eucherius, sometime high in the civil service of the empire, with his wife and sons, who became in their time bishops. He himself became Bishop of Lyons, and it was no empty compliment when Claudianus Mamertinus called him "by far the greatest of the great bishops of his age."

In Appendix A I have reprinted, with some slight alterations, the parallels to the *Quicunque* in the writings of Vincentius and Faustus, which I collected for my former book.

The parallels in the *Commonitorium* of Vincentius have been held by many writers to be quotations of the creed. Some, from Antelmi (1693) to Ommanney (1897), hold that they prove that he was the author. I prefer to discuss them in connection with the internal evidence of the creed, because there is no positive proof that they are quotations or he the author. But, regarded as parallels, they are close enough to warrant the conjecture that there is some relation between them and the creed, and it is easier to believe that Vincentius used the creed, than that anyone in a subsequent generation or century, of less exact scholarship, picked out his phrases and wove them into a document of this kind.[2] It has been argued that "there is no appearance that Vincentius was quoting any particular document."[3] This is true, but it does not exclude the supposition that he quoted phrases of the

---

[1] Hil. Arelat., *Vita S. Honor.* c. 4.   [2] *The Ath. Creed*, p. xcii.
[3] Swainson, *Hist. Creeds*, p. 224.

Quicunque by memory. If he had seen it written out, he would not think of it as an important document, in the sense in which he regarded the letter of S. Capreolus read at the Council of Ephesus, of which he speaks (c. 42), as important. The intrinsic merits of the creed, regarded as a sermon or private profession of faith, not Synodical sanction or connection with the name of Athanasius, would give it authority. He would only receive it as approved by his judgment, and possibly as recommended by his regard for the author.

Again, it is important to note the differences which distinguish these Vincentian parallels from the *Quicunque*. They are strongly anti-Nestorian. Vincentius says (c. 12) that Nestorius wished to make "two Sons of God," and quotes the title "Mother of God," which became a test phrase in the controversy, but is not found in the *Quicunque*, where we find *unus est Christus*, not *Filius*. He uses the term *humanitas* freely, and in c. 20 writes *Deus Uerbum assumendo et habendo carnem*, but seems to shrink from the compound phrase *assumptio humanitatis*. I think we may trace this to his fear of a Nestorian interpretation of the words. In c. 17 he argues against the theory that "postea in eum (the Man Christ) assumentis Uerbi persona descenderit; et licet nunc in Dei gloria maneat assumptus, aliquamdiu tamen nihil inter illum et ceteros homines interfuisse uideatur."

The *idem, idem* in the following parallel (c. 13) to clause 29 shows a train of thought foreign to the *Quicunque*, though it is found in the context of the parallel passage in Augustine, *Enchiridion*, 35:

    (a) *Aug.*: "Deus ante omnia sæcula."
        Quic.: "Deus est ex substantia Patris ante sæcula genitus."
        Vinc.: "idem ex Patre ante sæcula genitus."
    (b) *Aug.*: "homo in nostro sæculo."
        Quic.: "homo ex substantia matris in sæculo genitus."
        Vinc.: "idem ex matre in sæculo generatus."

The greater part of this c. 13 is taken up with confutation of Nestorian statements. In the same way I would explain the variation in the following parallel to clause 34:

Aug. : " non confusione naturæ sed unitate personæ."
Quic. : " non confusione substantiæ sed unitate personæ."
Vinc. : " non corruptibili nescio qua diuinitatis et humanitatis confusione sed integra et singulari qua-
dam unitate personæ."

The word *substantia* (= *natura*) was used freely by Augustine (*In Joh. Tract.* 78), as in the well-known Ambrosian hymn, " Procede de thalamo tuo geminæ gigas substantiæ." Elsewhere it is used freely by Vincentius, but he seems to substitute *diuinitatis et humanitatis* in this sentence as if he would prefer the plural *substantiarum* to the singular of the *Quicunque* form, and adds the epithet *singulari* to sharpen his sentence against Nestorianism.

The parallels in writings of Faustus show the same trend of thought. The epithet *simplicem* (personam) in *Ep.* 7 corresponds to Vincentius's use of *singularis*. And his use of *pariter* in the parallels to clause 28, which is found also in Vincentius, though it is doubtful whether it stood in the original text of the *Quicunque* (see p. 187), corresponds to S. Cyril's phrase Θεὸς ὁμοῦ καὶ ἄνθρωπος in anti-Nestorian sentences.[1]

§ IV. THE INTERNAL EVIDENCE OF THE "QUICUNQUE"

We are now in a position to discuss the internal evidence of the *Quicunque* from a wider point of view than has hitherto been attained. It is not enough to pick out certain test phrases and argue that they were inserted against this or that heresy, or that certain modifications would have been introduced if the creed had been written after a certain date. Such reflections are useful as affording, so to speak, a key to the problem of date; but we ought also to examine the wards of the lock in which the key turns, to be sure that

---

[1] Ommanney, *Diss.* p. 411, quotes a sentence from the contemporary Latin translation of S. Cyril's *Apology for the Twelve Chapters*, in which *pariter* is used with a similar purpose.

they correspond. We obtain this wider knowledge by comparing the creed with these other professions of faith which we have traced to the beginning of the fifth century. Standing as they do, midway between the teaching of Augustine and the parallels in Vincentius, they afford valuable corroboration of Waterland's opinion, that the *Quicunque* belongs to Apollinarian times, *i.e.* before the condemnation of Nestorius in 431.

In regard to the doctrine of the Trinity, these professions are less Augustinian than the *Quicunque*. They offer no parallels to the characteristic method of ascribing to each of the three persons in the Trinity the same attributes, "uncreate, eternal, omnipotent," while asserting in each case that they are one uncreate, one eternal, one omnipotent. Though S. Ambrose had written cautiously on these lines, it was only in the fifth book of Augustine *On the Trinity* that they were fully developed. Since then such balanced antitheses have become a commonplace of Christian thought, though sometimes weakened by a writer like Fulgentius,[1] who adds the word God, "one eternal God." This is, as Waterland[2] says, "a very insipid and dull way of expressing it."

On the other hand, these professions agree closely with the *Quicunque* in carefully distinguishing the persons, while they retain the Gallican terminology, *una substantia*. Pelagius and Bacchiarius lay similar stress on the scriptural terms for the Divine relationships, "begotten," "proceeding," and maintain their coequality as excluding grades of superiority in the Godhead.

In regard to the doctrine of the Incarnation, there is even more marked agreement of phraseology in opposition to Apollinarianism. The main thesis of the *Quicunque* in its second part (cl. 30) is the perfectness of the two natures in Christ, and the unity of His Divine-Human person is taught in relation to the Apollinarian error respecting the natures rather than the Nestorian puzzle respecting the mystery of their union.

The phrase *perfectus Deus perfectus homo* comes from a

[1] Appendix C. [2] P. 214.

doubtful treatise of Athanasius, *c. Apol.* i. 16; cf. *Orat.* iii. 41. The nearest parallel in Augustine is *Serm.* 238: "Aduersus Arium, ueram et perfectam Uerbi diuinitatem; aduersus Apollinarem, perfectam hominis in Christo defendimus ueritatem." Leporius writes: "Manente in sua perfectione naturaliter utraque substantia." Pelagius sums up in a sentence the argument of the *Quicunque* (cll. 24–35): "Sic autem confitemur in Christo unam Filii esse personam, ut dicamus, duas esse perfectas atque integras substantias, id est, deitatis et humanitatis, quæ ex anima continetur et corpore." And not only does Pelagius proceed to condemn Apollinaris by name, but he also condemns other unnamed teachers who had recently introduced a fresh development of that error teaching a confusion of Godhead and Manhood (Hahn[3], p. 290).

Thus it is plain that the author of the *Quicunque* used both phrases and arguments which were in current use before the rise of Nestorianism.

The mere repetition of such phrases in documents of the Nestorian period, such as the *Union Creed of the Antiochenes*, proves nothing against the priority of the *Quicunque*, unless it can be proved that its teaching on the "Unity of Person" is either the main point in the argument or distinctly directed against Nestorian denial of such unity. In the section clauses 32–35 the subject that Christ is "God and man" is explained to refute the theory of confusion of substance, and illustrated by the analogy of the union of soul and flesh in one man. Both in the explanation and in the illustration the "unity of His person" is postulated, but it is not put forward as if it was specially endangered. Nor is it guarded by the test phrases which were found so useful against Nestorius. "There is not a word of the Mother of God, or of one Son only, in opposition to two sons, or of God's being born, suffering, dying: which kind of expressions the creeds are full of after Nestorius's times, and after the Council of Ephesus."[1] It has been suggested that the error of Leporius was of a similar kind, and we certainly find in his confession

[1] Waterland, p. 149.

the statement : "Nec alter Deus, alter homo, sed idem ipse Deus, qui et homo, et uicissim idem ipse homo, qui et Deus." How easy it would have been to insert a clause of this kind in the *Quicunque* if it had been desired to labour this point. It is just this turn which we find given to the parallels in Vincentius and Faustus.

The illustration from the constitution of man (cl. 35) was used by S. Ambrose, and more freely by S. Augustine, before Nestorianism was thought of. It threw no light on the problem of personality, either suggesting the true view that the manhood assumed was impersonal, or that its personality was annihilated, according to the dangerous logic of Faustus, "persona personam consumere potest."

The teaching on the two nativities " ante sæcula . . . in hoc sæculo" finds a parallel in Augustine's *Enchiridion* (420), c. 35, in a chapter which certainly anticipates the arguments against Nestorianism, insisting on the unity of person with denial of two Sons. But this fact points the contrast to the *Quicunque*. Augustine may have had Leporius in his mind, who in his recantation quoted the two nativities to lead up to "unum *eundemque* Deum atque hominem." Pelagius, however, quotes the nativities with reference only to the perfectness of the natures. And this is the natural conclusion from clause 29 of the *Quicunque*, which leads up to the same point, "perfectus Deus perfectus homo," and lacks the " idem " " idem " so often inserted by Vincentius.

While the doctrine of the Two Natures is thus clearly defined for practical purposes, it is not elaborated in the way which became necessary after the rise of Eutychianism. Eutyches, whose difficulty may have been accentuated by the poverty of the Syriac language, was unable to distinguish accurately between " nature " and " person," and felt driven to deny the duality of the natures, after their union in Christ. He confessed that He, who was born of the Virgin Mary, was perfect God and perfect man, but had not flesh consubstantial with ours. Thus he virtually denied the true manhood, and it became necessary to enlarge dogmatic statements to exclude his theory of One Nature. There is no indication that such need was felt by the author of the *Quicunque*, who might so easily have inserted teaching that Christ is consubstantial with us in one nature, as He is consubstantial with the Father in the other. Such phrases were used in Gaul by Cassian[1] in 430, before the rise of Eutychianism. They did not need to be invented, only to be applied. Another argument to prove that the *Quicunque* is pre-Eutychian has been founded on the change of reading in clause 33, from accusatives *carnem, Deum*, to ablatives *carne, Deo*. Thus the creed would be made to condemn Eutychian teaching of a change of Godhead in the flesh, and that the manhood was assumed into God in such a sense as to be absorbed into the Divine nature, teaching which would be to some extent favoured by the accusatives.[2] And it is also an acknowledged fact that Catholic writers, after the rise of this heresy, shrank from using the illustration of clause 35, "as the reasonable soul," etc., which the Eutychians misused, pleading for one nature in Christ, as soul and body make one nature in man.

On these grounds it seems to me reasonable to support Waterland's opinion that the *Quicunque* was written before the condemnation of Nestorius in 431. And I am glad to claim the support of Kattenbusch,[3] who has studied minutely the whole question, and lays stress on the fact that beside the phrase of Leporius, "Jesus Christus unus Dei Filius," clause 33 of the creed is, so to speak, unbiased, expressing a mode of thought which was disturbed by Nestorius, and had to be defended against him with new phrases. Ommanney's arguments, in his careful chapter on the date of the creed,[4] are defensible against Waterland only on the assumption that the main argument of clauses 32–35 is to uphold the unity of Christ's person against the Nestorian denial, which I venture to think is mistaken. And I am confident

---

[1] *De Incarn.* vi. 13.
[2] Waterland, p. 144. I take this opportunity of withdrawing the mistake in this connexion on p. lxxiv. of my book, *The Athanasian Creed*, pointed out by a kind critic in the *Tablet*.
[3] *Theol. Lit. Z.* March 6, 1897. [4] *Diss.* pp. 350–374.

that further consideration of the evidence of contemporary Gallican Creeds will finally establish the soundness of Waterland's judgment.

There is one more point in the internal evidence which deserves special mention, the reference to the descent into hell. This was rare in forms of the Apostles' Creed at that time, but was common in the writings of Catholic teachers (Hilary, *de Trin.*; Aug. *Ep.* 164, etc.) before 431, and supplied a useful argument against the Apollinarian denial that the Lord had a human soul.

§ V. Priscillianism

These conclusions from the internal evidence of the creed may be confirmed by the suggestion that it was written with the special object of meeting the errors of Priscillianism.

Priscillian was a wealthy Spanish layman, who was unquestionably devout, and was well read in the Scriptures. But he had had no theological training, and was not, to say the least, a clear thinker. He quotes Hilary of Poitiers again and again without understanding his argument. With the best intentions such a man might fall into heretical modes of expression. We may charitably trace to this cause the Sabellian and Apollinarian teaching which he gives so confidently as gospel truth. He professed all the time to use and interpret in their primitive sense Church formularies, such as the Baptismal Formula and the Apostles' Creed. When we find him, however, making "Holy Church" precede "Holy Spirit" in the creed, we cannot but doubt his belief in the personality of the Holy Spirit. This doubt is not removed by the following passage from the same treatise, Tract II. § 45: "*In nomine Patris et Fili et Spiritus Sancti, non dicit autem 'in nominibus' tamquam in multis, sed in uno, quia unus Deus* trina potestate uenerabilis omnia et in omnibus Christus est sicut scribtum est: *Abrahæ dictæ sunt repromissiones et semini eius; non dicit 'et seminilis'* tanquam *in multis, sed quasi in uno 'et semini tuo' quod est Christus.* . . . Nobis enim Christus Deus Dei Filius passus in carne secundum fidem symboli baptizatis et electis ad sacerdotium *in nomine Patris et Fili et Spiritus Sancti* tota fides, tota uita, tota ueneratio est."

With this passage we may compare a fragment of esoteric teaching, his *Benedictio super fideles*, which begins with a quotation from Hilary's prayer, "Sancte Pater, omnipotens Deus," but falls away from the lines of his thought in the following sentence: "Tu enim es Deus, qui . . . unus Deus crederis, inuisibilis in Patre, uisibilis in Filio et unitus in opus duorum Sanctus Spiritus inueniris."

The accusation of Orosius in his *Commonitorium*,[1] that Priscillian omitted the *et* in the Baptismal Formula, is true as to the substance of his teaching, if not in the letter. He never uses the word Trinity, and it does not appear that he acknowledges the distinction of persons in the Godhead behind the manifestation of threefold power (*trina potestas*).

The same mist of vagueness obscures the outlines of his Christological teaching. The following passage is plainly Apollinarian. Tract VI. § 99: "Denique Deus noster adsumens carnem, formam in se Dei et hominis, id est diuinæ animæ et terrenæ carnis adsignans, dum aliud ex his peccati formam, aliud diuinam ostendit esse naturam, illudque *arma iniquitatis* peccato, hoc *iustitiæ arma* demonstrat in salutem nostram uerbum caro factus."

We are not concerned here with the events of his life, his consecration as bishop, the controversies which followed upon the propagation of his teaching, his appeal to the Bishops of Rome and Milan, Damasus and Ambrose, the final tragedy of his appeal to the usurper Maxentius, a suicidal step which led to his condemnation on political rather than religious grounds. He was, however, executed on the charge of heresy, being the first to suffer this fate which he had proposed for others, and many saintly minds were grieved. Certainly it brought no gain of peace to the Church, for he was venerated as a martyr, and the sect increased everywhere. We have

---

[1] Orosius, *ad Aug.*: "Trinitatem autem solo uerbo loquebatur, nam unionem absque ulla existentia aut proprietate adserens sublato 'et' Patrem, Filium Spiritum Sanctum hunc esse unum Christum docebat."

seen, in the case of Bacchiarius, how great was the suspicion of all monks coming from Spain. When language so inaccurate as the passages quoted above was declared with vehemence to be Catholic teaching, there was need for vigilance. And there was need of a summary of Catholic belief on the Trinity and the incarnation, which should lay due stress on the responsibility of the intellect in matters of faith, and at the same time do justice to the moral aspect of these problems, and prove that faith worketh by love, only "they that have done good shall go into life eternal." The *Quicunque* exactly meets these requirements. May it not have been written for the purpose ?

There is another side to Priscillian's teaching on which it is not possible to speak with any confidence, but it must be mentioned in justice to his opponents. I refer to his leaning towards Manicheism and Gnosticism. Against his emphatic denial of such heresies must be set the plain proofs of his acquaintance with many recondite forms of such errors, and with apocryphal literature in which they are taught. His doctrine of the elect throws light on his setting Holy Church before Holy Spirit in the creed, and suggests his connection with some theosophic sect. The prominence which he gives to the sufferings of Christ may be explained away, if, like Mani, he attributed to them only a symbolical meaning.[1] It must be remembered that the Western Manicheans of the fourth and fifth centuries made much more parade of Christian teaching than those of the East.

Orosius charges him with explaining S. Paul's words, Col. ii. 14, "the handwriting of the ordinances," as "the bond in virtue of which the soul was imprisoned in the body, and made subject to sidereal influences." It seems to have been supposed that the powers brought the different parts of the body into relation to the signs of the zodiac, while the soul was influenced by the twelve heavenly powers, represented under the names of the twelve patriarchs. There are vague hints in Tracts VI., VIII., X. of these doctrines.

Tract VI. § 111 : "Inter duodecim milia signatorum patriarchum numeris mancipati."

[1] Neander, *Hist.* iv. p. 509 (Trans.).

Tract VII. § 117 : " Perpetua luce contecti peccatorum supplicia respuere et requiem possimus habere iustorum per Iesum Christum."

Such words seem simply to imply that the soul is mystically purged by fellowship with the higher world, and enabled to defy (respuere) the punishments of sins. This is the sort of teaching which would encourage secret immorality among those who imagined themselves safe by election. It was the suspicion of evil-doing which ruined Priscillian and his cause, however far he may have been from countenancing such conclusions. The only remedy is to proclaim, as is done with no uncertain sound both by the Creed of Damasus and the *Quicunque*, the doctrine of a Future Judgment, when " all shall rise again with their bodies, and shall give account for their own works."

§ VI. Date and Authorship

My conclusions from all these considerations differ but little from those of Waterland. They seem to point to the decade 420–430 as the period when the creed must have been written.

Kattenbusch[1] would push the date ten years further back.

[1] *Theol. Lit. Z.* 1897, p. 144 : " Das Charakteristische an der Formel ist ihre eigenthümlich kunstmässige Gestalt. Man kann sie eine " Dichtung " heissen. In feierlich bemessener, gravitätischer Form präzisirt sie die ' *catholica fides*.' Sie hat kein Metrum, wohl aber einen unverkennbaren Rhythmus. In ihrer rhetorisch plerophorischen Art spricht sie speciell den trinitarischen Gedanken vielleicht kühner und consequenter aus, als es der Theologie noch geläufig war. Man sieht sich ja nothwendigerweise an die Gedanken erinnert, die Augustin ausgeführt hat. Es kann aber ein Vorurtheil sein, wenn man meint, das Quic. setze die augustinische Trinitätsconstruktion als solche voraus. Die Formel lässt sich füglich auch begreifen als eine Vorläuferin der Spekulation des Augustin. Mir scheint, in der That, als ob Augustin sie bereits kenne. Nicht als ob er sie irgendwie als eine 'Autorität, betrachte. Aber wenn sie in Lerinum entstanden sein sollte, kann sie bald auch in afrikanischen mönchischen Kreisen bekannt geworden sein. Es hat für mich mehr Wahrscheinlichkeit, dass dem Augustin einzelne ihrer Ausdrücke oder Sätze im Gedächtniss gehaftet haben und ihm gelegentlich in die Feder geflossen sind, als dass der Autor der Formel aus den Stellen, die u. a. Burn nachweist, seine überraschend ähnlichen oder geradezu gleichlautenden Wendungen geschöpft haben sollte."

He does not consider that its relationship to the theology of Augustine stands in the way. He would even regard it as antecedent to Augustine's speculations. It seems to him possible that Augustine knew it, and that the parallel passages scattered over his works represent reminiscences. It does not follow that he would regard it as an authority.

I have often wondered whether the following sentence in Augustine, *de Trin.* I. v. 5, referred to a formal profession: "But in this matter (*i.e.* the Catholic faith) some are disturbed when they hear that the Father is God, and the Son is God, and the Holy Ghost is God, and yet that they are not three Gods but one God." I do not know of any other passages which would bear out Kattenbusch's suggestion, and the reference in this case seems to me too weak to bear the weight of so important an argument. It comes to this. If the main portion of part i. clauses 7–19, which one has been accustomed to think of as pre-eminently Augustinian, and which (as I have shown, p. 138) distinguishes the *Quicunque* from the other professions of faith quoted in this chapter, is not the fruit of Augustine's influence upon the author, but exercised, on the contrary, a constraining influence upon Augustine, the Church owes an unacknowledged debt of gratitude to a mind superior to that of the great African thinker. Surely this is an incredible hypothesis, since we find no trace of such influence on Victricius or Vincentius. Vincentius was possibly prejudiced against Augustine, and we find no parallels to these clauses in the *Commonitorium*; but no prejudice, as far as we know, would exist in his mind against a Gallican writer, and he desired to set forth the fulness of the Trinity (*Trinitatis plenitudo*), which is just what these clauses do. The genius of Augustine had no rivals, and we may be thankful, for the advance which he made in the interpretation of the doctrine of Divine Personality was only won at the cost of bitter pains, revealed to us in his heart-searching *Confessions*.

The supposed dependence of the author of the *Quicunque* on Augustine leads us to set the date of the publication of his *Enchiridion, c.* 420, as the earliest possible date of the *Qui-*

cunque. The parallels to the second book "against Maximinus," published *c.* 427, are of less importance. His lectures on S. John were written in 416, and in the same year he finished his work *On the Trinity*.

The absence of any reference to Nestorianism gives us the lower limit *c.* 430. There is a good deal of truth in Kattenbusch's observation, that expositions of faith must usually be assumed to be up to date, whereas commentaries on creeds and expositions of faith tend to stop with the latest heresy against which their authors find arguments in the creed of their subject.

The question of authorship is not so easy to define. There are three modern claimants,—Victricius, Vincentius, and Honoratus. I consider Vigilius of Thapsus,[1] or his double, out of court.

The chief claim put forward for Victricius by Harvey[2] was the fact that he was accused of Apollinarianism or something like it, and that he wrote a *Confessio*, which has been lost. Yet we gather from the full account given by Paulinus, and the parallel passage in the *de Laude Sanctorum*, that it only partially corresponded to the *Quicunque*; roughly speaking, to clauses 4, 6, 15, 28, 29, 30. We have no right to dogmatise on the omission of parellels to other clauses. We do not know for certain what else it contained. But on the whole we seem to be justified in rejecting the theory of his authorship, unless some MS. should be found connecting the creed with him in any more definite way.

The theory that Vincentius was the author has been ably advocated by Ommanney. Nothing that I have written about the priority of the creed to the *Commonitorium* need hinder one from regarding the creed as an earlier work of Vincentius. There is no question of his knowledge or of his ability. But these general considerations do not amount to proof, and there are others which may be said to counterbalance them. "He was a poet-theologian, and the *Quicunque* represents rather the grammar than the poetry of theology. His intellect was imaginative rather than analytical, and there is true poetry

[1] See Appendix B. [2] *On the Creeds*, ii. p. 577.

in his illustrations. But his promise to treat of matters of faith in another work can only refer to a more elaborate form of the *Commonitorium*, equally diffuse in style, not to the terse clearly-cut sentences of the creed."

We come, lastly, to the theory of authorship which I advocated in my book on *The Athanasian Creed*, and to which I still cling with some fondness, though it has not been received with any favour. All the available evidence, both internal and external, points to the south of France as the home of the creed, and the parallels, not to say quotations, in writings of Vincentius, Faustus, and hereafter Cæsarius of Arles, point to Lerins. Nor can there be any question that the first brothers in that famous retreat of piety and learning were men of more than average calibre, and made their mark on their generation. There is no reason to suppose that their enthusiasm for their leader, so beautifully expressed in the funeral sermon written by Hilary of Arles, was in any way misplaced or mistaken. And it is certain that a preacher is to some degree influenced by his congregation, that he would be encouraged to give his best thoughts and choose his words when addressing disciples so able and so devout as the congregation which met in that happy island-home. I would therefore suggest that Honoratus was worthy to be the author of the creed, regarded as an instruction in the faith. And I maintain that there is some support for the theory in the references which Hilary of Arles and Faustus make to his dogmatic teaching.

Hilarius, *Vita Honorati*, c. 38 : " Quotidianus siquidem in sincerissimis tractatibus confessionis Patris ac Filii ac Spiritus Sancti testis fuisti : nec facile tam exerte tam lucide quisquam de diuinitatis Trinitate disseruit, cum eam personis distingueres, et gloriæ æternitate ac maiestate sociares."

Faustus, *In depositione S. Honorati* : " Sed et modo minus potest gaudere is . . . qui patriam uel parentes illius feruore contempserit . . . qui fideliter sanctam regulam custodierit ab illo allatam et per illum a Christo ad confirmationem loci istius constitutam. . . . Ergo carissimi, ut adipisci possimus illa quæ obtinuit sequamur illa prius quæ docuit ; teneamus in primis fidem rectam, credamus Patrem et Filium et Spiritum Sanctum unum Deum. Ubi enim est unitas esse non potest inæqualitas, et cum Filius quia Deus est perfectus consummatus et plenus sit, prorsus minor dici non potest plenitudo."

Only the first of these sermons was known to Waterland, who recognised an allusion to the *Quicunque*, but inferred that Hilary was quoting his own composition. Hilary's biographer speaks of his "admirable exposition of the symbol," but this, in the language of the day, usually meant a detailed exposition of the Apostles' Creed. The *Quicunque* cannot be called an exposition of that creed, for it does not comment on the articles which it quotes.

This theory of the authorship is at least not more speculative than others, and harmonises with my suggestion, that the creed was written to warn men against the loose pietism of the Priscillianists. " In such a case we are content with a probability." We do not receive the creed as the faith of any individual teacher, but as a form of faith sanctioned by the usage of the Catholic Church. We are content to trace it to the island-home which sent forth into the world so noble a band of confessors and martyrs. " Peace also has its martyrs," wrote Hilary of Honoratus. These men were ready to die and suffer, as Faustus had to suffer, for the truths they taught, because the creed on their lips was no mere assertion of formal orthodoxy, because they desired with true devotion "to acknowledge the glory of the eternal Trinity, and in the power of the Divine Majesty to worship the Unity."[1]

[1] Cf. my *The Ath. Creed*, p. xcvii.

CHAPTER VII

THE ATHANASIAN CREED II

§ I. The Sermons of Auitus, Cæsarius, and others.
§ II. The Canons of Toledo and Autun.
§ III. The Trèves Fragment.
§ IV. Of Eighth and Ninth Century Quotations.
§ V. Early Commentaries.
§ VI. Rival Theories of Origin.
§ VII. The Later History.
§ VIII. The Text and a Translation.

WE must now proceed to review the external evidence which may be shown for the use of the *Quicunque* from the fifth century. There is a certain advantage in considering it by itself, since we come to it in a detached frame of mind. And it is only fair that we should endeavour to meet rival theories, which are built up on the support of such evidence only, on their own ground.

§ I. THE SERMONS OF AUITUS, CÆSARIUS, AND OTHERS

The external evidence may be said to begin with the quotations found in the writings of Auitus and Cæsarius.

(i.) Auitus, Bishop of Vienne 490–523, in a work on the Divinity of the Holy Spirit, quotes clause 22: "Quem nec factum legimus, nec genitum nec creatum"; and again: "Sicut est proprium Spiritui Sancto a Patre Filioque procedere istud fides catholica, etiamsi renuentibus non persuaserit, in suæ tamen disciplinæ regula non excedit." Also, in Frag. xii. of *A Dialogue against Gundobad*,[1] first the negative and then the positive statement of clause 22 comes to light.

[1] Ed. Peiper, *Mon. Germ. Auct.* vi. 2.

And in Frag. xviii. are found parallels to clauses 3, 4. In another Fragment against the Arians there is a parallel to clause 32: "In Christo Deus et homo non alter sed ipse, non duo ex diuersis sed unus ex utroque mediator. Gemina quidem substantia sed una persona est."

(ii.) Cæsarius, Bishop of Arles 503–543, one of the leading theologians of Southern Gaul, quotes from both parts of the *Quicunque* in a sermon, Ps.-Aug. 244, which is now unanimously assigned by critics to his pen. I will print that portion of the sermon from the Benedictine text, which I have collated with *Cod. Sangallensis* 150, sæc. ix. *in.* :—

1. "Rogo et admoneo nos fratres carissimi ut *quicunque* [1]
(40.) *uult saluus esse fidem rectam* [2] *catholicam* discat, *firmiter* [3]
  teneat inuiolatamque conseruet.[4] Ita ergo oportet uni-
15. cuique obseruare ut credat Patrem credat Filium credat
16. Spiritum Sanctum. *Deus Pater Deus Filius Deus et*
7. *Spiritus Sanctus* sed *tamen non tres Dii sed unus Deus.*
  Qualis Pater talis Filius talis et Spiritus Sanctus.
  Attamen [5] credat unusquisque fidelis quod Filius [6]
31. *æqualis* [7] est *Patri secundum diuinitatem* et *minor est* [8]
  Patre [9] *secundum humanitatem* [10] carnis quam de nostro [11]
  assumpsit; [12] Spiritus uero Sanctus ab utroque procedens."

[1] Quicumque, G. [2] + et, G. [3] + que, G. [4] conseruat, G. [5] Et tamen, G.
[6] om. Filius, G. [7] equalis, G. [8] om. est, G. [9] Patri, G. [10] ma, *supra lin.*, G.
[11] nostra, G. [12] ads—, G.

About the beginning of the seventh century this sermon was combined with another, the authorship of which is by no means so certain. I will reserve discussion of it for Chapter X., and only note here that it contains parallels to phrases in clauses 6, 13, 15, 16, 29, 38.

There is an "Address to Clergy," which in one MS. is ascribed to Cæsarius (*Cod. lat. Monacensis* 5515, sæc. xii., xiii.): *Sermo beati Cæsarii episcopi in præsentia cleri*; also in the index: *Item sermo beati Cæsarii episcopi ad clerum*. It became very popular in the eighth and ninth centuries, and is found in several recensions, being incorporated in the *Ordo ad Synodum* of the Roman Pontifical. But in spite of the number of Cæsarian expressions which abound in it, and which seem to prove that portions of it came originally from the pen of Cæsarius, it is impossible to claim any recension as wholly free from interpolation. We cannot therefore claim as his the following reference, f. 119: " Sermonem Athanasii episcopi de fide trinitatis cuius inicium est Quicunque uult memoriter teneat."[1]

At this point I may refer to the evidence of a *Tractatus de Trinitate* printed among the works of Ambrose. Kattenbusch[2] calls it pre-Chalcedonian, and this date seems probable. But other critics are not likely to admit that the parallel sentences to the *Quicunque*, which it contains, are really quotations, unless they receive support from other sources. It includes a commentary on a form of the Apostles' Creed not distinguishable from R, expanding the doctrines of the Trinity and the Incarnation. In c. 2 the phrase *rectum et catholicum* is used with regard to faith in God. In c. 5 we find *uenerari Unitatem in Trinitate* and *Trinitatem in Unitate*. Kattenbusch points out that it is the formal connexion of these phrases which is noticeable, since the latter phrase by itself can be traced to Epiphanius, *Ancorat.* 118, τριάδα ἐν ἑνότητι. The procession of the Spirit is spoken of as *a Patre*.

Kattenbusch[3] also calls attention to a sermon published by Elmenhorst, probably of the sixth century, which contains an exact quotation of clause 3.

We may connect also with the sermon of Cæsarius the following quotation in the *Instructio* of Columban (+ 615), the founder of the monasteries of Luxeuil and Bobbio: " Credat itaque primum omnis *qui uult saluus esse* in primum et in nouissimum Deum unum ac trinum, unum subsistentem trinum substantia, unum potentia, trinum persona . . . ubi

---

[1] Malnory, *S. Césaire*, Paris, 1894, p. 285. Morin, *Rev. Bén.* Sept. 1895, p. 390.

[2] *Theol. Lit. Z.* 1897, p. 144; cf. i. p. 98, where Kattenbusch proves conclusively that it is not a work of Ambrose.

[3] *Gennadii liber de eccl. dogm. homilia sacra*, Hamburg, 1614.

CANONS OF TOLEDO AND AUTUN 153

habes in ueritate *Trinitatem in Unitate et Unitatem in Trinitate.*" Columban used the Rule of Cæsarius, and the words which I have italicised certainly look like quotations of clauses 1 and 25. Moreover, Columban's disciple and successor, Attalus, had been trained at Lerins.

§ II. THE CANONS OF TOLEDO AND AUTUN

(i.) The Fourth Council of Toledo, which met in 633, is perhaps the most important of a series of Spanish Councils which at this period embodied quotations from the *Quicunque* in their canons. The wording of the earlier parallels is quite as exact as that of the later, but the special characteristic of the Canon of 633 is the fact that the Creed of Damasus is quoted with the *Quicunque*.[1] I will print these quotations in italics, those of the *Quicunque* in small capitals. In both cases the authors of the canon seem to have quoted written documents :—

Canon 1 (*Cod. Nov.* sæc. x., *Spicilegium Casinense*, i. p. 300): " Secundum diuinas scripturas et doctrinam quam a sanctis patribus accepimus Patrem et Filium et Spiritum Sanctum unius deitatis atque substantiæ confitemur in personarum diuersitate Trinitatem credentes,
4. in diuinitate unitatem prædicantes NEC PERSONAS CON-
20. FUNDIMUS NEC SUBSTANTIAM SEPARAMUS. PATREM A
21. NULLO FACTUM uel GENITUM dicimus : FILIUM A PATRE NON
22. FACTUM SED GENITUM asserimus ; SPIRITUM UERO SANCTUM NEC CREATUM NEC GENITUM SED PROCEDENTEM ex PATRE
28. ET FILIO profitemur. Ipsum autem DOMINUM NOSTRUM IESUM CHRISTUM DEI FILIUM et creatorem omnium, EX
29. SUBSTANTIA PATRIS ANTE SÆCULA GENITUM, *descendisse ultimo tempore* pro redemptione mundi *a Patre, qui nunquam desiit esse cum Patre.* Incarnatus est enim ex Spiritu Sancto et sancta gloriosa Dei genetrice uirgine Maria, et natus ex ipsa, solus autem Dominus Iesus

[1] I owe this suggestion to Prof. J. A. Robinson.

Christus ; unus de sancta Trinitate, anima et carne
(33.) *perfectum,* sine peccato, *suscipiens hominem* manens *quod*
31. *erat* assumens *quod non erat*: ÆQUALIS PATRI SECUNDUM
DIUINITATEM, MINOR PATRE SECUNDUM HUMANITATEM;
habens in una persona duarum naturarum proprietates;
35. naturæ enim in illo duæ, DEUS ET HOMO, non autem duo
Filii et Dei duo, sed idem una persona in utraque
36. natura, preferens passionem et mortem PRO SALUTE
NOSTRA: non in uirtute diuinitatis sed infirmitate
humanitatis. DESCENDIT AD INFEROS, ut sanctos qui
ibi tenebantur erueret: *deuictoque mortis imperio re-*
37. *surrexit,* assumptus deinde in cœlum UENTURUS est in
futurum ad iudicium uiuorum et mortuorum: cuius
nos *morte et sanguine mundati* remissionem peccatorum
consecuti sumus, *resuscitandi ab eo in die nouissimo, in ea
qua nunc uiuimus carne* et in ea qua resurrexit idem
(39.) Dominus forma, percepturi *ab ipso* alii pro iustitiæ meritis
uitam æternam, alii *pro peccatis supplicii æterni* senten-
40. tiam. HÆC EST catholicæ ecclesiæ FIDES; hanc confes-
sionem conseruamus atque tenemus: QUAM QUISquis
FIRMissime custodierit perpetuam salutem habebit."

It will be noticed that the clauses of the *Quicunque* are
quoted in their proper sequence of numbers. We cannot
argue as to the form of text beyond what is quoted, but it
is obvious that it contained both parts. We can account
for the apparent omission of clause 33, with the characteristic phrase *assumpsit humanitatem*: the phrase of the
"Creed of Damasus," which is also the phrase of the *Te
Deum,* was preferred, *suscipiens hominem.*

The only argument which has been brought forward
against this series of quotations, to prove that they are mere
coincidences of diction, is the argument from the silence of
Isidore, Archbishop of Seville, who presided over this Council.
He wrote a book *On the Offices of the Church,* in which,
especially in the section *On the Rule of Faith,* Swainson[1]
searched in vain for quotations of the *Quicunque,* concluding

[1] P. 235,

"that it was not known to him, or, if known, it had no authority." Loofs[1] also thinks that it is perhaps more probable that the Toledan Councils did not use the *Quicunque* than the opposite. He argues that a reference to the *Quicunque uult saluus esse* would have had a stronger effect than Isidore's efforts to state in his own words what, according to tradition, was "the most certain faith after the Apostles' Creed."

"Hæc est autem post apostolorum symbolum certissima fides, . . . ut profiteamur Patrem et Filium et Spiritum Sanctum unius essentiæ, eiusdem potestatis et sempiternitatis . . . Patrem quoque confiteri ingenitum, Filium genitum, Spiritum Sanctum uero nec genitum nec ingenitum, sed de Patre et Filio procedentem. . . . Ipsum quoque Filium perfectum ex uirgine sine peccato hominem suscepisse. . . . Et quod diuinam humanamque substantiam, in utraque perfectus, una Christus persona gestauerit. . . . Hæc est Catholicæ traditionis fidei uera integritas de qua si unum quodlibet respuatur, tota fidei credulitas amittitur."[2]

It is obvious from this passage that Isidore wished to restate the substance of the general belief in his own words.

A good illustration of the way in which similar theological statements have been borrowed and adapted to express faith in the Trinity and the incarnation may be taken from the first of our Thirty-nine Articles:

De Fide in Sacrosanctam Trinitatem

"Unus est uiuus et uerus *Deus, æternus, incorporeus, impartibilis* impassibilis *immensæ potentiæ, sapientiæ ac bonitatis: creator et conseruator omnium* tum *uisibilium* tum *inuisibilium.* Et in unitate huius diuinæ naturæ *tres* sunt *personæ, eiusdem essentiæ potentiæ* ac æternitatis, *Pater Filius et Spiritus Sanctus.*"

The words in italics are quoted in the first Article of the Confession of Augsburg, in which the latter sentence runs as follows: "Et tamen tres sint personæ eiusdem essentiæ potentiæ et coæternæ Pater et Filius et Spiritus Sanctus."

[1] *R.E.*[3] art. "Athanasianum," p. 192; cf. 189.
[2] *De Eccles. Offic.* ii. 24, M.S.L. 83, 817.

We see in these Articles how theologians of another age have tried to condense a summary of their faith exactly as Isidore and his contemporaries desired to do. We note that in one Article two reminiscences of the *Quicunque, et tamen* (used conversely to emphasise the Trinity) and *coæternæ*, have dropped out. Yet it would be absurd to argue that they did not know and did not value that creed.

Is it not just as absurd to argue from Isidore's silence, in his own private teaching on the Rule of Faith, that he was ignorant of a creed manifestly quoted by the Council over which he presided?

(ii.) *The Canon of Autun.*—The famous Canon of Autun was passed by a Synod held at Autun, under Bishop Leodgar, some time between 663 and 680. It is usual to date it in a round number, 670. The earliest collection in which it is found is called the Collection of Angers, and was made at the beginning of the eighth century. Three out of the seven MSS. extant contain, in addition to disciplinary canons, a Canon on the Faith, which is called the first (hira prima). It seems reasonable to suppose that it was made at the same time, and that there has been some mistake in the numbering of the disciplinary canons which follow, and which are numbered from 1. The MSS. are as follows:—

P—*Cod. lat. Paris.* 1603, fol. 11, sæc. ix.
E—*Cod. Phillippsii nunc Berolinensis*, 1763, fol. 3, sæc. ix.[1]
X—*Cod. Vindob.* 2171, fol. 1ʳ, sæc. ix.

CANONES AGUSTODINENSIS HIRA PRIMA (*a*)

"Si quis presbyter aut diaconus subdiaconus (*b*) clericus (*c*) symbolum (*d*) quod Sancto inspirante (*e*) Spiritu apostoli tradiderunt, et fidem sancti Athanasii (*f*) presulis (*g*) irreprehensibiliter (*h*) non recensuerit (*i*) ab episcopo condamnetur (*k*)."

(*a*) Agustodinensis, P; Agustudunensis, X. (*b*) *om.* subdiaconus, E. (*c*) clericus, *pr.* aut, E. (*d*) symbulum, P*. (*e*) inspirante s. *supra lin.* P. (*f*)

---

[1] My collations of E and X are taken from *Mon. Germ. Hist.*, Legum sectio iii.; *Conc.* tom. i. p. 220.

Athanasi, P. (*g*) presolis, P*, u. *supra lin*. P *corr*. (*h*) inr—, P. (*i*) recen-siuerit, P. (*k*) condempnetur, X.

The only real difficulty connected with the Canon lies in the question whether the Faith referred to was the *Quicunque* or some other, *e.g.* the *Fides Romanorum*, which Ratramn of Corbey quoted, as he quoted the *Quicunque* under the title *Libellus de Fide Athanasii*. Hincmar also, following Ratramn, ascribed the *Fides Romanorum* to Athanasius. But there is not a single MS. in which it is so described, independent of the work of Vigilius of Thapsus *On the Trinity*, through which Ratramn and Hincmar came to ascribe it to Athanasius. On the other hand, there are at least twenty MSS. of the ninth century which describe the *Quicunque* as the Faith of Athanasius, and prove that it had obtained that title by common consent.

§ III. THE TRÈVES FRAGMENT

The Trèves fragment is part of a sermon in which clauses 27^b–40 of the *Quicunque* (with the exception of clause 35) have been incorporated. It is found in a MS. in Paris (B.N. *Cod. lat.* 3836), which contains the S. Blasien Collection of Canons. The MS. is of the eighth century, and is written in Lombardic characters. The scribe seems to have been a travelled man who had visited Rome, for he gives a list of books of Scripture which were read in the Church of S. Peter. He uses the fragment, which he says he found at Trèves, to illustrate the Definition of Faith of the Council of Chalcedon. He does not appear to know the *Quicunque*, for he uses the first words of the fragment as a title. Such ignorance on the part of an Italian scribe is not surprising. The use of the creed was as yet confined to Gaul. All trace of the original fragment has been lost. Trèves was sacked by the Normans in 882, and it probably perished. The present librarian of the town, Herr M. Keuffer, has only been able to find one MS., a copy of Prosper, written in a similar hand, *c.* 719.

Cod. lat. 3836, f. 89.:—

"HÆC INVINI TREVERIS IN UNO LIBRO SCRIPTUM SIC INCIPIENTE
27. DOMINI NOSTRI IHESU CHRISTI, ET RELIQUA. DOMINI NOSTRI
28. IHESU CHRISTI FIDELITER CREDAT. Est ergo fides recta ut credamus et confitemur quia dominus ihesus christus dei
29. filius deus pariter et homo est. deus est *de* substantia patris ante sæcula genitus, *et* homo *de* substantia matris in
30. sæculo natus. perfectus deus perfectus homo ex anima
31. rationabili et humana carne subsistens. æqualis patri sæcundum diuinitatem minor patri sæcundum humani-
32. tatem. qui licet deus sit homo non duo tamen sed unus est
33. christus. unus autem non *ex eo quod sit* in carne *conuersa diuinitas*, sed *quia est* in deo *adsumpta dignanter humanitas*.
34. unus *Christus est* non confusione substantiæ sed unitatem
36. personæ qui *sccundum*[1] *fidem nostram* passus *et mortuos*
37. ad inferna *discendens, et die tertia* resurrexit, *adque* ad celos ascendit, ad dexteram dei patris sedet, *sicut uobis in simbulo tradutum est*; Inde *ad iudicandos* uiuos et mortuos
38. *credimus* (f. 89ᵛ) *et speramus eum esse uenturum*. ad cuius aduentum *erunt* omnes homines *sine dubio in* suis corporibus
39. *resurrecturi* et reddituri de factis propriis rationem, *ut* qui bona egerunt *eant* in uitam æternam, qui mala in
40. ignem æternum. Hæc est fides *sancta et* catholica, quam *omnes homo qui ad uitam æternam peruenire desiderat scire integræ debet, et fideliter custodire.*"

We have here about a third of the creed, and it is possible that the other two-thirds were contained on the preceding page of the original Trèves MS., particularly since the fragment begins in the middle of a sentence. The variations from the usual text, which I have italicised, are all easy to explain, on the supposition that they represent free quotation, and not a first draft, which was afterwards polished. The preacher turns the precise antithesis of clause 33 into flowing relatival sentences. He adds from his Baptismal Creed, *et mortuus* and *die tertia*. He alters the form of clause 37*b*,

[1] In the MS. the *a* of sæcundum has been erased, and a second *m* in humana.

and of 38, altering "resurgere habent" into "erunt resurrecturi," naturally enough in parallelism to "reddituri," and weights his phrase with "sine dubio." The use of "habeo" with the infinitive for the synthetic future has been much discussed. It was often used in African Latin from the third century, and by Gallican writers in the fifth, so that it does not disprove the early date of a text containing it. A more important fact is the omission of clause 35, which seems to have been intentional, and to have led to a slight alteration of clause 36, where "omnino" is omitted, and "Christus est" is supplied in clause 34 from the omitted clause as antecedent to the relative "qui." The reason of the omission is not far to seek. The illustration from the constitution of man, in clause 35, was misused by the Eutychians, and came therefore to be regarded with disfavour by Catholic writers. The preacher probably omitted it for this reason. If we suppose the sermon to be some fifty or sixty years older than the date when the fragment was copied at Trèves, we are brought to a date at which Eutychianism was widely prevalent. Heurtley[1] has shown that "Bede mentions this [heresy] as the occasion of the assembling of the great Synod of Hethfield [in 680], and mentions it in such terms as to imply that it was one of the pressing dangers of the day to which the Church generally—not merely the English branch of it—was exposed." The danger was of long continuance. More than a century earlier, Nicetus, Archbishop of Trèves 527-566, wrote a letter remonstrating with Justinian on his lapse into a form of Eutychianism. He bade him remember his baptismal vow: "Unum Filium manentem in duabus substantiis cum Patre et Spiritu Sancto non duos Christos testatus es . . . talis Pater qualis et Filius."[2] There is another parallel to the wording of the *Quicunque* in his letter to Queen Chlodosinda on her husband's Arianism: "In die resurrectionis nec manere nec apparere potuit qui Trinitatem in Unitate non crediderit."

It is possible that we have in the Trèves Fragment a sermon of Nicetus. He was a friend of Venantius Fortunatus, and was brought into touch with the school of Lerins through

[1] *Hist. Earlier Form.* 1892, p. 126.   [2] Galland, iii. 776.

a friend Florianus, Abbot of Romanus (diocese of Milan), a pupil of Cæsarius. Indeed, he quotes Germanus, Hilary, and Lupus in his letter to the queen.

§ IV. OF EIGHTH AND NINTH CENTURY QUOTATIONS

The most important of the eighth century testimonies to the creed is a *Libellus de Trinitate* found by Caspari in a Milan MS., which formerly belonged to Bobbio (*Cod. Ambros.* D. 268 *inf.* sæc. viii., ix.). It contains, both in form and words, reminiscences of the *Quicunque*, since it combines teaching on the Trinity with teaching on the Incarnation.

Another testimony belonging to this period, or an earlier, is Ps.-Gennadius, *de Fide*, which contains a form of creed parallel in form to the *Quicunque*, and such sentences as the following: "Spiritum Sanctum dicimus et credimus eo, quod est ex Patre et Filio æqualiter procedens, non factus nec creatus nec genitus, sed coæternus et coæqualis per omnia Patri et Filio. Hanc uero Trinitatem, id est Patrem et Filium et Spiritum Sanctum, non tres Deos sed unum esse Deum certissime confitemur. . . . non tamen tres dii, sed unus Deus."

A sermon, which I have found in a MS. at Munich (*Cod. lat.* 14,508, sæc. x.), and published in the *Zeitschrift für Kirchengeschichte*, July 1898, contains a form of R, and is therefore probably older than the ninth century, when R had been superseded almost universally by our *Textus receptus*. It appears to quote the *Quicunque* as follows: "Sicut aliquis auctor dixit Deus Pater, Deus Filius, Deus et Spiritus Sanctus."

Another such testimony is in a sermon, which I found at S. Gallen (*Cod.* 230, sæc. ix. *in.*). After a quotation from the Fortunatus Commentary follows: "In hac Trinitate unum Deum colimus et adoramus et confitemur, nihil prius aut posterius, nihil maius aut minus, sed totæ tres personæ coæternæ sibi sunt et coæquales. Quia semper fuit Spiritus Sanctus in una diuinitate, æqualis gloria, coæterna maiestas." That this is more than a quotation from a shortened form of text found in the Fortunatus Commentary, is proved by the fact that the whole of clause 24 is here quoted, only half of which appears in that Commentary.

In *Cod. Sessorian.* 52 (see p. 232 *infra*), Morin [1] has found a very interesting profession of faith, such as was made by bishops at their consecration. The collection in which it is found was made in the ninth century, and it follows a sermon containing R, so we are fairly justified in assigning it to the eighth century, and in comparing it with the Profession of Denebert (p. 175 *infra*), made in 798. The last words, *seculum per ignem*, are a quotation from the form in which the *Fides Romanorum* appears in the *Gesta Liberii* (p. 215 *infra*):

"Fides autem catholica quam me secundum sanctorum patrum doctrinam retinere profiteor ac firmiter credere, hæc est. Confiteor itaque sanctam perfectam ueramque Trinitatem, id est Patrem et Filium et Spiritum Sanctum unum esse Deum omnium uisibilium et inuisibilium conditorem ; propter inseparabilem substantiam deitatis Unitatem, propter distinctionem uero personarum Trinitatem ueneramur. Neque personas confundimus nec substantium separamus. Alia est enim persona Patris, alia Filii, alia Spiritus Sancti. Sed Patris et Filii et Spiritus Sancti una est diuinitas, æqualis gloria, coæterna maiestas. Pater Deus, Filius Deus, Spiritus Sanctus Deus. Non tamen tres Dii sed unus est Deus. Idcirco in personis discretio est sed in diuinitate nulla distinctio. Pater a nullo est factus nec creatus nec genitus. Filius a Patre solo non factus nec creatus sed absque initio genitus. Spiritus autem Sanctus non factus nec creatus nec genitus sed ex Patre Filioque procedens est. Pater enim proprie Pater est et non est Filius. Filius uero proprie Filius est et non est Pater. Spiritus autem Sanctus proprie Spiritus Sanctus est et non est Pater uel Filius. Pater quidem semper est et erat et erit et nunquam fuit Pater sine Filio, uel Filius sine Pater, nec Spiritus Sanctus sine Patre uel Filio. In hac autem sancta Trinitate nihil prius aut posterius, nihil maius aut minus, sed totæ tres personæ coæternæ sibi sunt et coæquales. Omnis namque sancta Trinitas, inuisibilis, incorporalis, impalpabilis, infinita, immensa, sempiterna credenda est. De hac autem ineffabili Trinitate sola Uerbi Dei persona, id est Dominus noster Iesus Christus Dei Filius in ultimis diebus propter nos redimendos descendit de cœlis, unde nunquam recesserat. Incarnatus est de Spiritu Sancto et Maria uirgine. Natus ex ipsa solus et homo uerus factus per omnia similis nobis absque peccato. Uerusque permanet Deus æqualis

---

[1] *Rev. Bén.* 1897, p. 487.

Patri in diuina natura, minor Patre in humana. Perfectus Deus secundum diuinitatem, perfectus homo secundum humanitatem. Qui licet Deus sit et homo non duo tamen sed in utraque natura, diuina scilicet et humana, unus uerus et proprius est Dei Filius Dominus noster Iesus Christus. In diuina ergo natura in qua Deus noster impassibilis est et immutabilis est. Sed in humana substantia quam assumpsit ex uirgine dignatus est pati pro nobis, crucifigi, sepeliri, et die tertia resurgere et cum eadem glorificata carne ad cælos ascendit, sedetque nunc ad dexteram Patris cum qua etiam uenturus est iudicare uiuos et mortuos et sæculum per ignem. Amen."

Another document, which may be assigned to this date, is a sermon *de fide*, found among the works of Boniface, Archbishop of Mainz (f. 755). It contains the following parallels: "Necessarium est patres carissimi ... fidem rectam et catholicam siue dubitatione firmiter tenere ... Ista est fides catholica, ut credamus in unum Deum Patrem omnipotentem ... Filium Spiritum Sanctum ex Patre procedentem et Filio ... Pater æternus, Filius æternus, Spiritus Sanctus æternus ... sicut Christus tertia die resurrexit a mortuis sic omnes homines boni et mali in nouissime die cum propriis corporibus resurgere debent."[1]

§ V. The Early Commentaries

An important argument, to prove the existence of the entire text of the *Quicunque* in the eighth century or earlier, may be founded on the early commentaries, and is independent of others. There are some seven which come into consideration here. Four of them (Bouhier, Oratorian, Paris, Troyes) have been published by Ommanney,[2] who has made this subject specially his own, and for whose work as a pioneer all students must be grateful. The others (Orleans, Stavelot, Fortunatus) I have edited (in part from new MSS.) in my book on *The Athanasian Creed and its Commentaries*.[3] As I shall quote the readings of the texts of the creed embedded in them in my *apparatus criticus*, it will

[1] Ed. Giles, Oxford, 1841. [2] *Early History*, pp. 1-39, 311-386.
[3] *Texts and Studies*, iv. 1.

suffice here to give a short summary of the facts known about each:—

1. *The Orleans Commentary.*—The Orleans Commentary [1] has been found by Cuissard in a MS. (No. 94) which formerly belonged to the Abbey of Fleury, with some scraps of Theodulf's treatise against Adoptianism, and an exposition of the Mass. It is probably the MS. which the authors of the *Histoire Littéraire de la France* [2] found at Fleury with such a commentary on the first page. But it seems very doubtful whether they were right in ascribing it to Theodulf, as Cuissard has also done. It does not exhibit the learning shown in Theodulf's known writings. No doubt the copyist is to blame for many clerical errors and grammatical mistakes, but the laboured explanations and the loose use of terms like "percipere," "apprehendere," "accipere," are unworthy of the author of the *De Ordine Baptismi*, and his use of "suscipere," "assumere (humanitatem)." The quotations from the Gospels show no dependence on the Theodulfian recension of the Vulgate. The author quotes from other commentaries—Fortunatus, Troyes, Stavelot, Paris— but does not improve their sentences by alterations. Lastly, the title *Explanatio Fidei Catholicæ* does not agree with the title given to the Commentary of Theodulf in the list of the Abbots of Fleury, *Expl. Symboli s. Athanasii*, which is the title used in his book, *De Spiritu Sancto*.

2. *The Stavelot Commentary.*—The Stavelot Commentary is the original text of a commentary widely popular in the Middle Ages, and usually connected with the name of Bishop Bruno of Würzburg, who edited it in the eleventh century. The earliest MS. (B.M., Add. MSS. 18,043) of the tenth century comes from Stavelot Abbey, in the Forest of Ardennes, It is a glossed Psalter from the school of Notker, a teacher from S. Gall, whom Abbot Odilo summoned to help him when he restored the abbey after the Norman invasion. The internal evidence points to the ninth century as the date of its composition. The wording of the note on clause 27, "Non adoptiuum sed proprium Dei Filium," corresponds with the

[1] *Théodulfe Évêque d'Orléans*, Orléans, 1892.   [2] iv. 473.

wording of the letter of the Council of Frankfort. Perhaps it is one of the commentaries referred to by the synod held in the Diocese of Liège, c. 840–855, in their second canon: "Fidem enim S. Athanasii episcopi in hoc opere censuimus obseruandum, et simbolum apostolorum cum tradicionibus et exposicionibus sanctorum patrum in his sermonibus." Stavelot was attached to Liège from the ninth century. It has been suggested [1] that this is the missing commentary of Theodulf, but there is nothing to connect any of the MSS. with Fleury, or the text with Theodulf. The subject-matter is well thought out, and, together with the Fortunatus and Oratorian Commentaries, it was used as the foundation of several composite commentaries. One of these, under the name of the hermit, Rolle of Hampole, was widely used in England in the fourteenth century.[2]

3. *The Paris Commentary.*—The Paris Commentary is found in a MS. of the tenth century (B.N., Paris, *Cod. lat.* 1012) from the Abbey of S. Martial at Limoges. Some portions of it are found also in a Psalter of the tenth century, now in the British Museum (Reg. 2 B. v.), though the latter show traces of polish. It contains quotations from Gregory the Great and Gennadius, but no definite evidence as to the date of its composition. The readings in the Paris MS. are old, but this only proves that the author used the older text, omitting the second half of clause 4, and paraphrasing clause 27.

4. *The Bouhier Commentary.*—The Bouhier Commentary is found in some four MSS., the earliest of which is of the tenth century (Troyes, 1979), and belonged formerly to the Bouhier family of Dijon. The other MSS. also seem to have been written in France. The text of the creed cited in it shows late readings, and I cannot assign to it an earlier date than the beginning of the ninth century. It is mainly founded on the Oratorian Commentary, and was constructed with some literary skill. The personal statements of the preface are omitted or changed,

[1] Ommanney, *Diss.* p. 211.
[2] Another form of the commentary is found in a Psalter at Boulogne (*Cod.* 20) from the Abbey of S. Bertin at S. Omer, written c. 1000.

e.g. " in ueteribus codicibus inuenitur prætitulatum " for " eum uidi præt. etiam in uet. cod."

5. *The Oratorian Commentary.*—The Oratorian Commentary is by far the most learned, if not the most original, of all the early commentaries. At present there are only two MSS.[1] known. The earliest, *Cod. Vat. Reg.* 231, sæc. ix., x., contains works of Cassiodorus, Prosper, Alcuin, Isidore, with expositions of the Lord's Prayer and Apostles' Creed. The other, Troyes, 804, sæc. x., contains works of Theodulf, the Creed of Pelagius, Augustine on the Lord's Prayer and Apostles' Creed, followed by two other expositions of that creed and another of the *Quicunque*, to which I shall refer again as the Troyes Commentary. The Vatican MS. only contains a preface, which reappears in a condensed form in all MSS. of the Bouhier Commentary. The writer, apparently addressing a synod, states that he has carried out their instructions to provide an exposition of this work on the Faith, " which is here and there (*passim*) recited in our churches, and continually made the subject of meditation by our priests." He complains of the ignorance prevailing among the clergy, of the difficulty which they find in getting books for their sacred offices—a Psalter, or a Lectionary, or a Missal. " Since some have no desire to read or learn, it is the will of the synod that at least they should be compelled to meditate on this exposition of the Faith " which he has illustrated from the Fathers. Ignorance of God in a priest should be accounted sacrilege, like blasphemy in a layman. He goes on to speak of the tradition that this work had been composed by the blessed Athanasius," Bishop of the Alexandrian Church, " for I have always seen it entitled thus, even in old MSS." He had come to the conclusion that it was composed to meet the Arian heresy. The exposition contains extracts from Augustine, Prosper, Leo, the translation by Dionysius Exiguus of Cyril's Synodical Epistle, Fulgentius, Pelagius I., Vigilius of Thapsus, the Creed of Pelagius, and the Definition of the Sixth General Council (681).

[1] A third MS., mentioned by Swainson, p. 379, as Turin lxvi. sæc. xiii. contains a composite text in which notes from the Stavelot Com. are added.

From this last extract Ommanney concluded that the commentary was written while some fear of Monothelitism, the heresy condemned by that Council, still existed, *i.e.* about the end of the seventh century.[1] But there is no other such reference, and the words of the Definition are quoted rather as a statement of positive truth than a weapon against error. We may note, however, that there is very distinct emphasis laid on the Lord's unity of person, as if in fear of a revived Nestorianism. The phrase, *singularitas personæ*, found useful by Vincentius to define the *unitas personæ*, is quoted again and again, as in the Troyes Commentary. No doubt it is found in uncontroversial passages, *e.g.* the Gelasian Sacramentary, "unus es Deus, unus es Dominus, non in unius singularitate personæ."[2] But the question is not so much of the phrase as of its use. It seems to me to point to the Adoptianist period, and to confirm Swainson's suggestion that this might be the lost commentary of Theodulf.

The whole tone of the preface is worthy of Theodulf, and the situation is exactly that which he found in his diocese at the beginning of the Carlovingian revival of learning. The same series of authors are quoted in his book *On the Holy Spirit*, in which he speaks of the *Symbolum Athanasii*.[3] Is it fanciful to connect the remarks on clerical ignorance with a canon of the Sixth Council of Toledo, "Ignorantia mater cunctorum errorum maxime in sacerdotibus Dei uitanda est," which the author of the preface would know in his copy of Dionysius Exiguus, and with the fact that Theodulf was of Spanish extraction?

The Vatican MS. belongs to Queen Christina's collection, and came probably from Fleury. The Troyes MS. may be connected with Fleury, both by the fact that it contains works of Theodulf and through the Troyes Commentary, which is quoted by the Orleans Commentary itself in a Fleury MS.

[1] *Diss.* p. 189.
[2] Ed. Wilson. I owe this reference to Dr. Mercati's review of my book, *Revista Bibliog.*, 1896, p. 149, but disagree with his argument.
[3] The title given to his Commentary in the catalogue of the Abbots of Fleury was *Explanatio symboli Athanasii*. The Vatican MS. of the Commentary has no title, but is preceded by *Explanatio symboli Apostolici*.

Besides its use with the Stavelot Commentary, in Rolle of Hampole's edition, it was also combined with other notes in a Commentary found in an Oxford MS. (Bodleian Library, *Cod. Canonici Bibl.* 30).

6. *The Troyes Commentary.*—The Troyes Commentary precedes the Oratorian in the Troyes MS. (*Cod.* 804) of the tenth century. It is based in the first part on the Fortunatus Commentary, but in the second deviates from it widely. The author deals fairly with the text of the creed.

The date is not easy to determine. Ommanney notes " the entire omission of the terminology of the Præstinarian and Adoptianist controversies," and " the distinct employment of that in use when Monothelitism was the great subject of discussion," and would date it from the middle of the seventh century.[1]

We do not find any precise technical terms such as " non adoptiuus," but it seems to me that there are several indications of opposition to Adoptianism, which would bring the earliest possible date down to the end of the eighth century. "Felix of Urgel was at one with his orthodox opponents in admitting the whole doctrine of the two natures and two wills. But he spoke of our Lord in His human nature as Adopted Son, and therefore incurred the suspicion of introducing a double personality. This danger would account for the strong assertion in clause 33 of the singularity of His person, and a more emphatic condemnation of Nestorianism than is found in Fortunatus. Felix also held that our Lord assumed human nature in the state to which Adam's fall reduced it, not indeed as tainted by original sin, but as subject to mortality and other consequences of sin, a view which is clearly condemned in the note on clause 30 : " Perfectum hominem absque peccato de uirgine suscipere dignatus est, ut per eandem naturam, quæ in paradiso decepta mortem incurrerat, rursum eundem diabolum non potentia diuinitatis sed ratione iustitiæ uincerit."

" As the process of adoption was not held to be completed till the resurrection, the emphatic iteration in this and the

[1] *E.H.* p. 33 ; *Diss.* p. 187.

Stavelot Commentary (as in the ninth century recensions of the *Fides Romanorum* and the Fortunatus Commentary), that the Lord rose in the same flesh in which He died, may be supposed to guard against Adoptianist error. Paulinus made the same point in his speech at the Council of Friuli."[1]

"Another hint of the date is found in the reference to the genealogy in S. Matthew's Gospel, which was distinguished by Felix from that recorded by S. Luke as giving Christ's descent according to the flesh, while S. Luke gave the descent according to the spirit.[2] The commentary confutes this view, by pointing to the true contrast between the Divine generation and the fleshly, just as Paulinus, in the speech to which I have referred, contrasts the human birth in time with the Divine birth, irrespective of time." On these grounds we may assign the Commentary to the period when Adoptianism was an active heresy, c. 780–820.

7. *The Fortunatus Commentary.*—The Fortunatus Commentary is the earliest known, and must be allowed to take an important place in the argument for determining the date and earliest text of the creed. Waterland was only acquainted with two MSS., but we now hear of some twenty, nine of which at least belong to the ninth century.

By a curious clue I have been able to find and identify the lost S. Gall. MS., known hitherto only through the editions of Goldast in his *Manuale Biblicum*, Frankfurt, 1610, and of Card. Pitra in his *Analecta sacra et classica*. Having looked for it in vain at S. Gallen and Frankfurt, I went to Leiden to see Goldast's MS. copy, which had drifted thither in the collection of MSS. formed by the celebrated Voss. Finding in it no clue, I was turning over the pages of a written catalogue of MSS., when I came on a note, to the effect that certain Latin verses had been found in a MS. at Zürich (*Cod. Misc.* c. 78, sæc. ix.), which formerly belonged to S. Gallen. I recognised them at once as having been printed by Goldast from the lost MS. Through the kind offices of the librarian, Dr. Fäh, the MS. was sent to S Gallen for inspection. There could be no doubt as to the

[1] *Ath. Creed*, p. lv. f.   [2] Dorner, *Hist. Person of Christ*, ii. p. 256.

identification. But, alas! there was no trace of the name Euphronius, which Goldast had invented as the name of the author. The title was simply *Expositio Fidei Catholicæ*, to which Goldast had added in the margin, *Athanasii usque huc.* It would seem that anonymous treatises did not interest his reading public. One can appreciate the caustic complaint in the catalogue of MSS. at S. Gallen, that by giving false names to documents he has wrought confusion, but that it is hard to prove this, because the MSS. which he possessed, lawfully or unlawfully, are scattered over the world.[1]

Besides these ninth century MSS. of the full Commentary, we have also a ninth century MS. of an adaptation of the Commentary in the margin of a Psalter (*Cod. Sangall.* 27).[2] This, at any rate, would seem to throw back the archetype of all these MSS. at least as far as the eighth century.

The internal evidence points back to an earlier date. Apollinarianism is the latest heresy mentioned by name. Eutychianism, which revived in the sixth and seventh centuries, is ignored, and only a mild warning is given against the error of Nestorius: "Ne propter adsumptionem humanæ carnis dicatur esse quaternitas, quod absit a fidelium cordibus uel sensibus dici aut cogitari." "There is no reference to the Procession controversy of the eighth century, nor to the Monothelete controversy, which, in the seventh century, was a struggle for life or death." On the other hand, Sabellius, Arius, and Apollinaris are in turn branded as false teachers, and the warnings which the *Quicunque* contains against their errors are noted.[3] These facts incline us to suppose that the Commentary was written not long after the creed itself, since many sentences afforded, as we have seen in the case of other commentaries, the opportunity of saying something about

---

[1] This discovery confirms my argument, *The Ath. Creed*, p. lxxi., that the lost MS. was not to be identified with *Cod. Sangall.* 241, as Pitra suggests.

[2] The adaptation is also found in *Cod. lat. Monacensis*, 3729 sæc. x., and *C.L.M.*, 14,501, sæc. xii. I have described it fully on p. lx. of my book, *The Ath. Creed*.

[3] In the Troyes Commentary founded on this, apparently when the Adoptianists had revived his heresy, Nestorius is mentioned by name.

later controversies. Kattenbusch[1] urges with some force, that expositions of a creed tend to stop in their review of heresies with the latest heresy opposed therein, whether they were written a long or a short time after. This argument is not always borne out by the facts, e.g. the references to other heresies in the Oratorian and Bouhier Commentaries.

"Another indication of time has been found in the note on clause 29, 'In seculo, id est in isto sexto miliario in quo nunc sumus.' This 'sixth milliary' must mean the sixth period of a thousand years from the creation, with the close of which men expected the end of the world." During the fifth century the dread of barbarian invasion, with gloomy forebodings of disaster to the Roman arms, led to anxious anticipations of the last judgment. S. Augustine, while he taught that the exact date of the Second Advent must remain unknown, believed that the last years of the sixth milliary were passing. Speaking of the binding of Satan, in his book *On the City of God* (413–426), he says, xx. 7 : " Aut quia in ultimis annis mille ista res agitur, id est, sexto annorum miliario, tanquam sexto die, cuius nunc spatia posteriora uoluuntur."[2] He seems to have used the chronological system of Julius Africanus, according to which Christ was born in the year 5500 from the creation of the world. Thus the "sixth milliary" would end in A.D. 499.[3] In the fourth century, Eusebius of Cæsarea, while accepting most of the conclusions of his predecessor, found reason to postpone the date three hundred years, bringing it to A.D. 799. Since my discovery of Goldast's literary dishonesty, and the consequent collapse of speculations as to another Euphronius, I cannot contend for so early a date as the fifth century, and must therefore suppose that the author used the Eusebian chronology.[4] He does not suggest that the close of the

[1] *Theol. Ltz.*, 1897, see p. 147. [2] Cf. Sulpicius Severus, *Hist.* ii.
[3] Epiphanius seems to have made an independent calculation, which would bring it to A.D. 478.
[4] This system was used by Bede, *de Temporibus*, c. 22, and in Paris, B.N., *Cod. lat.* 1451, written c. 796 ; cf. the chronological notes in *Cod. Wirceburg*, M.P., th. f. 28, fol. 68, sæc. viii., and *Cod. Bodl. c. Mus.* 113 (*olim.* 94), fol. 114ᵛ and 115, sæc. vii. I owe the latter references to Dom. Morin.

milliary was at hand. We may fairly conclude that he wrote at least a century before the date 799.

We have yet to consider the abridged form of text found in this Commentary, and may compare it with that found in the Troyes Commentary. Both omit clauses 2, 12, 20–22, 26, 27; Fortunatus alone omits also clauses 14, 24.[b] As regards clauses 12, 14, the leading ideas, "uncreate, incomprehensible, omnipotent," have been explained with reference to clauses 8, 9, 13; and it does not fall within the scope of the author's argument to enlarge on the guarding clauses. There is no term in clauses 26, 27, which appears by analogy to need explanation. The author of the recension in *Cod. Sangall.* 27 inserts a new note on clause 2, as on clause 20–22, but he does not find it necessary to explain any of the terms in clause 2. It forms properly one sentence with clause 1, and was probably so regarded by the author of the Commentary. But when the creed was inserted in Psalters, and its clauses were pointed for singing as a canticle, it was detached from clause 1. This seems to have led the author of the recension to say something about it. As to clauses 20–22, the latter portions of which are found in the note on clause 5, it may be argued that he had already explained the terms *gignens, genitus, procedens*, and found nothing more to say. The author of the recension has nothing of importance to add.

As to authorship, we are once again dependent on the Milan MS. 79, sæc. xi., which ascribes the exposition to a Fortunatus. He has not unreasonably been identified with Venantius Fortunatus, some time Bishop of Poitiers, and a friend of Gregory of Tours, whose exposition of the Apostles' Creed is contained in this MS. at fol. 26 *v.* Waterland traced in the two commentaries "great similitude of style, thought, and expressions," and found in his poems phrases which seemed like poetical renderings of phrases in the *Quicunque*. "But the biographer of Fortunatus does not include such a commentary among his works; and the special case, founded on mere similitude of style and scraps of poetry, is much weaker than Waterland's sound general conclusion, that "the tenour of the whole comment, and the simplicity of the style and thoughts, are very suitable to that age, and more so than to the times following."

Thus it appears that the text embedded in these commentaries is simply an abridged form of the ordinary text current in MSS. of the eighth century.[1]

§ VI. Rival Theories of Origin

1. *The Two-Portion Theory.*—At this point it will be convenient to discuss a theory of the origin of the *Quicunque* which was first put forward by Swainson. From the suggestion that the Trèves fragment contains the earliest version of the part relating to the incarnation, he was led on to the conclusion that the Profession of Denebert, containing clauses 1, 3–6, 20–22, 24 f., and this Trèves fragment (clauses 28–40) represent the component parts of the creed in their earliest form. He argued that they were not brought together and moulded into their present form till the ninth century, and that the final shaping took place in the diocese of Rheims between the years 860–870.

He was followed by Lumby,[2] who stated the case succinctly as follows: "(i.) Before A.D. 809, there is no trustworthy evidence of any confession called by the name of S. Athanasius. (ii.) Before that date two separate compositions existed, which form the groundwork of the present *Quicunque*. (iii.) That for some time after that date all quotations are made only from the former of these compositions. (iv.) That the *Quicunque* was not known down to A.D. 813, to those who were most likely to have heard of it, had it been in existence. (v.) That it is found nearly as we use it in A.D. 870. (vi.) A comparison of the various MSS. shows that after the combination of the two parts, the text was for some time in an unsettled or transition state. On every ground, therefore, both of internal and external evidence, it seems to be a sound conclusion that somewhere between A.D. 813–850 the creed was brought nearly into the form in which we use it."

[1] This argument is accepted by Loofs, *R. E.*[3], Art. "Athanasianum."
[2] *Hist. of the Creeds*, ed. 3, p. 259.

In Germany this two-portion theory has been supported in a slightly modified form by Harnack,[1] who regards the first part as a Gallican Rule of Faith, based on the teaching of Augustine and Vincentius, written in the fifth century, and probably polished into its present artistic form in South Gaul in the course of the sixth century. It obtained popularity as an instruction for clergy, and was learnt by heart with the Psalms. Synods began to quote it, and it came into general use as a creed of the Frankish Church in the eighth and ninth centuries, when the second Christological part was added to it, the origin of which is lost in obscurity, though it was certainly not finished in the ninth century.

At first this theory appears spectral and intangible. It seems only too probable that when the evidence proving the existence of the entire text, and its continuous use from the eighth century on, has been collected and classified, and when the assumptions, which were adduced to prove that the completed form was only moulded in the ninth century, have been shown to have been unjustifiable, the theory will only betake itself a century further back, where there is less evidence available, and more scope for unverifiable assumptions, and thus continue to defy its enemies. Such fears are groundless. The evidence as to the separate existence of the two parts is incomplete, and the theory having gained a fictitious strength from mistaken assumptions, when they are exposed, vanishes.

Reference to Appendix D, a table of testimonies to the creed in the eighth and ninth centuries, which can be supported by entire texts, copied (so far as we can tell with any certainty) in the same localities, will show at a glance that these testimonies, e.g. quotations by Hincmar, or Ratramn, or Alcuin, were not from a mere fragment. Since the publication of my book, *The Athanasian Creed*, I have been able to find and collate some eight new MSS. of the eighth and ninth centuries, containing the entire text, to add to the lists there given. And there are others waiting for collation. Thus M. L. Delisle has lately published notes on a MS., which was given to the Church of Lyons by Archbishop Leidrad, 798–

[1] *D.G.*² ii. p. 299.

814, now in the "Bibl. des Pères Maristes de Sainte-Foi-les-Lyon."[1] He regards such a MS., whose date is approximately fixed by the autograph inscription "Leidrat . . . eps istum librum tradidi ad altare sci Stephani," as of great value for the clearing up of palæographical difficulties. The light which it throws on the history of handwriting is not more illuminating than the light which the list of its contents, including the *Quicunque*, throws on our present subject. For it appears to contain a collection of creeds, which Leidrad had compiled in preparation for his journey to Spain, to contend against Adoptianism. This proves that he not only knew of the creed, but valued it—a most important conclusion, as we shall see in the sequel.

The authors of the two-portion theory took advantage of the uncertainties attaching to palæographical arguments twenty years ago, which in respect of *Quicunque* MSS. have been minimised by the publications of the Palæographical Society. They were sceptical about the dates of MSS, *e.g.* B.N., Paris, *Cod. lat.* 13, 159, the date of which is fixed by some Litanies as 795-800.

Nowadays there is no question as to accepting that date,—in fact there is no question, from a palæographical point of view, that there is documentary proof that the *Quicunque* was read, as we have it, in the eighth century.

Apart from the eighth century MSS., the evidence was liable to collapse. It was argued that Hincmar with others of his contemporaries only quoted the first part. Yet all the time a quotation of clause 38, with the old idiom "resurgere habent," as from "the Catholic Faith," was overlooked in the second of Hincmar's treatises on Predestination.

The three fragments which were the stronghold of the theory were a twelfth century sermon at Vienna, the Profession of Denebert, and the Trèves fragment.

1. The Vienna sermon (*Cod.* 1261) is a collection of writings ascribed to Augustine, which, though copied in the twelfth century, contains materials of an earlier date. There are two references to the *Quicunque*, under the title *Fidis*

[1] *Notices et Extraits des manuscrits*, 1898.

RIVAL THEORIES OF ORIGIN 175

Catholica. In the first, the preacher quotes clause 3; in the second, clauses 1–6, 24, 26a, with variations, which find no support in other MSS. Since the preacher quoted S. Paul freely, it is probable that he intended to quote the creed freely, and the fragment may be safely ignored in any reconstruction of the earliest text.

2. The profession of Denebert, Bishop-elect of Worcester, was made to Ethelhard, Archbishop of Canterbury, in the year 798. It is found in a MS. in the British Museum (Cleopatra E. 1) of the twelfth century. It consisted of a promise of obedience, with a short exposition of the Catholic and apostolic faith, as Denebert had received it. He quoted from a written original (*Scriptum est*), clauses 1, 3–6, 20–22, 24, 25 of the *Quicunque*; and promised further to observe the decrees of the Popes, and the six Catholic synods and their Rule of Faith. Since he undertook to be brief, and would find the Incarnation fully expounded by those synods, it cannot be safely said that he knew no more of the creed than he quoted. I will quote the variants of Denebert's text on p. 192. Morin has found a MS. of the eighth century written in an Anglo-Saxon hand (*Cod. lat. Monacensis*, 6298), containing the whole creed, and agreeing in one variant (clause 5 > *enim est*) with Denebert against all other MSS. This is a small point, but it is interesting, and the text as a whole strongly confirms the argument that Denebert was likely to know more than he cared to quote.[1] Some clergy from England attended the Council of Frankfurt in 794. Perhaps they brought back some such MS. with them. The creeds of other English bishops of this century, preserved in the same collection, have, as Swainson[2] suggests, a Sabellian sound. They run as follows: "Credo in Deum Patrem et Filium et Spiritum Sanctum natum et passum," etc.[3] Such

---

[1] Denebert's readings of clauses 22, 25 correspond to those of another eighth century MS., B.N., Paris, *Cod. lat.* 1451, which contains a list of Popes, with a notice of the first six Councils. He may have quoted from a MS. of this collection.

[2] P. 286.

[3] The creeds referred to are those of Heabert, 822; Humbert, 828; Herefrith, 825; Ceolfrith, 839.

erroneous teaching might have been given ignorantly, but it is an interesting fact that Denebert quotes the same clauses as Benedict d'Aniane and Hincmar, when in the following century they reasoned against the heretical tendency of the phrase *trina deitas*.[1]

3. The Trèves fragment in B.N., Paris, *Cod. lat.* 3836, has already been sufficiently described (p. 157), and reasons have been stated which make it improbable that the original document contained no more than the copyist found at Trèves in 730.

The two-portion theory further depended on three questionable assumptions—(i.) That the silence of such men as Paulinus and Alcuin, and Alcuin's pupil, Rabanus Maurus, showed their ignorance of the *Quicunque*; (ii.) that the authority of the document from the hand (as was supposed) of Athanasius would constrain anyone, who knew anything of it, to use and quote it; (iii.) that the completed creed would be a useful weapon against Adoptianism, but was not discovered in time.

i. It must be admitted that Rabanus Maurus and Meginhard of Fulda are strangely silent at a time when, with the multiplication of copies, the creed was coming more and more into use, and was known to their contemporary Haito, Abbot of Reichenau.[2] Haito's successor, Walafrid Strabo, came from Reichenau to Fulda, and went back in 838. But the use of the creed was local as yet. None of the episcopal charges recorded would be binding on Rabanus. And his knowledge of some phrases at least of the creed may be attested by the following parallels: (*a*) "Oportebat ita insinuari Trinitatem ut, quamuis nulla esset diuersitas substantiæ, singillatim tamen commendaretur distinctio personarum"; (*b*) "Una substantia una natura una maiestas una gloria æternitas et Patris et Filii et Spiritus Sancti."[3]

[1] This quotation from Swainson was strongly objected to by some critics of my former book, *e.g.* Dr. Mercati in the *Revista Bibl. Ital.* 1896, p. 149, but without giving any reasons.

[2] We have now the testimony of the Karlsruhe MS., *Cod. Augiensis*, ccxxix., of the year 821.

[3] Rabani, *Opp.* MSL. 110, p. 210. Cf. my *Ath. Creed*, p. xxxviii. f.

When we turn to Alcuin we find it impossible to believe that he really was silent on the subject. There is the evidence of a work on the Procession of the Holy Spirit, which may, with some confidence, be ascribed to him.[1] It is found in a MS. of the early part of the ninth century, which was presented by Bishop Dido, who died in 891, to the Church at Laon. In this are quoted clauses 7, 20–22, 24–26.[2] Swainson admits that his thoughts, in a letter to Charlemagne (Ep. 33) " run curiously enough into the channel of the *Quicunque*,"[3] and "that the order of everything in the *Quicunque*, as well as many of its words and phrases,[4] are found in his book on the Trinity. Surely, in the light of accumulated evidence, Swainson would have abandoned the hopeless task of proving that Alcuin knew nothing of the creed.

The fact is that both Alcuin's quotations, and also those of Paulinus in his speech at Friuli in 796, show a tendency to paraphrase the creed, in order to meet the Nestorian tendency of the Adoptianists. Thus Alcuin writes, *adv. Elip.* i. 9: "Ut unus sit Christus et unus Deus et unus Dei Filius . . . diuinitate consubstantialis Patri, humanitate consubstantialis matri"; and Paulinus: "Naturaliter Patri secundum diuinitatem, naturaliter matri secundum humanitatem: proprius tamen Patri in utroque, quoniam sicut dictum est non sunt duo Filii, alter Dei et alter hominis, sed unus Christus Iesus propter unam personam, Dei et hominis Filius, Deus uerus et homo uerus in anima rationali et uera carne."

ii. "The supposed authority of the document is the second assumption with which we have to deal."

We can distinguish between two phases of the influence which the *Quicunque* might win in the ninth century. In the first it would be known as a sermon or treatise on the Faith, whether recommended by the name of Athanasius or not, on the same level of interest and importance as the *Fides Romanorum*. We may compare the degree of authoritativeness which the Te Deum possessed for Cæsarius of Arles, or Theodulf's hymn

---

[1] The differences in style which distinguish it from other of his works are unimportant. Cf. D.C.B. Art. "Alcuin."
[2] MSL. 101, §§ 750 756.   [3] P. 405.   [4] P. 412.

for Palm Sunday, "Gloria laus et honor," for ourselves. But when the *Quicunque* had been taken up by the bishops as an accredited expansion of the creed, and the clergy had been commanded to learn it, it would obtain the same measure of authority as the first of our Thirty-nine Articles. It does not follow that a teacher would feel constrained to mention its name when he quoted its phrases.

iii. To what extent could it be used as a weapon against Adoptianism? We can now give a precise answer to this question. It was included in the collection of creeds which Leidrad had in his possession when he went on his expedition to Spain. It was quoted by Agobard, his successor in the see of Lyons, c. 820 : " Beatus Athanasius ait Fidem Catholicam nisi quis integram inuiolatamque seruauerit, absque dubio in æternum peribit." But the orthodox theologians in this controversy found that its phrases were useless against heretics, who could take them up and give them a different turn, unless they were paraphrased as we have found them in sentences from Alcuin and Paulinus. All depended on the way in which they were applied. It never was, it never could be, " looked upon as a most satisfactory exposition of the doctrines in debate at Friuli."[1]

Thus it has been shown that these three assumptions have no foundation in fact. Deprived of their support, the two-portion theory completely breaks down. To use the words of Loofs,[2] " it is shattered on its best proof (the Trèves fragment). For all the arguments formerly brought forward for it are very weak."

2. *A Theory of Growth by Accretion.*—Another theory as to the origin of the *Quicunque* has been built up by Loofs[3] on the ruins of the two-portion theory.

He supposes that the original *Quicunque* was a sermon on the Apostles' Creed, like the sermons of Augustine at the giving of the creed (Nos. 212, 213, 214), containing an expansion of its teaching on the Trinity and the Incarnation. The Trèves fragment represents the original text of the latter

---

[1] Lumby, *Hist. of the Creeds*, p. 244. Cf. my *Ath. Creed*, p. xliv.
[2] In his able article "Athanasianum" in *R.E.*³. [3] *Ib.*

RIVAL THEORIES OF ORIGIN

portion, which has been polished into its present state by unknown hands. The quotations in the *Ps.-Aug., Serm.* 244 (Cæsarius) and in the less polished form combined with it (*Auscultate expositionem*) are from its original form in which the Apostles' Creed was still the faith which was to be held. By an unexplained process it was then transformed into an exposition of faith like the *Fides Romanorum*. In this stage, the reference or references to the Apostles' Creed having been removed, it became an authority on its own account, claiming belief in itself rather than the faith of which it was an exposition. The Milan MS., O. 212 *sup.*, preserves a trace of its yet unfinished state in clause 22, where "patri et filio coæternus" cannot be understood as an addition by some copyist. These words must be regarded as a relic from its first stage of existence before clause 10, "Æternus pater etc.," had been inserted. The relation of the forms thus quoted in *Ps.-Aug., Serm.* 244, the Trèves fragment, and the Milan MS., to the final *Quicunque*, revealed in MSS. and commentaries of the eighth century, is like the relation of rock boulders in a mountain glen to a boulder which was detached from the mountain at the same period, but has been carried down the valley by a stream, and polished and rounded by its waters.

When the process was completed, the form obtained greater celebrity by its connection with the name of Athanasius, without any intention to deceive. This point in the history of its development must have been reached before the date of the Canon of Autun, *c.* 630.

This theory is open to serious objections. It is very doubtful whether the Trèves fragment is part of a sermon preached at the giving of the creed. Kattenbusch[1] points out that it is just as likely that it was a document like *Ps.-Aug., Serm.* 236, the author of which wished to deliver "the right faith" to his brethren, so made use of a great part of the Creed of Pelagius.

It is still more doubtful whether we can think of the original text of the *Quicunque* as intended to be an exposition

[1] *Theol. Litz.* 1897, p. 145 f.

of the creed. Such expositions in the fifth century were not so formal, and explained the articles of the creed consecutively. There is not a trace of this in the Trèves fragment. Words are quoted from the creed, but no explanation is attempted of those particular words, though we know from many instances that they were considered to need explanation.

This theory also depends upon questionable assumptions, viz. the supposed late date of the Fortunatus Commentary, the silence of Isidore, and the theory that the Milan MS. contains a survival of an unpolished primitive text.

The date of the Fortunatus Commentary is, as we have seen, uncertain. It is probable that it belongs to the sixth century, if not an earlier. Certainly there is not a shred of positive evidence pointing to the eighth century as the date of its composition. A theory built on negations is built on sand. The silence of Isidore is not much less questionable beside the evidence of the Canon of 633, than the silence of Alcuin and Paulinus beside the quotations of Denebert. The question has been considered carefully above, and it only remains to point out that when Loofs asserts that a reference to the *Quicunque* would have had stronger effect than Isidore's own collaborations, he is arguing from a mistaken idea of the authority which the *Quicunque* would have had for the Church of that time. It could only have been regarded as an exposition of the faith side by side with others, *e.g.* the Creed of Damasus. This explains why it did not receive a name at an earlier date,[1] and why Isidore, even if he knew it, was as free to expound the faith in his own way as the authors of our First Article.

The Milan MS. contains another variation, which must be considered in relation to this theory, besides the addition, "patri et filio coæternus"; *e.g.* the repetition of "persona" in clause 5. This is an addition which was made by Hincmar when he was paraphrasing sentences from the creed (*de Una non Trina Deitate*; cf. Alcuin, *de Trin.* iii. 22). It is easy to understand that it would approve itself to an early copyist.

---
[1] Kattenbusch, art. cit.

On the other hand, it is not clear that the omission would really smooth the rhythm. This addition in clause 5 thus supports the theory of an addition in clause 22. Loofs says that they were implied in clause 10: "The Father is eternal," etc. He omits to add that the expression of certainty was not only implied but stated in clause 24^b: "All three persons are coeternal." The latter words are not quoted in the Fortunatus Commentary, and it would have been safer to suggest that they, rather than clause 10, were only inserted in a recension of the original text. It is inconceivable that clause 10 did not belong to the original text, and early copyists of the sixth or seventh century were not likely to spend much time considering what it implied. The actual phrase, "Patri et Filio coæternus," was familiar, being found four times in "this MS., twice in the Faith of Bacchiarus," and once in Gennadius's *Book of Dogma* and the Creed of Damasus, which is added in a slightly later hand.

This theory must go the way of its predecessor, but it will not have been put forward in vain if it rouses students to renewed efforts to find some new sixth century testimony, which shall patch up the threadbare controversy over the Sermon of Cæsarius and the Canon of 633. Loofs admits the weakness of his argument from negative conclusions, when he allows that such a discovery would link the early parallels to the later quotations, and prove the early date of the present text of the creed. He atones for it by the vigour of his criticism of weak points in the rival theory, and thereby earns our gratitude.

We may now retrace our steps to the fifth century, and maintain that none of the external evidence quoted, from the Sermon of Auitus onwards, has in any degree injured the theory that the creed was written in the early years of the fifth century, *c.* 425–430, by some one trained in the school of Lerins.

It is of no great importance that we should succeed in attributing it to any individual author. We do not receive it on one man's authority, but as the expression of the common faith which (as we gladly recognise) he had the gift to express in rhythmical language.

As I have said before, "the chief interest of these researches is centred in the hypothesis that the *Quicunque* belongs to the fifth century; that is to say, to an age of original thought, the age of S. Augustine himself, and not to an age which could only make a patchwork theology out of his writings. The author seems to have adapted phrases which he had borrowed from S. Augustine as current terms, not confining himself to slavish reiteration like later writers.[1] But, as we have seen, he was not tongue-tied by that phraseology, and took his own line. "Auitus and Cæsarius, the inheritors of lofty traditions, might be expected to quote the *Quicunque* with appreciation," as the work of a teacher in Christ of a former generation, more formally than Faustus or Vincentius were likely to do. "The sixth and seventh centuries were for Gaul an age of failing culture, of weakened and often crude theology, an age in which the composition of the *Quicunque* is unimaginable; in which, as a matter of fact, the very faculty of appreciating its terse, incisive style, and the accuracy of its definitions, had failed" in many quarters. We may contrast Gregory of Tours with Cæsarius, from whose time he was separated by one generation, and we find him bewailing his bad grammar, and that he had equal reason, though earnest and orthodox, to bewail his lack of theological training. Here we must leave the question, not despairing of a more satisfactory solution in the future by the help of the new evidence which will surely be brought to light.

§ VII. THE LATER HISTORY OF THE CREED.

From the ninth century the history of the creed is well known. Its use in the office of Prime, of which we hear first at Fleury, spread rapidly over the Frankish Empire. At the end of the tenth century, Abbo of Fleury writes that it was sung antiphonally in England, as well as in France. An Anglo-Saxon homily, "On the Catholic Faith," written about

[1] *The Ath. Creed*, p. xcix.

the middle of the tenth century by a monk, Ælfric,[1] quoted it for the instruction of the people. And from this time on we find many versions in Anglo-Saxon, Old French, Old German, and finally Greek.

The date of its reception at Rome is uncertain. Amalarius of Trèves, in his account of the Roman Office of Prime, written c. 820, made no mention of it, but it was quoted in this connection two centuries later by Honorius of Autun, as used in the four regions of the world, therefore probably in Rome. This fact is confirmed by the evidence of Abelard, who complained to S. Bernard, c. 1130, that the Cistercian Order had given up the ancient custom of daily recitation.[2] In the same letter, Abelard shows minute knowledge of Roman customs, and speaks of the fidelity with which the old offices were preserved in the Church of the Lateran. It is probable, therefore, that the creed had found its way into use in Rome at that date.

Its monastic use can be proved by the evidence of *Cod. Vat.* 84, of the tenth century, and by the oldest MS. Breviary (*Cod. Mazarin.* 364), written at Monte Cassino in 1099. But we may conjecture that it was used in sermons long before this.

Its earliest and only proper title is *Fides Catholica*, a Catholic Faith, clearly expressed in the ninth century by those writers who described it as *sermo*, an instruction, whether it was connected with the name of Athanasius or not. The name *symbolum* was not attached to it till the end of that century, first by Regino of Prum (c. 892). This marks the fact that it had been finally distinguished from other formularies of the same kind, and, by association with the Apostles' and Nicene Creeds in an increasing number of Psalters, was acquiring a new and, in the first instance, reflected authority as a creed authorised by the Catholic Church. By one MS. of that period (H) it was called a Hymn concerning Faith of the Trinity; and in the Constitutions of English Bishops of the thirteenth century it was called a Psalm. But, in the latter case, it does not follow

[1] Ommanney, *Diss.* p. 29.   [2] *Ep.* x., M.S.L. 178, p. 335.

that it was merely regarded as a Canticle. Waterland points out that a MS. of the twelfth century, called *Rhythmus Anglicus*,[1] gives this title also to the Apostles' Creed and the Lord's Prayer, like old German writings.[2] At the Reformation, popular translations (one by Wyclif?) were available in Old and Middle English, and in the recent Primer of Bishop Hilsey, 1539. In the first Prayer-book of Edward VI. it was "to be sung or said" after the Benedictus on the greater feasts. In the second Prayer-book seven other festivals were added, and in 1662 the rubric was altered to "at Morning Prayer, instead of the Apostles' Creed."

Thus in the English Church alone has it been made a popular creed, the Roman Church continuing to use it in the office of Prime on Sundays only. Some restriction of that use has resulted from "the gradual encroachment of the *Sanctorale* upon the *Temporale*, (1) through the multiplication of saints' days, and (2) to a less extent by the raising of the "ritus" or dignity of individual festivals. According to the general rubrics, if a "festum duplex" fall on an ordinary Sunday, "fit officium de festo, commemoratio de Dominica." How often this occurs depends largely on the particular calendar in use; *e.g.* English Jesuits use the Roman calendar supplemented by the *Proprium Soc. Jesu* and by the *Proprium Angliæ*, with the result that hardly a Sunday in the year escapes "occurrence." But occurrence — even with a "duplex"—does not crowd out the Sunday office in the case of the Sundays in Advent and Lent, or of Septuagesima, Sexagesima, and Quinquagesima, so the *Quicunque* (with the rest of the Sunday office) survives on these, and (as regards the *Quicunque*) on Trinity Sunday. In the case of the secular clergy there will be fewer cases of occurrence, and the Sunday office is more frequently, or less infrequently, recited."[3]

In the Eastern Orthodox Church it is not used in any office, though it has found its way into the Appendix of the modern Greek *Horologium*, without the words "and the

---

[1] Trin. Coll. Camb. c. 1180.   [2] Lambec. *Catal.* ii. 760.
[3] I am indebted for this clear statement of the modern use by the Roman Church to Father H. Lucas, S.J., Professor at S. Beuno's College.

Son." Thus Eastern theologians regard it (with that exception) as containing sound doctrine.[1]

§ VIII. THE TEXT AND A TRANSLATION OF THE "QUICUNQUE"

With reference to the following text of the *Quicunque*, a few words may be said about the new MSS. of which full collations are here printed for the first time, and about the light which they throw on disputed readings. Full descriptions of the others may be found in the works of Swainson and Ommanney.

K_1.—At Karlsruhe, in the Grand Ducal Library, in the fine collection of MSS., from Reichenau, *Cod. Augiensis*, ccxxix. It can be dated before 821 A.D., by a marginal note on f. 58v. It contains works of Isidore and Martin of Bracara, with expositions of the Lord's Prayer and Apostles' Creed.

K_2.—Another MS., *Cod. Aug.* xviii. of the same collection, was unfortunately out on loan when I visited Karlsruhe. It contains a collection of creeds and commentaries. I am indebted to the librarian, Dr. A. Holder, for collations of the *Quicunque* and the Creed of Damasus.

L_2.—At Leiden, in the University Library, *Cod. lat.* xviii. 67. F. sæc. viii., ix. This is a collection of creeds, including the Creed of Damasus, and the second form of the *Fides Romanorum*. It contains also a Latin glossary, which has attracted some interest.

L_3.—The Psalter of Lothaire[2] is now in a private collection, but I am indebted to the owner for the following collation.

M_1.—At Munich, in the Royal Library, *Cod. lat.* 6298, written in an Anglo-Saxon hand, sæc. viii., is a mixed collection. I am indebted for the collation to Dom. G. Morin.

M_2.—In the same library, *Cod. lat.* 6330[3], sæc. viii., ix. from Freisingen, is a collection of so-called *Doctrinæ diuersorum*

---

[1] For further information on the whole question of Reception and Use, see Ommanney, *Diss.* pt. ii. chap. vi.

[2] A description of this MS. has been published by the Palæographica Society, with three facsimiles, vol. ii. 69, 93, 94.

[3] Since I collated it, I have found a description of the MS. in Arnold's *Cæsarius von Arelate*, p. 452.

patrum. I was attracted by the names, Athanasius, Effrem, Cæsarius, and found the *Quicunque* preceding *Fides Romanorum* ii.

N.—In the Cathedral Library at Vercelli, a collection of creeds, including also the two Nicene Creeds, *Cod.* clxxv. sæc. ix.

R.—At Rheims, in the Town Library, *Cod.* 20, sæc. ix. A Psalter with creeds and canticles.

T.—At Troyes, in the Treasury of the Cathedral, the so-called Psalter of Count Henry, sæc. ix. It formerly belonged to the Chapter of the Church of S. Etienne.[1]

V_2.—In the Vatican Library, *Cod. Vat. Pal.* 1127, sæc. ix., is a collection of creeds and canons.

W.—In the University Library at Würzburg, an interesting Psalter from Ebrach, *Cod. Mp. th.*, f. 109, in a Lombardic hand, sæc. ix. It contains the Fortunatus Commentary in the margin (see p. 168).

I may add that I have verified collations of other MSS. at Paris, Rome, Milan, and can testify to the great importance of two in particular. Paris, B.N., *Cod. lat.* 13,159, and Milan, *Cod. Ambros.* O. 212, *sup.* P_1.—Paris, B.N., 13,159, is a Gallican Psalter, which was written before 800 A.D. The date is fixed by the evidence of two Litanies, in which petitions are offered for a Pope Leo and a King Charles. These must have been written before Charlemagne's coronation as Emperor by Leo III. After f. 160, two folios have been torn out, one of which was "remade in the eleventh century,"[2] including clause 1–12*a*, of the *Quicunque.*

B.—Milan, *Cod. Ambros.*, O. 212 *sup.*, is a small collection containing the Book of Ecclesiastical Dogmas (ascribed to Gennadius), the Faith of Bacchiarius, a Sermon on the Ascension, and (in a slightly later hand) the Creed of Damasus. It has often been described and discussed. Dr.

---

[1] This MS. is difficult of access, since it is kept in a glass case under three locks, the keys to which are in the possession of different officials. I am indebted to them, and in particular to M. L'Abbé Chaudron, Arch-priest of the Cathedral, for permission to examine it.

[2] Delisle, *Le Cabinet des Manuscrits*, iii. p. 239; cf. Ommanney, *Diss.* p. 107.

Ceriani thinks that it was written in Ireland, and pointed out to me the great similarity between it and the *Bangor Antiphonary*.[1] He thinks that it may even be of the end of the seventh century.

The number of readings which are really doubtful is not large.

Clause 22.—All the new MSS., with the exception of N, *omit* est. This gives a better rhythmical ending, *cursus uelox*, *génitus sed procédens*. On the Rhythm, see p. 248.

Clause 28.—*Om.* pariter, $K_2 L_3 M_2 N R U_2 W$; + pariter, $K_1 L_2 M_1 T$. In this case the MSS., taken altogether, are almost equally divided, but in five of those which originally contained it, it has been erased. I have seen similar erasures in many other MSS., of later dates, showing that the feeling against it was widespread. The fact that it was found in A B $M_1 L_2 P_1$ is strongly in its favour. But it is not found in the first quotation of the verse in the Fortunatus Commentary, though it appears when the latter half is repeated in the exposition. This shows how easy it would be for anyone to insert it in the text, to sharpen a sentence against Nestorianism. By omitting it, we obtain a good rhythmical ending, *Déus et hómo est* (*pl.*), but this is no argument by which to prove its omission from the original text, since it might only explain the reason why it became unpopular, after the use of the creed as a canticle had become general.

Clause 33.—A majority of MSS., including the earliest, are in favour of the ablatives, *carne* . . . *Deo*, with the earliest MSS. of the Fortunatus Commentary. But Ommanney[2] has argued strongly against this reading, on the ground that "it is difficult to perceive what doctrine precisely, what phase of thought, the readings *in carne* and *in Deo*, in their literal interpretation, symbolise; they jar like a discordant note upon our sense of the fitting and appropriate." He quotes Waterland's opinion that they were not the original readings, and shows that it would be very easy for a copyist to omit the contractions over "e" and "m" thus—CARNĒ-DM̄, after which "another copyist would be tempted to substitute 'o' for 'm' in

[1] May, 1898. [2] *Diss.* p. 416.

the latter word, in order to make it harmonise with the former, adding the mark of contraction (manifestly omitted) over it."

It is perfectly true that the parallels in Augustine and Vincentius support the readings *carnem . . . Deum*, and that, from the point of view of the internal evidence, these are likely to be the original readings. The Eutychians admitted a change of the Godhead in the flesh, and taught that the manhood was assumed into God, so that the change to the ablatives may have been, as Waterland [1] has shown, a direct confutation of their principles. But this would be to give to the ablatives, regarded as an emendation, a strong dogmatic meaning, which is just what Ommanney refuses to them.

The corrupt Latinity of the sixth and seventh centuries extended further than Ommanney suggests; it included utter confusion about cases. The copyists were indifferent to such distinctions. Under these circumstances it seems to me remarkable that so many of the earlier MSS., A B $M_{1, 2}$, $P_{1, 4}$ should agree on ablatives, and I prefer to follow them without further argument. The meaning, as I have shown from Waterland, is clearly antagonistic to Eutychian confusion of the two natures in Christ, and as such appropriate for our present use.

Clause 36.—There is an overwhelming majority of MSS. against *ad inferna*, and yet I think that one is justified in adopting it, for the following reasons:—

It is found in A, W, Fort, Or, Stav. It is one of the cases in which copyists would be influenced by their reading of the Apostles' Creed; and, on the other hand, the author, presuming him to have lived in Gaul, at all events before 500 A.D., when he was obviously quoting his Baptismal Creed, would surely quote it exactly, even if he, like S. Augustine, preferred *ad inferos* as an improvement on the teaching *ad infernum* or *ad inferna*. Now, the reading *ad inferos* had not come into the Gallican creeds in the time of Cæsarius, Gregory of Tours, or Eligius of Noyon, *i.e.* before 600 A.D. And it became common with the appearance and spreading of the *Textus receptus* from c. 700 A.D. Thus there is a strong presumption against the

[1] P. 146.

change from *inferna* to *inferos* before 700, and in favour of it after that date. The reading of B may be accounted for by the reading of the Apostles' Creed in the *Bangor Antiphonary*.

Clause 37.—The readings *Dei* and *Omnipotentis* in the later MSS. have been plainly inserted, to make the creed correspond to the *Textus receptus* of the Apostles' Creed, in which they formed a very natural accretion.

The translation in the Book of Common Prayer needs several slight amendments. In clauses 9, 12, for "incomprehensible" read "infinite." In this case the translators were influenced by the Greek version, which they imagined to be the original, and which has ἀκατάληπτος. In clause 27 "believe rightly" is obviously a translation of ὀρθῶς πιστεύσῃ, where the Latin text has "fideliter credat." In clause 28 they quoted the Greek γάρ not the Latin *ergo*, and for the same reason omitted to translate *firmiterque* in clause 40, which has no place in the Greek text.[1]

The word "must" in clause 26 represents an Old English idiomatic use of the word, which still survives in the North of England = may, shall. "Must I give you some tea?"

The other changes in my translation are unimportant, with the exception of the rendering of *saluus*, "in a state of salvation." The word is used in Holy Scripture with three references, to past, present, and future, according to the point of view, redemption, grace, or glory. It is obvious that it is the second of these which the author had in mind. It may be paraphrased in the words "spiritually healthy."

THE TEXT OF THE QUICUNQUE, FROM MSS. OF THE EIGHTH AND NINTH CENTURIES.

SYMBOLS.*		SÆC.	TITLE.
A (a)	Paris, B.N.3836, (Trèves fragment)	viii.	
B (b)	Milan, O. 212 *sup.*	viii.	
C (g)	A lost Paris MS., S. Germains 257	viii.	F.S.A. Epi.
D (t)	Paris, B.N., 1152. Psalter of Charles the Bald	ix.	F.S.A.
E (x)	Utrecht Psalter (formerly Brit. Mus., Claudius, C. vii.)	ix.	F.C.

[1] The other instances quoted by Ommanney, p. 312, are doubtful, since they might be explained by variants in the Latin text.

AN INTRODUCTION TO THE CREEDS

Symbols.[*]		Sæc.	Title.
F (z)	B.M., Galba, A. xviii. Psalter	ix.	F.S.A.A.
G₁ (u)	S. Gallen, Cod. 20 ,,	ix. in	F.C.S.A. epi.
G₂ (l)	,, 15 ,,	ix.	F.C. edita a S.A.A. epo.
G₃ (n)	,, 23 ,,	ix.	F.C.S.A. epi.
G₄ (m)	,, 27 ,,	ix.	F.S.A. epi.
H (ac)	B.M., Reg. 2. B.V. ,,	ix. x.	Hymnus A. de fide Trinitatis.
K₁	Karlsruhe, Cod. Aug. ccxxix.	ix. in.	
K₂	,, ,, xviii. .	ix.	
L₁	Lambeth Palace, Cod. 427. Psalter	ix. x.	F.C.S.A. epi.
L₂	Leiden, Cod. xviii. 67. F	viii. ix.	F.S. Athanasii epi.
L₃	Psalter of Lothaire . . .	ix.	F.C. tradita a S.A.A.
M₁	Munich, cod. lat. 6298 . . .	viii.	
M₂	,, ,, 6330 . . .	viii. ix.	F.C.S. Athasii(+na corr.) epi.
N	Vercelli, Cod. clxxv. . . .	ix.	F.S. Athanasia cpi A.
P₁ (k)	Paris, B.N.,13,159. Psalter, clauses 12b–40 . .	viii.	
P₂ (h)	,, 4858, clauses 1-11	viii.	
P₃ (d)	,, 1451	viii.	Inc. exemplar fidei cht. sci. atanasii epi alex. ecclesiæ.
P₄ (bb)	,, 3848, B . . .	ix.	F.S.A. epi.
Q (q)	C.C.C.Cambridge,272.0.5. Psalter	ix.	F.C.
R	Rheims, 20. Psalter . . .	ix.	F.S.A. epi.
S (s)	C.C.C. Cambridge, 411 N. 10. Psalter	xi. ?	F.S. Anasthasii epi.
T	Troyes (Psalter of Count Henry)	ix.	
U₁ (c)	Rome, Cod. Vat. Pal. 574 . .	ix.	F.C. b. Atanasi epi.
U₂	,, Cod. Vat. Reg. 1127 . .	ix.	Inc.exemplar F.C.S. Atanasi epi. Alex. ecclesiæ.
V (e)	Vienna, 1032	ix	F.C.S. Atanasi epi.
W	Würzburg, Cod. Mp. th. f. 109. Psalter	ix.	
Y (y)	Vienna, 1861 (Golden Psalter) .	ix.	F.C. trad. a S.S.A. epo.

[*] A-F and H are so designated by Lumby. I have given Swainson's symbols in brackets (a) etc.

COMMENTARIES.

Symbols.		Sæc.	Title.
Fort	Fortunatus, in Oxford Bodl. Junius 25	ix.	F.C.
Tr	Troyes, in Troyes, 804 . .	x.	F.C.
Or₁	Oratorian in Troyes, 804 . .	x.	F.C.

TEXT OF THE "QUICUNQUE" 191

SYMBOLS.		SÆC.	TITLE.
Or₂	Oratorian, *Cod. Vat. Reg.* 231	ix.	
Bou₁	Bouhier in Troyes, 1979	x.	F.C.S.A. epi.
Bou₂	„ B.M. Add. MSS. 24,902	x. xi.	F.C.
Orl	Orleans, in Orleans, 94	ix.	F.C.
Paris	Paris, in B.N. 1012	x.	F.C.
Stav	Stavelot in B.M. Add. MSS. 18,043	x.	F.C.S.A.
Den	Denebert, 798 A.D. (B.M. Cleopatra E. 1)	xii.	(F.C.)
Tol	Conc. Toletanum, 633, A.D. (*Cod. Novar.*)	x.	

To these add MSS. uncollated.

Sæc. viii. ix.—The MS. given by Leidrad to the Church of Lyons, 798–814 (p. 173 *supra*).

Sæc. ix.—A MS. among the Archives of the Münster Kirche at Essen,[1] containing the Latin text of most of the Psalms in three versions, with the Greek text in a fourth column in Latin letters. Also the usual canticles, including the *Quicunque*. It is assigned to the Carolingian period, *c.* 850.[2]

Sæc. ix. x.—A MS. at Ivrea (*Cod.* xlii.), f. 59ʳ, "Fides sc̄i Athanasi epi alexandrini."

Sæc. ix.—A MS. at Paris, B.N., Nouv. acq. lat. 442 (Libri 94), a Psalter written in Tironian notes or shorthand signs.

The Text of the "Quicunque" from MSS. of the Eighth and Ninth Centuries, and Commentaries

[1] Quicunque uult saluus esse ante omnia opus est ut teneat cathólicam fídem,ᴾˡ [2] quam nisi quisque integram inuiolatamque seruauerit, absque dubio in ætérnum perίbit.ᵗ

I. i. (*a*) [3] Fides autem Catholica hæc est, ut unum Deum in Trinitate et Trinitatem in Unitātĕ uĕnĕrēmur; [4] neque confundentes personas neque substántiam separántes.ᵛ [5] Alia est enim persona Patris, alia Filii, alia Spíritus

---

[1] *Theol. Literaturblatt,* 14th Dec. 1894, p. 600.
[2] Hitherto the oldest MS. of the kind known has been *Cod. Bambergensis,* of 909.

Sáncti,[pl] ⁶ sed Patris et Filii et Spiritus Sancti una est diuinitas, æqualis gloria, coætérna maiéstas.[pl]

(b) ⁷ Qualis Pater talis Filius talis et Spíritus Sánctus.[pl] ⁸ Increatus Pater increatus Filius increatus et Spíritus Sánctus.[pl] ⁹ Immensus Pater immensus Filius immensus et Spíritus Sánctus.[pl] ¹⁰ Æternus Pater, æternus Filius, æternus et Spíritus Sánctus,[pl] ¹¹ et tamen non tres æterni sed únus aetérnus:[pl] ¹² sicut non tres increati nec tres immensi, sed únus increatus et únus imménsus.[pl] ¹³ Similiter omnipotens Pater, omnipotens Filius, omnipotens et Spíritus Sánctus,[pl] ¹⁴ et tamen non tres omnipotentes sed únus omnípotens.[t]

(c) ¹⁵ Ita Deus Pater Deus Filius Deus et Spíritus Sánctus,[pl] ¹⁶ et tamen non tres Dei sed únus est Déus.[pl] ¹⁷ Ita Dominus Pater Dominus Filius Dominus et Spíritus Sánctus.[pl] ¹⁸ et tamen non tres Domini sed únus est Dóminus.[t] ¹⁹ Quia sicut singillatim unamquamque personam et Deum et Dominum confiteri christiana ueritáte compéllimur[v] ita tres Deos aut Dominos dicere catholica religiōnĕ prŏhĭbēmŭr.

ii. ²⁰ Pater a nullo est factus nec creátus nec génitus.[t] ²¹ Filius a Patre solo est, non factus nec creátus sed génitus.[t] ²² Spiritus Sanctus a Patre et Filio, non factus nec creatus nec génitus, sed procédens.[v] ²³ Unus ergo Pater non tres Patres, unus Filius non tres Filii, unus Spiritus Sanctus non tres Spíritus Sáncti.[pl] ²⁴ Et in hac Trinitate nihil prius aut posterius, nihil maius aut minus, sed totæ tres personæ coæternæ sibi sunt ét coæquáles:[pl] ²⁵ ita ut per omnia sicut iam supradictum est, et Trinitas in Unitate et Unitas in Trinitātĕ uĕnŏrāndă sit. ²⁶ Qui uult ergo saluus esse ita de Trinitate sentiat.

II. ²⁷ Sed necessarium est ad æternam salutem, ut incarnationem quoque Domini nostri Iesu Christi fidéliter crédat.[pl] ²⁸ Est ergo fides recta, ut credamus et confiteamur, quia Dominus noster Iesus Christus Dei Filius Déus et hómo est.[pl]

i. ²⁹ Deus est ex substantia Patris ante sæcula genitus, et homo est ex substantia matris in sáeculo nátus.[pl] ³⁰ Perfectus Deus, perfectus homo, ex anima rationali et humana cárne

TEXT OF THE "QUICUNQUE" 193

subsístens.^pl ^31 Æqualis Patri secundum diuinitatem, minor Patri secúndum humanitátem^v.

ii. ^32 Qui licet Deus sit et homo non duo tamen sed únus est Chrístus.^pl ^33 Unus autem, non conuersione diuinitatis in carne, sed assumptione humanitátis in Déo.^pl ^34 Unus omnino non confusione substantiæ sed unitáte persónæ.^pl ^35 Nam sicut anima rationalis et caro unus est homo, ita Deus et homo únus est Chrístus^pl :

iii. ^36 qui passus est pro salute nostra, descendit ad inferna, resurréxit a mórtuis,^t ^37 ascendit ad cælos, sedet ad dexteram Patris: inde uenturus indicare uíuos et mórtuos,^t ^38 ad cuius aduentum omnes homines resurgere habent cum corporibus suis et reddituri sunt de factis própriis ratiónem.^v ^39 Et qui bona egerunt ibunt in uitam æternam, qui uero mala in ígnem ætérnum.^pl

^40 Hæc est fides catholica quam nisi quisque fideliter firmiterque crediderit, saluus ésse non póterit.^t

1-27. *deest in* A. 1. Quicumque, B F H K$_{1, 2}$ L$_3$ N P$_4$ R T U$_{1, 2}$. ult, L$_1$. > esse saluus, B. est] + enim, H. tenead, U$_2$. fidem cath. Den. chatolicam, F P$_{1, 3}$ Paris. 2. nisi] ni, *supra lin*. L$_2$. quisque] quis, B. intigram, B. inuiolatamque, B. *om.* absque dubio, P$_2$ *ad fin*. Incipit de fide, H. 3. hec, U$_2$. Trinitatem] Triuitate, K$_1$ M$_2$ P$_1$. 4. confudentes, B ; confundantes, H P$_3$. substanciam, L$_2$] substantia, M$_2$ N P$_2$ U$_2$. seperantes, W*. 5. > enim est, M$_1$ Den. *om.* est, P$_1$. alia persona Filii alia persona Spiritus Sancti, B. alia, 2°] —a, *supra ras. sec. man.* (?) N. personam, K$_1$*. Spiritus, *pr.* et, G$_{1, 2, 3, 4}$ K$_2$. 6. sed Patris et Filii et Spiritus Sancti, *supra lin. e recentiori manu*, B. Spiritus] s̄pu, R. diuinitas] diuitas, P$_1$. equalis, P$_1$ R. coæterna, *pr.* et, Or. ; quoeterna, P$_1$; quoæt—, P$_{2, 3}$ Orl. Paris. magestas, P$_3$. 7, 8, 9, 10, 13, 15, 17. *om.* et, K$_1$ L$_1$ R S *corr*. W *corr*. Bou. Orl. 7, 9, 10, 15, 17. *om.* et, Stav. 13, 15, 17. *om.* et, B. 8. et, *supra lin. sec. man.* (?) N. *om.* et, B P$_4$ Or$_2$. 8, 9, 10 > 10, 8, 9. æternus . . . increatus . . . immensus, P$_3$ U$_2$ (*cf.* 11, 12). 9. inmensus (*semper*), B D F H G$_2$ G$_4$* K$_{1, 2}$ L$_{1, 2}$ M$_2$ N P$_{1, 4}$ Q R S T U$_{1, 2}$ Fort. Tr. Or. Bou. Paris Stav. *om.* et, B Or$_2$ Paris. 10. æternus, 1° . . . æt. 3°] et— . . . et—, P$_1$. *om.* et, B G$_2$ P$_4$. 11. *om.* et, E F. tres] .III. B. unus æternus] *def*. P$_2$. eterni . . . eternus, P$_1$. 12. > unus inmensus et unus increatus, B. 14. *om.* tamen, B. nec tamen, Bou. tres] III. M$_2$. omnipotentis, P$_3$ T. unus] + ÷ P$_4$ *ras*. N. 16, 17 > 17, 16, Or. 16. tres] .III. B. Dii, D F H K$_2$ L$_{1, 2}$ N P$_{3, 4}$ Q R S T U$_{1, 2}$. *om.* est, B L$_2$ P$_1$. 18. tres] .III. B. *om.* est, B. 19. *om.* sicut, P$_1$. singulatim, L$_1$. unaquamque persona, K$_1$. et, 1°] ad, M$_1$. *om.* et, 1° C E F G$_{1, 2, 3, 4}$ H K$_1$ L$_{1, 3}$ N *corr*. P$_{1, 3}$ Q R S T U$_1$ *corr*. U$_2$ Or. Bou. Orl. Stav. et, 2°] ac, Or. Orl. Stav. ; hac, K$_1$. confitere, L$_2$ P$_4$. christiane, P$_1$. ueritate trinitate, L$_2$. conpellimur, B F H K$_1$ L$_2$ M$_2$ N P$_{1, 3, 4}$ Q S T U$_1$. tris, P$_1$. aut] ac, Bou$_2$. Dominos] Deos, *ras*. U$_1$, *pr.* tres, D E K$_1$ M$_1$ P$_3$ T Or.

Bou₁. dicere] dici, N P₄; dicire, U₁. catholicam religionem, K₁; relegione, M₂ N U₁ corr. (?) Paris. prohibimur, M₂, h supra lin. N corr. P₄; proibemur, Q Paris; ita tres . . . prohibemur, in marg. G₄. 20. >factus est, Den. 21. solus, K₁. om. est, K₁. non] nec, K₁. nec] aut, Or. 22. non] nec, K₁. nec, 1°] aut, Or. genitus] + est, C E F M₁ N V. procedens P₁] + Patri et Filio coeternus est, B (cf. Symb. Damasi). 23. unus, 1°] + est, K₁M₁; unus, 2°] + est, K₁. om. Sanctus, P₁. non, 3°]pr. sed, Or₂; tris, P₁, ter; .III. B(ter). Sancti]Sanctos, P₄. 24. et, 1°] supra lin. M₁; sed, Or. K₁; om. et in hac, C. hac] ac, P₃*; a, Paris; + enim, M₁. maius, pr. est, M₁. tote, K₁ L₂ P₃,₄ R T U₂. persone, L₂ P₃ U₂ W. coeterne, K₂; coeterne, L₂; quoeterne, K₁ P₁; quohæternæ, P₃; quoæt—, Or. Orl. Paris. quoæq. K₁ Q U₂ Or. Or]. Paris; quoæqualis, L₂ (co—,U₁). 25. om. supra, Bou.; superius dictum, supra lin. P*₁. om. et, 1° K₁. et, 1°] ut, N P₄. om. et Trinitas in Unitate, M₁. > Unitas in Trinitate et Trinitas in Unitate, C D F N P₄ R corr. S* Y (Fort.?) Bou₂ Orl.; + et Trinitas in Unitate, in marg. D; Unitatem . . . Trinitatem, U₁*. ueneranda sit] ueneremur, K₁. 26. Qui]Quicumque, K₁ P₄ U*. ergo] supra lin. N corr. U₁; om. K₁ P₄. senciat, K₂ M₂ Paris. 27. om. est, P₁. incarnatione, K₁. quoque, supra lin. U₁. Domini] hic inc. A. Jesu] iħu, B D F H K₂ L₁,₂ M₂ N P₁,₃,₄ Q R S T U₁,₂ W. fideliter] pr. unusquisque, in marg. c recentiori manu Q. credat] + s. qui uult saluus esse, supra lin. S. 28. est] pr. hec, K₁. Dei]Deus, L₂. >Filius est Dei. Deus, K₁. om. Dei Filius, Or. Deus] pr. et, B C G₁ M₁ P₃ Paris; + pariter, A B C D G*₂ H K¹ L₁* L₂ M₁ P₁* S* T U₁* Fort. (?) Tr. Or. Paris, Stav., in marg. Q corr. 29. om. est, 1° K₁ Bou₁, supra lin. W corr. ex]de, A D bis. substantia, 1°] substancia, L₂. ante sæcula genitus est, in marg. c recentiori manu B. om. et, B C F P₄ Tr. Or. Bou₁. om. est, 2° A C D F H K₁ W Tr. Bou₁. in] a, Y. seculo, R, supra lin. W corr.; secula, H P₁ W*; sæculum, K₁ U₁. 30. rationale, M₂ N P*₁,₄ (e fere eras. R) U₁ corr.; rationabili, A B C D M₁ Q* Tr.; racionabili, Fort. umana, P₃. carne] carnis, L₂. 31. Equalis, M₂ P₁,₃ W; + est, Or₂. Patri] Patris, K₁* U₁ corr. secundum] sedum, P₂. Patri, 2°] Patre, B C D G₁, ₂, ₃, ₄ H L₃ N corr. P₄ Q R S U₂ W corr.; Patris, K₁* (?) L₂ M₂* U₁ corr. 33. unus autem] una, K₁. conuers × × ione (at ut mid. eras.), B. diuinitates, K*₂; —is, K₂ corr. in carne . . . Deo, A B C D E F G₂ H L₁, ₃ M₁, ₂ P₁, ₃,₄ (carnæ, Q) R S T V Fort. Or₁ Paris; carne . . . diuinitate, Tr.; carnem . . . Deum, G₁ K₂ L₂ Or₂ Bou. Orl.; carnem . . . Deu × (m eras.), G₃ U₁ (Deo, U₁ corr.); carne . . . Deum, K₁ W Bou₂ Stav.; carne × (m eras.) . . . Deum, G₄; carnem . . . Deo, Y. adsumptione, B E F H K₁,₂ N P₃ corr. T Stav.;—ni, P₃*;—nem; U*₁, ₂; adsumtione, L₂; adsuptione, P₁; adsumpsione, Paris. humanitatis] h eras. P₃; a, 1° supra lin. B. 34. unitatis, P₃. persone, K₁ L₂ N P₃, ₄ U₂. 35. rationabilis, B M₁ Tr.; racionabilis, Paris. om. hunc uers, A. 36. saluta, V. salutem nostram, K₁ L₂. >pro sal. n. passus est, Or₂. discondit, B M₂ N U₁; descendet, P₃. ad inferna, A W Fort. Or. Stav.] ad infernum, Tr. Paris; ad inferos, B (—nos, C) D E F G₁, ₂, ₃, ₄ H K₁ K₂ L₁, ₃ M₂ N P₁, ₃, ₄ Q R S T U₁, ₂ V Y Bou. Orl. Tol.; inferus, L₂. resurrexit] surrexit, B K₁ P₃ U₂ Fort. Tr. Bou₂. re—ras. supra lin. U₂; pr. tertia die, E (cum lin. G₄) H K₂ L₁ Q corr. R S corr. T (supra lin. sec man. W) Or. Bou. Orl.; pr. die tertia, A Tr.; pr. et, M₁ (ascendit ad inferos et resurrexit in cælos, M₁). cuelos, F. sedit, B E H P₁, ₃, ₄ T U₁. ad] a, P₁. dexteram] + Dei, D E F G₁, ₂, ₃, ₄ H K₁, ₂ L₃ M₂ N P₁, ₃, ₄ Q R S T U₁ corr. U₂ Y W Orl. Stav. Patris] + omnipotentis, C D E F G₁, ₂, ₃, ₄ H K₁, ₂ L₁, ₃ M₂ N P₁, ₃, ₄ Q R S T U₂ W Y

TEXT OF THE "QUICUNQUE"

Orl. Stav.; omnipotentis. Inde ... mortuos, *in marg.* U_1 *corr.* 37. uenturus] + est, H K_1. et] ac, B K_1. 38. ad] A, K_1; ad ... et] *om.* a ... e, F. > habent resurgere (D) omnes homines, M_1; resurgere\\(nt *cras?*) habent, *supra lin.* R. cum] in, A B. racionem, M_2. 39. *om.* Et, N P_4. Et procedunt qui bona fecerunt in resurrectionem uitæ, U_2. ægerunt hibunt, U_1. uitam æt.]+ fecerunt in res. uitæ, P_3. æternam, a *eras bis* L_1. qui, 2°] *pr.* et, D E F H N P_4 T (*supra lin.* U_1) (K *sec. man.* W) Paris; *pr.* nam, M_1; qui uero m. *sec. man. ut uid.* Q. uero] autem, K_1. *om.* uero, A B E F M_1 N P_1, $_4$ T, Paris; uọrọ, U_1. mala] + egerunt, Or. eternum, K_1. 40. Hæc] *pr.* hẹc eras. K_1; a *eras.* L_1. est] + ergo, K_1. fides] + fides, P_3. chatolica, P_3 U_2. quisque] quis, M_1. fidiliter hac, U_1. firmiterquæ, P_3; *om.* que, G_3. crediderit] credederit, U_1 (?); + atque scruauerit, G_2. poterrit, L_2.

The paraphrases in A and the Paris Commentary are not included in this apparatus. See above, p. 157. I have used Swainson's collations of the following MSS. C V Y, and they are not represented in their completeness.

A NEW TRANSLATION OF THE ATHANASIAN CREED

[1] Whosoever willeth to be in a state of salvation, before all things it is necessary that he hold the Catholic Faith, [2] which *Faith* except everyone shall have kept whole and undefiled without doubt he will perish eternally.

[1] S. John vii. 17. Heb. xi. 6. S. Mark xvi. 16.
[2] 2 Thess. ii. 10-12. 2 Pet. ii. 21.

I. i. (*a*) [3] Now the Catholic Faith is this that we worship One God in Trinity and Trinity in Unity, [4] neither confounding the Persons nor dividing the substance. [5] For there is one Person of the Father, another of the Son, another of the Holy Ghost. [6] But the Godhead of the Father, of the Son, and of the Holy Ghost, is One, the Glory equal, the Majesty co-eternal.

Divine Personality is Triune.

[3] S. Mark xii. 29. S. Matt. xxviii. 19.
[4] (*a*) S. John xiv. 16, 17. (*b*) S. John x. 30. (*c*) Acts v. 3, 4, 9.
[6] (*a*) Ex. iii. 14. (*b*) S. John viii. 58. (*c*) 1 Pet. iv. 14.

(*b*) [7] Such as the Father is, such is the Son, and such is the Holy Ghost; [8] the Father uncreate, the Son uncreate, and the Holy Ghost uncreate; [9] the Father infinite, the Son infinite, and the Holy Ghost infinite; [10] the Father eternal, the Son eternal, and the Holy Ghost eternal. [11] And yet *they are* not three eternals but one eternal, [12] as also *they are* not three infinites, nor three uncreated, but one uncreated, and one infinite. [13] So, likewise, the Father is almighty, the Son almighty, and the Holy Ghost

Attributes of the Godhead expressed in subsidiary antitheses.

[8] Gen. i. 1. S. John i. 1. Gen. i. 2.
[9] Ps. cxxxix. 7. Jer. xxiii. 24.
[10] Ps. xc. 2. Col. i. 17. Heb. ix. 14, iii. 8.
[12] Isa. lvii. 15.
[13] Rev. xxi. 22. S. John v. 19. S. Luke i. 35.

almighty; ¹⁴ and yet *they are* not three almighties but one almighty.

^(c) ¹⁵ So the Father is God, the Son God, and the Holy Ghost God; ¹⁶ and yet *they are* not three Gods but one God. ¹⁷ So the Father is Lord, the Son Lord, and the Holy Ghost Lord; ¹⁸ and yet *they are* not three Lords but one Lord. ¹⁹ For like as we are compelled by Christian truth to acknowledge every Person by Himself to be both God and Lord; so are we forbidden by the Catholic Religion to say, *there be* three Gods or three Lords.

¹⁵ (a) S. John vi. 27. (b) S. John i. 1, xx. 28. Acts xx. 28. Rom. ix. 5. (c) S. John iii. 6; cf. 1 John v. 4. 1 Cor. iii. 16, vi. 19.
¹⁷ (a) S. Matt. xi. 25. (b) 1 Tim. vi. 15; cf. Acts x. 36. (c) 2 Cor. iii. 17.
¹⁸ Deut. vi. 4.

in which Christian Truth acknowledges the Trinity.

ii. ²⁰ The Father is made of none, neither created nor begotten. ²¹ The Son is of the Father alone, not made nor created but begotten. ²² The Holy Ghost is of the Father and the Son, not made nor created nor begotten but proceeding. ²³ So there is one Father not three Fathers, one Son not three Sons, one Holy Ghost not three Holy Ghosts. ²⁴ And in this Trinity there is nothing afore or after, nothing greater or less, but the whole three Persons are co-eternal together and coequal.

²⁰ S. John v. 26.
²¹ S. John i. 14; cf. i. 18, iii. 16, 18.
Heb. i. 5, 6, 8, 10.
²² S. John xv. 26; cf. xvi. 7, 14, 15, xx. 22. 1 Cor. xii. 4–6. Eph. iv. 4–6.

Divine Relationships in scriptural terms are unique, coeternal, coequal.

²⁵ So that in all things, as is aforesaid, the Trinity in Unity and the Unity in Trinity is to be worshipped. ²⁶ He therefore who willeth to be in a state of salvation, let him thus think of the Trinity.

²⁶ S. John iii. 33–36.

II. ²⁷ But it is necessary to eternal salvation that he also believe faithfully the Incarnation of our Lord Jesus Christ. ²⁸ The right Faith therefore is that we believe and confess that our Lord Jesus Christ, the Son of God, is God and Man.

²⁷ 1 Tim. iii. 16. 1 John iv. 2, 3.
²⁸ S. John xiv. 2.

The Incarnation. We confess that Christ

i. ²⁹ He is God of the substance of the Father begotten before the worlds, and He is Man of the substance of His Mother born in the world; ³⁰ perfect God, perfect Man of a reasoning soul and human flesh subsisting; ³¹ equal to the Father as touching *His* Godhead, inferior to the Father as touching *His* Manhood.

²⁹ Gal. iv. 4.
³⁰ (1) Col. i. 15; cf. Heb. i. 3. (2) S. Luke ii. 52. S. John xiii. 1. S. Mark iii. 5. Heb. ii. 14, 16 f.
³¹ (1) S. John x. 30; cf. S. John v. 18. (2) S. John xiv. 28.

in Two Natures

ii. ³² Who although He be God and Man yet He is not two but one Christ; ³³ one however not by conversion of the Godhead in the flesh, but by taking of

³² 1 Tim. ii. 5; cf. Cor. viii. 6.
³³ Phil. ii. 6 ff.

is One Person

the Manhood in God; [34] one altogether not by confusion of Substance but by unity of Person. [35] For as the reasoning soul and flesh is one man, so God and Man is one Christ.

iii. [36] Who suffered for our salvation, descended into hell, rose again from the dead, ascended into heaven, sitteth at the right hand of the Father, [37] from whence He shall come to judge the quick and the dead. [38] At whose coming all men shall rise again with their bodies and shall give account for their own works. [39] And they who have done good shall go into life eternal, and they who indeed *have done* evil into eternal fire.

[40] This is the Catholic Faith, which except a man shall have believed faithfully and firmly he cannot be in a state of salvation.

The Redeemer,

The Judge.

[34] cf. Heb. i. 2 f.
[35] Gen. ii. 7. S. Matt. xvi. 15 f.
[36] Rom. iii. 24 f; cf. S. Luke xxiii. 43. 1 Pet. iii. 18 f. S. Luke xxiv. 46, 51. Acts i. 11. Rom. viii. 34. Col. iii. 1; cf. Acts vii. 56.
[37] Acts x. 42.
[38] Rom. xiv. 12. S. Matt. xvi. 27; cf. 2 Cor. v. 10.
[39] S. John v. 28 f. Heb. x. 26, 27.

CHAPTER VIII

THE APOSTLES' CREED IN THE FOURTH CENTURY

§ I. Rome. § IV. Africa.
§ II. Aquileia. § V. Spain.
§ III. Milan. § VI. Gaul.

THE path along which we may trace the growth of the ancient historic faith, dignified from the fourth century by the name of "the Apostles' Creed," now widens out considerably. Many forms demand attention, and it is difficult to compress within the limits of a single chapter all that may be said about them. A line of cleavage begins from the middle of the century between Eastern and Western forms. The Eastern Churches began to adapt their forms of Baptismal Creed, as we have seen in the case of our Nicene Creed, by the insertion of Nicene terms. Eventually it obtained universal currency as the Creed of the Fathers.

Beginning with the Creeds of Rome and Aquileia, upon which Rufinus commented, we may extend our survey to the Creeds of Milan, Africa, Spain, and Gaul.

§ I. THE OLD ROMAN CREED

We must pick up again the thread of the history of the Old Roman Creed at the point where we dropped it. We discussed the text quoted in Greek by Marcellus, and in Latin by Rufinus. We were in search of a complete form from which to look back. Now we seek to reverse the process, and trace the stages by which this normal type of historic faith was enlarged.

In Rome itself the type was most carefully preserved, and remained unaltered possibly for two centuries to come. Rufinus gives two reasons for this: (i.) that no heresy had its origin there; (ii.) that the candidates for baptism were made to rehearse their creed publicly, and no alterations were allowed. The author of the *Explanatio ad initiandos* writes to the same effect: " Where faith is whole, the precepts of the apostles suffice."

We may now bring forward some corroborative evidence, gleaned from MSS. of a later date than the fourth century, which preserve the ancient text most correctly.

For the Greek text we may use the so-called Psalter of Æthelstan (B.M., Galba, A. xviii.), which was written by an Anglo-Saxon hand in Latin letters of the ninth century. Here the creed is found, with collects, a litany, the Lord's Prayer, and the Sanctus, also in Greek. It probably represents the Greek text of the Old Roman Creed brought to England by Roman missionaries. I will denote its variant readings by A, those of Marcellus by M.

For the Latin text we may use: (i.) The celebrated *Cod. Laudianus*, 35 (L), in the Bodleian Library, best known as Cod. E of the Acts of the Apostles. Of the story of its wanderings it must suffice to say that it was written most probably in Italy at the end of the sixth century, was brought to Sardinia, and thence to England, where it came into the hands of the Venerable Bede by the beginning of the eighth century.

(ii.) A MS. in the British Museum (2 A xx.), called by Kattenbusch[1] *Cod. Swainsonii* (S), of the eighth century, contains sections from the Gospels, the Lord's Prayer, and the creed, with Saxon versions, canticles, and prayers. The title, Symbol*um* Apos*tolorum*, has been added in a later hand; and in the margin the names of Jesus Christ and eleven apostles (excluding Andrew) have been assigned to the Twelve Articles.

(iii.) An interesting form has been published by Dom. Morin,[2] from a sermon in *Cod. Sessorian.* 52 (V), of the

[1] i. pp. 74 f.   [2] *Rev. Bén.*, Nov. 1897, p. 486.

eleventh or twelfth century, now in the Victor Emmanuel Library at Rome. The collection in which it is found will come under our notice again (p. 232), and was made probably in Rome. The sermon begins: "Simbolum enim in greca lingua"; and ends: "pœnas corporis et animæ."
These MSS. enable us to check the text, which may be gleaned from Rufinus (R). It is true that they are of a later date, and that they are not free from interpolations, *e.g.* *catholicam*, SV; *uitam æternam*, V. Their general agreement, however, is decisive in favour of *Deum Patrem omnipotentem*, in place of the ablatives quoted by Rufinus from the Creed of Aquileia, and implicitly suggested for that of Rome; also in favour of *et* in Art. 3, and *qui* in Art. 4.

THE OLD ROMAN CREED

I. 1. Πιστεύω εἰς Θεὸν πατέρα παντοκράτορα,

II. 2. Καὶ εἰς Χριστὸν Ἰησοῦν, τὸν υἱὸν αὐτοῦ τὸν μονογενῆ τὸν κύριον ἡμῶν,

3. τὸν γεννηθέντα ἐκ πνεύματος ἁγίου καὶ Μαρίας τῆς παρθένου,

4. τὸν ἐπὶ Ποντίου Πιλάτου σταυρωθέντα καὶ ταφέντα,

5. καὶ τῇ τρίτῃ ἡμέρᾳ ἀναστάντα ἐκ τῶν νεκρῶν,

6. ἀναβάντα εἰς τοὺς οὐρανοὺς

7. καὶ καθήμενον ἐν δεξιᾷ τοῦ πατρός,

8. ὅθεν ἔρχεται κρίνειν ζῶντας καὶ νεκρούς.

III. 9. Καὶ εἰς τὸ ἅγιον πνεῦμα,
10. ἁγίαν ἐκκλησίαν,
11. ἄφεσιν ἁμαρτιῶν,
12. σαρκὸς ἀνάστασιν.

I. 1. Credo in Deum Patrem omnipotentem,

II. 2. Et in Christum Jesum, Filium eius unicum, Dominum nostrum,

3. qui natus est de Spiritu Sancto et Maria uirgine,

4. qui sub Pontio Pilato crucifixus est et sepultus,

5. tertia die resurrexit a mortuis,

6. ascendit in cœlos,

7. sedet ad dexteram Patris,

8. unde uenturus est indicare uiuos et mortuos.

III. 9. Et in Spiritum Sanctum,
10. sanctam ecclesiam,
11. remissionem peccatorum,
12. carnis resurrectionem.

---

1. *om.* πατέρα, M.
2. τὸν υἱὸν] *om.* τὸν, A.

1. Deo Patre omnipotente, R.
2. Christo Iesu, RL, > Ihesum Christum, SV, > unico Filio eius, R. Domino nostro, R.
3. et] ex, R.

… AQUILEIA 201

5. om. καί, A.
τῶν νεκρῶν] om. τῶν, A.

7. om. καί, A.

8. κρίνειν] κρῖναι, A.
9. τὸ ἅγιον πνεῦμα] πνεῦμα ἅγιον, A.
10. ἁγί[αν ἐκκλησίαν], A.

12. ἀνάστα[σιν], A.
+ ζωὴν αἰώνιον, M.

4. om. qui, R, > cruc. sub P. P., R.
om. est, R.

6. ad cęlos, V ; in cœlis, L.
7. sedit, S. dextera, L. Patris] pr.
Dei, S*; Dęi, S. corr.
8. inde, RV.   et] ac, S.
9. Spiritu Sancto, RL.
10. sancta ecclesia, L] + catholicam
SV.
11. remissione, L.
12. resurrectionis, L.
+ uitam æternam, V.

§ II. AQUILEIA

The creed which Rufinus quotes as the creed of his native town is distinguished by some important additions. For convenience of comparison, I will print with it the Creeds of Milan and Africa, to be discussed in succeeding sections.

The other Aquileian Creeds, printed in Hahn,[3] pp. 43 ff., cannot be used to confirm this text, since their testimony is doubtful, and they lack its chief characteristics. The first is ascribed to a patriarch Lupo of the ninth or tenth century. The second is the Creed of Venantius Fortunatus, who came from Aquileia, and ended his days as Bishop of Poitiers, at the beginning of the seventh century. In Art. 6 they both read *in cœlum*. Lupo adds, in Art. 5, uiuens;[1] in Art. 10, *catholicam*; and at the end, *et uitam æternam*. Fortunatus records the descent into hell, but in the form *ad infernum*; and in Art. 8 reads *iudicaturus*. It is quite plain that these are not forms derived from the Aquileian Creed.

The town of Aquileia was destroyed by Attila in 452, and it is possible that when it was rebuilt much that belonged to its old life was altered.[2]

Rufinus was careful to explain that the preposition *in* is reserved to distinguish belief in the Three Divine Persons from belief in created beings and mysteries. He does not

[1] Cf. the Creeds of Niceta, the Spanish Church from the sixth century, Theodulf of Orleans, and some old English translations which add *ad uitam*.
[2] Kattenbusch, i. p. 107.

AQUILEIA.	MILAN.	AFRICA.
Rufinus.	Ambrose, *Expl. ad init.* Aug. Serm. 212, 213, 214.	Aug. Serm. 215.
1. Credo in Deo Patre omnipotente *inuisibili et impassibili*;	1. Credo in Deum Patrem omnipotentem;	1. Credo in Deum Patrem omnipotentem, *uniuersorum creatorem, regem saeculorum, immortalem et inuisibilem.*
2. Et in Christo Jesu, unico Filio eius domino nostro,	2. Et in Jesum Christum Filium eius unicum dominum nostrum,	2. *Credo* et in Filium eius unicum Dominum nostrum Iesum Christum,
3. qui natus est de Spiritu Sancto *ex* uirgine Maria,	3. qui natus est de Spiritu Sancto et uirgine Maria,	3. natum de Spiritu Sancto *ex* uirgine Maria;
4. crucifixus sub Pontio Pilato et sepultus, *descendit in inferna,*	4. *passus* est sub Pontio Pilato crucifixus et sepultus,	4. qui crucifixus sub Pontio Pilato et sepultus est,
5. tertia die resurrexit a mortuis,	5. tertia die resurrexit a mortuis,	5. tertia die resurrexit a mortuis,
6. ascendit in coelos,	6. ascendit in caelum,	6. ascendit in caelum,
7. sedet ad dexteram Patris,	7. sedet ad dexteram Patris,	7. sedet ad dexteram Patris,
8. *inde* uenturus est indicare uiuos et mortuos;	8. *inde* uenturus est indicare uiuos et mortuos;	8. *inde* uenturus est indicare uiuos et mortuos.
9. Et in Spiritu Sancto,	9. Et in Spiritum Sanctum,	9. Credo et in Spiritum Sanctum,
10. sanctam ecclesiam,	10. sanctam ecclesiam,	10. remissionem peccatorum, carnis et
11. remissionem peccatorum,	11. remissionem peccatorum,	11. resurrectionem uitam aeternam
12. *huius* carnis resurrectionem.	12. carnis resurrectionem.	12. *per* sanctam ecclesiam.

seem to attach any importance to the use of the ablative case. In fact, from this time onwards ablatives and accusatives seem to have been used indifferently, and in the early Middle Ages no consciousness seemed to remain of any difference of case. But in Latin translations of our Nicene Creed, which had *in* repeated before *unam* . . . *ecclesiam*, the distinction required by Rufinus was kept up by the use of the Ablative to denote the Divine Persons.

The words *inuisibili et impassibili* were an unfortunate addition, intended to guard against Sabellianism, but made use of by the Arians to their own purpose. This objection was clearly pointed out by S. Ambrose.[1] The clause *descendit in inferna* is not found in any earlier Baptismal Creed, though it occurs in the manifestoes of three Arian Synods during this century. Rufinus calls attention to the fact that it is not in the Roman or any Eastern Creed.

SIRMIUM, 359.	NIKÉ, 359.	CONSTANTINOPLE, 360.
Καὶ εἰς τὰ καταχθόνια κατελθόντα, καὶ τὰ ἐκεῖσε οἰκονομήσαντα· ὃν πυλωροὶ ᾅδου ἰδόντες ἔφριξαν.	Καὶ ταφέντα καὶ εἰς τὰ καταχθόνια κατελθόντα· ὃν αὐτὸς ὁ ᾅδης ἐτρόμασε.	Καὶ ταφέντα καὶ εἰς τὰ καταχθόνια κατεληλυθότα· ὅντινα καὶ αὐτὸς ὁ ᾅδης ἔπτηξεν.

The first of these, the famous Dated Creed of Sirmium, was drawn up by Mark of Arethusa. It is based on the fourth Creed of Antioch, which he and a few other bishops had drawn up to take to Constans in 340. It is said to have been translated rather freely from a Latin original now lost.[2] But this has not been actually proved, and the connection with the fourth Creed of Antioch tends, on the contrary, to confirm the suggestion that it was Mark's composition. The reference to the descent into hell, coupled with the quotation of Job xxxviii. 17 (LXX. πυλωροὶ δὲ ᾅδου ἰδόντες σε ἔπτηξαν), seems to have been introduced as equivalent to "buried," which is here omitted. This is exactly in harmony with the teaching of Cyril of Jerusalem, " whose influence is

---

[1] *Explanatio ad initiandos*, quoted on p. 207 *infra*. Rufinus is careful to guard against the Arian inference.
[2] Kattenbusch, i. p. 261, n. 16; Zahn, p. 72.

seen in other features of the Sirmian ecthesis."[1] Cyril refers to the descent in several of his lectures, but in his list of ten *dogmata* it appears as subordinate to the burial, or rather as an explanation of it.[2] Thus he says (*Cat.* iv. 11): Κατῆλθεν εἰς τὰ καταχθόνια, ἵνα κἀκεῖθεν λυτρώσηται τοὺς δικαίους ; and at the beginning of the following section on the Resurrection (*ib.* 12): 'Αλλ' ὁ καταβὰς εἰς τὰ καταχθόνια πάλιν ἀνῆλθε, καὶ ὁ ταφεὶς 'Ιησοῦς πάλιν ἀνέστη τὸ τριήμερον ἀληθῶς.

Zahn suggests that the Sirmian Creed was drawn up with some reference to the Creed of the Church in that part of Pannonia, and that we may conclude that this clause has already found a place in it. It is true that Martin, Bishop of Bracara, a native of Pannonia, who came into Spain in the seventh century, had these words in his creed. But it is easy to account for them at that date as derived from a Gallican or Spanish source, and it must be remembered that they are only found in one of Caspari's three MSS. (*Cod. Toletanus*). This suggestion cannot be regarded as yet proved.

The Creeds of Niké and Constantinople are dependent upon the Dated Creed, and need not be considered apart from it. Indeed, it is doubtful whether the reference to these Synods throws any light on the history of the Aquileian Creed, in which the clause had probably stood for two centuries when Rufinus wrote. "At any rate" (says Dr. Swete), "Rufinus had lost the clue." He regards it merely as a gloss on *sepultus*: "uis tamen uerbi eadem uidetur esse in eo quod sepultus dicitur." Compared with the dramatic descriptions common in the fourth century, the clause seems severely simple ; but it is scriptural, for *descendit in infernum* (*ad infernum, ad inferna*) are old Latin and Vulgate renderings of LXX., εἰς ᾅδου κατέβη ; *e.g.* Ps. liv. (lv.) 16, and xvi. (xv.) 10, quoted by S. Peter (Acts ii. 27).[3]

It may therefore have been added in protest against docetic denials of the Lord's true death at the end of the second century, for the Church of Aquileia claimed a high antiquity, or it may have been added, without reference to

---

[1] Swete, pp. 56 f.
[2] Swete goes too far in saying that he made it "one of his ten primary *credenda.*" [3] Swete, p. 59.

false teaching, to express what reverent Christian imagination has always held, that the Lord by sharing sanctified the condition of departed souls.

One more variation in the Creed of Aquileia needs mention, *huius carnis resurrectionem*, " possibly a relic of some early struggle of the Aquileian Church with docetic Gnosticism. Rufinus interprets *huius carnis* as teaching the absolute identity of the future with the present body."[1] This was the popular teaching of the time of Jerome and the latter writings of Augustine, and it is emphasised in several creeds, *e.g.* of Phœbadius, Niceta, and others. It ministers, however, to a materialistic view which is opposed, as Origen had pointed out long before, to S. Paul's teaching; for the apostle's illustration from the growth of a seed points to continuity of life under changed and glorified conditions: " First that which is natural, and afterwards that which is spiritual."

§ III. Milan

We look instinctively to the writings of the great bishop and statesman Ambrose for information about the Creed of Milan. Caspari[2] has restored to a place among them a very interesting sermon, *Explanatio symboli ad initiandos*. It is found in three MSS., and he has analysed their mutual relations with great care. The best, in which the authorship is ascribed to Ambrose, has come from Bobbio to the Vatican (*Cod. Vat.* 5760, sæc. ix., x.). It is a copy of what might be called rough notes taken down by a hearer. The other MSS. (*Cod. Lamb.* sæc. xiii., from the monastery of Lambach, and *Cod. S. Gall.* 188, sæc. vii., viii.) depend upon a common archetype, and represent a more polished recension of the text. They ascribe the authorship to Maximus of Turin and Augustine. The claims of Maximus are easily set aside by reference to a sermon which he preached on the delivery of the creed, and which contains the Old Roman Creed.[3] Nor is the style in the least like that of Augustine, of whose sermons on the creed several specimens survive.

[1] Swete, pp. 95 f.   [2] II. 48 ; III. 196.   [3] Hahn,[3] p. 40.

On the other hand, the authorship of Ambrose is confirmed by a number of small points:—(1) The preacher argues against alterations of the text of the creed, which he affirms is identical with that of the Church in Rome: " Hoc autem est symbolum quod Romana ecclesia tenet." In a letter of Ambrose to Pope Siricius the same opinion is expressed: "Credatur symbolo Apostolorum, quod ecclesia Romana intemeratum semper custodit et seruat."[1] As a matter of fact, when we compare his creed with the Roman, the only variation of any importance[2] is the addition of the word *passus*, which is in any case implied in *crucifixus*. (2) Arianism, when the sermon was preached, was still a power to be combated. (3) The author shows acquaintance with the Creed of Aquileia, and argues that it was a mistake to add in it the words *inuisibilis et impassibilis*, because the Arians argue therefrom that the Son, on the contrary, is visible and passible. When we remember that Ambrose presided over a Council at Aquileia in 382 which deposed the Arian Bishops Palladius and Secundianus, we see at once how natural the references to Arianism and to the Aquileian Creed would be from his mouth. (4) Some of the phrases repeated in this short discourse may be proved to be favourite words of Ambrose in the anti-Arian treatises, *de Fide, de Spiritu Sancto, de Incarnationis Dominicæ Sacramento*, e.g. the use of *derogare, accipere, videre*, and *denique*.[3]

These arguments have been opposed by Kattenbusch,[4] who admits that the rhetorical style is like that of Ambrose, but thinks that it would be easy to imitate. This is true, and no doubt it was a common thing to attach the name of a great man to any anonymous writing, but the fact remains that it is the oldest text in this case which preserves the name Ambrose. The reference to Arianism as a present power which is fatal to the claims of Maximus, who wrote before and after 450, when, as Kattenbusch admits, "Arianism had long been conquered in the Church of the Roman

---

[1] *Ep.* 42.
[2] The order Iesus Christus, and the repetition of *in* before *ecclesiam* and *remissionem* (*Cod. Vat.*), might be due to copyists.
[3] Caspari, ii. pp. 82 ff. [4] i. pp. 84-91.

Empire,"[1] would seem to be equally fatal to the claims of the unknown Italian prelate of the beginning of the fifth century whom he postulates as the author. His strongest point is the assertion that the author quoted the Commentary of Rufinus. He goes so far as to say that the preacher first understood his position when he had read Rufinus, and found a creed which contained the additions to be forced upon his Church that the door might be opened to Arianism. But he at once admits in a note [2] that this may be to read too much into the words of the sermon. And it is difficult to understand how, if the author was dependent upon Rufinus, he failed to quote the written words more exactly, *e.g.* the emphatic and repeated "Constat." The passages are of interest in themselves, and I will therefore quote them in full:—

Explanatio symboli.

Sed dicis mihi, postea emerserunt hæreses. Quid ergo? uide simplicitatem, uide puritatem. Patripassiani cum emersissent, putauerunt etiam catholici in hac parte addendum *inuisibilem et impassibilem,* quasi Filius Dei uisibilis et passibilis fuerit. Si fuit uisibilis in carne, caro illa fuit uisibilis non diuinitas. Denique quid dicat audi : "Deus, Deus respice in me : quare me dereliquisti?" In passione hoc dicit; dominus noster Iesus Christus hoc secundum hominem locutus est, quasi caro dicat ad diuinitatem, "quare me dereliquisti?" Ergo esto medici fuerint maiores nostri; uoluerint addere ægritudini sanitatem ; medicina non quæritur. Ergo si medicina non fuit eo tempore necessaria, quo erat hæreticorum quorundam grauis ægritudo animorum ; et si fuit tunc temporis quærenda, nunc non est. Qua ratione? Fides integra aduersus Sa-

Rufini *Commentarius.*

His additur, *inuisibili et impassibili.* Sciendum quod duo isti sermones in Ecclesiæ Romanæ symbolo non habentur. Constat autem apud nos additos, hæreseos causa Sabellii, illius profecto quæ a nostris "Patripassiana" appellatur ; id est, quæ et Patrem ipsum uel ex Virgine natum dicit, et uisibilem factum esse, uel passum affirmat in carne. Ut ergo excluderetur talis impietas de Patre, uidentur hæc addidisse maiores, et "inuisibilem " Patrem atque "impassibilem" dixisse. Constat enim Filium non Patrem, incarnatum et ex carne natum, et ex natiuitate carnis Filium uisibilem et passibilem factum. Quantum autem spectat ad illam deitatis immortalem substantiam, quæ una ei eademque cum Patre est, ibi neque Pater, neque Filius, neque Spiritus Sanctus uisibilis aut passibilis creditur. Secundum dignationem uero carnis

---

[1] P. 86.   [2] P. 87, n. 7.

| *Explanatio symboli*—contd. | Rufini *Commentarius*—contd. |

Explanatio symboli—contd.
bellianos. Exclusi sunt Sabelliani maxime de partibus occidentis. Ex illo remedio Arriani inuenerunt sibi genus calumniæ: et quoniam symbolum Romanæ ecclesiæ nos tenemus, ideo uisibilem et passibilem Patrem omnipotentem illi æstimarent et dicerent: uides quia symbolum sic habent, ut uisibilem Filium et passibilem designarent. Quid ergo? Ubi fides integra est, sufficiunt præcepta apostolorum. Cautiones licet sacerdotum non requirantur. Quare? quia tritico immixta zizania sunt.

Sic dicite: *Filium eius unicum.* Non unicus dominus? Unus Deus est, unus et dominus: sed ne calumnientur et dicant, quia una persona; dicamus Filium etiam unicum dominum nostrum.

Rufini *Commentarius*—contd.
assumtæ Filius et uisus et passus est in carne.

Hic est ergo Christus Iesus, Filius unicus Dei, qui est et dominus noster. Unicus et ad Filium referri et ad dominum potest. Unicus est enim et uere Filius et unus dominus Iesus Christus.

It is surely impossible to prove a "literary relationship" from such parallels. In the second case, as Kattenbusch admits, the point of view is different, though both writers maintain that in the text of the creed *unicus* is to be connected with *Filius*. But the author of the *Explanatio* permits the teaching of *unicus dominus* against Sabellianism, while Rufinus connects it with the Lord's work of redemption. On the other hand, it is easy to explain how Rufinus, an admirer of Ambrose, might have quoted what had been handed down as the teaching of Ambrose, though not in the exact words.

Another authority for the Creed of Milan is Augustine, the disciple of Ambrose, who in his writings quotes two Creeds of Milan and Africa, the former in Sermons 212, 213, 214.

The authorship of 213, denied by Pearson and suspected by Heurtley, has been confirmed by Caspari's discovery of the only known MS. in the University Library at Breslau (*Cod.* I. Q. 344, sæc. xv.). The three sermons contain a creed-text practically identical with that of the *Explanatio*. It is true that in 212 the words "inuisibilem, immortalem, regem sæculorum, uisibilium et inuisibilium creatorem," follow the first article, but not in the correct order of the African Creed, as in Sermon 215, and the phrases *passus* and *in cælum* show that he is quoting the Creed of Milan.¹

From a dogmatic point of view the creed is chiefly interesting as the Baptismal Creed of Augustine. It only differs from the Roman Creed by the addition of the word *passus*, which is so plainly included in the idea of the word *crucifixus* following, that no one would regard it as a departure from the teaching there set forth. In many short Interrogative Creeds (see p. 232) *passus* is used to sum up all the teaching of the Lord's passion and burial. Possibly it came into the Milanese Creed under the influence of the writings of Irenæus, in whose Rule of Faith it had a prominent place. Once established in that form, it may, in return, have influenced the later Gallican Creed. In his researches, the Abbé Duchesne has tried to prove that the Church of Milan had considerable influence in the development of liturgical forms in Gaul. It is possible that *passus* came into the Gallican Creeds of the fourth century from the Milanese, but it is more probable the writings of Irenæus were the source in both cases.

§ IV. AFRICA

The following passages from the letters of S. Cyprian, Bishop of Carthage, c. A.D. 255, witness to the use of an African form, though only a fragment is quoted.² The varying order of articles 10–12, which was stereotyped in the later African form, may have come through the interrogatories used at baptism.³

Ep. 69. 7, *ad Magnum* : " Quodsi aliquis illud opponit ut

[1] For 213 *Cod.* Breslau has "et uirgine Maria"; cf. Bäumer, p. 63, n. 2, and *Cod. lat. Monac.*, 8826 f. 326 f.

[2] Lumby, *Hist. Creeds*,² p. 115, n. 1, remarks with reason that "we cannot suppose that Cyprian's Creed was shorter than that of his 'Master,' Tertullian," and proposes to combine the forms in restoring the Creed of Carthage (p. 28). Elsewhere, pp. 18, 115, he argues that the form as quoted is complete.

[3] Kattenbusch, i. p. 136.

dicat, eandem Novatianum legem tenere, quam catholica ecclesia teneat, eodem symbolo quo et nos baptizare, eundem nosse *Deum Patrem*, eundem *Filium Christum*, eundem *Spiritum Sanctum*, ac propter hoc usurpare eum potestatem baptizandi posse, quod uideatur in interrogatione baptismi a nobis non discrepare, sciat quisquis hoc opponendum putat, primum non esse unam nobis et schismaticis symboli legem, neque eandem interrogationem. Nam cum dicunt: *Credis in remissionem peccatorum et uitam æternam per sanctam ecclesiam?* mentiuntur in interrogatione, quando non habeant ecclesiam. Tunc deinde uoce sua ipsi confitentur, remissionem peccatorum non dari nisi per sanctam ecclesiam posse; quam non habentes ostendunt, remitti illic peccata non posse."

Ep. 70. 2, *ad Januariam*: " Sed et ipsa interrogatio, quæ fit in baptismo, testis est ueritatis. Nam cum dicimus: *Credis in uitam æternam et remissionem peccatorum per sanctam ecclesiam?* intelligimus, remissionem peccatorum non nisi in ecclesia dari."

S. Augustine's writings form a connecting link at this period between the Churches of Milan and Africa. There is some uncertainty about the form or forms of creed embedded in them. In the Sermons 212, 213, 214, which have been quoted above, he used the Creed of the Church of Milan, where he had been baptized. On the whole he seems to have kept closely to it. But there is one sermon (215) which manifestly contains an African text, and some small variations in other passages point to the influence of this African type. Surely this is what might be expected. Anyone who is familiar with two forms will find words come into his mind which do not belong to the form which he is expounding. We must keep before our minds the possibility of subsequent alteration of the text by copyists, and the strong objection which S. Augustine expresses to any writing out of the creed with ink and pen.[1] Indeed, in his book *de Fide et Symbolo*, an address originally delivered as a presbyter to the Council of Hippo Regius in 393, he says distinctly that the exact form given to the catechumens

[1] Serm. 212, see p. 281 *infra*.

is not repeated. This address was afterwards, as he tells us in his *Retractations* (i. 17), published by request. But it would be unwise to lean much on the text found in this book. Heurtley reads *unigenitum*, which is indeed found in a corresponding passage of *de Genesi ad Literam*. In this passage it is immediately explained by *unicum*, and appears to be due to the context, possibly to a reminiscence of the Nicene Creed: "Filium Dei Patris unigenitum id est unicum." In Sermon 57 there is the following definite quotation: "Filius Dei Dominus noster Iesus Christus docuit nos orationem, et cum ipse sit dominus sicut in symbolo accepistis et reddidistis filius Dei unicus tamen uoluit esse unus."

Perhaps it would be simplest to exhibit the variations in the *de Fide et Symbolo, de Genesi, Sermo ad catechumenos*, and *Enchiridion* (written within the last ten years of his life), by means of a table:

De F. et S.	De Genesi.	Serm. ad catech.	Enchir.
2. unigenitum, *i.e.* unicum.	unigenitum.	unicum.	unigenitus, *i.e.* unicus.
3. *per* Spiritum Sancto *ex* uirgine Maria.	de . . . et.	de . . . et.	de . . . et.
4. sub. P.P. crucifixus.		passus sub. P.P.	
12. carnis res.	...	res. carnis.	res. carnis.

The preposition *per* in Art. 3 is a unique use; *ex* showing an approximation to African usage like the omission of *passus*. But the fact that in none of these cases does he quote the last three articles in the African order, shows that the Milanese type was dominant in his mind.

When we come to Sermon 215, we find the African type shown by the addition of words in Art. 1 and by the altered order of the concluding articles familiar to us from the time of Cyprian.

This type may be tested by comparison with some Ps.-Augustinian sermons,[1] which, from the strong language used

[1] Ed. Hahn,³ p. 60, from Aug., ed. *Bened.* viii. 1609-1648.

against the Arians, appear to belong to the period of the Vandal persecutions at the end of the fifth century. We may also use the creed proposed by Fulgentius, Bishop of Ruspe,[1] at the beginning of the sixth century. It is preserved in a fragment of his treatise against the Arian Fabianus.

AUG. Serm. 215 (A); Ps.-AUG. Serm. (B); FULG. c. *Fab. Ar.* Frag. xxxvi. (F).

I. 1. Credo in Deum Patrem omnipotentem,
    universorum creatorem, regem sæculorum,
    immortalem et inuisibilem.
II. 2. Credo et in Filium eius unicum Dominum
    nostrum Iesum Christum,
  3. natum de Spiritu Sancto ex uirgine Maria;
  4. qui crucifixus sub Pontio Pilato et sepultus est,
  5. tertia die resurrexit a mortuis,
  6. ascendit in cælum,
  7. sedet ad dexteram Patris,
  8. inde uenturus est iudicare
    uiuos et mortuos.
III. 9. Credo et in Spiritum Sanctum,
  11. remissionem peccatorum,
  12. carnis resurrectionem et uitam æternam
  10. *per* sanctam ecclesiam.

1. Credo (*ter*)]; Credimus (*ter*), A B; sæculorum] cælorum, B. 2. *om.* et F; *om.* unicum, A B; *om.* Dominum nostrum, B; >Iesum Christum, Filium eius unicum, F. 3. Caspari, iii. p. 92, n. 174, suggests for B the readings natum ... crucifixum ... sepultum. Qui natus est, F. 4. *om.* est, B. 5. >a mortuis resurrexit, B. 6. >ascendit] assumptus, B. ad cælos,[2] A. 7. Patris] *pr.* Dei, A. 9. *om.* et F. 12. >resurrectionem carnis, A.

There are several readings in this restored African type which need explanation. Did S. Augustine himself use the plural *Credimus*, which is found in Sermon 215? His ordinary use was undoubtedly the singular, and in the

[1] Fragm. xxxvi., Hahn,[3] p. 61.
[2] *Ad cælos* and *Dei* in the following articles are plainly due to copyist's error.

repeated use of *Crede* in this sermon, where *credite* would be more natural, if it stood in the text, I find a hint of this: "Crede ergo Filium Dei crucifixum sub Pontio Pilato et sepultum."

Upon this quotation I rely also for the exclusion of *mortuus*, which has been inserted by Lumby[1] in his text of the creed extracted from this sermon. In this passage, *mortuus*, if not a copyist's addition, may be said to belong to the comment. The *insuper* introduced precludes the idea of exact quotation. Some lines below in the transition to *resurrexit* we read "crucifixus sub Pontio Pilato et sepultus est," and *mortuus* again follows in a comment. Here I have the support of Kattenbusch.[2]

Both Lumby and Heurtley add *mortuus* to the text of the creed quoted in *Sermo ad Catechumenos*. There, also, it seems to belong rather to the exposition. After the definite quotation, "passus sub Pontio Pilato," follows in the comment, "passus est, crucifixus mortuus et sepultus," the last four words being repeated.

As to the order *resurrectionem carnis*, it may be pointed out that the form of the sentence is artificial: "per ipsam remissionem ... per ipsam resurrectionem ... per ipsam uitam." This would explain the repetition of the words in that order in § 9, though it must be admitted that it would not explain the order in the *Sermo ad Catechumenos* and the *Enchiridion*.

The addition *uitam aeternam* had been in use in the African Church since the third century, and it is interesting to note how frequently S. Augustine introduces it in his comment when the Milan type of creed is before his eyes.

[1] P. 155.
[2] I. p. 137, n. 4, "Dass das Symbol nicht etwa ein 'mortuus' aufgenommen habe, darf ohne Umstand präsumiet worden."

§ V. Spain

The type of creed used at this time in Spain may be partially restored from the quotation found in the writings of Priscillian :

I. 1. (Credimus) *unum* Deum Patrem omnipotentem,
II. 2. et *unum* Dominum Iesum Christum, . . .
    3. natum *ex* Maria uirgine *ex* Spiritu Sancto, . . .
    4. *passum* sub Pontio Pilato, crucifixum . . . sepultum ;
    5. tertia die resurrexisse . .
    6. ascendisse in cælos,
    7. sedere ad dexteram *Dei* Patris *omnipotentis* . . .
    8. inde uenturum et iudic*aturum de* ui*ui*s et mortu*i*s.
    10. (Credimus) *in* sanctam ecclesiam,
III. 9. Sanctum Spiritum (baptismum salutare); . . .
    11. (Credimus) *in* remissionem peccatorum ; . . .
    12. (Credimus) *in* resurrectionem carnis.

The peculiar tenets of Priscillian are manifested in this version of the creed. His Sabellianism is shown by the position of the words Holy Spirit after the Virgin Mary, and as subordinate to the idea of Holy Church.

We gather that the Spanish Creed was almost identical with that of Milan, though it seems that *Dei* and *Patris* had already been added in Art. 7. *Iudicaturus* is confirmed by the reading of the Mozarabic Liturgy.

§ VI. Gaul

The Creed of the Church in Gaul at this period is of great importance, in view of the development of its form in the following century, when it attained almost the full form of our *Textus receptus*. It may be conjecturally restored from the writings of Phœbadius and Victricius.

i. Phœbadius (+ after 392), Bishop of Agen in the Church province of Bordeaux, was the author of a vigorous polemical treatise against the Arian Second Creed of Sirmium. He was one of the most stalwart Orthodox bishops at Ariminum in 359, and is supposed[1] to have written the formulary issued by them, which is quoted by Jerome.[2] The following extract is interesting, as it contains the earliest appearance of the phrase "conceived of the Holy Ghost." But it is not to be depended on as quoting a Gallican form of creed, since it does not contain the word "suffered," for which there is other evidence:

Credimus in unum uerum *Deum Patrem omnipotentem. Credimus in unigenitum* Dei *Filium,* qui ante omnia sæcula et ante omne principium natus est ex Deo, natum autem unigenitum solum ex solo Patre, Deum ex Deo, similem genitori suo Patri secundum scripturas, cuius natiuitatem nullus nouit nisi qui solus eum genuit Pater. Qui de cœlo descendit, *conceptus est de Spiritu Sancto, natus ex Maria uirgine, crucifixus a Pontio Pilato, tertia die resurrexit a mortuis ascendit in cœlum, sedet ad dexteram Dei Patris, uenturus iudicare uiuos et mortuos.*

A more important form of confession, also attributed to Phœbadius, subsequently obtained a wide popularity, under the title, "The Faith of the Romans." This theory of authorship was first suggested by the Benedictines of S. Maur, and has been confirmed by Kattenbusch,[3] who quotes the following words from the writing of Phœbadius, de Fide Orth. c. 8: "Quem etsi *passum* credimus et sepultum . . . tertia quoque die resurrexit . . . ascendit in cœlos . . . consedit ad dextram Patris."

The confession is found in the 50th oration of Gregory Nazianzen, where it is called *de Fide Nicæna Ruffino presbytero interprete tractatus.* Also among the writings of Vigilius of Thapsus, in the 7th Book, "On the Trinity" attributed in the Middle Ages to S. Athanasius. In this way it came to be quoted by Hincmar as "The Faith of S. Athanasius." It is also found in no less than eight collections of canons, comprising a very large number of MSS., in some of which it is divided into two parts, the second having the title of *Sermo.* The greater part was quoted in the apocryphal Acts of Liberius, which were written not later than the fifth century.[4] They are

---

[1] By the Benedictines of S. Maur, Hahn,[3] p. 208.
[2] *Dial. adv. Lucif.* c. 17.   [3] i. p. 171 ff.
[4] O. Marucchi, *Le memorie dei SS. apostoli,* p. 108, Rome, 1894. I owe this reference to Dom. G. Morin.

contained in six collections of canons, the earliest of which, that of S. Blasien, was completed in the sixth century.[1] It is also quoted in a composite document, known as the Creed of Damasus (p. 244 *infra*), and in a mixed text in which the two creeds are combined. Thus we have striking testimony to its popularity.

I am able to print a critical text from the following MSS:—

A	Paris, B.N., *Cod.* 3836 in the *Gesta Liberii* .		*s.* viii.
L	Leiden, *Cod.* xviii. 67 F	. . . .	*s.* viii., ix.
M₁	Munich, *Cod. lat.* 6330	. . . .	*s.* viii., ix.
M₂	Munich, *Cod. lat.* 14,008	. . . .	*s.* x.
P	Paris, B.N., *Cod.* 1451 .	. . . .	*s.* viii. *ex.*
Q	Paris, B.N., *Cod.* 3848 A	. . . .	*s.* viii., ix.
R	Paris, B.N., *Cod.* 2341	. . . .	*s.* x.
V	Rome, *Cod. Vatic.* 1342	. . . .	*s.* ix., x.

FIDES ROMANORUM.

Credimus in unum *Deum Patrem omnipotentem et in* unum *unigenitum Filium eius Ihesum Christum,* Deum et *Dominum* saluatorem *nostrum* et Spiritum Sanctum Deum. Non tres Deos, sed Patrem et Filium et Spiritum Sanctum unum Deum esse confitemur : non sic Deum
5 quasi solitarium, nec eundem, qui ipse sibi Pater sit, ipse et Filius, sed Patrem uerum, qui genuit Filium uerum, id est, Deus de Deo, lumen de lumine, uita ex uita, perfectum ex perfecto, totum a toto, plenum a pleno, non creatum sed genitum, non ex nihilo, sed ex Patre, unius substantiæ cum Patre. Spiritum uero Sanctum Deum,
10 non ingenitum neque genitum, non creatum nec factum, sed Patris et Filii, semper in Patre et Filio coæternum ueneramur : unum tamen Deum, quia ex uno Patre totum quod Patris est, Deus natus est Filius, et in Patre totum quod inest, totum genuit Filium. Pater Filium generans non minuit nec amisit plenitudinis suæ Deitatem.
15 Totum autem quod est Deus Pater id esse et Filium ab eo natum certissime tenentes cum Spiritu Sancto unum Deum piissime confitemur. *Credimus Ihesum Christum dominum nostrum* Dei *Filium* per quem omnia facta sunt, quæ in cælis et quæ in terra, uisibilia et inuisibilia propter nostram salutem descendisse de cælo, qui nunquam
20 desierit esse in cælo, et *natum de Spiritu Sancto ex Virgine Maria.* Uerbum caro factum non amisit quod erat, sed cœpit esse quod non erat, non demutatum sed Deum permanentem etiam hominem natum, non putatiue sed uere, non ærium sed corporeum, non phantasium sed carneum, ossa, sanguinem, sensum et animam
25 habentem. Ita uerum hominem ut uerum Deum unum eundemque uero hominem et uerum Deum intelligimus, ita ut uerum Deum

---

[1] Maassen, p. 504.

FIDES ROMANORUM 217

uerum hominem fuisse nullo modo ambigimus confitendum. Hunc eundem Ihesum Christum adimpleuisse legem et prophetas, *passum sub Pontio Pilato, crucifixum* secundum scripturas, *mortuum*
30 *et sepultum secundum scripturas tertia die a mortuis resurrexisse, adsumptum in cœlum, sedere ad dexteram Patris, inde uenturum iudicare uiuos et mortuos.* Expectamus in huius morte et sanguine mundatos *remissionem peccatorum* consecutos resuscitandos nos in his corporibus et in eadem carne, qua nunc sumus, sicut et ipse in eadem
35 carne, qua natus passus et mortuus est et resurrexit, et animas cum hac carne uel corpora nostra accepturos ab eo aut uitam æternam præmium boni meriti, aut sententiam pro peccatis æterni supplicii.

LINE 1. *om.* in, Q. *om.* patrem, L$M_{1, 2}$, PQR. *om.* in, 2° M_1PQ *corr. om.* unum, P. 2. Filium] + Dei, L. *om.* Ihesum Christum, Q. *om.* Dominum, P. Salbatorem, M_2. 3. et] + in, R. *om.* Deum, R. *om.* Non ... Sanctum, R. Non ... unum, LM_2. *om.* sed, Q. 4. *om.* Deum, 1° LM_2PR. sic] si, P. 5. *om.* quasi, P. *om.* et, P. 6. uerum, 1°] uero, L. *om.* uerum, 2° M_2, id] et, L; ut, $M_{1,2}$Q.V *hic inc.* A. Deum de Deum, A. 7. lumen] *pr.* et, A. *om.* uita ... toto, A. uitam, V. perfecto de perfectum totus a totum plenus, M_1. ex 2°] de, M_2QRV. 8. creatum] creaturam, Q. sed, 1°] set, V. 9. substantie, V_1; substancie, L. Spiritum] *pr.* et, Q. *om.* Spiritum ... 10. genitum, M_2. Deum] + nostrum, A. 10. nec] neque, A LM_1R. sed] + de patre procedentem, A M_1 (procedente, R). Patris] Patri, M_2. 11. Filii] fi *supra lin.* A. in] cum, A M_1R. quoæternum, R_1. coæt—, V. 12. Patre? V. Deus Natus, L V. 13. Filius] + est Filius, M_2. *om.* et, P. Patre] Patrem, M_1. in est] Deus est, P; dm. *supra lin.* Q. *om.* Deus, M_2. totam, P. genuit] ingenitum, M_2. filium] filio, LR_1. *pr.* in, LM_2RV. 14. non] no n *supra lin.* M_2. suę, V. 15. *om.* est, LR. *om.* Deus, L. > Deus Pater est, A$M_{1,2}$QV. id esse] idem se, M_1. ab eo] a Deo, PQ. 16. Certissime, L. tenentis, A P V; confitentes, A_1; credentes, V + una, M_1. credimus, M_2. *om.* Deum, M_2. *om.* piissime, M_2V. 17. *om.* Credimus, Q. Ihesum] *pr.* dominum, V. > Christum Ihesum, Q. 18. *om.* omnia, Q. quæ, 1°] que, L_1. *pr.* et, M_2. cęlis, V. *om.* quæ, 2° AQRV. cęlo (*bis*) V. discendisse, P_1. descendit, A Q. 19. propter] *pr.* et M_1; propter nos homines et, R. numquam, A L P R. desiit, L R. *om.* qui ... nunquam ... 20. cælo, M_2; cælum, A. ex] et, $M_{1, 2}$V. uirginem maria, M_1. > maria uirgine, M_2V. 21. caro] carne, M_2; —em, V. erat, fuerat, M_2QRV. *om.* sed ... erat, M_2V. cœpit, QR. 22. demutabile, LR. sed] se, M_2. Deum] qm̄, V.; *om.* Deum. Q. ętiam,V. 23. putatinum, A_1; potaui, L; putatiuę, Q; potatiue, R. uere] uiri, L. ærium] ęreum, A LM_1; ereum, M_2; hereum, R_1; ereum,V. 24. phantasenm, A_1; fantasia, V_1; fantasiam, L; —ium, M_1QR; fatasiam, P. carneum] carnium, L; carnem, M_2V. *om.* et, Q. 25. Ita] Iterum, M_2. *om.* hominem ut uerum, LR. *om.* unum ... Deum, 1° M_2V. 26. uero] uerum, A L. *om.* et ... hominem, A. intellegimus, L$M_{1, 2}$. —amus, Q. ut] et, M_2. *om.* ut, LQ. 27. uerum] *pr.* et, M_1. modo] nodo, P. ambigamus, P; —emus, R; ambiguimus, M_2. confiteudum] confitendo, L. hunc] nunc, M_2V. 28. eundem] + que, M_1P. Ihesum] *pr.* dominum, A$M_{1, 2}$QRV. *pr.* nostrum, QR. adimplesse, A R V, adimples se, Q; adimplesset, M_2; adimplisse, P. legem] leges V; legimus. et] uel, A. passus, M_2V. 29. crucefixum, A. *om.* secundum scripturas, R. scribturas, A. *om.* mortuum . . . 29. scripturas, A. mortuum] + esse, P. 30. *om.* sec. scripturas, M_1. tercia, L Q. resurrexit, R.; resurrexisset, M_2. 31. assumptum, Q. cęlum, M_2 V]; cœlis, A L M_1 P Q R. uenturus, L M_2. 32. uius, L. mortuus, L. spectamus] + et sæculum per ignem, A. *hic. def.* A. mortem et sanguinem emundatus, L. 33. emundatos, M_2 R + nos, L. remissione, M_2. peccatorum] + ō, V. consecutus, Q; consuetus, L; consequuturos, M_1; consec—, V. + nos, M_1. resuscitandu, L M_2; resuscitando, V. s. *cras. ut ind.* M_2. nos] *om.* uos, L. + ab eo, L $M_{1,2}$ Q V. his] is, L*. 34. corporibus] cordibus, M_2. *om.* et, L M_2. carne] caruem, M_2 R. qua] quọ, M_2. *om.* qua . . . carne, L V. eandem, Q. *om.* in eadem carne, M_2. 35. qua] qui, M_2. natus] + est, L Q. passus] *pr.* et L $M_{1,2}$ Q R V. *om.* et, 1° M_1 P. *om.* et, 2° Q. mortuos, P V. *om.* est, Q. 36. *om.* hoc, L. hanc carnem, M_2. vel] et L. *om.* accepturas, Q. accepturas, L P M_1. eo] + accepturos, M_1. aut] ad, P. ęternam, V. 37. præmium] pro premio, M_1. æterni, ęt— V] æternis, M_2. *om.* æterni, M_1. supplicii] æternam, M_1; recepturos, Q.

ii. Another confession of great interest is found in the treatise by Victricius, Bishop of Rouen (+409), *On the Praise of Saints.* He was probably by birth a Briton, and an enthusiastic missionary among the neighbouring tribes. It may be compared with the Creed of Pelagius. His quotation of the Apostles' Creed was first notified by **Kattenbusch**.[1]

We may compare the forms to be extracted from these writings, thus:

	PHŒBADIUS.	VICTRICIUS.
I. 1.	(Credimus) in Deum Patrem omnipotentem,	(Confitemur Deum Patrem
II. 2.	Et in (*unigenitum*?) Filium eius Ihesum Christum Dominum nostrum,	*Confitemur* Deum Filium)
3.	natum de Spiritu Sancto ex uirgine Maria,	(de) Maria uirgine . . .
4.	*passum* sub Pontio Pilato (*mortuum et*?) crucifixum et sepultum;	*passus* est, crucifixus, sepultus;
5.	tertia die resurrexisse,	tertia die resurrexit a mortuis,
6.	*adsumptum* in cœlum,	ascendit in cœlum,
7.	sedere ad dexteram Patris,	sedet ad dexteram *Dei* Patris,
8.	inde uenturum iudicare uiuos et mortuos	inde uenturus iudicare uiuos et mortuos;
9.	(. . . Spiritum Sanctum)	Et in Spiritu Sancto
10.		
11.	remissionem peccatorum	
12.	(carnis resurrectionem)	

---

[1] i. p. 174. I have quoted more of this confession on p. 130.

The net result is a creed almost identical with that of Milan. It is doubtful whether the phrase *unigenitum* of Art. 2 belonged to the underlying Baptismal Creed of Phœbadius. The influence of Nicene phraseology is apparent throughout, and would suffice to account for it. Or it may be a translation from a Greek text of the Apostles' Creed. Certainly it reappears in the Creed of Cyprian of Toulon in the sixth century. The participial accusatives (*natum*, *passum*, etc.) also look like a translation from a Greek text. In Art. 3 *ex* reminds us of the African Creed. In Art. 4 *mortuum et* is, as Kattenbusch says, uncertain. In Article 6 the reading *cœlum* is preserved by the MSS. V and M_2 only, but confirmed by the text of Victricius. The Vatican MS. alone preserves *Patrem* in the first line, which, with the evidence of Irenæus in the background, we are constrained to insert in Art. 1.

The only variations to be noticed in the Creed of Victricius are the addition of *Dei* in Art. 7 (cf. the Creed of the Orthodox at Ariminum, quoted by Jerome), and the Ablative *Spiritu Sancto*. The probable fact that Victricius was a Briton suggests that this may have been a variation adopted by the Church in Britain as in Spain (cf. the Creed of Pelagius). In any case, communications were frequent between the Gallican and British Churches. Victricius went on a mission to Britain in 393, probably of the same kind as that of Germanus and Lupus twenty years later. Their creeds were probably identical. Victricius addressed his treatise, *de Laude Sanctorum*, to S. Ambrose, and the remarkable agreement which I have pointed out between the Creeds of Phœbadius and Victricius and that of Milan offers further confirmation of the theory of the Abbé Duchesne, as to the influence of the Church of Milan in liturgical matters over the Church in Gaul.

The conclusions to be drawn from these six Western creeds are not in themselves very important. At least we have met with three of the additions to the Old Roman Creed, familiar to us in our own Baptismal Creed, the words "suffered," " descended into hell," " eternal life." Of a fourth, the word " dead," we cannot speak so confidently, though we have found it in the expositions of Phœbadius and Augustine. Without hesitation we may express our indebtedness to the Churches of Milan, Spain, and Gaul for the word, which reminds us of the moral aspect of the crucifixion of our blessed Lord, who "suffered for our sins," as He "rose again for our justification." To the Church of Aquileia belongs the merit of preserving in a creed the simple primitive teaching of the descent into hell, though we shall find reason to doubt whether this was the source from which the clause ultimately passed into our creed. The words " eternal life " had stood from the days of Cyprian in the Creed of Africa, and it may be as long in the Creed of Jerusalem. They come down to us from the days of the great persecutions, to explain the secret of the courage and the constancy with which Christians faced death. In the words of Cyril[1] : " Ours is no trifling aim ; eternal life is the object of our pursuit."

[1] *Cat.* iv. 28.

CHAPTER IX

OUR APOSTLES' CREED

§ I. Gallican Creeds in the fifth, sixth, and seventh centuries. Salvianus, Faustus, Cæsarius, Cyprian, Gregory of Tours, Eligius.
§ II. Creeds of the British Church. Pelagius, *Bangor Antiphonary*.
§ III. Roman and Italian Creeds. Turin, Ravenna, Rome.
IV. The origin of the *Textus receptus*.

THE archetype of our Apostles' Creed is usually sought in Gaul. The completed form is found in the writings of Pirminius, a Frank missionary of the eighth century; and forms which approximate to it are found in Ps.-Aug., Serm. 241, as in the so-called *Missale Gallicanum* and *Sacramentarium Gallicanum*, which were used in Gaul about that time. There seemed to be good reason for supposing that our *Textus receptus* (T) was a Gallican recension, which obtained widespread use, and was finally adopted in Rome. But a fatal objection to this view may be raised in the fact that the phrase *creatorem cœli et terræ* is not found in any purely Gallican Creed till the twelfth century.[1] There is also some new evidence that the Roman Church, while sanctioning the additional use of the Nicene Creed (C) at baptism, never really dropped the use of her old Baptismal Creed. In the following Chapter I shall endeavour to prove that R was transformed into T in Rome itself, by the gradual absorption of clauses, and that Rome was the centre from which its use spread. Some of the new clauses were distinctly of Gallican origin; there is this amount of truth in the old theory.

[1] Moreover, the Gallican Creeds generally repeat *credo* in Art. 2, and read *in* in Art. 6.

§ I. Gallican Creeds in the Fifth, Sixth, and Seventh Centuries

Salvianus supplies the following fragment: *De gub. Dei*, vi. 6: "Credo, inquis, in Deum Patrem omnipotentem et in Iesum Christum Filium eius." There is a less exact quotation in the profession of Leporius. "Nascitur . . . de Spiritu Sancto et Maria semper uirgine, Deus homo Iesus Christus Filius Dei . . . crucifixus est, mortuus, resurrexit."

Bacchiarius, whose treatise, as we have seen, was probably written in Gaul, quotes a form which may be compared with the Creed of Victricius of Rouen, though the mention of the Blessed Virgin before the Holy Spirit reminds us of Priscillian. He writes: "Natum esse de uirgine et Spiritu Sancto . . . passum et sepultum, resurrexisse a mortuis . . . ascendisse in cœlum, indeuenturum expectamus ad iudicium uiuorum et mortuorum. Carnem quoque nostræ resurrectionis fatemur integram."[1]

A more important witness of the Creed of Gaul in this century is Faustus, Bishop of Riez. In acknowledged writings we find the following: i. "Credo et in Filium Dei Iesum Christum qui conceptus est de Spiritu Sancto natus ex Maria uirgine.[2] ii. (Credo et) in Spiritum Sanctum, sanctam ecclesiam, sanctorum communionem, abremissa peccatorum, carnis resurrectionem, uitam æternam."

With these agrees fairly well the creed form embedded in the two sermons of the Eusebian collection, which have been edited by Caspari, and are now generally attributed to Faustus. But the difficulty of deciding what is part of the creed quoted from, and what is explanation, leaves one with a sense of insecurity about any argument based only on these homilies, to which I will refer as H_1 H_2.

There is a third source of information, but of a more doubtful kind, in a sermon found by Caspari in a MS. at Albi, *Cod.* 38. s. ix., and published under the title, *Tractatus s. Faustini de symbolo* (T).[3] The *in* of Faustini has been

---
[1] *Ep. ad Fratrem Græcum diaconum*, ed. Engelbrecht, p. 205.
[2] *De Spiritu Sancto*, i. 2.   [3] *A. u. N. Quellen*, 1879, p. 250.

erased, and there can be little doubt that the sermon is a compilation from the works of Faustus. The title Sanctus points to the beginning of the sixth century as the date when it was made, before the Synod of Orange (529) condemned his semi-Pelagian teaching, probably in his own diocese. Caspari was prepared to accept the evidence of this sermon without reserve, but this confidence is not shared by Engelbrecht. Here again we are dealing with a somewhat intangible argument, but it seems clear that the creed quoted in this sermon can be relied on as the Creed of the Diocese.

The differences in the Creed of the Homilies lead one to suppose that Faustus is quoting his personal creed, which was possibly British. It is remarkable for the omission of *unicum*, of *passus sub Pontio Pilato*, though this is not certain, of *mortuus* and *omnipotentis*, and for the form *abremissio peccatorum*, which occurs in the Creed of the Antiphonary of Bangor. But it lacks other marks of relationship to the latter creed.

CREED OF FAUSTUS

I. 1. Credo in Deum Patrem
    omnipotentem ;
II. 2. Credo et in Filium eius
    Domiuum nostrum   *om.* Dom. n., H_1
    Iesum Christum,   >I. C. d. n., T.
  3. qui conceptus est
    de Spiritu Sancto,
    natus ex Maria uirgine,
  4.   passus sub Pontio Pilato, T.
    crucifixus et sepultus,[1]   +mortuus H_2 (a_2), T.
  5. tertia die resurrexit,
  6. ascendit in caelum,[2]   ad caelos, H_1 H_2.
  7. sedet ad dexteram Dei
    Patris,   +omnipotentis, H_1.

---

[1] Kattenbusch reads (*qui* ?) *sub Pontio Pilato crucifixus est*. He quotes for *passus*, *mortuus*, the doubtful support of Ps.-Aug., Serm. 243, which contains quotations from Faustus.

[2] The singular, preserved by T, is remarkable (cf. Phœbadius, Victricius). The Homilies have *ad cælos* in their text, but the Second Homily has the singular *ad cælum* in the exposition.

8. inde uenturus iudicare [1]
uiuos et mortuos ;
III. 9. Credo et in Spiritum *om.* et, T.
Sanctum,
10. sanctam ecclesiam catholicam,
sanctorum communionem,
11. abremissa [2] peccatorum,
12. carnis resurrectionem uitam æternam.

We turn next to the sermon of Cæsarius of Arles (Ps.-Aug., 244), which has already come under our notice as containing quotations of the *Quicunque*. The first sentence and the latter part, which is hortatory, have been found combined with another sermon in two Paris MSS. (B. N., *lat.* 3848 B and 2123). Caspari came to the conclusion that the composite *expositio fidei* thus formed was compiled in Gaul at the end of the sixth or beginning of the seventh century. I have been fortunate enough to find three MSS. of the other sermon, with its proper beginning, *Auscultate expositionem*, but must reserve discussion of its creed-form for my chapter on "Unsolved Problems" I have also found the first sentence and hortatory part of Ps.-Aug., 244, as a *Sermo ad neophytos* in a Rouen MS. (A. 214).

I will print the whole passage containing the creed from the Benedictine edition, with the variants of *Cod. Sangallensis*, 150, sæc. ix. *in* (G) and *Cod. lat. Monacensis*, 14, 470, sæc. viii., ix. (M.):

"Credite ergo, carissimi, in Deum Patrem omnipotentem, credite et in Iesum Christum Filium eius unicum Dominum nostrum, credite eum conceptum esse de Spiritu Sancto, natum ex Maria uirgine, quæ uirgo ante partum et uirgo
5 post partum semper fuit, et absque contagione uel macula peccati perdurauit. Credite eum pro nostris peccatis passum sub Pontio Pilato, credite crucifixum, credite

---

[1] Hom. 2 (a₂) has *uenturus iudicaturus de uiuis et mortuis.* This variant is found in Priscillian. Aug. Serm. 213; Cyprian of Toulon, Venantius Fortunatus, Mozarabic Liturgy have *iudicaturus.*

[2] *Abremissa* is the reading of three MSS. of *de Spiritu Sancto,* i. 1, and must be quoted as neuter plural, cf. ii. 4: "In baptismo peccatorum abremissa donantur." In H₂ (*Cod. Madrit.*) it is used as feminine singular, followed by *abremissio* in the Commentary, which is the reading of Tr.

mortuum et sepultum, credite eum ad inferna descendisse,
diabolum obligasse, et animos sanctorum, quæ sub custodia
10 detinebantur liberasse secumque ad cælestem patriam
perduxisse. Credite eum tertia die resurrexisse et nobis
exemplum resurrectionis ostendisse. Credite eum in cælis
cum carne quam de nostro adsumpsit ascendisse. Credite
quod in dextera sedit Patris. Credite quod uenturus sit
15 iudicare uiuos et mortuos. Credite in Spiritum
Sanctum, credite sanctam ecclesiam catholicam, credite
communionem sanctorum, credite resurrectionem carnis,
credite remissionem peccatorum, credite et uitam æternam."

LINE 1. car.] *pr.* fratres, G. 2. *om.* et, G. 4. *pr.* et, B G. *om.* et u. p. p. M.
5. fuit] fidelis, G. 7. cruc.] *pr.* eum, G. 8. disc., G. 9. diabulum, M. alligasse,
G. anima, M ; +que, M. 10. detine-] ne, *supra lin. man.* 2, M. 10. eumque,
M. celestem, GM. tercia, G. *pr.* a mortuis, BG. 12. celis, G. 13. nostra, G.
14. sed // *duo litt. ras.* G. sedet, B. 17. >s. c. B. >c. r. B. 18. *om.* et, G.

Closely parallel to this Creed of Cæsarius is the following
Creed of Cyprian, Bishop of Toulon, recently recovered from a
letter [1] to Maximus, Bishop of Geneva, in which he makes a
respectful reference to Cæsarius. The whole passage is as
follows :—

"Certe symbolum, quod et tenemus et credimus, hoc
continet : Credo in Deum Patrem omnipotentem, credo et
in Iesum Christum, Filium eius unigenitum dominum nostrum—ecce explicitæ sunt personæ Patris et Filii secundum
5 deitatem. Quid uero pro redemptione nostra Filius unigenitus Deus egerit, audi quod sequitur. Qui conceptus
de Spiritu Sancto, natus ex Maria uirgine—utique sub-
audis unigenitus Deus, quia non aliam nominasti personam—passus, inquit, sub Pontio Pilato—qui utique
10 Filius unigenitus Deus — crucifixus et sepultus—qui
nihilominus unigenitus Deus—tertia die resurrexit a
mortuis ascendit in cælos, sedet ad dexteram Patris, inde
uenturus indicaturus uiuos ac mortuos—qui utique quem
superius es confessus Filius unigenitus est."

LINE 4. *Cod.* persone. 8. *Cod.* nomen—. 9. *Cod.* inquid sup. 13. *Cod.* niuis.

[1] *Monumenta Germ. Hist.*, Epp. iii., ed. W. Gundlach, from *Cod. Colon.*
212 (Darmstad. 2326), sæc. vii.

From these passages we may extract the following creeds, and say with confidence that they were used in Southern Gaul at the end of the fifth century:—

Cæsarius.	Cyprian of Toulon.
I. 1. Credo in Deum Patrem omnipotentem ;	Credo in Deum Patrem omnipotentem ;
II. 2. Credo et in Iesum Christum, filium eius unicum, Dominum nostrum,	Credo et in Iesum Christum filium eius unigenitum, Dominum nostrum,
3. conceptum de Spiritu Sancto, natum ex Maria uirgine,	qui conceptus de Spiritu Sancto, natus ex Maria uirgine,
4. passum sub Pontio Pilato, crucifixum mortuum et sepultum ; ad inferna descendit,	Passus sub Pontio Pilato, crucifixus et sepultus.
5. tertia die resurrexit,	Tertia die resurrexit a mortuis,
6. ascendit in cælis ;	ascendit in cœlos,
7. sedit in dextera Patris,	sedet ad dexteram Patris,
8. inde uenturus iudicare uiuos et mortuos.	inde uenturus iudicaturus uiuos ac mortuos.
9. Credo in Spiritum Sanctum,	
10. sanctam ecclesiam catholicam, communionem sanctorum,	
11. remissionem peccatorum,	
12. resurrectionam carnis et uitam æternam.	

Some years ago I attempted to combine the evidence of these creeds with the Creed of Faustus and others, and so reconstruct the average Gallican Creed of the fifth century.[1] The result was a purely artificial form, and was criticised as such by Morin.[2] But he admitted that the threefold repetition of *credo* was proved to be common Gallican usage. This adds to the artistic character of the form and improves the rhythm. Faustus gives us a hint that this was considered when he speaks of *symboli salutare carmen*, or *perfectio symboli*.[3] My object might just as well be gained by quoting the Creed of Cæsarius alone, to prove that nearly the whole

---

[1] Art. in *Guardian* of 13th March 1895. [2] *Rev. Bén.*, 1895, p. 199.
[3] Ed. Engelbrecht, p. 102 f.

of our *Textus receptus* was current in Gaul at the end of the fifth century.

Our next witness, Gregory of Tours (+594), does not add much to our knowledge in the following sentences, which he incorporates in the prologue to his History: "Credo in Deum Patrem omnipotentem. Credo in Iesum Christum Filium eius unicum, dominum *Deum* nostrum. . . . Credo eum die tertia resurrexisse . . . ascendisse in cœlos, sedere ad dexteram Patris, uenturum ac iudicaturum uiuos et mortuos. Credo Sanctum Spiritum a Patre et Filio processisse." But the mention of the procession from the Son is interesting, and the participle *iudicaturus* agrees with the Creed of Cyprian.

Much the same creed was used by Eligius of Noyon (+659) in his *de Rectitudine Catholicæ Conversationis Tractatus*. I will quote the passage from *Cod. lat. Monacensis*, 6430, sæc. ix., which gives a slightly different and probably purer form of text:—

FOL. 57. " Promisistis e contra credere uos Deum Patrem omnipotentem et in Ihesum Christum Filium eius unicum Dominum nostrum, conceptum de Spiritu Sancto ex Maria uirgine, passum sub Pontio Pilato, tertia die resurrexisse a mortuis, ascendisse in cælis. Promisistis deinde credere uos et in Spiritum Sanctum sanctam ecclesiam catholicam, remissionem peccatorum, carnis resurrectionem et uitam æternam."

The form is plainly shortened, not imperfect, since it would be inconceivable that this preacher on the Last Judgment did not confess Christ as Judge in his creed.

Exactly the same form is contained in the sermon following, which I cannot trace to any author. It begins (f. 59 r.): " Rogo uos et admoneo fratres carissimi ut diem iudicii semper pertimescatis. . . ."

§ II. Creeds of the British Church.

The Creed of the heretic Pelagius contains the following:—

I. 1. Credimus in Deum Patrem, omnipotentem cunctorum uisibilium et inuisibilium conditorem.
II. 2. Credimus et in Dominum nostrum Iesum Christum . . . (unigenitum et uerum Dei) Filium . . .
3.
4. passus est . . . mortuus est
5. . . . resurrexit tertia die,
6. ascendit in cœlum,
7. sedet ad dexteram Dei Patris . . .
8. uenturus est . . . ad iudicium uiuorum mortuorum.
9. Credimus et in Spiritum Sanctum;[1]
10.
11.
12. resurrectionem carnis.

This form is to be compared with the creed in the *Bangor Antiphonary*, which preserves the creed of the Irish Church in the seventh century:

I. 1. Credo in Deum Patrem omnipotentem, inuisibilem omnium creaturarum uisibilium et inuisibilium conditorem.
II. 2. Credo in Iesum Christum, Filium eius unicum Dominum nostrum, Deum omnipotentem,
3. conceptum de Spiritu Sancto, natum de Maria uirgine,
4. passum sub Pontio Pilato,[2] qui crucifixus et sepultus descendit ad inferos,

---

[1] I have transferred these words from their place following the confession of the Son.   [2] *Cod.* Pylato.

5. tertia die resurrexit a mortuis,
6. ascendit in cœlis,
7. seditque ad dexteram Dei
   Patris omnipotentis,
8. exinde uenturus iudicare
   uiuos ac mortuos.
III. 9. Credo et in Spiritum Sanctum,
   Deum omnipotentem, unam
   habentem substantiam cum
   Patre et Filio;
10. sanctam esse ecclesiam [1]
    catholicam,
11. abremissa [2] peccatorum,
(10). sanctorum communionem,[3]
12. carnis resurrectionem.
    Credo uitam post mortem et
    uitam æternam in gloria Christi.

The repetition of *Deum omnipotentem* and the emphatic assertion of the one substance of the Deity are marks of teaching which was current in Gaul from the fifth century. This is shown in a crystallised form in the *Quicunque*. Its influence on the Irish Church is easy to explain, since S. Patrick had visited Lerins. The creed seems to be Gallican, omitting *creatorem cœli et terræ*, the place of which is supplied from the Nicene Creed or from Cassian.[4] But there are several peculiarities for which it is less easy to account: *de Maria*, cf. Victricius, *Gall. Miss.* A, *Gall Sacr.* C, etc.; *ad inferos*, cf. Lambeth, 427, Bratke's Berne MS.

It is most closely related to the sermon, *Auscultate expositionem* (p. 243), which appears to be Gallican of the fifth century. I therefore agree with Hahn [3] (p. 85, n. 222) that it is neither founded on the *Textus receptus* nor an independent recension of the Old Roman Creed. But I do not think that it is possible at present to prove anything more.

[1] Æcclesiam. [2] Abremisa. [3] Commonionem.
[4] Hahn,[3] p. 84, n. 207, compares the so-called Creed of Palmatius found in *Martyrium Sancti Calixti Papæ et Sociorum eius*, but this reference is of very doubtful value.

§ III. Roman and Italian Creeds

Before we attempt to discuss the evidence of documents containing our *Textus receptus*, it will be well to review the history of the creed in Italian Churches, especially in Rome, up to the end of the seventh century.

The Creed of Turin, found in a sermon of Maximus, who was Bishop of Turin in the middle of the fifth century, shows that the Old Roman Creed was preserved unaltered, with the exception of the order *Iesum Christum* and the reading *in cœlum*.

The sermons of Peter Chrysologus, who was Bishop of Ravenna at the same period, show an even closer adherence to the form, though there is some doubt whether *uitam æternam*, which appears in the exposition of lxi., and in the other sermons, had not crept (as we have seen happen in other cases) into the text of the creed.[1]

The lack of information on the creeds of Milan and Aquileia at this period is at once explained by the fact of their sufferings under barbarian invasion.

Of Rome there is more to say, for the letters of some of the Popes, though they do not prove that the form of creed had yet been altered, show unmistakably that the modifications, which are characteristic of T, were already valued and used. Leo's famous letter to Flavian (449), while it quotes the old type, *natus de Spiritu Sancto et Maria Uirgine*, contains the explanation, *conceptus de Spiritu Sancto*. The statement is made (c. 5): "unigenitum Filium Dei crucifixum et sepultum omnes etiam in symbolo confitemur," but the word "dead" soon follows, and the mention of the Lord's words to the penitent thief in the preceding chapter shows that Leo had also in his mind the descent into hell.

In the following century Pelagius I. wrote a letter to King Childebert I., to prove his loyalty to the old faith of the Church defined at Chalcedon. His language about the crucifixion seems to be influenced by the Nicene Creed, but it shows the same turn of thought towards a fuller expression of the central fact of our redemption: "Quem sub Pontio

[1] Hahn,³ p. 42, n. 58. *Catholicam* is certainly an interpolation.

Pilato sponte pro solute nostra passum esse carne confitemur, crucifixum carne, mortuum carne, resurrexisse tertia die. . . ."

The Creed of Gregory the Great, printed in the appendix to his letters, is extant in many MSS.,[1] and there seems to be no reason to doubt its authenticity. It begins with a confession of the Trinity, in terms like those of the *Quicunque*, and, with some phrases borrowed from the Nicene Creed, proceeds to the following : " Conceptus et natus ex Spiritu Sancto et Maria uirgine; qui naturam nostram suscepit absque peccato, et sub Pontio Pilato crucifixus est et sepultus tertia die resurrexit a mortuis, die autem quadragesimo ascendit in cælum, sedet ad dexteram patris, unde uenturus est iudicare uiuos et mortuos."

Need we hesitate to conclude that R was still in use in the Roman Church, a fact which is confirmed by the discovery of the Old Roman form (with *uitam æternam*) side by side with T, in a collection of liturgical documents made in Rome in the ninth century ? It appears to have been the form brought to England in the sixth century by Gregory's mission (see p. 243 *infra*), and it survives in several sermons, which cannot be referred to an earlier date than this, nor to any other Church.

There is some evidence to prove that the Nicene Creed had been added to it in the service of baptism. Both the Gelasian Sacramentary and the seventh *Ordo Romanus* (as printed in Migne, 78, 993) quote the Nicene Creed only in this connection. The priest asked in what language the profession of faith for the children should be made. The acolyte answered, in Latin, and sang : " Credo in unum Deum Patrem omnipotentem."

The Gelasian Sacramentary, in its present form, is clearly a compilation, which was introduced into France about the end of the seventh century.[2] It is based on a Roman liturgi-

---

[1] *E.g.* Rouen, *Cod.* 516 (O. 16), from Jumièges, sæc. xi., which I have collated with the Benedictine text given in Hahn,[3] p. 337. There is no variation.

[2] Duchesne, *Origines*, p. 123 : " Par sacramentaire gélasien il faut entendre un recueil liturgique romain."

cal collection, and has been enlarged from Gallican sources. In the service of baptism there are two creeds mentioned at the *Traditio symboli*, the Nicene (C); at the time of baptism the questions asked manifestly represent a shortened form of R.

"Interr.: Credis in Deum Patrem omnipotentem?—Resp.: Credo.—Interr.: Credis in Iesum Christum, Filium eius unicum, Dominum nostrum, natum et passum?—Resp.: Credo. —Interr.: Credis et in Spiritum Sanctum, sanctam ecclesiam, remissionem peccatorum, carnis resurrectionem?—Resp.: Credo."

Kattenbusch[1] lays stress on the marks of antiquity which distinguish the preface and concluding words that form the setting of the *Traditio symboli*, and argues that R not C was obviously the original form employed in the service. But the highest antiquity allowed to the preface would not guarantee it against interpolation, and the question is simply this, To what extent was the use of the interpolated creed (C) carried on?

It was too readily assumed that this was the only form used, and the conclusion was drawn that it had been substituted for the old creed, to meet the constant pressure of Gothic Arianism during the reign of Odoacer, 476-493.[2] Bäumer indeed pointed out a discrepancy, in the fact that the creed was said to have been sung *dicit symbolum decantando*, whereas Leo III. wrote to Charles the Great that the Nicene Creed was not sung in Rome. But he was unable to explain the problem except by suggesting that some enlarged form of the Apostles' Creed, like the *Bangor Antiphonary*, might have been used.[3]

The mystery has now been cleared up by Morin's publication[4] of another text of the seventh *Ordo Romanus* from *Cod. Sessorianus* 52, sæc. xi., xii. This interesting MS. comes from the Abbey of Nonantula, and is now in the Victor Emmanuel library at Rome. The collection in which the *Ordo* is found comprises fol. 104–177°, and includes solemn acclamations for use on festivals characteristic of the Carlovingian epoch, and containing the names of a Pope Nicholas

[1] ii. p. 20.   [2] Caspari, ii. 114.   [3] P. 46.   [4] *Rev. Bén.*, 1897, p. 481.

and an Emperor Louis. These must be Nicholas I. (858–867) and Louis II. (855–875). We may therefore assume with some confidence that the collection was made in the ninth century.

Now in this text of the Ordo it is the *Textus receptus* which the acolyte sings at the baptism of an infant. On the other hand, in the account of the *redditio symboli* on Thursday in Holy Week it is the form, *Credo in unum deum Patrem omnipotentem*, etc., which the priest recites over the catechumens. The custom of the recitation of the Nicene Creed on that day is an evident importation from the East, but we see clearly that it did not involve the disuse of the Old Roman Creed transformed into our Apostles' Creed. We cannot on this evidence alone argue that the completed form was found in Rome before the ninth century, when the collection was made.

§ IV. The Origin of T

It remains to pass in review the earliest documents in which T is found. We may begin with the Psalter of Pope Gregory in the library of Corpus Christi College, Cambridge (N. 468). The MS. is of the fifteenth century, and was probably written in England. But there seems no reason to doubt the evidence of the title, *Psalterium Latinum et Græcum, Papæ Gregorii*, which implies that the archetype came from Rome. Caspari's judgment on a point of this kind is always weighty, and he decided to refer it to Pope Gregory III. (731–741).[1] The text of the creed only varies from T by the omission of *est* in Art. 8 and *et* in Art. 12. This would be an insecure foundation for a theory by itself, but it may be supported by a number of small details.

It is usual to quote Pirminius, a celebrated Benedictine monk and missionary of the eighth century, as the first writer who quoted the modern form of the creed. But no sufficient answer has been given to the question, How did it come to him? He belonged to the kingdom of Neustria,

[1] iii. pp. 11, 215.

and came into Southern Germany c. 720, where he founded the Abbey of Reichenau, and many others. His creed is found in an interesting treatise called *Dicta Abbatis Pirminii de singulis libris canonicis scarapsus*,[1] carefully edited by Caspari.[2] There is an interesting detail in it which seems to have escaped notice. Pirminius speaks of the delivery of the creed to the catechumens immediately after their renunciation of the devil and his works. This was a distinctly Roman custom, whereas in Gallican usage an interval elapsed before the giving of the creed.[3] This at once establishes a presumption that it was from Rome that he obtained the form of creed. His contemporary Boniface was most enthusiastic in extending the influence of the Apostolic See, and there is every reason to believe that they worked on similar lines, though the references to the creed in the epistles of Boniface [4] do not decide the question of the form used. Before the days of Boniface, the Roman liturgy had begun to exercise influence in Gaul. Duchesne [5] points out how the country had been traversed continually during the seventh century by Roman missionaries on their way to England. The mixture of Roman and Gallican rites and prayers which we find in the Gelasian Sacramentary, *Miss. Gallic.*, *Sacr. Gallic.*, is not surprising.

The so-called *Miss. Gallic.* (*Cod. Vat. Pal.* 493, sæc. viii. in.) is not a missal, but a sacramentary, and was written most probably in France. It contains, however, a large proportion of Roman elements. The ceremonies of the *Traditio symboli* follow Gallican usage. There are three forms of creed quoted, to which I will refer as A, E, B, since it is possible to distinguish a second creed (E) in the exposition of the first (A).

The *Sacr. Gallic.*, which is really a missal, is in the Bibliothèque Nationale at Paris (*Cod. lat.* 13,246, sæc. vii.). It presents a peculiar mixture of Gallican and Roman rites

---

[1] Scarapsus, from scarpsus = excarpsus, excerpt, Hahn,[3] p. 96, n. 247.
[2] *Anecdota*, p. 151.
[3] Duchesne,[2] *Origenes du Culte Chrétien*, p. 308, n. 3.
[4] *Epp.* 6. 8.   [5] *Op. cit.* p. 94.

so that it is hardly possible to decide from internal evidence where it was compiled. The MS. itself was probably copied at Bobbio, where Mabillon found it, and the archetype may have belonged to Luxeuil, "the monastic metropolis of the Italian convent."[1]

In it there are four forms of creed, which I will call A, E, B, C, distinguishing the creed of the exposition (E) from the first form quoted (A). With these documents should be compared one of the most important of the Ps.-Augustinian Sermons, No. 242. It is known to exist in many MSS.,[2] and it is a pity that it has not been critically edited. At present there are questions regarding it which cannot be answered with any certainty. It is a compilation drawn chiefly from the sermons of Faustus, in the Eusebian collection, but including quotations from Augustine, Serm. 212, and from the exposition of the first sermon in the *Sacr. Gallic.*, the latter passage containing also a reminiscence of Serm. 241.[3] It is fully reproduced in the *Miss. Gallic.*

As printed in the appendix to S. Augustine, it manifestly contains two forms of creed, the first (A) being interpolated. Kattenbusch points out that the preacher at that point only proposes to quote the first words: "Iam ad . . . symboli professionis sacramentum textumque ueniamus, quod in hunc modum incipit." The true creed of the preacher, to be extracted from the exposition, agrees with the Creed of Faustus in the threefold repetition of *credo*, and in omitting *unicum, mortuus, a mortuis*.

Of the date, it is only possible to say that it was in existence at the date of the formation of the *Miss. Gallic.*, c. 700, and was probably compiled in France. It was found in two MSS. of the Herovall Collection of Canons (Paris, 2123, 3848, B). Perhaps the most practical way of presenting the evidence in these documents will be to draw up a table of their principal variations from the normal type of T, quoting the different creeds in each case as A, B, C, and the expositions as E.

---

[1] Duchesne, *Origines*,[2] p. 151.   [2] Caspari, iv., xviii. n. 1.
[3] Kattenbusch, i. p. 210, n. 16.

AN INTRODUCTION TO THE CREEDS

	PS.-AUG. 242	MISS. GALLIC. A E	MISS. GALLIC. B	SACR. GALLIC. A E	SACR. GALLIC. BC
1.	+creatorem c. et t., A B	+creatorem c. et t., A E	+creatorem c. et t., B	+Credo, A; om. et, A	+Credo, BC; om. et, C
2.	+Credo, B	+Credo, A E	(in expos. Credo in Filium)		
3.	om. unicum, B	unigenitum sempiter-num, A E		unigenitum sempiter-num, A	
	om. Dom. nost., B (in expos. Dominus n., B)	om. Dom. nost., A E natus + est, A E de Maria, A E	ex, B	om. Dom. nost., A conceptum ... natum, A	Dom.] pr. Deum et, C
4.	om. est, A	om. est, E	om. est, B		
	om. mortuus, B (in expos. in ueritate mortuus et sepultus)				om. mortuum, B
5.	om. desc. ad inf., B	om. desc. ad. inf., E	om. desc. ad. inf, B uictor ad caelos, B		
6.	om. a mortuis, B			in E	in, B; in, C
7.	om. sed. ad d. P. o., B (in expos. in Dei Patris, B)	sedit, A; sedet, E om. Dei	sedit, B om. Dei, B	sedit, A E om. Dei, A E	
8.					
9.	Credo + et, B		Spiritu Sancto, B		+Credo, C
10.			sancta ecclesia cath., B		om. s. c., C
11.		om. rem. pecc., A E	ac remissionem, B	om. sanctorum com., E	pr. per baptismum sanctum, C
12.	huius carnis, A; carnis h., B			uitam habere, post mortem in gloria Christi resurgere, B	uitam pr. in, C

The other creed forms from Ps.-Augustinian Sermons, 240, 241, joined with this by Hahn[3], p. 50, cannot be the work of the same pen. He suggests that they belong to Italy, but does not give any reasons. Having rightly pointed out the objections raised above (p. 221), that no pure Gallican Creed contains *Creatorem cœli et terræ* till the twelfth century, he founds on these sermons a theory that T had its origin in North Italy. It seems to me useless to speculate about their origin till we find some further clue. They deserve to be critically edited from new MSS., paying regard to the sources of the collections in which they are found.

I may add here a short section on the evidence, so far as it goes, of the various lists of apostles' names attached to particular clauses of the creed, whether R or T. It is difficult to arrange it clearly, but the following may suffice:—

I. *Sermons founded on R.*—I have come across two sermons in which the clauses of R are assigned to apostles, following the order of Matt. x. 2–4, *Cod. Sangallensis*, 40, sæc. viii., ix. and *Cod. Vat. Pal.* 220.[1] I will print all the

SÆC. VIII., IX. *Cod. Sangallensis*, 40	SÆC. IX., *Cod. Vat. Pal.* 220	SÆC. XI. XII. *Cod. Sessorian*, 52 B	SÆC. X. *Cod. Vésoul*, 73
1.			+creatorem c. et., t.
2. om. Filium eius	>I. C.	>I. C.	>I. C.
3. et] ex			qui conc. est de S.S. natus ex
4. om. est	>cruc. et sep. est		Passus sub P. P. cruc. mortuus
5.	>res·t.d.a mort.		
6. celum	uictor ad cælos	ad celos	uictor ad cælos
7. +Dei +omnipotentis			+Dei +omnipotentis
8. Inde om. est	Inde	Inde om. est	Inde om. est
9.		+catholicam	+catholicam
10.			+ sanct. com.
11.			
12.	+uitam futuri sæculi	+uit. æt.	+uit. æt.

[1] Another MS. is found in *Cod. Vat. Pal.* 212, sæc. ix., x.

variations from the pure text of R, given p. 200 *supra*, in a table. Another sermon, which is partly dependent on *Sangallensis*, 40, is found in *Cod. Sessorian* (B). Another version of it with many phrases of T is in *Cod. Vésoul*, 73,[1] but without names of apostles.

II. *Sermons founded on T.*—Some of the sermons containing T follow the order given in Acts i. 13, with two slight variations, *i.e.*, John James for James John, and Matthias for Judas Iscariot. These are Ps.-Aug. 241, the sermon of Pirminius (though this by an obvious error repeats Thomas for Matthias), and the third sermon in *Sacr. Gallic* (C).

The first sermon in *Cod. Sessorian*, 52 (A) follows the order of the Roman Canon, the names being added in the margin. In this case it is impossible to say whether they belonged to the original sermon before it was copied into this collection. Two other sermons, *Cod. Augiensis*, ccxxix. (Karlsruhe) of the year 821, and Ps.-Aug. 240, omit S. Paul's name after S. Peter's, and add Matthias at the end. It is true that the Karlsruhe MS. also omits Simon the Cananæan, but a blank space proves that this was an oversight.

MATT. x. 2.	ACTS i. 13.	ROMAN CANON.
Cod. Sangallensis, 40	Ps.-Aug. 241	(1) *Cod. Sessorian*, 52 (A)
Cod. Vat. Pal. 220	Pirminius	(2) *Cod. Augiensis*, ccxxix.
Cod. Sessorian 52 (B)	*Sacr. Gallic.* (C)	(3) Ps.-Aug. 240
Peter	Peter	Peter
Andrew	John	(1) Paul or (2)(3) Andrew
James	James [2]	Andrew
4 John	Andrew	James
Philip	Philip	John
Bartholomew	Thomas	Thomas
Thomas	Bartholomew	James
8 Matthew	Matthew	Philip
James of Alphæus	James of Alphæus	Bartholomew
Thaddæus	Simon Zelotes	Matthew
Simon the Cananæan	Judas of James	Simon (1) the Cananæan
12 Matthias	Matthias [3]	Thaddæus
		(2) (3) Matthias

---

[1] Cf. also *Cod. Sangallensis*, 732, sæc. ix.   [2] Order in R.V., A.V.—James, John.
[3] Pirminius repeats Thomas.

THE ORIGIN OF T   239

I do not think that these lists lead to any certain conclusion at the present time. But I am confident that future research on these lines will throw light on the origin of the Ps.-Augustinian sermons, which are so puzzling an element in the problem. At least the comparison shows up, so to speak, in a clearer light the important evidence of the two sermons in *Cod. Sessorian*, 52, in which a text of R survives almost untouched, while the sermon based on T supports the evidence of the order of baptism.

For the present we must fall back on the hypothesis with which we began this chapter, that the Old Roman Creed was revised in Rome itself before 700. All the details which have been brought forward converge upon this conclusion. The Psalter of Gregory III., the witness of Pirminius, as an exponent of Roman customs, the similar witness of the *Miss. Gallic.* and *Sacr. Gallic.*, the short Creed of the Gelasian Sacramentary—above all, the new evidence of *Cod. Sessorian*, 52, proving that R had been used consecutively though the Nicene Creed was used. It is impossible to believe that the Church, which in the ninth century refused to insert the *Filioque* in N to please an emperor, should during that very period have accepted from outside a brand new recension. All analogy points to a process of gradual growth.

Everyone of the additions made had stood the test of time, and was recommended by the usage of teachers held in honour at Rome. The phrases *passum, mortuum, catholicam, sanctorum communionem, et uitam æternam* were found combined in the Creeds of Niceta[1] (see p. 252) and Cæsarius, who visited Rome, and were received with distinction. Niceta's sermon may also be the source from which *Creatorem cœli et terræ* was taken, though it is perhaps more probable that it was taken from the Nicene Creed. Cæsarius has both the remaining phrases, *conceptus* and *descendit ad inferna*.

Kattenbusch suggests that T is not, as a matter of fact, the richest or most circumstantial (*weitläufigste*) form.[2] He quotes " *Deum et Dominum*, resurrexit *uiuus*, omnium pecca-

[1] For my present quotation it does not matter whether Niceta was a Gallican or a Dacian Bishop.   [2] i. p. 196.

torum" from the Spanish Creeds, "*ascendit uictor*" from *Miss. Gallic.* (and elsewhere), "*per baptismum* remissionem" from *Sacr. Gallic.*, the peculiarities of the form in the *Bangor Antiphonary*, and "*huius* carnis" from the creed of Aquileia, as specimens of phrases by which T might have been enriched, had it included everything in the way of rhetorical embellishment. But this is a matter of opinion. We may well rest content with the form which has survived, and with the conclusion that the present Baptismal Creed of Western Christendom is not the effect of chance causes combining to thrust an obscure provincial creed into the place once occupied by the venerable archetype of many varied forms. Our Apostles' Creed is the Old Roman Creed of the second century, sanctified by continuous usage of eighteen hundred years in its Mother Church, like a precious jewel which in the new generation has been recut and polished, that it may reflect new beauties of incommunicable light.

OUR APOSTLES' CREED [1]

Nicene Creed
Niceta (?)
1. Credo in Deum Patrem omnipotentem, *creatorem cœli et terræ*.
2. Et in Iesum Christum Filium eius unicum dominum nostrum,

Phœbadius (?)
Cæsarius
3. qui *conceptus* est de Spiritu Sancto natus ex Maria uirgine,

Milan, Phœbadius
Cæsarius
Aquileia
4. *passus* sub Pontio Pilato, crucifixus *mortuus* et sepultus *descendit ad inferna*,
5. tertia die resurrexit a mortuis,

Augustine
6. ascendit *ad* cœlos,

Victricius, Faustus
(Priscillian)
7. sedet ad dexteram *Dei* Patris *omnipotentis*,

Cæsarius, Faustus
8. *inde* uenturus est iudicare uiuos et mortuos

Cæsarius, Faustus
9. *Credo* in Spiritum Sanctum,

Cæsarius, Faustus
10. Sanctam ecclesiam *catholicam, sanctorum communionem*,

Cæsarius, Faustus
11. remissionem peccatorum

Cæsarius, Faustus
12. carnis resurrectionem *et uitam æternam*.

---

[1] This text with slight variations of spelling is found in *Cod. Sessorian*, 52, the *Ordo Romanus* (O), the first sermon (A); in the Psalter of Gregory III. (C), and *Cod. Sangallensis*, 27 (G). Art. 4. mortuus]+est, A. ad infernum, A. Art. 8. *om.* est, A C G. Art. 12. *om.* et, A C G.

CHAPTER X

UNSOLVED PROBLEMS

§ I. Bratke's Berne MS.
§ II. The Sermon *Auscultate expositionem.*
§ III. The Creed of Damasus.
§ IV. The Rhythm of the *Te Deum* and the *Quicunque.*
§ V. The Creed of Niceta of Remesiana.

THE following chapter is designed to relieve former chapters of unwieldy sections which would hinder the progress of the argument. In each of the cases now proposed for discussion it is desirable to enter into details, which would be out of place if these creeds were introduced in their proper chronological order. And it will be convenient to take them in the reverse of such order, in order to connect the section on Niceta with the following Chapter on the *Te Deum.*

§ I. THE CREED IN BRATKE'S BERNE MS.

The following creed was published in 1895 by Professor Bratke,[1] from a MS. at Berne (*Cod. N.* 645) of the seventh or eighth century.[2] Most of the other contents are of a geographical or chronological character; *e.g.* it is preceded by the Easter cycle of Victorius of Aquitaine, and a catalogue of Church provinces made in Gaul, and it is followed by the forged Acts of a supposed Synod of Cæsarea, which were written in Britain during the controversies about the keeping of Easter in the seventh century.

[1] *Theol. Stud. u. Krit.* i. pp. 153 ff.
[2] Bratke compares the specimen of Merovingian writing in Sir E. M. Thompson's *Manual of Palæography,* p. 230.

Bratke concludes that it is a copy made in Gaul of an ancient form of Gallican Creed as it existed before 400, which was brought to England and used in the British Church in the seventh century.

Hahn [3] (p. 95, n. 237) classes it as a South German Creed, having regard to the place where the MS. is now found. There is little to be said for this view, since the whole collection in which it is found was clearly put together in England, and there is nothing else to connect it with Germany. I agree with him in calling it a mixed creed, and have printed the interpolated words in italics.

I. 1. Credo in Deo Patrem omnipotentem,
II. 2. Et in Iesum Christum Filium eius,
unicum dominum nostrum,
3. natum de Spiritu Sancto et
Maria uirgine,
4. *Passus* sub Pontio Pilato
crucefixum et sepultum,
descendit ad inferos,
5. tertia die resurrexit a mortuos,
6. ascendit ad cælos,
7. sedit ad dexteram Patris,
8. inde uenturus iudicare
uiuos ac mortuos.
III. 9. Credo in Spiritu Sancto,
10. sancta ecclesia *chatholica,*
11. remissionem peccatorum,
12. carnis resurrectionis,
in uitam æternam.

Thus the creed appears to be a recension of the Old Roman Creed, formed by adding the words *passus, descendit ad inferos, in uitam æternam.* I do not attach any importance to the ablatives *Deo, Spiritu Sancto,* etc., which remind one of the Aquileian Creed. They are unevenly distributed, and are more probably due to an illiterate copyist. If they had belonged to the original type, surely one ablative would have survived in the second Article.

SERMON "AUSCULTATE EXPOSITIONEM" 243

There are very interesting points of resemblance to the creed in *Cod. Laudianus*, which was brought into Britain before the beginning of the eighth century, and represents the normal type used by Augustine of Canterbury and other Roman missionaries.[1] It is easy to understand how such a copy of the Old Roman Creed might have been altered under the influence of creeds brought from Ireland by Celtic missionaries, such as that of the *Bangor Antiphonary*, from which might have come *passus, descendit ad inferos, uitam æternam*.

§ II. THE SERMON "AUSCULTATE EXPOSITIONEM"

The sermon *Auscultate expositionem* has been edited by Caspari and Ommanney from the Paris MSS. (B.N. *lat.* 3848 B and 2123), in which it is combined with the sermon of Cæsarius (Ps.-Aug. 244). I have found three MSS. in which it occurs alone: (i.) Bodleian Library, Oxford, *Cod. Junius* 25, from Murbach Abbey; (ii.) Munich, *Cod. lat.* 14,508, from the Abbey of S. Emmeran at Ratisbon; (iii.) Wolfenbüttel, *Cod.* 91, from the Abbey of Weissenburg, all of the ninth century. Having published the text of the whole sermon in the *Zeitschrift für Kirchengeschichte*, July 1898, I will now only quote the creed form:—

I. 1. Credo in Deum Patrem omnipotentem,
  inuisibilem, uisibilium et inuisibilium
  (omnium)[2] rerum conditorem.
II. 2. Et in Iesum Christum, Filium eius unicum,
  dominum nostrum,
  3. conceptum de Spiritu Sancto, natum
  ex Maria uirgine,
  4. crucifixum sub Pontio Pilato
  et sepultum,
  5. tertia die resurgentem ex mortuis,
  6. Victor (ascendit ad cælos),

---

[1] See p. 199 *supra*. Art. 9. sp̄u sc̄o; 10. sancta ecclesia, *om.* catholica; 12. carnis resurrectionis.
[2] The words in brackets are added by Hahn[3] from the later recension.

7. sedit in dexteram Dei Patris,
8. inde uenturus iudicare uiuos ac mortuos.
III. 9. Et in Spiritum Sanctum *Deum omnipotentem, unam habentem substantiam cum Patre et Filio,*
10. ecclesiam catholicam,
11. remissionem peccatorum,
12. *communem omnium corporum* resurrectionem *post mortem (et* uitam æternam).

This form is apparently Gallican, and of an earlier date than the Creed of Cæsarius in Ps.-Aug. Serm. 244, with which it has been associated from the sixth century. It lacks the additions *passum, mortuum, ad inferna descendisse, communionem sanctorum.* Nor does the sermon contain the characteristics of Cæsarius's style, which have been pointed out in the other. If it is still conceivable, as Morin thinks, that Cæsarius wrote it, we must suppose that he used differing forms of one creed, one belonging to his birthplace Châlons, the other to Arles, his diocese. We have no data by which to connect it with any locality. The Creed of the *Bangor Antiphonary* has the words *inuisibilem . . . conditorem* in the first Article, and the words *Deum omnipotentem unam habentem substantiam cum Patre et Filio* in the eighth. It was evidently founded on some such form, though it contains the latter additions found in the Creed of Cæsarius. *Victor ascendit ad cœlos* recurs in *Miss. Gallic. B, Cod. Vat. Pal.* 220, Ps.-Aug. Serm. 238, and a sermon in a Vésoul MS., *Cod.* 73. (see p. 238). The present participle *resurgentem* is unique, and so are *in dexteram* (cf. Fulgentius de fide ad Petrum, c. 20) and the turn of the sentence *communem omnium corporum resurrectionem post mortem.*[1]

§ III. THE CREED OF DAMASUS

The Creed of Damasus[2] in its original form is always ascribed to Jerome, and in some MSS. is called a Letter or

---

[1] Cf. the addition in Art. 12, *post mortem,* in the *Bangor Antiphonary.*
[2] It is called in Hahn,[2] "The Second Creed"; in Hahn,[3] "The First Creed," ascribed to Damasus. The change is somewhat misleading.

THE CREED OF DAMASUS

Faith addressed by him to Damasus. It is generally found in collections of creeds, and in one MS. (*Cod. Augiensis* xviii., sæc. ix., at Karlsruhe) it follows two Rules of Faith ascribed to Councils of Toledo. Its history is important in connection with the *Quicunque*, since it was quoted by the Fourth Council of Toledo in 633 with that creed.

I am able to edit the text from the following MSS. :—

G₁ *Cod. Sangallensis* 125	sæc. viii.
G₂ *Cod. Sangallensis* 159	sæc. x.
K *Cod. Augiensis* (Karlsruhe) xviii. . .	sæc. ix.
L *Cod. Leidensis* xviii. 67 F.	sæc. viii., ix.
M *Cod. Mediolan. Ambros.* O. 212 *sup.* . .	sæc. viii.
P *Cod. Paris.* B.N. 1684 [1]	sæc. xi. *ex.*

Fides Hieronimi ad Damasum Papam, G₁ ; *Epistola Hieronimi ad Papam Damasum de symbulo*, G₂ ; *Fides beati Hieronimi presbyteri ad Damasum Papam*, K ; *Exemplar fidei chatolice sancti Hieronimi presbiteri*, L ; *Hieronimi incipit fides*, M ; *(Hieronimi) de Fide apud Bethleem*, P.

THE CREED OF DAMASUS

CREDIMUS[2] IN UNUM DEUM PATREM OMNIPOTENTEM ET in unum Dominum nostrum IHESUM CHRISTUM FILIUM Dei ET in SPIRITUM SANCTUM DEUM. NON TRES DEOS SED PATREM ET FILIUM ET SPIRITUM SANCTUM UNUM Deum colimus et CONFITEMUR : NON SIC
5 UNUM DEUM QUASI SOLITARIUM, NEC EUNDEM, QUI IPSE SIBI PATER SIT, IPSE et FILIUS, SED PATREM esse QUI GENUIT, FILIUM esse qui genitus sit, SPIRITUM UERO SANCTUM, NON GENITUM NEQUE INGENITUM, NON CREATUM NEQUE FACTUM, SED de Patre procedentem, Patri et Filio COÆTERNUM et coæqualem et cooperatorem, quia
10 scriptum est : *uerbo Domini cæli firmati sunt*, id est, a Filio Dei, et *Spiritu oris eius omnis uirtus eorum*, et alibi : *Emitte Spiritum tuum et creabuntur et renouabis faciem terræ*. Ideoque in nomine Patris et Filii et Spiritus Sancti unum confitemur Deum, quia Deus nomen est potestatis non proprietatis. Proprium nomen est Patri
15 Pater, et proprium nomen est Filio Filius, et proprium nomen est Spiritui Sancto Spiritus Sanctus. In hac trinitate unum Deum credimus, quia ex uno Patre, quod est unius cum Patre naturæ uniusque substantiæ et unius potestatis. Pater Filium genuit, non uoluntate, nec necessitate, sed natura. Filius ultimo tempore ad
20 nos saluandos et ad implendas scripturas descendit a Patri, QUI NUNQUAM DESIIT ESSE cum Patre, et conceptus est de Spiritu Sancto, et NATUS EX UIRGINE, CARNEM ANIMAM ET SENSUM, hoc est perfectum

---

[1] Collated by Ommanney.
[2] The words in capitals are found in the *Fides Romanorum*.

suscepit hominem, NEC AMISIT QUOD ERAT, SED COEPIT ESSE QUOD NON
ERAT; ita tamen ut perfectus in suis sit et uerus in nostris. Nam
25 qui Deus erat homo natus est, et qui homo natus est operatur ut
Deus; et qui operatur ut Deus ut homo moritur; et qui ut homo
moritur ut Deus surgit. Qui deuicto mortis imperio cum EA CARNE
QUA NATUS ET PASSUS ET MORTUUS fuerat, RESURREXIT, ascendit ad
Patrem, sedetque ad dexteram eius in gloriam, quam semper habuit
30 habetque. IN HUIUS MORTE ET SANGUINE credimus EMUNDATOS NOS
ab eo RESUSCITANDOS die nouissima IN HAC CARNE QUA NUNC uiuimus
et habemus, consecuturos ab ipso AUT UITAM ÆTERNAM PRÆMIUM BONI
MERITI aut pœnam PRO PECCATIS ÆTERNI SUPPLICII. Hæc lege, hæc
retine, huic fidei animam tuam subiuga, a Christo Domino et uitam
35 consequeris præmia.

LINE 2. *om.* nostrum, L P. *om.* in, M. 3. *om.* Sanctum ... 4. Sanctum,
G_2. *om.* Deum, M. 5. *om.* Deum, L P. ipse, *supra lin.* G_2. 6. qui]
quem, G_1. genuit] + Filium, G_1. Filium] *pr.* et, G_2 (K, *supra lin.*). 7. sit]
est (sit, *supra lin.*), K. 8. Patre] + et Filio, G_1 L (K*). 9. coequalem, K;
quoœqualem, M. 10. scribtum, M*. celi, G_1. *om.* id ... Dei, M; a, *supra
lin.* K; *om.* a, L. 11. emittes, $G_{1, 2}$. 12. innouabis, G_1. terre, L P. 13.
quia] quod, G_2 *corr.* *om.* Deus, G_2 > nomen est potestatis Deus, K L M.
14. *om.* Proprium, L. *om.* est, $2°$ G_2. 15. proprium $1°$] proprio, L. 16.
Spiritu, P. In] *pr.* Et, K. hac] + autem, G_1. Deum] + colimus, *supra
lin.* K. 17. uno] ũo, L. naturæ] nature, G_1; natura, L_1; + est, G_2 M; ei,
K; esse, L. 18. uniusquæ substanciæ, L. genuit, *supra lin.* G_2 *corr.* *om.* et
unius, G_1. 19. uoluptate, P. 20. saluandus, L. implendos, G_1. scribturas,
M; scriptura, G_1. discendit, K* L M. 21. numquam, K M. desiuit, M. *om.*
et, G_1. *om.* est, M. 22. et, $1°$ *supra lin.* M. uirgine, *pr.* Maria, G_1 K L M.
carnem] CARNEUM, G_1* L. ANIMAM, eras G_1; *pr.* et, G_2. 23. suscipit, M.
nec] non, L. 24. nostris] + sit, G_1. 25. *om.* Deus ... (26) qui, $1°$ M.
om. est ... est, G_1 L, *hæc uerba supra lin.* K. 26. moritur] moreretur,
L *bis.* 27. surgit, G_2 P] resurgit, G_1 K L. Qui] *pr.* et, L. *om.* Qui, M.
mortis imperio] mortis, *supra lin.* K; imperio diabuli, K* M (diaboli, L).
28. *om.* et passus, M. mortuus] mortus, G_1. resurrexit] surrexit, G_1, *pr.* et,
$G_{1, 2}$ K M_1, + ter(c)ia die, K L. 29. sedit, K M; *om.* que, C_2. gloria, G_2 M.
30. huius] cuius, G_1. emundatos] e, *supra lin.* K; MUNDATOS, L M. nos]
+ esse, G_1; + et, $G_{1, 2}$. 31. ab eo] habeo, L. nouissimo, G_1. IN hac CARNE
QUA NUNC uiuimus] IN QUA NUNC uiuimus CARNE, P. 32. habemus] + spem,
G_2 *corr. supra lin.* consecuturos] + nos, G_1, *pr.* nos, G_2. *om.* ab ipso, G_2.
uitam] *pr.* ad, G_1. *om.* aut uitam æternam, G_2 K *corr.* premium, K L. 34.
om. Domino, G_2. 35. præmia] præmium, G_1 K M_1, *pr.* et, G_1 M.

In the *Cod. Sangallensis* 125 is added the following:—
"Spiritus uero Sanctus Patris et Filii communiter Spiritus.
Sicut generare solius Patris et nasci solius Filii et procedere
de ambobus solius confitemur Spiritus Sancti. Credimus in
Spiritum Sanctum, Spiritum Sanctum Deum dicimus, nec

tamen dicimus Patrem et Filium et Spiritum Sanctum tres Deos sed unum quia una est æternitas una maiestas una potestas. Pater non est Filius sed Pater est. Filius non est Pater sed Filius est Patris. Spiritus Sanctus nec Pater est nec Filius sed Spiritus est Patris et Filii, tres personæ sed unus Deus est. Credo in Spiritum Sanctum. Spiritus Sanctus Deus est a Patre Filioque non minor sed una maiestas una potestas inseparabilis trinitas, inuisibilis sanctitas, simulque Deus Pater Deus Filius Deus Spiritus Sanctus. Non tres Dii sed trinitas unus Deus est. Quo modo procedit Spiritus ex Patre ita procedit ex Filio."

The fact that it was quoted by the Council of Toledo has led me to the suggestion that it was the reply of Damasus to the treatise addressed to him by Priscillian. There are two or three sentences which reply directly to statements in that treatise, and cut away the roots of his error. Thus (1) "Deus nomen est potestatis non proprietatis" is a sentence which afterwards found its way into the Fortunatus commentary on the *Quicunque*, and with good reason. It explains why Priscillian's frequent and loose use of the term *potestas* was wrong. Power is an attribute of the Godhead, not a proper name like Father or Son or Holy Ghost. In this treatise Priscillian uses the term twice—§ 41: "unita unius Dei potestate";[1] and § 45 (where he is speaking of the Baptismal Formula): "in uno (nomine) quia unus Deus trina potestate uenerabilis *omnia et in omnibus Christus est.*" As I have shown above (p. 142), the tendency of all such untheological argument is Sabellian.

Again, in his Christological teaching, the author of the creed defines the perfect Manhood which the Lord took upon Him as including flesh, soul, and feeling: *ut perfectus in suis sit et uerus in nostris . . . qui ut homo moritur ut Deus surgit.* Thus he replies to the vague teaching, leaning, as it seems, to the Apollinarian error, in the passage quoted above (p. 143) from Tract. VI. 99, where Priscillian himself uses the words

[1] Cf. V. § 88: "Christum nulli nomini uel potestati parte concessa unum Deum crederet."

dum moritur homo resurgit ut Deus, though in the context he seems to deny that the Lord had a human soul.

This conclusion is borne out by the following passage from the same treatise (§ 95), though it is only fair to add two other references in which a tripartite division of human nature is given, the first a quotation from Wisdom ix. 15. But they do not throw light on his Christology.

Tract. VI. § 95 : " Dum in utrisque testamentis corpore et spiritu, sicut fuit Christus in carne, uelut in duobus perfectus homo quæritur, uetus testamentum castificandi corporis Deo et nouum animæ institutione mancipatur et non dissentaneum sibi sed ratione diuisum est, ut sicut hæc duo testamenta Deus unus est, sic in nobis perfectio boni gloria sit." . . .

Ib. § 97, *Sap.* 9, 15 : " *Corpus* . . . *anima* . . . *sensus.*"

Ib. § 105 : " Post sapientiæ sæcularis institutione reiecta corpore anima et spiritu in quibus homo uincitur triformi decalogi in nobis lege reparata mensis fiat domini." . . .

I have already pointed out (p. 145) that the teaching on eternal rewards and punishments is a complete answer to the Antinomian theory, which might be deduced from his mystical teaching. Tract. VII. § 117 : " Perpetua luce contecti peccatorum supplicia respuere et requiem possimus habere iustorum per Iesum Christum."

Lastly, the appeal, " Hæc lege, hæc retine, huic fidei animam tuam subiuga," fits in well with my theory of authorship. The connexion with S. Jerome suggested by the MSS. may be explained by the fact that he was at this time in Rome, and in constant communication with Damasus.

§ IV. The Rhythm of the "Te Deum" and the "Quicunque"

The researches of Meyer[1] prove that the work of S. Cyprian, *de Mortalitate*, in which we have found an important parallel to verses 7, 8, 9 of the *Te Deum*, was written in metrical prose; that is to say, prose which had

---

[1] *Göttingsche gel. Anzeigen*, 1893, p. 1. I owe my introduction to this interesting subject to Mr. J. Shelly. Cf. article in *Guardian*, March 10, 1897.

RHYTHM OF "TE DEUM" AND "QUICUNQUE" 249

strictly regulated metrical endings to its sentences. These were used by many rhetoricians of the Silver Latin period, and were known as *clausulæ rhetoricæ* (cf. Terentianus Maurus V. 1439). The passage may be scanned as follows :—

"Illīc ăpōstŏlōrūm | glŏrĭōs|ūs chŏrūs ³ ||, illīc prŏphētārum ēxūlt|āntĭūm | nŭmĕrūs ⁶ ||, illīc mārtўrum īnnŭmĕr|ăbĭlīs | pŏpŭlūs ⁶ || ōb cērtămĭnĭs ēt pāssĭōnĭs glōrĭam ēt uīctōrĭām cŏrōnātūs ⁹ || "

At the end of the fourth century these metrical endings were superseded by less artificial, though not less musical, endings or cadences, in which the rhythm was marked by accent. Sometimes, though this shows a further decadence of style, the new rhythmical endings were combined with rhymes. At a later period the new method was dignified by grammarians with the name of the *Cursus Leoninus*. There were three ordinary forms of endings, which were known as—

cursus planus $\acute{-} \smile \smile \acute{-} -$ (pl)

cursus tardus $\acute{-} \smile \smile \acute{-} \smile \smile$ (t)

cursus uelox $\acute{-} \smile \smile \smile \smile \acute{-} \smile$ (v)

These cadences are found throughout the writings of Cassian, Pomerius, his pupil Cæsarius, Cassiodorus, and other writers of the fifth and sixth centuries. After two centuries the method fell into disuse, and was restored by the Chancellor John Cajetan, the future Gelasius II., under Pope Urban II. (1088). Definite rules were drawn up by another chancellor, Albert de Mora, the future Gregory VIII.,[1] according to which the beginning of the sentence should contain spondees (rhythmical, not metrical), the middle spondees and dactyls mixed.

The results of such ruling were what might be expected. All the freshness of the early method evaporated, and in the sixteenth century, though Dante used it effectively in his letters, it died a natural death.

We are not now concerned with later developments of

[1] Chevalier, *Poésie liturgique du moyen age*, p. 36.

the system, but with its use in liturgical books. The Gelasian Sacramentary is full of these cadences, and they are found in all the most beautiful of Latin collects. Thus the collect of the Angelus contains three typical specimens.

The ears of the translators of our Prayer Book were so tuned to them, that they have reproduced these cadences in many most familiar and most musical prayers.[1]

The importance of the subject is not confined to the æsthetic valuing of harmonious phrases. The date when the method came into use being known, the very fact of its use may in some cases help to determine the date of documents. We must, of course, be on our guard against fanciful extensions of the theory to support doubtful theories of date. But it is to be hoped that the rhythms will be marked in future editions of writings known to be written according to these rules. Thus in Arnold's great work on Cæsarius, the treatise *on Humility* is, for the first time, printed in such a way as to show the rhythms.

The application of the method to the *Te Deum*[2] revealed the fact that the rhythmical endings stopped with verse 21, the Psalm verses which follow being, as we know from other sources, not part of the original composition. I have en-

---

[1] Mr. Shelly writes: "Taking the collects for the Sundays and those for Christmas Day, Ash Wednesday, Good Friday, Easter Eve, and Ascension Day, I find they contain one hundred and seventy-one distinct clauses, of which at least seventy have endings that correspond with one or other of the usual forms of the *cursus*. I do not think this can be accidental. Anyway, it is very curious, because, though I do find similar cadences in other portions of English literature, they are nothing like so frequent nor so regular in their occurrence." Thus—

    Planus—hélp and défend us.
         mán's understánding.
         áble to pléase thee.

    Tardus—hélp and delíver us.
         contínual gódliness.
         wórship the Unity.

    Velox—noúrish us with all góodness.
         sérvice is perfect fréedom.
         glóry of His resurréction.

[2] In the first instance by Lejay.

deavoured to mark them independently. It must be admitted that there are several very doubtful endings, which may be explained by the fact that they illustrate the transition from the metrical to the rhythmical style. Thus we find the fifth of the metrical endings classified by Meyer both in the *Te Deum* and the *Quicunque*—

  Verse 2.—Te aeternum Patrem omnis terră uĕnĕrātur.
  Clause 3.— Trinitatem in Unitātĕ uĕnĕrēmur.

Meyer [1] shows that this was allowed as a sixth form of the *cursus*, but not, it would seem, till a much later time.

Among the *Quicunque* endings there are several which do not conform to the usual rules of the *cursus*, *i.e.* clauses 3, 20, 25, 26. Mr. Shelly suggests that "a slight alteration of the words in each case would form a recognised cadence." Thus—

  Clause 3.—ueneremur et Trinitatem | in Uni|táte.^{pl}
  " 20.—religione Cathólica | prohib|émur.^{v}
  " 25.—in Unitate | sít uene|ránda.^{pl}
  " 26.—ita sentiat | dé Trinitáte.^{pl}

In three of these cases, clauses 3, 20, 27, such a proposal is not necessary, since they are covered by the suggestion that the metrical ending ‾ ˘ ˘ ‾ ˘ passed into the *cursus*, though it was only formally recognised at a late period. In the fourth case there is no such explanation available, but I am still unwilling to resort to so violent a rectification of the text with no MS. authority.

There is one other case in which the *cursus* may be used to decide between doubtful readings. In clause 22 there is little doubt that *est* should be omitted, giving a good specimen of the *cursus velox*, génitus | sed pro|cédens.^{v} This reading is of small consequence in itself, but the argument for it lends some additional probability to Mr. Shelly's theory.

The fact that the creed was thus written in rhythmical prose does not prove that it was written for singing. The address of Cæsarius *on Humility* was not intended for singing. At the same time, we must note that it was just because it was written in this style that it was found so

[1] P. 25.

suitable for singing at a later time. In an interesting lecture on "Art in Liturgical Melodies, Ancient and Modern," by the Abbé A. Bourdon,[1] director of the cathedral music at Rouen, some stress is laid on the fact that there is a musical *cursus* which corresponds to the literary *cursus*, and is founded on it.

He quotes the following words of Dom. Mocquereau: " Dans les répertoires liturgiques des trois principaux dialectes du plain-chant (ambrosien, grégorien, mozarabe), ou trouve, reproduites des *milliers de fois*, plus de cent cadences imitant les ondulations rhythmiques du cursus planus littéraire, sur lesquelles on les a évidemment calquées."

§ V. Niceta of Remesiana

Niceta was Bishop of Remesiana [2] in Dacia, the modern Bela-Palanka on the Servian railway from Nisch to Pirot. In 398 and 402 he visited Paulinus of Nola, the friend of many leading churchmen in Italy and Gaul, among others of S. Ambrose, Sulpicius Severus, and Eucherius of Lyons. Paulinus wrote enthusiastically of his character and ability, and used terms such as holy Father, Father, and teacher, which seem to imply that he was the older, *i.e.* born before 353. This date agrees with the chronological setting of the short reference in Gennadius, who seems to date his life *c.* 370–420. Paulinus wrote in 398 of the success of his missionary work among the wild tribe of the Bessi. Shortly before this S. Jerome mentions the fact that even the wild Bessi had given up their inhuman customs to make heard the sweet songs of the Cross. Work so successful must have been going on for some time, and there is a possible reference to it in a decree of the Second Roman Synod held under Pope Damasus *c.* 369–371, which they sent to the Bishops of Illyria. Reports of the revival of Arianism had been sent them by brethren among the Gauls and Bessi.[3]

---

[1] *Mémoires sur la Musique Sacrée en Normandie.*
[2] Gennadius, c. 22 in B.N. Paris, *Cod. lat.* 12,161.
[3] *Spicilegium Casinense*, i. 98.

NICETA OF REMESIANA 253

Possibly Niceta was the messenger, for his treatise on the titles of our Lord shows acquaintance with the *Decretum Gelasii*, which was discussed at a Synod held under Damasus. Paulinus implies that his activity was not confined to the Bessi in the Balkans (*Carm.* xvii. 321: *non unius populi magistrum*), but that it extended to the Scythians in the Dobrudscha, and even to the Getæ north of the Danube. He taught also among the gold-diggers of the neighbourhood.[1]

Latin seems to have been his native tongue, but he was probably acquainted also with Greek, since he quotes the *Catecheses* of Cyril of Jerusalem, and in some cases appears to give his own translation from the Greek Testament.

At Rome his learning made a great impression. Paulinus wrote of it to Sulpicius Severus: "Quo genere te et uenerabili episcopo atque doctissimo Nicetæ, qui ex Dacia Romanis merito admirandus aduenerat . . . reuelaui."[2] Paulinus also delighted in his gifts as a hymn-writer, beside whom he felt himself poor.[3]

Kattenbusch[4] makes the interesting suggestion that he was the Bishop Nichæ referred to in the letter of Germinius of Sirmium in 367. He quotes the form Niceas as found in the MSS. of Gennadius. It is more probably a corruption of Nicetæ, since the specimens of handwriting from Dacian wax tablets given by Maunde Thompson[5] show that *et* could easily be corrupted into *h*.

Niceta is mentioned with another Bishop of Sirmium in a letter of Pope Innocent I. to Marcianus, Bishop of Nisch, in the year 409; and in another letter of 414 is referred to with Marcianus among bishops of Macedonia and the surrounding district.

Gennadius (c. 22) informs us that he wrote in simple and clear language six books of instruction for neophytes, of which the fifth was *On the Creed*. By the evidence of some fragments found by Morin[6] in a MS. at Rouen, in an

---

[1] Paulinus, *Carm.* xviii. 213, 269. [2] *Ep.* 29.
[3] *Carm.* xxvii. 193-199. [4] *Theol. Lit. Zeit.* 1896, p. 303.
[5] *Greek and Latin Palæography*, p. 216. [6] *Rev. Bén.* 1897, p. 97.

Ordo de catechizandis rudibus, cod. A, 214, sæc. xi., xii., this fifth book may be identified with the *Explanatio symboli* attributed to Nicetas of Aquileia.[1] On fol. 123 *v.* an extract from that sermon is called *de Immortalitate Animæ Nicetæ in libro quinto ad competentes.*[2] This evidence seems completely to remove the doubt expressed by Hahn[3] (p. 47, n. 72), who argued reasonably that if the author was not Nicetas of Aquileia, some further evidence was required to prove that he was a Nicetas. The sermon is an eloquent one, addressed to a cultured congregation, and specially interesting as containing the first mention of *sanctorum communionem* in a creed form. The appeal to renounce theatres and pomps is not out of place, since the Roman colonies in that district were probably wealthy and luxurious. If further investigation should confirm Kattenbusch's[3] doubts upon this point, another explanation could easily be found, in the suggestion that this was a sermon preached to an Italian congregation at Rome or Nola.

The form of creed is not easy to extract from the sermon. I have therefore shown in notes how my reconstruction differs from those of Caspari (C), Hümpel (H[1]), Hahn[3] (H[3]), and Kattenbusch (K). It seems to be a provincial form of R, and the accusatives *natum, crucifixum* seem to point to independent translation from a Greek text.[4] I have somewhat doubtfully included *cœli et terræ creatorem*, because the note following *hunc confitere Deum* in connexion with the use of *confessio* after the first words of Art. 1, and of *confiteberis* after the first words of Art. 2, seem to me to imply that he is quoting the creed. The words were found in the Jerusalem Creed, which he would know through Cyril, and it may have been through Niceta that they found their way into our Apostles' Creed.[5] The words *uiuus a mortuis* are found in the Creeds of Martin of Bracara, a native of

---

[1] M.S.L. 52, 865.

[2] Morin, Art. cit., points out that the third and fifth fragments, edited by Denis from another MS. (*Cod. Vindob.* 1370, sæc. x.), are said to have been taken from the fifth book of Niceta, and are not found in the *Explanatio*. I do not see that this affects the evidence of the Rouen MS.

[3] *Das ap. Symbol.* i. p. 406.   [4] Cf. p. 200 *supra.*   [5] P. 240 *supra.*

Pannonia, and in Spanish Creeds, Ildefonsus, Etherius, Beatus, Mozarabic Liturgy, possibly dependent on Martin; also in Theodulf's Creed, which is explained by the fact of his Spanish extraction.

NICETA

I. 1. Credo in Deum Patrem omnipotentem
   cœli et terræ creatorem:
II. 2. Et in Filium eius Iesum Christum,
   3. natum ex Spiritu Sancto et ex
      uirgine Maria,
   4. *passum* sub Pontio Pilato, crucifixum,
      mortuum;
   5. Tertia die resurrexit *uiuus* a
      mortuis,
   6. ascendit in cœlos,
   7. sedet ad dexteram Patris,
   8. inde uenturus iudicare
      uiuos et mortuos :
III. 9. Et in Spiritum Sanctum,
   10. sanctam ecclesiam *catholicam*,
       communionem sanctorum,
   11. remissionem peccatorum,
   12. carnis resurrectionem
       et uitam æternam.

1. *om.* cœli et terræ creatorem, C H[1] H[3] K.   2. + Dominum nostrum, K.
3. natum . . . uirgine, *in expos.* C.   4. >sub Pontio Pilato passus est (passum, H[3]), C H[3].   mortuum, *pr.* et, 11[3]; mortuus, *in expos.* C.   7. Patris, *pr.* Dei, H[3].   10. sanctæ ecclesiæ catholicæ, C.   11. remissionem, *pr.* in H[3].
12. carnis, *pr.* huius, H[3].   uitam, *pr.* in H[3].

CHAPTER XI

THE "TE DEUM"

§ I. MSS. and Quotations.
§ II. The Authorship.
§ III. The Sources upon which the Author may have drawn.
§ IV. The Text.

THE history of the *Te Deum* touches the history of the Apostles' Creed at so many points, that it is scarcely necessary to apologise for the addition of the following Chapter. Since the publication of the Bishop of Salisbury's exhaustive article in the *Dictionary of Hymnology*, an entirely new turn has been given to the discussion of the subject by Dom. G. Morin's brilliant discovery of the probable author in Niceta of Remesiana, whose commentary on the creed has already interested us. His suggestion has been accepted as a probable solution of a very puzzling problem by leading critics at home and abroad. It may therefore be of interest to collect the principal arguments for the new theory in a concise form. The materials are not yet available for a critical edition of the text of the hymn in all the three versions known to us. But I have compiled a provisional list of the earliest MSS.,[1] and have attempted to reconstruct the original text in the light of the new theory. The result is only tentative, but may serve to illustrate the progress of modern criticism in this subject. At least, it is comforting to find that, with the exception of some Psalm verses, which for some time have been recognised as additions to the hymn, the whole of the text dear to us is original.

[1] Appendix E.

§ I. MSS. AND QUOTATIONS

The hymn *Te Deum laudamus* is found in a large number of MSS., most of them psalters and collections of hymns. The earliest known are a Vatican Psalter (*Cod. Vatic. Alex.* xi.) of the seventh century, or earlier, and the *Bangor Antiphonary*, which may be dated A.D. 680–691. These contain the forms of text known as the Milan and Irish versions. A third form, the version of the Prayer Book, is probably the most ancient, but apart from the question of the antiphons, or psalm verses, added to the original hymn, the differences between the versions are of small importance.

The evidence of quotations carries us back to the fifth century. The Rule of Benedict of Nursia, which was written *c.* A.D. 530, contains the following direction: c. xi., "Post quartum responsorium incipit Abbas *Te Deum laudamus*, quo prædicto legat Abbas lectionem de Euangelio cum honore et tremore, stantis omnibus, qua perlecta respondeant omnes Amen, et subsequatur mox Abbas hymnum Te decet laus."

To this we may add the Rule of Aurelian: "Omni Sabbato ad Matutinos Cantemus Domino et *Te Deum laudamus.*"

The Rule of Cæsarius, who was consecrated Bishop of Arles in 502, is said to have been written while he was still Abbot of Lerins. He directs: c. xxi. "Perfectis missis dicite matutinos directaneo: Exaltabo te Deus meus et rex meus. Deinde Confitemini. Inde Cantemus Domino, Lauda anima mea Dominum, Benedictionem, Laudate Dominum de cælis. *Te Deum laudamus.* Gloria in excelsis Deo: et capitellum."

To this testimony of Cæsarius may be added an important quotation in the letter of Cyprian, Bishop of Toulon, which has been quoted as a new authority for the Creed of Gaul. He mentions Cæsarius by name, and his use of the *Te Deum* seems to have been exactly parallel to the directions given in his friend's rule. He writes thus to Maximus, Bishop of Geneva:

"Sed in hymno quem omnes ecclesia toto orbe receptum canit, cottidie dicemus: 'Tu es rex gloriæ, Christus, tu patri sempiternus es filius';

et consequenter subiungit: 'Tu ad liberandum subcepturus hominem non orruisti uirgines uterum ; te ergo quaesumus tuis famulis subueni, quos praetioso sanguine redimisti."[1]

Two quotations of a more doubtful kind may be added, which will appear worthy of consideration in the light of the new evidence as to the authorship. It has been suggested[2] that Prudentius in his *Apotheosis*, l. 1019, uses the three words, suscipere, liberare, tenere, just as they are used in verse 16 of the hymn. He may have become acquainted with it during his long stay in Rome, A.D. 400–405.[3]

The other is a passage in the *Commonitorium* of Vincentius of Lerins : c. xvi. *ad fin*. "Beata igitur ac ueneranda, benedicta et sacrosancta, et omnino supernae ille angelorum laudationi comparanda confessio, quae unum Dominum Deum trina sanctificatione glorificat."

I do not know if it has ever been suggested that Vincentius refers here to the *Te Deum*, but the words imply more than a mere reference to the *Sanctus*. They imply that it was set in a *Confessio Trinitatis*, which was worthy to be called *Laus angelorum*, and acknowledged one Lord God. The title *Laus angelica* is found in a MS. at Cambridge (S. John's C. 15), and *Laus angelorum* in a MS. at Rouen, Cod. 227 (A. 367), saec. xii.

§ II. The Authorship

In the ninth century there were two conflicting traditions held as to the authorship. Hincmar of Rheims believed the beautiful story, that it was composed by S. Ambrose and S. Augustine on the eventful day of S. Augustine's baptism. In his treatise on Predestination (A.D. 856) he writes : " Ut a maioribus nostris audiuimus, tempore baptismatis sancti Augustini hunc hymnum beatus Ambrosius fecit, et idem Augustinus cum eo." This tradition is confirmed by the title which is given to the canticle in a S. Gall. Psalter of the beginning of the century (*Cod.* 23): " Hymnum quem S.

---

[1] *Cod. Colon.* 212 (Darmstad. 2326) f. 113 f., quoted by Morin, *Rev. Bén.*
[2] M. C. Weymann in a letter to Dom. Morin.
[3] Zahn, *Neuere Beiträge*, p. 119, n. 1.

Ambrosius et S. Augustinus inuicem condiderunt." It is also found in the titles of the Vienna Psalter, S. Gall. 27, and B. M., Add. MSS. 9046.

The Irish Book of Hymns of the tenth, B. M., Vitellius, E. xviii., and Bodleian Laud, 96, both of the eleventh century, show the tradition continued. In the eleventh century the whole story was reported in the Chronicle of Milan, erroneously called by the name of Dacius, who was bishop c. A.D. 527.

On the other hand, Abbo of Fleury, in a letter to some English monks (A.D. 985), attributed the hymn to S. Hilary of Poitiers: " Dei palinodia quam composuit Hilarius Pictauensis Episcopus." This tradition is the more interesting, because Fleury Abbey possessed one of the greatest monastic libraries, and Abbo, even if he seems pedantic, was a real student. Moreover, it is carried back probably to the preceding century by the title in one of Daniel's Munich MSS.,[1] which belonged to the Abbey of S. Emmeran.

From the tenth century, however, there is evidence of a third tradition, which has been preserved in some ten MSS. It was first noticed by Archbishop Ussher, who wrote to Voss about a collection of Latin and Irish hymns in which he had found the *Te Deum* attributed to a Niceta. This MS. has at last been identified with the Irish Book of Hymns (sæc. xi.), belonging to the Franciscan Convent at Dublin, by Prof. J. H. Bernard of Dublin, who has edited it with a most interesting introduction. There is a curious preface to the *Te Deum* written in Latin and Old Irish, which may be translated as follows[2]: " Neceta, coarb [*i.e.* successor] of Peter, made this canticle. In Rome, now, it was made. Incertum autem quo tempore et ob quam causam factum, nisi Necetam Deum laudare uoluisse diceremus, dicens *Laudate pueri Dominum, Laudate nomen Domini, Te Deum laudamus,*" etc.

Ussher found in the Cotton Library another MS., which ascribed the *Te Deum* to a Nicetius, *i.e.* a Gallican Psalter, which he supposed to have been written in the reign of Henry I. (1120–1134). This is missing, but with inde-

[1] *Thesaurus Hymnologicus*, ii. 288. [2] Bradshaw Society vol. xiii. 59.

fatigable labour Dom. Morin has collected references to nine others.

The earliest is—(1) A Roman Psalter from the Abbey of S. Aubin, at Angers (*Cod.* xv.), of the tenth century. The others are (2) B. M., Harleian, 863, sæc. xi.; (3) B. M., Arundel, 60, sæc. xi., in which Vicetius is obviously a mistake for Nicetius; (4) Bibl. Laurent. Florence, Plut. xvii. *Cod.* iii. sæc. xi.; (5) *ib. Cod.* ix., sæc. xi.; (6) *ib. Cod.* viii. sæc. xiii.; (7), Munich, *Cod. lat.* 13067, sæc. xi., xii., in a Scotch or Irish hand, from the Belgian monastery of Hastière on the Meuse; (8) Bibl. Vatican., *Cod. Palat. lat.* 35, sæc. xiv., xv.; (9) an early printed Psalter, *ad usum ecclesiæ Sarisburiensis*, London, 1555, in which is "the rubric, *Canticum beati Niceti*," and a note stating that the traditional account respecting S. Augustine's baptism is untrue : " Quod non est uerum sed decantauerunt usum prius compositum per beatum Nicetum episcopum Vien(n)ensem quod innuit Cassiodorus de institutione sanctorum scripturarum."

In a few MSS. the names of Sisebut and Abundius are connected with the hymn. They are coupled together in the Breviary of the Collegium Anicianum at Rome, Bibl. Vatican. *Cod. Basil. Vat.* n. xi. *Cod. Vat.* 4928, sæc. xii. Sisebut alone is mentioned in a Breviary at Monte Casino, which was written under Abbot Oderisius, Paris, Bibl. Mazarin, *Cod.* 364 (759), Bibl. Vatican. *Cod.* xi. They were probably monks, who either introduced it into some new district of Italy, or composed the musical setting. Sisebut, a Goth, is mentioned among early disciples of Benedict. S. Gregory, who narrates, *Dial.* ii. 6, how a Goth was received by Benedict, mentions also a clerk, Abundius, who was *mansionarius* at S. Peter's in the sixth century.

The natural inclination to assign popular creeds or hymns to great men will account for the first and second of these traditions, neither of which can be traced back beyond the ninth century. And it may be worth while to point out that the MS. which ascribes the hymn to Hilary was not written in France, that the MS. which ascribes it to Ambrose and Augustine was not written in Italy, and that no MS. of the

Milan version, where we should expect the latter tradition to survive, if anywhere, has any such title.

There remains the interesting series of MSS. which connect it with the name Niceta or Nicetius. Most of them belong to Great Britain, and there is some likelihood that such a tradition would be longer preserved in these isles, which were often cut off from much communication with the Continent.[1]

There are strong reasons for identifying him with Niceta of Remesiana. Since Professor Bernard has found the missing MS. which alone preserved the Greek form of the name, the claims of Western writers like Nicetius of Trèves, or Nicesius of Vienne, to be regarded as possible authors, become void. It is easy to understand how the Greek name was Latinised in the other MSS. Another point of interest in the MS. is the statement that Niceta was Bishop of Rome. Evidently the scribe had seen the inscription, *Civitatis Romanæ episcopus.* Now *Romanæ* is one of the forms in which Remesiana is found in the MSS. of Gennadius.

The internal evidence of the treatises *On the Good of Psalmody* and *On Vigils* points quite away from the times and circumstances of Nicetius of Trèves, or of his namesake of Vienne. The writer defends the practice of keeping vigils with psalm-singing and hymns as something new, to which older Church-folk object, and at which the heathen mock. He speaks of Saturday and Sunday as observed with these night watches. This fact points decisively to some Church influenced by Eastern usage, and to the latter part of the fourth century, a description which would suit Remesiana in the time of Niceta. A reference to the Song of Moses and Miriam shows that the congregation were divided into two choirs, by sex. The whole congregation sang, and did not merely respond " Amen " or " Hallelujah " to a singer or choir.

Antiphonal psalm-singing by the whole congregation began in Antioch about the year 350, when two Orthodox laymen, Flavianus and Diodorus, afterwards Bishops of Antioch and Tarsus, gathered a congregation and taught them to sing hymns, in opposition to the influence of an Arian bishop,

[1] M. S. Berger, *Hist. of Vulgate*, Paris, 1893, pref. p. 12.

Leontius. S. Basil introduced the practice into Cæsarea (Cappadocia) in 375, and was heavily reproached for it.[1] It soon spread to Upper Egypt and Mesopotamia, but Basil does not mention one town of Europe where it was found. Opposition did not come so much from conservative congregations as from bishops. A synod held at Laodicea, 360, decreed: "Besides the canonical psalm-singers, who climb into the gallery and sing from the book, shall none sing in the church."

Dom. Morin[2] has found in the Vatican Library a new MS. of the tract, *On the Good of Psalmody, Cod. Vat.* 5729, containing several passages which are not found in the printed editions, but seem to belong to the original text. In one of these, the author answers the objection that S. Paul (Eph. v. 9) intended congregations to sing silently, when he wrote, "in gratia cantantes et psallentes Deo in cordibus uestris." In another he quotes a treatise of Cyprian.[3] This throws light on the extent of his reading, and is an interesting parallel to the quotation of Cyprian "On Mortality," in the *Te Deum.*

Though the writer distinguishes his people from Easterns, his list of the canticles sung at their services exactly corresponds with Eastern usage. Dom. Morin shows this by an interesting list:

NICETA.	CONSTANTINOPLE.	MILAN.	GAUL.
Moses, Exodus	Moses, Exodus	Isaiah xxvi. 9	Benedicite
„ Deut.	„ Deut.	Anna	Moses, Exodus
Anna	Anna	Habbakuk	„ Deut.
Isaiah xxvi. 9	Habbakuk	Jonah	Isaiah lx. 1-14
Habbakuk	Isaiah xxvi. 9	Moses, Deut.	„ lxi. 10-lxii. 7
Jonah	Jonah	„ Exodus	Anna
Jeremiah, (?)	Benedicite, i.	Zachariah, Luke	Mary
Benedicite	„ ii.	i. 68	Isaiah xxvi. 9
Elizabeth, Luke i. 46	Mary, Luke i. 46	Mary, Luke i. 46	Judith
		Benedicite	Ezechiel
			Jeremiah, Lam. v. 1-22
			4 Esdras viii. 20-36
			Azarias, Dan. iii. 26-44

---

[1] *Ep.* 207. [2] *Revue Bénédictine*, 1897, p. 385.
[3] *Ep. ad Donat.* c. 16, ed. Hartel.

It will be seen that the list of Niceta agrees with that of Constantinople with two exceptions, the inversion of the order Isaiah, Habbakuk, and the addition of Jeremiah, which is possibly a point of connection with the Gallican list.

In fact, the internal evidence of these tracts exactly fits in with the words which Paulinus of Nola used about his friend. He anticipated much pleasure from the enjoyment of Niceta's gifts as a hymn writer, beside whom he felt himself poor.[1] He hoped to gain inspiration,[2] and that Niceta would visit the church of his patron-saint Felix, with psalm-singing and hymns.[3] He imagined the sailors on the ship, which would carry Niceta over the Adriatic, taught to sing hymns in chorus, as in "the silent land"; the barbarians had already learnt to hymn Christ:—

> "Navitæ læti solitum celeusma
> Concinent uersis modulis in hymnos
> Et piis ducent comites in æquor
>   Vocibus auras.
>
> Præcinet cunctis, tuba ceu resultans,
> Lingua Nicetæ modulata Christum :
> Psallet æternus citharista toto
>   Æquore Dauid.
>
> Audient Amen tremefacta cete,
> Et sacerdotem Domino canentem
> Læta lasciuo procul admeabunt
>   Monstra natatu."[4]

Gennadius and Cassiodorus praise the writings of Niceta for their brevity, and the clearness and simplicity of their style. The same characteristics are certainly found in the *Te Deum* to a marked degree. The effect which the whole composition has on the mind is felt to be strong. But this is through the grandeur and rapidity of the thoughts which are expressed, rather than from mere brilliancy of expression.[5]

The parallels to the *Te Deum* scattered in the writings of Niceta are not perhaps so striking as one could wish, but they show that his mind was working on similar lines.

---

[1] *Carm.* xxvii. 193–199.   [2] *ib.* 243–272.   [3] *ib.* 500–510.
[4] *Carm.* xvii. 109.   [5] Morin, *Rev. Bén.* 1894, p. 75.

Ver. 7. In the *Explanatio* he writes: In cuius *gloriam* etiam angeli prospicere concupiscunt; qui et sedes et dominationes uniuersasque coelorum uirtutes sua *maiestate* sanctificat.

Ver. 8. In the same sermon he writes of patriarchs, prophets, apostles, martyrs, and the just, as united with angels in one church. And in what seems to be the best text [1] of his letter, *de lapsu Susannæ*, if that can be attributed to him, we find mention made of apostles, an army of prophets (exercitus), and the holy angels.

Vers. 11–13. Gennadius gives one title, *de fide unicæ maiestatis*, for the treatises on the faith, and on the Holy Spirit, in which maiestas is repeatedly used of the Godhead. The *immensitas* of God's works is spoken of in a way which implies that the writer would argue back to the *immensitas* of His Being. He speaks of Christ as *uerus* (*dei*) *filius* (Mai, p. 315). He uses the title *spiritum sanctum paraclitum* (Mai, p. 322).[2]

Ver. 16. *Expl. symboli.*—Carnem suscepit humanam (cf. Mai, p. 314, corpus suscepisse).

Ver. 20. Cf. sanguinis sui pretio nos redemit (Mai, p. 331).

Ver. 21. Cf. de remuneratione iustitiæ, de coelestis gloriæ expectatione (Mai, p. 332).

For the thoughts worked out in the whole of this section of the hymn, we may compare *de Psalmodiæ Bono*. "Et quod his est omnibus excelsius Christi sacramenta cantantur. Nam et generatio eius exprimitur, et rejectio plebis impiæ et gentium credulitas nominatur. Uirtutes domini cantantur, passio ueneranda depingitur, resurrectio gloriosa monstratur, sedisse quoque ad dexteram non tacetur. Tunc deinde igneus domina manifestatur aduentus, terribile de uiuis ac mortuis iudicium panditur. Quid plura? Etiam Spiritus [3] creantis emissio et terræ renouatio reuelatur. Post quæ erit in gloriam domini sempiternam iustorum regnum impiorum perenne supplicium."

This theory of the authorship has also the merit that it offers an explanation of the fragment of an original Greek version, which has been preserved in four MSS.

---

[1] *Epistula Nicetæ Episcopi*, in the MS. d'Epinal, sæc. vii., viii.
[2] Zahn, Art. cit.　　　　　　[3] *Cod. Vat.* xī̆s.

THE SOURCES

Niceta must have been competent to translate it himself, and we may even hope some day to find the rest of the version.

1. Σὲ Θεὸν αἰνοῦμεν· σὲ κύριον ἐξομολογοῦμεν·
2. Σὲ αἰώνιον πατέρα πᾶσα ἡ γῆ. . . .
3. Σοὶ πάντες ἄγγελοι, σοὶ οὐρανοὶ καὶ πᾶσαι ἐξουσίαι,
4. Σοὶ χερουβὶμ καὶ σεραφὶμ ἀκαταπαύστῳ φωνῇ ἀνακράζουσιν·
5. Ἅγιος Ἅγιος Ἅγιος κύριος ὁ Θεὸς σαβαώθ·
6. πλήρεις οὐρανοὶ καὶ ἡ γῆ τῆς μεγαλωσύνης τῆς δόξης σοῦ.
7. Σὲ δεδοξασμένος ἀποστόλων χορός·
8. Σὲ προφητῶν αἰνετὸς ἀριθμός·
9. Σὲ μαρτύρων ἔκλαμπρος αἰνεῖ στρατός·
10. Σὲ κατὰ πᾶσαν τὴν οἰκουμένην ἡ ἁγία ἐξομολογεῖ ἐκκλησία.

The absence of a verb in verse 2 should be noted. Either the MS. from which the scribe copied was mutilated, or, more probably, if the Greek version was written as an interlinear gloss, some word like σέβεται was forgotten.[1] These ten verses are all that remain at present of the original. The attempts made in some MSS. to continue the translation are very unsuccessful.

§ III. The Sources

The word "sources" is a convenient term, which we may use generally to include any parallel passages in Christian literature of the period to which we have traced the *Te Deum*. If they were not the actual source of the author's thoughts, they at all events represent the current teaching of his age.

1. THE GLORIA IN EXCELSIS.—First among them we may set the *Gloria in excelsis*, which in its earliest form can be traced back to the fourth century. The earliest Greek MS. is the famous *Codex Alexandrinus* of the fifth century. But

[1] Wordsworth, Art. cit.

it is also found in part in the treatise *de Virginitate*[1] wrongly ascribed to Athanasius, which must have been written in Syria in the fourth century. In the *Apostolic Constitutions*, vii. 47, a somewhat different version of the hymn is found in a collection of hymns and prayers, which was made in or near Antioch in the latter half of the century. This version of the text offers an illustration of the way in which the

THE GLORIA IN EXCELSIS

Codex Alexandrinus.	*Bangor Antiphonary.*
1. Δόξα ἐν ὑψίστοις Θεῷ	Gloria in excelsis Deo,
2. καὶ ἐπὶ γῆς εἰρήνη ἐν ἀνθρώποις εὐδοκία.	et in terra pax hominibus bonæ uoluntatis.
3. αἰνοῦμέν σε,	Laudamus te.
4. εὐλογοῦμέν σε,	benedicimus te,
5. προσκυνοῦμέν σε,	adoramus te,
6. δοξολογοῦμέν σε,	glorificamus te, *magnificamus te,*
7. εὐχαριστοῦμέν σοι	gratias agimus tibi
8. διὰ τὴν μεγάλην σου δόξαν.	propter magnam misericordiam tuam.
9. κύριε βασιλεῦ	Domine rex
10. ἐπουράνιε,	coelestis,
11. Θεὲ πατὴρ παντοκράτωρ,	Deus Pater omnipotens,
12. κύριε υἱὲ μονογενῆ	Domine Fili unigenite
13. Ἰησοῦ χριστὲ	Ihesu Christe,
14. καί ἅγιον πνεῦμα.	Sancte Spiritus Dei, *et omnes dicimus, Amen.*
15. κύριε ὁ Θεὸς	Domine
16. ὁ ἀμνὸς τοῦ Θεοῦ,	Fili Dei Patris,
17. ὁ υἱὸς τοῦ πατρὸς,	agne Dei
18. ὁ αἴρων τὰς ἁμαρτίας τοῦ κόσμου	qui tollis peccata mundi,
19. ἐλέησον ἡμᾶς.	miserere nobis.
20. ὁ αἴρων τὰς ἁμαρτίας τοῦ κόσμου	
21. ἐλέησον ἡμᾶς.	
22. πρόσδεξαι τὴν δέησιν ἡμῶν ὁ καθήμενος ἐν δεξιᾷ τοῦ πατρὸς ἐλέησον ἡμᾶς.	Suscipe orationem nostram, qui sedes ad dexteram Dei Patris, miserere nobis.
23. ὅτι σὺ εἶ μόνος ἅγιος.	Quoniam tu solus sanctus.
24. σὺ εἶ μόνος κύριος.	tu solus Dominus. tu solus gloriosus.
Ἰησοῦς χριστὸς εἰς δόξαν θεοῦ πατρός.[2]	*cum Spiritu Sancto.* in gloria Dei Patris. Amen.

---

[1] Robertson, *Athanasius*, p. lxv. [2] Phil. ii. 11.

writer, known as Ps. Ignatius, "has taken and simply manipulated it to square with his curious views and terminology."[1]

The following is the form found in the *Apostolic Constitutions*. As it really depends on one MS. (X), I will quote it separately from Lagarde's edition:—

X. *Cod. Vindobonensis gr.* 46, sæc. xiv. Y. *Cod. Vindobonensis gr.* 47, sæc. xvi. Z. *Cod. Parisinus gr.* 931, sæc. xvi.

προσευχὴ ἑωθινή X Y. [ἐ Z].

δόξα ἐν ὑψίστοις Θεῷ καὶ ἐπὶ γῆς εἰρήνη, ἐν ἀνθρώποις εὐδοκία· αἰνοῦμέν σε, ὑμνοῦμέν σε,[2] εὐλογοῦμέν σε, εὐχαριστοῦμέν σοι, δοξολογοῦμέν σε, προσκυνοῦμέν σε, διὰ τοῦ μεγάλου ἀρχιερέως, σὲ τὸν ὄντα Θεὸν ἀγέννητον
5 ἕνα ἀπρόσιτον μόνον διὰ τὴν μεγάλην σου δόξαν, κύριε βασιλεῦ ἐπουράνιε Θεὲ πατὴρ παντοκράτωρ, κύριε υἱέ μονογενῆ Ἰησοῦ Χριστέ, καὶ ἅγιον πνεῦμα· κύριε ὁ Θεὸς ὁ ἀμνὸς τοῦ Θεοῦ, ὁ υἱὸς τοῦ πατρός, ὁ αἴρων τὰς ἁμαρτίας τοῦ κόσμου ἐλέησον ἡμᾶς· ὁ αἴρων τὰς ἁμαρτίας τοῦ
10 κόσμου, πρόσδεξαι τὴν δέησιν ἡμῶν· ὁ καθήμενος ἐν δεξιᾷ τοῦ πατρός, ἐλέησον ἡμᾶς· ὅτι σὺ εἶ μόνος ἅγιος, σὺ εἶ μόνος κύριος Ἰησοῦς Χριστὸς εἰς δόξαν Θεοῦ πατρός. ἀμήν.

3. om. 2° σε, Y Z. 6. πάτερ παντοκράτορ, Y. υἱέ . . . 8. ἁμαρτίας, X. ὁ Θεὸς ὁ πατὴρ τοῦ Χριστοῦ τοῦ ἀμώμου ἀμνοῦ ὃς αἴρει τὴν ἁμαρτίαν, Y. 9. om. ἐλέησον κόσμου, Y. 10. ἐν . . . 11. ἡμᾶς, X. ἐπὶ τῶν Χερουβείμ, Y. om. εἰ bis, Y. 12. Χριστὸς + τοῦ Θεοῦ πάσης γεννητῆς φύσεως τοῦ βασιλέως ἡμῶν εἰς . . . ἀμήν, X. δἰ οὗ σοι δόξα τιμὴ καὶ σέβας, Y.

The following parallels show that "in all but two details the language of the version is thoroughly characteristic of Ps. Ignatius, and in those two details, since they are quotations from Holy Scripture, he is quite himself, since he quotes Holy Scripture on every possible occasion":[3]—

---

[1] Rev. F. E. Brightman, to whom I am indebted for a list of parallels in the work of this person, which I will quote after the version.

[2] This seems to be a "conflate" of the ordinary text with that in *de Uirginitate*.

[3] Brightman.

Διὰ τοῦ μεγάλου ἀρχιερέως. *Ap. Const.* ii. 25, § 5, v. 6, § 7 : διὰ Ἰησοῦ Χριστοῦ τοῦ μεγάλου ἀρχιερίως ; vii. 38 : διὰ τοῦ μεγάλου ἀρχιερέως Ἰησοῦ Χριστοῦ ; viii. 16 : ἥτις μίμησιν περιέχει τοῦ μεγάλου ἀρχιερέως Ἰησοῦ Χριστοῦ. Cf. viii. 46 : τῇ φύσει ἀρχιερεὺς ὁ μονογενὴς Χριστός. *Smyrn.* 9 : τῇ φύσει τοῦ Πατρὸς ἀρχιερέα. *Ap. Const.* viii. 46 : τοῦ Πατρὸς ἀρχιερέα Χριστὸν Ἰησοῦ τὸν κύριον ἡμῶν ; 6 : ἀρχιερέα σόν. *Magn.* 7 : Ἰησοῦν Χριστὸν τὸν ἀρχιερέα τοῦ ἀγεννήτου Θεοῦ.

Σὲ τὸν ὄντα Θεόν. *Ap. Const.* v. 12, § 3 : περὶ τοῦ ὄντος Θεοῦ ; viii. 12 : ἀνυμνεῖν σε τὸν ὄντως ὄντα Θεόν.

Ἀγέννητον ἕνα ἀπρόσιτον μόνον. Eph. 7 : ὁ μόνος ἀληθινὸς Θεὸς ὁ ἀγέννητος καὶ ἀπρόσιτος. *Ap. Const.* viii. 6 : ὁ ἀγέννητος καὶ ἀπρόσιτος ὁ μόνος ἀληθινὸς Θεός. *Antioch*, 14 : ὁ ὢν μόνος ἀγέννητος. 2 : τὸν ἕνα καὶ μόνον Θεόν ; 4 : τὸν ἕνα πατέρα μόνον ἀληθινὸν Θεόν.

Ὁ Θεὸς ὁ πατὴρ τοῦ Χριστοῦ τοῦ ἀμώμου ἀμνοῦ. *Smyrn.* 1, *Ap. Const.* viii. 6, etc. : ὁ Θεὸς καὶ πατὴρ τοῦ κυρίου ἡμῶν Ἰησοῦ Χριστοῦ (a favourite quotation : notice change from original of *Smyrn.* 1). vii. 42 : τὸν πατέρα τοῦ Χριστοῦ, and 41.

The rest does not seem to occur elsewhere (cf. 1 Pet. i. 19).

Ὁ καθήμενος ἐπὶ τῶν χερουβείμ. Ps. lxxix. 2, xcviii. 1. Τοῦ Θεοῦ πάσης γεννητῆς φύσεως τοῦ βασιλέως ἡμῶν. *Philip.* 5 : ὁ πάλαι μὲν πᾶσαν αἰσθητὴν καὶ νοητὴν φύσιν κατασκευάσας. *Smyrn.* 8 : διανομεῖ πάσης νοητῆς φύσεως. *Ap. Const.* viii. 12 : βασιλέα δὲ καὶ μύριον πάσης νοητῆς καὶ αἰσθητῆς φύσεως ; *ib.* : τοῦ Θεοῦ πάσης αἰσθητῆς καὶ νοητῆς φύσεως τοῦ βασιλέως ἡμῶν ; vii. 46 : τὸν βασιλέα πάσης αἰσθητῆς καὶ νοητῆς φύσεως. Cf. viii. 12 : προσφέρομέν σοι τῷ βασιλεῖ καὶ Θεῷ ; 46 : Ἰησοῦ Χριστοῦ τοῦ βασιλέως ἡμῶν.

Δι' οὗ σοὶ δόξα τιμὴ καὶ σέβας. ἀμήν. *Ap. Const.* vii. 38 : σοὶ ἡ δόξα καὶ τὸ σέβας μετὰ Χριστοῦ καὶ πνεύματος ἁγίου νῦν καὶ εἰς τοὺς αἰῶνας· ἀμήν ; viii. 5 : μεθ' οὗ καὶ δι' οὗ σοὶ δόξα τιμὴ καὶ σέβας ἐν ἁγίῳ πνεύματι νῦν καὶ ἀεὶ καὶ εἰς τοὺς αἰῶνας τῶν αἰώνων· ἀμήν. Cf. 6, 7, 8, 11.

THE AUTHORSHIP

After the *Gloria* in the *Apostolic Constitutions* follows another hymn, the latter part of which, σοὶ πρέπει αἶνος, still accompanies it in the offices of the Eastern Church:[1]

Αἰνεῖτε, παῖδες, κύριον, αἰνεῖτε τὸ ὄνομα Κυρίου, αἰνοῦμέν σε, ὑμνοῦμέν σε, εὐλογοῦμέν σε διὰ τὴν μεγάλην σου δόξαν, κύριε βασιλεῦ ὁ πατὴρ τοῦ Χριστοῦ τοῦ ἀμώμου ἀμνοῦ, ὃς αἴρει τὴν ἁμαρτίαν τοῦ κόσμον· σοὶ πρέπει αἶνος, σοὶ πρέπει ὕμνος, σοὶ δόξα πρέπει τῷ πατρὶ καὶ τῷ υἱῷ καὶ τῷ ἁγίῳ πνεύματι εἰς τοὺς αἰῶνάς τῶν αἰώνων· ἀμήν.

It is beside my purpose to enter into a full discussion of the earlier history of the *Gloria*. Having shown that there is reason to believe that it was used in Antioch in 378, when Niceta probably visited that city, there seems to be no incongruity in the suggestion that he may have taken it as the model of his hymn. The Angels' Hymn of the New Testament, which led the author of the *Gloria* to his triumphant "We praise Thee," may have led Niceta to the thought of the Angels' Hymn of the Old Testament, the *Sanctus* of the Liturgy. Then follows in the *Gloria*, as in the *Te Deum*, the enumeration of worshippers, leading up to a short creed. It is important to note that in the earliest text of the *Gloria*, in both versions, mention of the Holy Spirit is inserted here instead of the last sentence. It is possible that the double insertion found in the *Bangor Antiphonary* implies that the original text had neither, that mention of the Holy Spirit was only thought of after the Macedonian controversy. But in that case it is difficult to believe that the interpolator would have been content with the simple words, "and the Holy Spirit," without adding the epithets familiar in the teaching of the fourth century, such as "Paraclete," which was indeed used by Niceta in his hymn. I regard the first mention, therefore, as primitive, and the second as an interpolation, which is the more marked because it obscures the fact that the last words are a quotation from Phil. ii. 11. It is by a mere accident that the first mention has dropped out

[1] In Ὄρθρος (*Horolog.* 1870, p. 72) and Ἀποδεῖπνον (*ib.* pp. 108, 170). I owe this information also to Mr. Brightman.

of our text. Then follows an address to Christ, ending with a threefold prayer for mercy. This finds a parallel in the modern text of the *Te Deum*, but in the present uncertainty about the original text, to which these antiphons may not have belonged, this point cannot be pressed.

If this theory, that the structure of the *Te Deum* was moulded on the lines of the *Gloria*, be accepted, some confirmation is given to the opinion that the first words are addressed to God the Father. And it fits in with a suggestion made by Zahn,[1] that the setting of the hymn following the *Gloria* in the *Apostolic Constitutions* was used by Niceta for his hymn. This hymn begins with the Psalm verse, *Laudate pueri dominum*, familiar to us in the so-called Irish text of the *Te Deum*. And it ends with some words of praise, *Te decet laus*. In MSS. of the modern text of the *Te Deum*,[2] in which the Gospel is appointed to be read after it, these words follow. But, unfortunately, no MS. has both the psalm verse and the *Te decet laus*.

2. Gothic and Gallican "Contestationes"

Another source of the *Te Deum* may be sought in the *Sanctus* and *Contestationes*, or Prefaces of the so-called Gallican and Gothic Missals, and the Gallican Sacramentary. The parallels are indeed so close that Dr. Gibson was able to argue with much force that, "whoever he was, the compiler of the hymn moved naturally and easily in the circle of phrases and expressions found in the fragments that remain to us of the Gallican Liturgy, but *not* found in that of the Church of Rome; and that the source on which he drew must have been the Eucharistic service of his Church, and more especially the variable *Contestatio* or Preface."[3] Our knowledge of these ancient liturgies is still very imperfect. We can only say that it is probable that these prayers are as old or older than the *Te Deum*, and with reference to the new theory of authorship it may be pointed out that there

[1] Art. cit., p. 119. [2] *e.g.* Oxford Bodl. Lib. Canon 83.
[3] *C. Q. R.*, April 1884, p. 19.

are more parallels to the Gothic Missal than to either of the Gallican books. Does that represent the Liturgy used in Dacia ?
1. Dignum et iustum est . . . ut *Te Dominum ac Deum totis uisceribus humana conditio ueneretur*, *Miss. Goth.*, p. 604; *Miss. Gall.*, p. 753.
2, 3, 4. *Omnis terra* adorat te, et *confitetur* tibi: sed et *cœli cœlorum* et *angelicæ potestates* non cessant *laudare* dicentes, *Sanctus*, *Miss. Goth.*, p. 518.
Quem *angeli* et archangeli, quem throni et dominationes, quem *Cherubin et Seraphin incessabili uoce proclamant* dicentes,[1] *Sanctus*, Mone ii.
Cui *omnes angeli* atque archangeli incessabili uoce *proclamant* dicentes, *Sanctus*, *Miss. Gall.*, p. 751.
Totus in orbe terrarum mundus exultat: sed et supernæ concinnunt potestates hymnum gloriæ sine fine dicentes, *ib.*, pp. 473, 750.
Cui merito *omnes angeli* atque archangeli sine cessatione proclamant dicentes, *Sanctus*, *Miss. Goth.*, p. 525.
Omnes angeli atque archangeli, *Cherubin* quoque *et* Seraphin sine intermissione *proclamant* dicentes, *Sanctus*, *ib.*, p. 557.
Cuius regnum . . . *incessabili uoce* proclamabant dicentes, *Sacr. Gall.*, p. 925.
7. Apostolorum chorus, *Miss. Goth.*, p. 528.
8. Tam copioso *prophetarum numero*, Mone v.
13. *Spiritus Sanctus Tuus Paraclitus*, *Sacr. Gall.*, p. 873.
14. *Tu rex gloriæ Christus*, *ib.*, p. 919.
15. *Tu Patris sempiternus es Filius*, Mone ix.
16. Secundum humanam conditionem *liberauit hominem*, Mone v.
17. *Aculeo mortis* extincto, *Miss. Goth.*, p. 532; *mortis* uicit *aculeum*, *ib.*, p. 623; aculeus mortis obtritus, *Sacr. Gall.*, p. 858; *cælorum regna*, *Miss. Goth.*, p. 543; ianuam *regni cælestis aperiat*, *ib.*, p. 540.

[1] The Irish and Milan versions in most MSS. add dicentes, probably a reminiscence of some such liturgical form.

19. Quem *credimus* et fatemur ad *iudicandos* uiuos et mortuos in gloria *esse uenturum*, *Sacr. Gall.*, p. 857; quem omnes gentes expectant *uenturum iudicem* ad iudicandum, *Miss. Goth.*, p. 752.

20. *Quos sanguinis* tui effusione *redemisti*, *Miss. Goth.*, pp. 601, 607; *Sacr. Gall.*, p. 858; oues, *quas pretioso sanguine* Filii tui *redemisti*,[1] *Miss. Gall.*, p. 706.

Another parallel to the *Te Deum* may be found in the Preface of the Liturgy of S. James, where mention is made of "the heavens," "prophets," "martyrs and apostles," with "angels," "Cherubim and Seraphim."

§ IV. The Text

ATTEMPTED RECONSTRUCTION OF THE ORIGINAL TEXT OF THE "TE DEUM"

YMNUS MATUTINALIS

Antiphon, Ps. cxii.
Laudate pueri Dominum laudate nomen Domini

1. To God the Father, a hymn of praise from things visible and invisible.
1. Te Deum laudamus, te Dóminum cónfitémur.ᵛ
2. Te æternum Patrem omnis térra uenerátur.ˢ
3. Tibi omnes angeli, tibi cæli et uniuérsæ potestátes.⁵
4. Tibi cherubim et seraphim incessabili uóce proclámant:ᵖˡ
5. SANCTUS, SANCTUS, SANCTUS, DOMINUS DÉUS SABÁOTH.ᵖˡ
6. PLENI SUNT CÆLI ET TERRA MAIESTATIS GLÓRIÆ TÚÆ.ᵖˡ

Founded on Apostles, Prophets, Martyrs, the Church;
7. Te gloriosus ápostolórum chórus.ᵛ
8. Te prophetarum laudábilis númerus.ᵗ
9. Te martyrum candidatus laúdat exércitus.ᵗ

confesses the Trinity,
10. Te per orbem terrarum sancta confitétur ecclésia:
11. PATREM ÍMMENSÆ MÁIESTÁTIS.ᵛ
12. UENERANDUM TUUM UERUM UNIGÉNITUM FÍLIUM.ᵗ
13. SANCTUM QUOQUE PARÁCLYTUM SPÍRITUM.ᵗ

the glory and
14. Tu rex glóriæ Christe.ᵖˡ

---

[1] The prayer in which these words occur is also found in *Sacr. Leon.* c. 304; *Sacr. Gelas.* cc. 531, 554, 699 (Invocation).

TEXT OF THE "TE DEUM"

mystery of the Incarnation,
15. Tu Patris sempitérnus es Fílius.ᵗ
16. Tu ad liberandum suscépturus hóminem, non horruisti uírginis úterum.ᵗ

echoing the creed
17. Tu deuicto mórtis acúleo,ᵗ aperuisti credentibus régna cælórum.ᵖˡ

as the ground of her petition to be granted
18. Tu ad dexteram Dei sedes in glória Pátris.ᵖˡ
19. Iudex crederis ésse uentúrus.ᵖˡ

grace now and glory hereafter.
20. Te ergo, quæsumus, tuis fámulis súbueni,ᵗ quos prætioso sánguine rédemísti.ᵛ
21. Æterna fac cum sanctis glória múnerári.ᵛ

Capitellum, Ps. xxviii. 0.
22, 23. Saluum fac populum tuum Domine et benedic hæreditati tuæ, et rege eos et extolle illos usque in æternum.

Capitellum of the *Gloria in excelsis*.

Ps. cxlv. 2.
24, 25. Per singulos dies benedicimus te, et laudamus nomen tuum in sæculum et in sæculum sæculi. Amen.

Prayers after the *Te Deum*—
(i.) From antiphons of the *Gloria in excelsis* or *Preces* in the Daily Office.
26. Dignare Domine die isto sine peccato nos custodire.

Ps. cxxiii. 3.
27. Miserere nobis, Domine, miserere nobis.
(ii.) In the Irish version, suggested by its use twice during the Fraction in the Celtic Liturgy?

Ps. xxxiii. 22.
28. Fiat misericordia tua Domine super nos, quemadmodum sperauimus in te.
(iii.) Found in the *Bangor Antiphonary* as the opening clause of a prayer after *Gloria in excelsis*.

Ps. xxxi. 1.
29. In te, Domine, speraui non confundar in æternum.

A prayer of the Celtic Church after the *Te Deum* from the *Bangor Antiphonary*—

"Te Patrem adoramus æternum : te sempiternum Filium inuocamus : teque Spiritum Sanctum in una diuinitatis substantia manentem confitemur. Tibi uni Deo in Trinitate debitas laudes et gratias referamus ut te incessabili uoce laudare mereamur per æterna sæcula."

A few words may be said about the analysis which I have printed in the margin.

Verses 1–7.—" To God the Father a hymn of praise from

things visible and invisible." This interpretation alone gives a plain meaning to the words *æternum patrem* in verse 2. It is rendered necessary by the *tuum* of verse 12. And it is confirmed by the analogy of the train of thought in the *Gloria in excelsis*, the first part of which is addressed to the Father. Since both canticles may be said to have been composed in the same age, this argument from analogy is quite independent of the theory that a closer relationship existed between them. Dr. Gibson has indeed pointed attention to a remarkable parallel in the first quotation from the *Missale Gothicum* given above (p. 271), in a special preface, which is the only one addressed to God the Son, and contains accusatives instead of the usual vocatives :—

> Dignum et iustum est ... ut *Te Dominum* ac *Deum* totis uisceribus humana conditio *ueneretur*.

If, on other grounds, it were possible to believe that the whole is a hymn to Christ, this would be a remarkable confirmation of it. But no reasonable explanation has ever been given of *æternum Patrem* as addressed to Christ. It was never adopted by Latin writers as an equivalent of πατὴρ τοῦ μέλλοντος αἰῶνος in Isaiah ix. 6, the closest parallel to it. Another argument has been sought in the wording of an ancient hymn to Christ, which is undeniably moulded by the thought of the *Te Deum* throughout.[1] It begins: "Christe Rex coeli." But this argument carries its own refutation with it in the line, "Thou Word of the Eternal Father."

On the other hand, a curious rendering of the hymn into Latin hexameters by Candidus, a monk of Fulda under Ratgar, 802–817, leaves no doubt as to the opinion held in the ninth century :[2]

> "Te ergo Deum laudamus te dominumque fatemur
> Te genitorem perpetuum terra ueneratur."

Verses 7–13.—Founded on apostles, prophets, martyrs, the Church comfesses the Trinity.

---

[1] Daniel, *Thesaurus*, i. p. 46.

[2] *Mon. Hist. Poet. Lat. aevi Carolini*, ed. Duemmler, ii. I owe this reference to Dr. Gibson.

TEXT OF THE "TE DEUM" 275

Verses 14–21.—(The Church confesses) the glory and mystery of the incarnation, echoing the creed as the ground of her petition to be granted grace now and glory hereafter. The outline of the Apostles' Creed is followed closely in the references to the nativity, passion, resurrection, session, and return to Judgment. Here the original hymn ends, a fact which is brought out very clearly by an interesting Irish text printed by Rev. F. E. Warren from a MS. in the British Museum (*Harl.* 7653, s. viii, ix.).[1] It was the work probably of an Irish nun, and contains a Litany and other prayers. Among them without title are introduced verses 1–21 of the *Te Deum*.

In this attempt to reconstruct the original text of the hymn in the light of the new theory, we assume that Niceta sent or brought it to Italy, possibly in time to be sung by S. Ambrose and S. Augustine in 386, or in the last decade of the century. It may have been passed on by Paulinus to his friends at Lerins. From Lerins it came into the possession of the Celtic Church in Ireland, possibly through S. Patrick. Our debt to the Irish version, which has preserved the author's name and the opening antiphon and the tradition respecting the limits of the original hymn, must not tempt us to regard it as necessarily the purest text. Its corruptions, however, are easily explained.

The first important variant is found in verse 6, where the Irish text has: " Pleni sunt cæli et *uniuersa* terra *honore* gloriæ tuæ." The other texts omit *uniuersa*, and for *honore* read maiestatis gloriæ tuæ,[p1] or in the Milan version " gloriæ maiestatis tuæ." The reading *honore* may be explained by the presence of the word *honor* in the Spanish[2] form of the Gloria Patri, which is found in the *Bangor Antiphonary*, and was therefore known to the Irish Church. To a scribe it might seem to introduce a familiar thought, and it was a less unwieldy phrase than *maiestatis*. To fill up the line, he or someone else would introduce *universa*. The order of the Milan version *gloriæ maiestatis* is found in the Mozarabic text of the *Te Deum*. But the familiar idea in Christian

[1] Bradshaw Society, vol. x. pp. 83 ff. [2] *Conc. Tolet.* iv. c. 15.

worship is to give glory, and it seems more natural to predicate majesty of glory than the contrary. There is an interesting parallel sentence in the sermon of Hilary of Arles, which he preached after the death of Honoratus, the founder of Lerins : " Nec facile tam exerte tam lucide quisquam de diuinitatis trinitate disseruit cum eam personis distingueres et gloriae aeternitate ac maiestate sociares." We have therefore early authority for the phrase in this order "majesty of glory" apart from the question of the text of the hymn, and apart also from the fact that " maiestatis gloriae tuae " ^{p1} makes a better rhythmical ending.

In verse 12 the Irish version in all MSS. and the oldest MS. of the Milan version (*Cod. Vat.* 82) have *unigenitum filium*,^{t} though all other MSS. have *unicum*. This is a case in which the copyists would be misled by remembrance of the Apostles' Creed, in which *unigenitum* is rare, though found in the Creed of Cyprian of Toulon, an early witness to the *Te Deum*. *Unicum*, on the other hand, is common in the creed. The rhythm is decisive in favour of *unigenitum*.

We now come to the much-disputed reading of verse 16. New light has been thrown upon it by the publication of the letter of Cyprian of Toulon, to which reference has been made,[1] and from which we learn that the reading used in the south-east of Gaul at the beginning of the sixth century was, "Tu ad liberandum suscepturus hominem non horruisti uirginis uterum." Thus it was not a mere pedantic correction made by Abbo of Fleury in the tenth century. The Irish text adds *mundum* after *liberandum*, with *suscepisti* for *suscepturus*. It has been suggested that *mundum* may have dropped out through *homoeoteleuton*. This is quite possible, but it is more probably an interpolation by an Irish copyist who was familiar with the idea of the phrase *Saluator mundi*. The word *mundus* recurs frequently in the collects of the *Bangor Antiphonary*. Since none of the MSS. of the other versions insert the word, it seems inadvisable to adopt it.

[1] P. 257 *supra*.

In verse 20 in one MS. of the Milan version (*Cod. Monac. lat.* 343), and in some six or seven MSS. of the ordinary version, *sancte* has been added after *ergo*. In the Milan Breviary it is added after *quæsumus*. This was at one time a widely spread reading, and has been traced by Dr. Gibson to the influence of the last stanza of an old Sunday morning hymn, *O rex æterne*, which begins, *Te ergo sancte quæsumus*.

In the Munich MS. I found that hymn immediately after the *Te Deum*.

In verse 21 the true reading of all MSS., *gloria munerari*, has been changed into *gloria numerari* in printed editions of the Breviary from 1491 onwards.

Our Prayer Book translation suffers in consequence. Dr. Gibson thinks that it originated in an attempt at textual criticism, and was suggested by the well-known words added by Gregory the Great to the Canon of the Mass, "in electorum tuorum iubeas grege numerari."

We come now to the problem of the antiphons or Psalm verses with which the hymn is concluded. A simple diagram will serve to show at a glance the relations of the different combinations, the full text being as follows:—

	Vv. 22, 23.	Saluum fac populum tuum Domine et benedic hæreditati
Ps. xxviii. 9.		tuæ, et rege eos et extolle illos usque in æternum.
	24. 25.	Per singulos dies benedicimus te, et laudamus nomen
Ps. cxlv. 2.		tuum in sæculum et in sæculum sæculi.
	26.	Dignare Domine die isto sine peccato nos custodire.
Ps. cxxiii. 3.	27.	Miserere nobis, Domine, miserere nobis.
Ps. xxxiii. 22.	28.	Fiat misericordia tua, Domine, super nos quemadmodum sperauimus in te.
Ps. xxxi. 1.	29.	In te, Domine, speraui non confundar in æternum.
Dan. iii. 26.	-	Benedictus es Domine Deus patrum nostrorum et laudabile et gloriosum nomen tuum in sæcula.

O Ordinary Version in our Prayer Book.
I Irish Version in the *Bangor Antiphonary*.
G The *Gloria in excelsis* (*Cod. Alexandrinus* and *Bangor Antiphonary*).
A *Cod. Vat. Alex.* xi.
M Milan Version in *Cod. Vat.* 82.

Verses						
22, 23	O	I		A	24, 25	M
24, 25	O	I	G		22, 23	M
			*	*		
26, 27	O		G	A		
			*			
28	O	I				
29	O					

Dr. Gibson's most interesting suggestion, that some of these antiphons were transferred from the *Gloria in excelsis*, has been commonly misunderstood. It will be remembered that the Rule of Cæsarius directed the use of *Te Deum laudamus, Gloria in excelsis, Deo et capitellum*.

The Council of Agde in 506 directed in their canon that the *capitula* from the Psalms should always be read after the lessons. These *capitula* = *capitella*, or antiphons, seem to have been in common use in the whole Church, for we find them in a fifth-century MS. of the *Gloria in excelsis* (*Cod. Alexandrinus*). It seems therefore natural to suppose that such were added to the *Te Deum* from the fifth century.

The simplest explanation of the enlargement is as follows: that Ps. xxviii. 9, 10, *Saluum fac populum* = verses 22, 23 of the Ordinary Version, was the *capitellum* appointed for the *Te Deum* in the Gallican Church. On the other hand, Ps. cxlv. 2, *Per singulos dies* = verses, 24, 25, was the *capitellum* for the *Gloria in excelsis*. When the *Gloria in excelsis* was transferred to the Liturgy, its *capitellum*, specially mentioned by Cæsarius, was attached to the *Te Deum*. It is an interesting fact that *Saluum fac* is not found among the *capitella* appended to the *Gloria* in any of the three Irish texts printed by Mr. Warren,[1]

[1] *Bangor Antiphonary*, ii. p. 78.

whereas Ps. cxlv. 2, *Per singulos dies*, with variant readings, *Cotidie* or *In omni tempore*, heads each list.

We have yet to explain the appearance of the additional verse, Ps. xxxiii. 22, *Fiat misericordia* = verse 26 in the Irish text of the *Te Deum*. That it did not originally belong to it is hinted by the Amen which precedes it in the *Bangor Antiphonary*. It was prescribed for use twice during the Fraction in the Celtic Liturgy.

The text of the antiphons in A is plainly formed by adding to the *capitellum* of the *Te Deum* two *capitella* from the *Gloria*.

The text in M represents the ordinary Milan version preserved down to the eleventh century. There is a curious inversion of verses 22, 23 following 24, 25, and followed by the verse from Daniel. It is not likely that this was the original text.

The ordinary version simply consists in the addition of 26, 27, which were familiar as *preces*, apart from the use after the *Gloria*, together with 28 found in the Irish version, and 29, Ps. xxxi. 4, which is found in the *Bangor Antiphonary* as the opening clause of a prayer after the *Gloria*. This offers an additional proof that our version is founded on the Irish rather than the Milan version.

CHAPTER XII

OF THE USE OF CREEDS

§ I. Of the Early Use of a Baptismal Creed.
§ II. The History of the term *Symbolum*.
§ III. Our Use of our Apostles' and Nicene Creeds.
§ IV. The Athanasian Creed.

Thus far my purpose has been mainly historical, to trace the development of the chief creeds of Christendom to the point at which each attains the form in which it is used to-day. It remains to justify this use. With this object it will be necessary to review briefly some of the theological statements made by way of explanation of historical facts. "Trahit sua quemque uoluntas." Faith still includes an act of will to believe all that the Scriptures have spoken as summarised in the creeds. Its reasonableness is found in recognition of the continuity of thought which unites the saints of to-day with the Church of the first century in one communion and fellowship.

§ I. THE EARLY USE OF A BAPTISMAL CREED

Our historic faith began with a simple confession of loyalty to Christ, of belief in His Person, which carried with it belief in His words. The Church required this as the minimum of knowledge which a Christian ought to have and believe to his soul's health.

Confession of faith in Jesus as the Lord, or the Son of God, was to a Jew or a proselyte the pledge of faith in one living and true God, who had visited His people Israel. It was inseparably bound up with the teaching of the Lord's

Prayer. The cobwebs which Scribes and Pharisees had spun out of the law were brushed aside. They knew that they were treading the way of life in the light of God's presence, having seen the light of the knowledge of the glory of God in the face of Jesus Christ.

The heathen had more to learn, if he had nothing to unlearn. For him, as for the Jew, it was all summed up in the Baptismal Formula, when he was baptized "into the name of the Father and of the Son and of the Holy Ghost."

The Old Roman Creed, which we have traced back to the generation immediately succeeding the apostles, is to be regarded as containing a summary of the catechetical instruction given *c.* 100 in the ancient Church to which both S. Peter and S. Paul had ministered in the great capital where they laid down their lives for their faith. It was truly a Rule of apostolic teaching, and the strength and simplicity of its style secured for it acceptance in other Churches from very early times. At that time the Roman Church was bilingual, and it is probable that its Latin and Greek forms were composed by the same hand. With one possible exception, this form remained unaltered to the fifth century. Enough has been said elsewhere of the exact and rigid fidelity with which it was preserved. It was only given to the catechumen (*Traditio symboli*) when he had been taught and tested, and he was required to repeat it publicly before his baptism (*Redditio symboli*). The earliest expositions delivered at the *Traditio* which have come down to us belong to the fourth century. Both Cyril and Augustine[1] lay stress on the prohibition to commit it to writing. It was to be written in the heart only. This strong feeling lasted on to the fifth century. Peter Chrysologus, Archbishop of Ravenna, taught: "Let the mind hold and the memory guard this pledge of hope, this decree of salvation, this symbol of life, this safeguard of faith, lest vile paper depreciate the precious gift of the divinity, lest black ink obscure the mystery of light, lest an unworthy and profane hearer hold the secret of God."[2] His rhetoric

[1] Cyril Hieros. *Cat.* v. 12; Aug. *Serm. ad Catech.* i.   [2] Serm. 59.

strikes one as artificial and inflated, and marks the period when the custom died out. It is not possible to assign a precise date to its origin, which was probably contemporaneous with the first use of fixed forms in the second century.

§ II. The History of the Term "Symbolum"

The use of a distinctive name for the Baptismal Creed marks the beginning of a new stage in its history; but it is not easy to determine when that stage was reached. As in the New Testament, such a phrase as "the Faith" referred rather to the subject-matter of teaching than to any form; so, in subsequent history, we must beware of giving too precise a meaning to terms like Justin Martyr's παρειλήφαμεν, δεδιδάγμεθα, μεμαθήκαμεν, or even to phrases of Irenæus: I. 9. 4, τὸν κανόνα τῆς ἀληθείας; I. 22. 1, regulam ueritatis; III. 3. 1, traditionem apostolorum. There is a controversy, as yet unsettled, as to the meaning of the term Rule. Some writers maintain that the creed itself, the bare form, was the Rule of Faith; others, that the Rule was the enlarged interpretation of the creed, though the creed would certainly be the groundwork of the interpretation.[1]

Certainly Irenæus included in his Rule of Truth some articles not yet added to the Roman Creed, which he probably knew. Nor are they found in the Creed of Gaul, when it comes to light in the fourth century, e.g. III. 4: "Maker of heaven and earth," taught with an anti-Gnostic reference.

Tertullian, however, proves a much more definite use of a fixed form, identified with the Rule of Faith common to the Churches of Rome and Africa, as a *tessera*, or token of fellowship.

The illustration is derived from the *tessera hospitalitatis*, an earthenware token, which two friends divided and passed on to their descendants, making the duty of friendship hereditary. Tertullian's words may refer to the way in which the creed was used as a badge of a Christian's

[1] Kattenbusch, ii. p. 81.

profession, admitting him to social meals in churches where he was a stranger.

This seems to be the root-idea of the term *symbolum* also as a Christian phrase. The word is used by Tertullian several times, but only in two passages with any reference to baptism or the use of a formal creed. He calls baptism *symbolum mortis*, where the word is easy to explain as a sign or sacrament in our sense. And he challenges Marcion, as a merchant in spiritual wares, to show the *symbolum* or token of their genuineness, *adv. Marc.* v. 1 : " Quamobrem, Pontice nauclere, si nunquam furtiuas merces uel illicitas in acatos tuas recepisti, si nullum omnino onus auertisti uel adulterasti, cautior utique et fidelior in dei rebus, edas uelim nobis, *quo symbolo susceperis apostolum Paulum*, quis illum tituli charactere percusserit, quis transmiserit tibi, quis imposuerit, ut possis eum constanter exponere." Kattenbusch [1] points out that the term had affinities to the terms *sacramentum* and *regula*.

It is indeed doubtful if the term had a technical sense in Tertullian's time, but it is plain that it was on the point of acquiring one. Cyprian, in his letter to Magnus, arguing against the validity of Novatianist baptism, deals with the objection that these " schismatics used the same symbol and law of the symbol and questions," [2] where the phrase " law of the symbol " appears to refer to the creed. But Firmilian of Cappadocia, in his letter to Cyprian, uses the term *symbolum Trinitatis* of the Baptismal Formula, so that it is not quite safe to appropriate the word *symbolum* as it stands in Cyprian's sentence for the complete creed.

The questions to which Cyprian refers are plainly the short interrogative creed put to the candidates at the very moment of baptism, which we find coexisting with the longer declaratory form certainly from the third century. Perhaps it is to such a form that Tertullian refers, *de Cor. Mil.* 3 : " Dehinc ter mergitamur amplius aliquid respondentes quam Dominus in euangelio determinauit."

[1] ii. p. 80, n. 43.
[2] *Ep. ad Magn.*: ("symbolum et lex symboli et quæstiones."

CYPRIAN, *Ep.* 70, 76.

Credis in Deum Patrem,
in Filium Christum,
in Spiritum Sanctum?

Credis in uitam æternam
et remissionem
peccatorum
per sanctam ecclesiam;

or

Credis in remissionem peccatorum
et uitam æternam
per sanctam ecclesiam?

CYRIL OF JERUSALEM,
Cat. x. 4.

Πιστεύεις εἰς τὸ
ὄνομα τοῦ Πατρὸς
καὶ τοῦ Υἱοῦ
καὶ τοῦ ἁγίου
Πνεύματος;

GELASIAN SACRAMENTARY.

Credis in Deum Patrem
omnipotentem?

Credis in Iesum Christum
Filium eius unicum
dominum nostrum,
natum et passum?

Credis et in Spiritum Sanctum,
sanctum ecclesiam,
remissionem peccatorum,
carnis resurrectionem?

Many more of these forms might be quoted,[1] but with the exception of the short Creed of Cyril it is impossible to believe that any of them represent earlier forms than the declaratory creeds to be connected with the Churches to which they belong.[2]

In the fourth century the term *symbolum* was firmly established in the West, and was identified by Augustine with the Rule of Faith, though Cyril still clung to the simpler name "the Faith." The interpretations which began to gather round the term, by their very variety prove its antiquity. The most important in after times was founded on the confusion of σύμβολον with συμβολή = *collatio*. The creed was regarded as a collation or epitome of doctrine contributed by the twelve apostles. This explanation, founded on the legend of the apostolic origin of the creed, was given by Rufinus and Cassian,[3] and was most popular in later expositions.

But Rufinus comes nearer to the truth when he explains it as *indicium* or *signum*, a token of orthodox belief, the watchword of the Christian soldier.[4]

The title *symbolum apostolorum* was first used by S. Ambrose, and occurs in the letter of the Council of Milan, which was possibly drawn up by him.[5] S. Jerome also wrote of the *symbolum fidei* . . . *quod ab apostolis traditum*.[6] In some old

[1] Hahn,[3] pp. 34-36.
[2] On this ground I differ from Lumby, p. 18.
[3] *De Incarnatione Uerbi*, VI. iii. : "Collatio autem ideo, quia in unum collata ab Apostolis Domini, totius catholicæ legis fide, quicquid per uniuersum diuinorum uoluminum corpus immensa funditur copia, totum in symboli colligitur breuitate perfecta."
[4] *In Symb. Apost.*: "Symbolum enim Græce et indicium dici potest et collatio, hoc est, quod plures in unum conferunt. Id enim fecerunt apostoli in his sermonibus, in unum conferendo unusquisque quod sensit. . . . Idcirco istud indicium posuere, per quod agnosceretur is qui Christum uere secundum apostolicas regulas prædicaret. Denique et in bellis ciuilibus hoc obseruari ferunt: quoniam et armorum habitus par, et sonus uocis idem, et mos unus est, atque eadem instituta bellandi, ne qua doli subreptio fiat, symbolo distincta unusquisque dux suis militibus tradit, quæ Latine 'signa' uel indicia nuncupantur; ut si forte occurrerit quis de quo dubitetur, interrogatus symbolum, prodat si sit hostis uel socius."
[5] *Opera*, v. p. 292.
[6] *Ad Pammach. c. Ioann. Hier. Opera*, ii. col. 380.

MSS. the form *symbolum apostolicum* is found, but it is not so common as the other (which occurs in the *Bangor Antiphonary*, seventh century).

It is more probable that the belief suggested the name. The plain title *symbolum* continued to be used for a long time side by side with it.

Thus Niceta explains it as the covenant made with the Lord, as a summary of Christian mysteries collected from the Scriptures for the use of the unlearned, like a crown set with precious stones.[1] Faustus of Riez, though it is possible that he has some sentences of Niceta in mind, gives a different derivation from the use of the plural *symbola*, contributions to a common feast, gathered by the Fathers of the Churches for the good of souls.[2]

The legend of apostolic origin, attached in the first instance to the Old Roman Creed, was naturally transferred to its later form, and was received without question in mediæval times.

§ III. Our Use of our Apostles' and Nicene Creeds

Besides the universal use of the Apostles' Creed as the Baptismal Creed of Western Christendom, it has been used in the Hour Offices since the ninth century.[3] Its voluntary use at such times was very ancient. Bede reminds Egbert that S. Ambrose exhorted the faithful to recite it at Matins

[1] "Retinete semper pactum, quod fecistis cum domino, id est hoc symbolum, quod coram angelis et hominibus confitemini. Pauca quidem sunt uerba, sed omnia continent sacramenta. De totis enim scripturis hæc breuitatis causa collecta sunt, tanquam geminæ pretiosæ in una corona compositæ, ut, quoniam plures credentium literas nesciunt, uel, qui sciunt, per occupationes sæculi scripturas legere non possunt, habeant sufficientem sibi scientiam salutarem."

[2] *Hom.* i. ed. Caspari, *Anecdota*, i. p. 315: "Sicut nonnullis scire permissum est, apud ueteres symbola uocabantur, quod de substantia collecti in unum sodales in medio conferebant ad solemnes epulas, ad cœnæ communes expensas. Ita et ecclesiarum patres, de populorum salute solliciti, ex diuersis uoluminibus scripturarum collegerunt testimonia diuinis grauida sacramentis. Disponentes itaque ad animarum pastum salubre conuiuium, collegerunt uerba breuia et certa, expedita sententiis, sed diffusa mysteriis, et hoc symbolum nominauerunt."

[3] Amalarius, *de Eccl. Offic.* iv. 2, M.S.L. 105, 1165.

as an antidote to the poison of the devil by night and day.[1] Thus it passed at our Reformation into our Daily Offices, and was included in the Catechism put into the hand of every child. Its value for educational use is increased by the fact that it allows the teacher freedom of detailed exposition. It does not attempt to narrate the whole history of the Lord Jesus, when He went in and out among His people; nor to furnish "a character sketch," which would be as impossible as painters have found it to paint His face. For frequent liturgical use it meets our need, in that it is not crowded with subjective impressions. The same thing is true of our Nicene Creed, considered generally as a form of Apostles' Creed. Even the added theological clauses have no taint of modern subjectivity.

The Apostles' Creed "paints before our eyes in broad outline the wonderful works of God, which, as long as we cherish them in faith and apply them to ourselves, will as little grow old and wearisome as the rising and setting of the sun every day on which God permits us to see the beauty of His works."[2]

In Eastern Christendom the Nicene Creed has superseded every other form as a Baptismal Confession, and as the Creed of Communicants in the Liturgies. From the former point of view it is interesting to point out characteristics in which this as an Eastern Creed differs from Western forms. It gives reasons for facts stated, e.g. Who *for us men and for our salvation* came, crucified also *for us*, rose . . . *according to the Scriptures*, One *baptism for* the remission of sins.[3] It preserves the word "One" in the first Article, which the Western archetype (R) has lost, and it adds "Maker of heaven and earth," words which, amid the conflicts of Gnostic speculations, were soon needed in the East, though they serve a catechetical rather than controversial purpose.

From the latter point of view, since this use of a theological creed has spread into the West (Toledo 589, Rome

---

[1] Hadden and Stubbs, iii. p. 316.
[2] Zahn, *Das ap. Symbol.*, p. 101.
[3] Gibson, *The Thirty nine Articles*, i. p. 302.

c. 1000),[1] something must be said of the present day usefulness of theological creeds.

Such usefulness is of two kinds, negative and positive; the first local and transitory, the second universal and lasting. As a sign-post in days of controversy, such a creed may be set, like the first Nicene Creed, to repudiate partial and rationalising explanations of Christ's perfect Godhead or perfect Manhood. As Mr. Balfour [2] has clearly stated, " the Church held that all such partial explanations [as the great heresiarchs attempted] inflicted irremediable impoverishment on the idea of the Godhead which was essentially involved in the Christian revelation. They insisted on preserving that idea in all its inexplicable fulness; and so it has come about that, while such simplifications as those of the Arians, for example, are so alien and impossible to modern modes of thought that if they had been incorporated with Christianity they must have destroyed it, the doctrine of Christ's Divinity still gives reality and life to the worship of millions of pious souls, who are wholly ignorant both of the controversy to which they owe its preservation, and of the technicalities which its discussion has involved."

This is not all. The formula which was found to exclude the Arian hypothesis, and is at all times available for that purpose, may also be used to aid worship, to guide the prophets of each new generation, who see the old truths in a new light.

We may know our way about a district fairly well, and not be able to draw a map of it. Yet with a map how much more definite will be the advice which we can offer to wayfarers. A theological creed is like a map, a survey of a certain region of thought drawn with a sense of proportion. Our Nicene Creed witnesses to " the spiritual power of a complete belief," complete because it interprets the Gospel history with due regard to the proportion of faith.

We cannot ask to be as if the old controversies had never been, as if through 1800 years no one had ever asked a question. If we could start as some would wish, as S. Cyril himself

[1] Swainson, p. 136.   [2] *Foundations of Belief*, p. 279.

wished in his early days, with the Bible, and the Bible only, we know, from the experience of every town parish priest, that the old errors would reappear in the form of new questions, and we should have to traverse again the same dreary wilderness of controversy from implicit to explicit dogma, from "I believe that Jesus is the Lord" to the confession that the Only-begotten Son of the Father is of one substance with the Father.

§ IV. Our Use of the Athanasian Creed

It is difficult to estimate the usefulness of this creed in the present day, without suffering from some bias of judgment through impressions produced by study of its early history. Yet its dogmatic value is really independent of historical theories as to its origin. Men so unlike as Charles Kingsley and John Henry Newman were united by a common admiration of its theological teaching without reference to its history. Neither from the Anglican nor from the Roman point of view does it matter in what century the creed was written, or its clauses received their final polish. They were concerned solely with the question, "Is it a true analysis of Christian experience?" History alone cannot decide this. Its proper task is to show us the original home of the creed, the changing figures and groups of the men who first voiced its measured rhythms, whose hopes and fears changed like lights and shadows on the landscape of their common Church life. That task ended, it is for theology to complete the argument and bear witness to the truth of its teaching as the common heritage of the Church since the days when her unity was unbroken, and, despite trial and tribulation, her cup of joy was full.

At least, it may be hoped that the bitterness, too often caused by extraneous considerations, which has been imported into modern controversies, may be in some measure allayed by the triumph of the theory that the author belonged to the school of Lerins. For Lerins was a true home of saints and confessors. Her sons did not prefer peace to truth. The very reproach of semi-Pelagianism, which rested upon some of her most honoured names, witnessed to the fact that they had sought to keep on that *via media* which is seldom the way of peace. The revealed truths of Free Will and Grace are rooted in what seemed to the apostles an insoluble mystery,[1] and the merit of Faustus and Cæsarius, so far as their teaching was anti-Augustinian, consisted in an honest endeavour to do justice to the obscurer aspect of a difficult problem. It is really the same problem under changed conditions of thought which faces us in our present inquiry. The responsibility of intellect in matters of faith was then acknowledged without question. It was the responsibility of man for conduct which was in dispute. In an interesting letter (*Ep.* 5), Faustus discusses the question whether believers in a United Trinity can be eternally lost. His correspondent Paulinus was concerned to know, not whether those who live a good moral life, but fall into intellectual error, should perish, but whether those who profess a correct creed will be saved in spite of sins against morality. Faustus replies, that "in Divine things not only is a plan of believing required, but also of pleasing." A baptized person must remember that he is the temple of God, and he quotes 1 Cor. iii. 17: "If any man defile the temple of God, him shall God destroy." The whole tone of the letter is sympathetic and spiritual. It shows a mind as far removed from a barren scholastic orthodoxy as from an undisciplined readiness to believe "anything good." And it enables us to guess how Faustus would have interpreted the damnatory clauses of the *Quicunque* in relation to a heresy like that of Priscillian. In all ages the tendency of such an esoteric doctrine of election is to encourage secret immorality, however sternly its author may have upheld moral law. And the teaching of the Catholic Church, to which both Faustus and the *Quicunque* witness, does not subordinate moral law to metaphysical arguments, but claims the highest truth of the Christian religion as the strongest motive power of a good life.

[1] Rom. ix. 20; Phil. ii. 12.

From this point of view let us approach the question of the so-called damnatory clauses of the creed. They do not judge any individual case. They assert only the principle that a man's faith influences his conduct, and that he must be judged by conduct. Falsity to faith must inevitably bring blemish on his character, and his conduct will show it. This is not a mere dogma of the Church, since Carlyle has written: "When belief waxes uncertain, practice becomes unsound"; and Emerson: "A man's action is the picture-book of his creed." As Dean Hook used to say, the only really damnatory clause is the 39th: "And they who have done good shall go into life eternal, and they who in deed *have done* evil into eternal fire." We should be false to the stern side of the Lord's teaching if we said less. And the truth expressed is quite independent of our interpretation of the words "eternal" or "fire." The question is one of fact. Every Christian believes in future punishment. Bishop Butler has shown that it is a fundamental doctrine of natural religion. In any age men may interpret such teaching in a more or less materialistic manner, but the mistaken form in which they receive it does not undermine the position which it holds either in revealed or in natural religion.

The reply is sometimes urged that the second clause goes beyond the limits thus assigned to monitory teaching: "Which *faith* except everyone shall keep whole and undefiled without doubt he shall perish eternally." It is said that in this clause we condemn Arius and other heretics, and all who are prevented by conscientious scruples from using the creed.

This is not so. The grammatical connexion of this clause to the preceding is that of a simple relative sentence. It is not the principal sentence. The result of printing the creed as a canticle has been to force into prominence what is a subordinate idea. It has been truly said that "the Church has her long list of saints. She has never inserted one name in any catalogue of the damned." The clause asserts only that disloyalty to faith must lead to spoiling of character, and thus to the eternal perishing from which in our Litany we pray to be delivered. As to Arius, we judge not before the time. As to the scruples of those who cannot accept the faith in the form here presented, we reply that it is not the creed which is taught to all the baptized, nor the creed which is recited by communicants. Assent to it, with the other creeds, is required only from Church teachers on the ground that they ought thoroughly to be received and believed, "for they may be proved by most certain warrants of Holy Scripture."[1] No one who believes every word of the Apostles' Creed is condemned by the Athanasian Creed, which, to speak technically, requires an implicit rather than explicit assent to its definitions; or, to speak popularly, assent to the facts of Christian experience rather than interpretations of those facts, faith in Divine Persons, faith in the Divine Christ. It is maintained that the interpretations are logical. A man may illogically refuse to accept them while he accepts the facts. Faith, not logic, will save him. Does he believe in the Blessed Trinity? His Catechism will teach him that out of the Apostles' Creed. Does he believe in the incarnation of our Lord Jesus Christ, that Christ crucified is to us who are being saved the power of God? This is the present salvation spoken of in the second clause, and the point of view is grace, of which he is not ignorant, nor from which has he fallen. He is at one with the author of the creed, who leads up to his main statement in clause 3: "Now the Catholic faith is this," not that we define or dogmatise unduly, but "that we worship One God in Trinity."

Most unjustly has this creed been pilloried as containing "man's dogma of damnation." The words are quoted from an exquisite tale of Indian life called "The Old Missionary," by Sir William Hunter, which has been sold by thousands. Such an expression could only be used rightly of a particular tenet such as Calvin's doctrine of Predestination. But the objections are not always thus based on moral principles. To the spirit of easy-going indifferentism, which is the besetting sin of a self-indulgent age, morality and the creed are alike stumbling-blocks. "Morality is so icy, so intolerant; its

[1] Art. viii.

doctrines have the ungentlemanlike rigour of the Athanasian Creed."[1] Such a judgment is profoundly anti-Christian, and is contradicted by the whole tenour of the New Testament.

A more serious objection is founded on the supposed necessity of explaining away the meaning of the author when his words are qualified. It is said that the clergy can put their own gloss on them, but cannot explain them in plain English to plain people, who must regard so much qualification as a more or less dishonest attempt to evade the literal meaning. This objection has no real weight. "It is an acknowledged principle in the interpretation of the damnatory language of Scripture regarding unbelief, that it is to be understood with conditions: the same rule of interpretation applies to the damnatory clauses of the Athanasian Creed. The omission of conditions is one of those expedients of which language has frequently availed itself for the sake of convenience,—making absolute statements when that which qualifies them is left to be understood."[2] We agree that the commands "Give to him that asketh of thee" and "Resist not evil" require qualification. "And just as *moral instruction* requires its liberty of speech, and has modes of statement which must not be tied to the letter, so has *judicial and condemnatory language.*"[3] People say, "We will have the Bible, and the Bible only." It is precisely in the Bible language that the difficulty lies; and if the letter of the grammar gives an artificial and false sense in Scripture, it cannot give the natural sense in the creed.

Many drastic proposals have been made for the alteration of these clauses, for what Dean Goulburn called in a trenchant phrase "the mutilating or muffling of the creed." It is proposed to cut them out. What assembly short of a General Council would have the right to treat thus a formulary sanctioned by use during a thousand years in the whole Church Catholic? It would establish a new and unheard of precedent. Again, it is proposed to do away with the rubric and

[1] An objection quoted by the Archbishop of Armagh, *Epistles of S. John*, p. 263.
[2] Mozley, *Lectures and Theological Papers*, p. 194. [3] Mozley, *ib.*

the creed, or relegate it to obscure retirement with the Thirty-nine Articles. This has been done by the American and Irish Churches. Of the former it has been said [1] that "the American Church shelved the creed at a time when people did not go very accurately into the meaning of what they did, and only aimed at a certain convenience in excluding anything which had an explanation wanted for it." This cannot be said of the Irish Church, by whose General Synod the question was fully debated. Strong disapproval of the step was expressed by some of her foremost theologians.[2] Time has not yet justified the wisdom of these Churches, and similar proposals in the Church of England were met and successfully resisted. Laymen combined with clergy to defend the creed. They said with truth that the question concerned them.

The proposal made by Bishop Lightfoot, that the rubric should be altered from "shall" to "may," leaving the use on the appointed days to the discretion of the clergy, would give relief in some cases where a genuine difficulty exists, because the congregations are not prepared for it. But it is open to the objection, which is really insuperable, that a congregation could be denied what they regarded as a privilege at the caprice of an individual.

No such objection could, however, be made to the proposal that the clergy should be permitted by episcopal authority to read it to their congregations rather than with them when this was desired. This, as we have seen, was the primitive congregational use, and such permission would bring our practice into strict conformity with that of the undivided Church Catholic. It sometimes offends one's sense of reverence to hear this solemn statement of the mysteries of our faith chanted too sonorously by a choir, or gabbled by Sunday-school children. Its solemn warnings need to be received rather with silent awe than either recited or sung in a jubilant tone.

Among the words which the late Archbishop Benson

---

[1] Mozley, *Lectures and Theological Papers*, p. 191.
[2] *E.g.* the present Archbishop of Armagh.

addressed to the last Diocesan Conference over which he presided, were the following: "I want to know whether our English people are really so stupid. I do not believe that they are. . . . I have heard many sermons preached against the Athanasian Creed by some who would be glad now to have their utterances forgotten, but I never did hear a sermon preached to explain in simple language to a village congregation the Athanasian Creed, except once, and that was by Charles Kingsley, who, with tears running down his face, explained like a man the Athanasian Creed to his poor people at Eversley."[1]

To conclude—the usefulness of this creed is, like that of the Nicene Creed, negative and positive. We may say with Waterland:[2] "As long as there shall be any men left to oppose the doctrines which this creed contains, so long will it be expedient, and even necessary, to continue the use of it in order to preserve the rest." The expansion of the English Church in the last fifty years aids us to confirm the argument with such testimonies as the following. Bishop Cotton of Calcutta, who went to India prejudiced against the creed, found that he was mistaken, "for the errors rebuked in the Athanasian Creed resulted from tendencies common to the human mind everywhere."[3] But this negative use is less important than the other, to use it as a subject for devout meditation, as being in Hooker's words "a most Divine explication of the chiefest articles of our Christian belief."[4] He thought it worthy "to be heard sounding in the Church of Christ, whether Arianism live or die." And the fact that we connect it with S. Augustine rather than S. Athanasius, in so far as the writer uses forms of thought which S. Augustine had made part of the common heritage of Christian theology, does not alter the case. The special characteristic of the theology of the creed is in the first part, and it is there that the influence of S. Augustine is most clearly seen. Led on in his strivings after self-knowledge, of which the *Confessions* give so vivid a record, he was enabled

[1] Reported in the *Guardian* of July 22, 1896, p. 1161. [2] P. 247.
[3] *Charge*, 1863. [4] *Works*, ed. Keble, ii. p. 187.

to analyse the mystery of his own triune personality, and illustrate it with psychological images. "I exist and I am conscious that I exist, and I love the existence and the consciousness; and all this independently of any external evidence." He carried on a step further S. Hilary's argument from self-consciousness, and applied it to the doctrine of the Holy Spirit, "the first to draw out the thought of the Holy Spirit as the bond of union, the coeternal Love, which unites the Father and the Son." Thus he rises to the thought of God, "whose triunity has nothing potential or unrealised about it; whose triune elements are eternally actualised, by no outward influence, but from within; a Trinity in Unity."[1] This teaching embodied in the *Quicunque* supplements the teaching of the Nicene Creed, and we therefore value it as possessing permanent and positive usefulness.

The history of the *Te Deum* brings our subject to a fitting close. Listening to its solemn strains, we seem to retrace our steps from the developed doctrine of the Blessed Trinity to the simple historical faith in Jesus as the Lord, who has "overcome the sharpness of death." But no longer with weary steps, mounting up with wings as eagles, borne up by the power of the poet's insight to the light of the knowledge of the glory of God in the face of Jesus Christ.

When we look at the sun with the naked eye, we seem to see a dark spot. We know that it does not exist there, because through a darkened glass we see no such thing. In the same way we may use the creeds as the darkened glass of thought, to assure us that if our spiritual sight were stronger all seeming contradictions would vanish in the clear light of truth. They help us to worship without the continual distraction of definition, to believe that we live and work in the light of His Eternal Presence whose love can make hard tasks light and rough paths smooth, and with the vision of peace cause sorrow and sighing to flee away.

[1] Illingworth, *Personality, Human and Divine*, p. 74.

APPENDICES

APPENDIX A.—List of Parallels to the *Quicunque* in Augustine, Vincentius, Faustus, Eucherius.

,, B.—Vigilius of Thapsus.

,, C.—Fulgentius of Ruspe.

,, D.—Early Testimonies to the *Quicunque*.

,, E.—MSS. of the *Te Deum*.

,, F.—Creed of the *Didascalia*.

APPENDIX A.—LIST OF PARALLELS TO "QUICUNQUE"

"Quicunque."	Augustine.
1. Quicunque uult saluus esse ante omnia opus est ut teneat catholicam fidem,	1. *De Util. Cred.* 29.—Catholicæ disciplinæ maiestate institutum est, ut accedentibus ad religionem fides persuadeatur ante omnia. *c. Max.* ii. 23.—Hæc est fides nostra, quoniam hæc fides est recta, quæ fides etiam Catholica nuncupatur. *Enarr. in Ps.* x. 3.—Hæretici . . . simplici fide catholica contenti esse nolunt; quæ una paruulis salus est.
2. quam nisi quisque integram inuiolatamque seruauerit, absque dubio in æternum peribit.	
3. Fides autem catholica hæc est, ut unum Deum in Trinitate, et Trinitatem in Unitate ueneremur;	
4. neque confundentes personas neque substantiam separantes.	4. *De Trin.* vii. 6.—Ut neque personarum sit confusio, nec talis distinctio qua sit impar aliquid.

VINCENTIUS.

1. c. 36.—Catholica fides.
   c. 4.—Inter sacraria catholicæ fidei salui esse potuerunt.

2. c. 7.—Qui uiolauerunt fidem tutos esse non posse, inuiolatamque illibatamque conserua.
   c. 34.—Catholicorum hoc fere proprium, . . . damnare profanas nouitates: et sicut dixit, atque iterum dixit apostolus: si quis annunciauerit, præterquam quod acceptum est, anathemate.
3. c. 22. 18.—Catholica ecclesia unum Deum in Trinitatis plenitudine, et item Trinitatis æqualitatem in una diuinitate ueneratur;
4. Ib.—ut neque singularitas substantiæ personarum confundat proprietatem, neque item Trinitatis distinctio Unitatem separet Deitatis.

FAUSTUS, EUCHERIUS.

3. Faustus, Serm. 9.—Trinitas sine separatione distincta. Pater et Filius et Spiritus Sanctus unus Deus credantur tres personæ et non tres substantiæ.
4. Ib.—Credatur a nobis Unitas sine confusione coniuncta, Trinitas sine separatione distincta.
   Cf. de Spu. Sco. II. i. 12.—Inseparabilem in personis Trinitatem.

APPENDIX A

"QUICUNQUE"—*contd.*

5. Alia est enim persona Patris, alia Filii, alia Spiritus Sancti,

6. sed Patris et Filii et Spiritus Sancti una est diuinitas, æqualis gloria, coæterna maiestas.
7. Qualis Pater talis Filius talis et Spiritus Sanctus.

8. Increatus Pater increatus Filius increatus et Spiritus Sanctus.
9. Immensus Pater immensus Filius immensus et Spiritus Sanctus.
10. Æternus Pater æternus Filius æternus et Spiritus Sanctus,
11. Et tamen non tres æterni sed unus æternus:
12. sicut non tres increati nec tres immensi, sed unus increatus et unus immensus.
13. Similiter omnipotens Pater, omnipotens Filius, omnipotens et Spiritus Sanctus,

14. et tamen non tres omnipotentes sed unus omnipotens.
15. Ita Deus Pater Deus Filius Deus et Spiritus Sanctus,

16. et tamen non tres Dii sed unus est Deus.

17. Ita dominus Pater dominus Filius dominus et Spiritus Sanctus,

AUGUSTINE—*contd.*

6. Serm. 126.—Trinitas est sed una operatio, una æternitas, una coæternitas.

10. Serm. 105.— Æternus Pater coæternus Filius coæternus Spiritus Sanctus.

13. *De Trin.* v. 8.—Itaque omnipotens Pater, omnipotens Filius, omnipotens Spiritus Sanctus.

14. *Ib.*—Nec tamen tres omnipotentes sed unus omnipotens.
15. *De Trin.* i. 5.—Hæc est catholica fides ... sed in ea nonnulli perturbantur cum audiunt Deum Patrem et Deum Filium et Deum Spiritum Sanctum.
16. Et tamen hanc Trinitatem non tres Deos sed unum Deum. Cf. viii. 1.—Deus Pater, Deus Filius, Deus Spiritus Sanctus, nec tamen tres Dii.
17. *c. Maxim.* ii. 23.—Sic et dominum si quæras, singulum quemque respondeo.

APPENDIX A

VINCENTIUS—contd.

5. c. 19.—Quia scilicet alia est persona Patris alia Filii alia Spiritus Sancti,

6. *Ib.*—sed tamen Patris et Filii et Spiritus Sancti non alia et alia sed una eademque natura.

FAUSTUS, EUCHERIUS—contd.

5. Faustus, *de Spu. Sco.* I.—Alter ergo in persona est Deus Pater alter Spiritus Dei Patris.
Ib.—In proprietate personæ alter est P. a. est F. a. S. S.

6. Faustus, Serm. 30.—Coæternitatem . . . maiestatis.

7. Philastr. *Hær.* 45.—Qualis immensa est Patris persona talis est et Filii, talis est Sancti Spiritus.

13. Eucherius, *Lib. sp. int.*—Omnipotens Deus Pater et Filius et Spiritus Sanctus unus et trinus. . . . Solus inuisibilis immensus atque incomprehensibilis.

15. Faustus, Serm. 31.—Pater itaque Deus Filius Deus Spiritus Sanctus Deus, non tres Dii sed unus Deus est.

"Quicunque"—contd.

18. et tamen non tres domini sed unus est dominus.

19. Quia sicut singillatim unamquamque personam et Deum et dominum confiteri christiana ueritate compellimur; ita tres Deos aut dominos dicere catholica religione prohibemur.

20. Pater a nullo est factus nec creatus nec genitus.

21. Filius a Patre solo est, non factus nec creatus sed genitus.

22. Spiritus Sanctus a Patre et Filio, non factus nec creatus nec genitus, sed procedens.

23. Unus ergo Pater non tres Patres, unus Filius non tres Filii, unus Spiritus Sanctus non tres Spiritus Sancti.

24. Et in hac Trinitate nihil prius aut posterius, nihil maius aut minus, sed totæ tres personæ coæternæ sibi sunt et coæquales:

25. ita ut per omnia, sicut iam supradictum est, et Trinitas in Unitate et Unitas in Trinitate ueneranda sit.

26. Qui uult ergo saluus esse ita de Trinitate sentiat.

Augustine—contd.

18. *Ib.*—Sed simul omnes non tres dominos Deos, sed unum dominum Deum.

19. *De Civit. Dei*, xi. 24.—Cum de singulis quæritur, unusquisque eorum et Deus et omnipotens esse respondeatur; cum uero de omnibus simul, non tres Dii, uel tres omnipotentes, sed unus Deus omnipotens.
De Trin. v. 14.—Nam et singillatim si interrogemur de Spiritu Sancto.

20. Serm. 140.—Dicimus Patrem Deum de nullo.

21. *Ep.* 170.—Filius Patris solius. Hunc quippe de sua substantia genuit non ex nihilo fecit.

22. *De Trin.* xv. 11.—De Filio Spiritus Sanctus procedere reperitur.
Ib. v. 14.—Neque natus est sicut unigenitus, neque factus.

23. *c. Maxim.* ii. 23.—Unus est Pater, non duo uel tres; et unus Filius, non duo uel tres; et unus amborum Spiritus, non duo uel tres.

24. Serm. 214. In hac Trinitate non est aliud alio maius, aut minus.

25. *De Trin.* vii. 4.—Unitas Trinitatis.

VINCENTIUS—*contd.*   FAUSTUS, EUCHERIUS—*contd.*

22. Faustus, *Ep.* 3.—Genitus ergo ingenitus et ex utroque procedens personas indigitat.
Cf. *de Spu. Sco.* I. 13.—Mitti a Patre et Filio dicitur et de ipsorum substantia procedere.

24. Faustus, Serm. 31.—Maius autem aut minus ignorat Trinitatem. . . . Nam etsi distinctionem recipit Trinitas gradum tamen nescit æqualitas.

25. c. 22.—Neque item Trinitatis distinctio unitatem separet deitatis.
c. 34.—Trinitatis Unitatem descindere . . . Unitatis Trinitatem confundere.
26. c. 18.—Recta sentiens nec in Trinitatis mysterio, nec in Christo incarnatione blasphemat.

25. Faustus. . . . Trinitatem in Unitate subsistere.

"Quicunque"—contd.

27. Sed necessarium est ad æternam salutem, ut incarnationem quoque domini nostri Iesu Christi fideliter credat.

28. Est ergo fides recta, ut credamus et confiteamur, quia dominus noster Iesus Christus, Dei Filius, Deus et homo est.

29. Deus est ex substantia Patris ante sæcula genitus, et homo est ex substantia matris in sæculo natus.
30. Perfectus Deus, perfectus homo ex anima rationali et humana carne subsistens.

31. Æqualis Patri secundum diuinitatem, minor Patri secundum humanitatem.

32. Qui licet Deus sit et homo non duo tamen sed unus est Christus.

33. Unus autem, non conuersione diuinitatis in carne, sed assumptione humanitatis in Deo.

Augustine—contd.

27. Serm. 264.—Necessariam fidem incarnationis Christi.
Ib. 264.— Necessariam fidem incarnationis fidei Christi.

28. *Enchirid.*35.—Proinde Christus Iesus Dei Filius est et Deus et homo.

29. *Ib.*—Deus ante omnia sæcula: homo in nostro sæculo, unus Dei Filius idemque hominis Filius.
30. Serm. 238.—Aduersus Arium, ueram et perfectam Uerbi diuinitatem ; aduersus Apollinarem, perfectam hominis in Christo defendimus ueritatem.

31. *Ep.* 137.—Æqualem Patri secundum diuinitatem, minorem autem Patre secundum carnem, hoc est secundum hominem.

32. *In Ioh. Tract.* 78.—Agnoscamus geminam substantiam Christi ; diuinam scilicet qua æqualis est Patri, humanam qua maior est Patri... utrumque autem simul non duo sed unus est Christus.

33. *Enchirid.* 34. — Uerbum caro factum est, a diuinitate caro suscepta, non in carnem diuinitate mutata.

APPENDIX A

VINCENTIUS—*contd.*

28. c. 19.—Unus idemque Christus, unus idemque Filius Dei ... unus idemque Christus Deus et homo.

29. *Ib.*—Idem ex Patre ante sæcula genitus, idem in sæculo ex matre generatus.

30. c.20.—Perfectus Deus, perfectus homo; in Deo summa diuinitas, in homo plena humanitas, ... quippe quæ animam simul habeat et carnem.

31. c.19.—Duæ substantiæ sunt ... una ex Patre Deo, altera ex matre uirgine; una coæterna et æqualis Patri, altera ex tempore et minor Patre.
Idem Patri et æqualis et minor.

32. c. 18.—Unum Christum Iesum, non duos, eundemque Deum pariter atque hominem ... et hoc totum unus est Christus.

33. *Ib.*—Unam personam .... quia mutabile non est Uerbum Dei ut ipsum uerteretur in carnem.

FAUSTUS, EUCHERIUS—*contd.*

27. Faustus, *de Spu. Sco.* II. 25.—Hoc loco necessarium uidetur ut in Christo Deo pariter et homine unam personam et duas substantias testimoniis adseramus.

28. *Ib.* ii. 4.—Si in Christo Deo pariter et homine duas substantias dicimus.
Eucherius, *ad. Ioh.* 2.—Quia licet assumpserit hominem, tamen homo et Deus, hoc est Christus, una persona est.

30. Faustus (Euseb.), *de Nat. Dom.* ii. — Perfectus Deus et uerus homo, unus Christus ... sed tamen Dei et hominis una persona: ita coniunctus Deus homini sicut anima corpori ... assumpta est enim humanitas: non absumpta diuinitas.

31. Faustus, Serm. 2.—Secundum diuinitatem æqualis Patri, secundum humanitatem minor etiam angelis.
Eucherius, *ad. Ioh.* 10.—Iuxta quam rationem diuinitatis atque humanitatis, etiam in reliquis quæ aut æqualitatem cum Patre, aut humilitatem eius sonant, facile intellectus patebit.

32. *Ib.* 2.—Quia licet assumpserit hominem, tamen homo et Deus, hoc est Christus, una persona est.

33. Faustus (Euseb.), *Hom. de Latrone beato.*—In una eademque persona quam bene manifestantur humana pariter et diuina?

"QUICUNQUE"—*contd.*

AUGUSTINE—*contd.*
Cf. Serm. 187.—Adsumpta humana substantia.

34. Unus omnino non confusione substantiæ sed unitate personæ.

35. Nam sicut anima rationalis et caro unus est homo, ita Deus et homo unus est Christus :

34. Serm. 186.—Idem Deus qui homo, et qui Deus idem homo, non confusione naturæ sed unitate personæ.

35. *In Ioh. Tract.* 78.—Sicut enim unus est homo anima rationalis et caro sic unus est Christus Deus et homo.

36. qui passus est pro salute nostra, descendit ad inferna, resurrexit a mortuis,

37. ascendit ad cœlos, sedet ad dexteram Patris : inde uenturus indicare uiuos et mortuos,

38. ad cuius aduentum omnes homines resurgere habent cum corporibus suis et reddituri sunt de factis propriis rationem.

39. Et qui bona egerunt ibunt in uitam æternam, qui uero mala in ignem æternam.

40. Hæc est fides catholica, quam nisi quisque fideliter firmiterque crediderit, saluus esse non poterit.

36. *Ep.* 164.—Quis ergo, nisi infidelis negauerit fuisse apud inferos Christum ? . . . antequam dominus in inferna descenderet.

40. Serm. 205.—Cauete, dilectissimi, ne quis uos ab ecclesiæ catholicæ fide ac unitate seducat. Qui enim uobis aliter euangelizauerit præter quam quod accepistis, anathema sit.

APPENDIX A

VINCENTIUS—*contd.*
c. 20.—Uerbum Deus absque ulla sui conuersione . . . non confundendo, non imitando factus est homo, sed subsistendo . . . in se perfecti hominis suscipiendo naturam.
34. c. 19.—Unus autem non . . . diuinitatis et humanitatis confusione sed . . . unitate personae.
35. c. 20.—(Igitur) sicut anima connexa carni nec in carnem uersa, non imitatur hominem, sed est homo, . . . ita etiam Uerbum Deus . . . uniendo se homini . . . factus est homo, . . . et ex duabus substantiis unus est Christus.

FAUSTUS, EUCHERIUS—*contd.*

35. Faustus, *Ep.* 7.—Nos uero . . . in Christum ita perfecta et inseparabili distinctione credamus ut Dei et hominis simplicem personam et duplicem nouerimus esse substantiam, sicut anima et corpus hominem facit, ita diuinitas et humanitas unus est Christus.
Cf. Claudianus Mamercus, *de Statu Animae*, i. 3.

37. Eucherius, *Lib. Formul.*—Secundum corpus sepultus est, secundum uero animam in inferna descendit.
38. Faustus (Euseb.), *Hom.* I., *de Ascensione.*—(Anima) resumere proprii corporis desideret indumentum.

APPENDIX B

VIGILIUS OF THAPSUS

THERE is some hope that the mist of obscurity which has hung round the life of Vigilius of Thapsus, and rendered doubtful the authenticity of the works attributed to him, will soon vanish. I have already referred to the article in which Morin [1] has endeavoured to trace the books on the Trinity to an Italian theologian. And the excellent monograph by Ficker [2] has begun the work of collecting new MSS., and of sifting the materials already gathered by Chifflet. Under these circumstances, it seems best to collect the parallels to the *Quicunque* in an additional Appendix, and await further developments of criticism before attempting to analyse them fully.

At the same time, it must be pointed out that the internal evidence of these Vigilian writings is against the theory that their author, or one of their authors, could have written the *Quicunque*. In the books against Eutyches the phrase *unitas personæ* is not found, though the writer speaks of *unio*.[3] The descent into hell is expressed in the form, "Descendit ad (in) infernum."

The Double Procession is not clearly asserted, cf. *de Trin.* xi.: "Ut ipse idem sit Spiritus Sanctus procedens a Patre qui est et Filii." To use Waterland's words, "there does not appear in Vigilius's pieces anything of that strength, closeness, and acuteness which we find in the Athanasian Creed."

It is probable that the creed obtained its connexion

[1] *Rev. Bén.* 1898.
[2] Halle, 1897.
[3] Le Quien, *Dissert. Damasc.* p. 10.

with the name of Athanasius through association in some MS., e.g. the *Codex Thuaneus*, quoted by Waterland [1] from Quesnel, with a Vigilian treatise written under that name. I may note the following parallels :—

Clause 3, c. *Arr. Sabell. Phot.* iii. 11 : " Probabilis igitur et omni ueritatis adsertione subnixa, utpote apostolicis traditionibus communita, ex eorum ueniens regulis Athanasii fides apparuit. Euidentius namque nobis secundum normam fidei catholicæ unum Deum ostendit, non tripertitum, non singularem, non confusum, non divisum, . . . sed ita Patrem et Filium et Spiritum Sanctum propriis exstare atque distingui personis, ut tamen secundum communis naturæ unionem unus sit Deus."

Ib. iii. 9 : " Ac si Trinitas unus Deus est secundum naturæ unionem, et unus Deus Trinitas est secundum personarum distinctionem."

c. Pallad. : " Perfecta Trinitas in Unitate consistens."

5. *De Trin.* ii. : " Alius est Pater in persona qui uere genuit, et in hoc alter est Filius."

[1] P. 82.

APPENDIX C

FULGENTIUS OF RUSPE

THE writings of Fulgentius of Ruspe (+533), Bishop of Ruspe in North Africa, contain many parallels to the *Quicunque*. There is no distinct evidence of quotation, unless we accept Kattenbusch's [1] suggestion that the forty chapters in which Fulgentius treats of the parts of true faith in his *de Fide ad Petrum* are moulded on the forty clauses of the creed. This seems very far-fetched, and the way in which the phraseology of Augustine is weakened is unlike the language of the creed.

Thus *ad Ferr. Ep.* xiv.: "Cum una sit naturaliter sempiterna uirtus ac diuinitas Patris et Filii et Spiritus Sancti. . . . Nec tamen tres Dii sed unus naturaliter Deus est Pater et Filius et Spiritus Sanctus. Omnipotens est Pater sed omnipotens est Filius omnipotens est Spiritus Sanctus; nec tamen tres Dii omnipotentes sed unus Deus omnipotens est Pater et Filius et Spiritus Sanctus. Æternus est sine initio Pater, æternus est sine initio Filius, æternus est sine initio Spiritus Sanctus; nec tamen tres Dii æterni sed unus Deus æternus est Pater et Filius et Spiritus Sanctus. Immensus est Pater sed immensus est Filius et immensus est Spiritus Sanctus: nec tamen tres Dii immensi sed unus Deus immensus est Pater et Filius et Spiritus Sanctus." In this passage there are obvious parallels to clauses 15, 14, 13, 9, but the reversed order seems to imply that the writer was quoting current theological phrases rather than the creed. It is true that he deserts his teacher Augustine in the matter of the term *substantia*,—*Obj. Arr.*: "nec personas

[1] *Theol. Lit. Zeit.* 1897, p. 540.

confundere nec substantiam separare,"—thus accepting the creed's phrase. And we find him using the language, *ad Tras.* iii.: "(Christi) in quo perfectus homo plenus est gratiæ, et in quo perfectus Deus plenus est ueritatis," which is closer to clause 30 than any sentence in Augustine. But if he knew the creed, at any rate it seemed to need further pointing by the insertion of such words as *naturaliter, e.g. Ep. ad Cor.* I. xii.: "Spiritus Sanctus qui naturaliter a Patre Filioque procedit." Cf. *ad Ferr. Ep.* xiv.: "Sanctam et ineffabilem Trinitatem unum esse naturaliter Deum."

APPENDIX D—

ENTIRE TEXTS

Ref. No.	Text.	Title.	Date.
C	Cod. Corbeiensis, S. Germain 257.	F. S. Ath. Epi.	790
P_1	B.N. Paris, Cod. lat. 13,159.		795
P_3	B.N. Paris, 1451.	F. C. S. Ath. Epi. Alex.	795
Y	Golden Psalter (Vienna).	F. S. Ath. Epi. Alex.	867
Q	Psalter of Fulco.	F. C.	c. 850
D	Psalter of Charles the Bald.	F. S. Ath.	c. 850
E	Utrecht Psalter.	F. C.	c. 830
K	Cod. Augiensis ccxxix. (Karlsruhe).		821
Orl.	Lyons MS. Orleans Cod. 94.		c. 800 c. 850
G_1	Cod. Sangall. 20.	F. C. S. A. Epi.	c. 820
B	Milan O. 212 sup.		c. 700

—APPENDIX D

TESTIMONIES

Date.	Province.	Diocese.	Testimony.	Title.
892	Cologne.	Liège.	Regino of Prum.	Sermo Ath. de F. S. Trin.
889	Rheims.	Soissons.	Riculfus.	Sermo F. C.
880	Rome.	Tarentum?	SynodusOrientana.	F. C.
870	Rheims.	Morinum.	Adalbert.	Sermo b. Ath.
868	,,	Rheims.	Ratramn of Corbey.	Libellus de F. b. Ath. Alex. cp̄i.
868	Sens.	Paris.	Æneas.	F. C. S. Ath. Epi. Alex.
865	Hamburg, Bremen.	Hamburg, Bremen.	Anskar.	F. C. a b. Ath.
859	Rheims.	Rheims.	Hincmar—	
			i. *De Prædest.*	C. F.
852			ii. *Capitula.*	Sermo Ath. de Fide.
848			iii. *De u. non t. deitate.*	C. F.
			iv. Pastoral.	Sermo C. F.
836	Mainz (Moguntia).	(?)	Haito of Reichenau.	F. S. Ath.
834	Lyons.	Lyons.	Florus Diaconus.	F. C.
821	Sens.	Orleans.	Benedict d' Aniane.	F. C.
820	Lyons.	Lyons.	Agobard, *adv. Dogm. Fel.*	F. C. (b. Ath. ait.).
	Sens.	Orleans.	Theodulf—	
			i. Address to Clergy.	C. F.
			ii. *De Spu. Sco.*	Symbolum Ath.[1]
810	Mainz.	S. Gallen.	Sermon.	
800	Milan.	Bobbio.	Libellus de Trin.	

---

[1] Loofs, art. "Athanasianum," *R.E.*[3] p. 178, thinks the text of this passage faulty, and calls attention to Sirmond's note on this passage (M.S.L. 105, 247).

APPENDIX E

MSS. OF THE *TE DEUM*

THE following is a provisional list of the more important MSS. of the *Te Deum*. I have affixed symbols to those which have been recently collated:—

I. IRISH VERSION.

			S.ÆC.
A	Milan	Cod. Ambros. C. 5 *inf.*	vii.
F	Dublin	Franciscan Convent, *Lib. Hymnorum*	xi.
H	London	Brit. Mus. Harleian MS. 7653	viii., ix.
T	Dublin	Trin. Coll. *Cod.* E. 4. 2.	xi.

II. MILAN VERSION.

			S.ÆC.
V_1	Rome	*Cod. Vat. Reg.* 11	vii.
V_2	Rome	*Cod. Vat.* 82	x.
M	Munich	*Cod. lat.* 343	x.
Mil.	Milan	Cathedral Breviary	xi.

III. ORDINARY VERSION.

			S.ÆC.
K	Cambridge	Univ. Lib. Ll. 1. 10	viii., ix.
L	Cambridge	Corpus Christi Coll. 272. 0. 5	ix.
	Essen	Münster Kirche (Psalter)	ix.
Lam.	London	Lambeth, 427	ix.
B_1	London	Brit. Mus. Galba A. xviii.	ix.
	Munich	Cod. S. Emmeran lxvii.	viii., ix.

APPENDIX E

III. ORDINARY VERSION—*contd.*

			SÆC.
W	Paris	B.N. *Cod. lat.* 1152	ix.
	Rheims	*Cod.* 20	ix.
	Troyes	(Psalter of Count Henry)	ix.
G$_{1, 2, 3, 4}$	S. Gallen	*Codd.* 15, 20, 23, 27	ix.
U	Utrecht	Psalter (Claudius, C. vii.)	ix.
V	Vienna	*Cod.* 1861	ix.
	Würzburg	*Cod.* Mp. th. f. 109	ix.
		Psalter of Lothaire	ix.

IV. GREEK VERSION.

			SÆC.
	Essen	Münster Kirche	ix.
G	S. Gallen	*Cod.* 17	ix.
B$_2$	Bamberg	*Cod.* A. i. 14	x.
C	Cologne	*Cod.* 8	ix., x.

APPENDIX F

CREED OF THE "DIDASCALIA"

IT may be of interest to add the following Creed, which has been conjecturally restored by Zahn[1] from the *Didascalia*. The book was written in the third century, probably not far from Antioch. Zahn calls attention, in the first place, to a passage which follows a free reproduction of Acts xv.: "Since danger has arisen lest the whole Church should fall into heresy, we Twelve Apostles assembled together in Jerusalem and discussed what should be done, and it pleased us all to write with one accord this Catholic *Didascalia*, for the confirmation of you all, and we established and determined that you should pray to *God* [the Father] *the Almighty, and Jesus* [His Son] *Christ, and the Holy Spirit*, and use the Holy Scriptures, and believe in the resurrection of the dead, and enjoy all creatures with thanksgiving." There is no trace here of Western influence, yet we find a Trinitarian Creed traced back to an Apostolic Council. This renders it probable that the legend of apostolic origin came to Rufinus from the East, where he would feel more at home than at Rome. S. Ambrose also was dependent on Greek literature. The conjectural character of Zahn's form makes me unwilling to found any argument on it at present.

[1] *Neuere Beiträge zur Geschichte des apost. Symbolums*, p. 23.

THE CREED OF THE "DIDASCALIA"

I. 1. Πιστεύω εἰς Θεὸν παντοκράτορα,
II. 2. Καὶ εἰς τὸν κύριον ἡμῶν Ἰησοῦν Χριστὸν (τὸν υἱὸν αὐτοῦ ?), τὸν (δι᾽ ἡμᾶς ἐλθόντα καὶ)
3. γεννηθέντα ἐκ (Μαρίας τῆς ?) παρθένου
4. καὶ σταυρωθέντα ἐπὶ Ποντίου Πιλάτου καὶ ἀποθανόντα,
5. τῇ τρίτῃ ἡμέρᾳ ἀναστάντα ἐκ (τῶν ?) νεκρῶν
6. καὶ ἀναβάντα (ἀνελθόντα ?) εἰς τοὺς οὐρανοὺς
7. καὶ καθήμενον ἐκ δεξιῶν Θεοῦ τοῦ παντοκράτορος,
8. καὶ ἐρχόμενον μετὰ δυνάμεως καὶ δόξης, κρῖναι νεκροὺς καὶ ζῶντας.
III. 9. Καὶ εἰς τὸ ἅγιον πνεῦμα . . .
10. (ἁγίαν ἐκκλησίαν ?) . . .
12. νεκρῶν ἀνάστασιν. . . .

INDEX

Abbo, 182, 259, 276.
Abelard, 183.
Abundius, 260.
Acacius, 87, 91, 94.
Ado, 117.
Adoptianism, 167 f., 177.
Ælfric, 117, 183.
Æthelstan, Psalter of, 199.
Aetius, 108, 113.
Agobard, 178.
Alcuin, 173, 176 seq.
Alexander, 80.
Amalarius, 183.
Ambrose, S., 20, 70, 77, 126, 138, 143, 203, 205 f., 208, 219, 252, 258 ff., 275, 285 f.
Anomœans, The, 91 f., 96.
Antelmi, 135.
Apelles, 55.
Apollinaris, 100, 106 f., 112, 125, 139 ; heresy of, 169, 247.
Apostles' Creed, The, 1, 8, 12, 286 f.
Apostolic Constitutions, The, 87, 266 ff.
Aquinas, 20.
Aristides, 30, 40 f.
Arius, 74 f., 77, 81 f., 169, 291 ; heresy of, 96, 126, 203, 206 ff., 232, 288, 295.
Asterius, 86 f.
Athanasius, S., 48, 69, 76, 80, 82, 85 f., 87, 91, 94 f., 97, 99 f., 101 f., 104, 114, 120 f., 123 f., 125 f., 130, 136, 139, 176 f., 179, 183, 215, 266, 295.
Attalus, 153.
Attila, 201.
Augustine of Canterbury, S., 243.
Augustine of Hippo, S., 44, 62, 70, 122, 124-128, 133, 136 f., 140, 146, 170, 173, 178, 182, 188, 205, 208 f., 235, 258 ff., 275, 281, 285, 295 f.
Auitus, 116, 150, 181 f.
Aurelian, 257.
Autun, Canon of, *156* f.

Bäumer, Dom. S., *31*, 63, 232.
Balfour, Right Hon. A. J., 288.
Bangor Antiphonary, 187, 189, 257, 266, 269, 273, 275 f., 279.
Baptismal Formula, The, 9, *20-25*, 33 ff., 64, 70.
Basil of Ancyra, 92, 94 f.
Basil of Cæsarea, S., 95, 99, 101, 105, 110, 262.
Bede, Ven., 286.
Benedict d'Aniane, 176.
Benedict of Nursia, S., 119, 257.
Benson, Archbishop, 23, 294.
Bernard of Clairvaux, S., 183.
Bernard, Prof. T. H., 259, 261.
Boniface, 162.
Bonn Conference, The, 123.
Bornemann, Prof., 39.
Bourdon, Abbé, 252.
Bratke's Berne MS., 63, 229, 241.
Bright, Prof., 96.
Brightman, Rev. F. E., 267, 269.
Butler, Bishop, 291.

Cælestine, Pope, 111.
Cæsarius, 148, *151-153*, 160, 179, 181 f., 188, 249, 250 f., 257, 290.
Cajetan, John (Gelasius II.), 249.
Callistus, 59, 61.
Candidus, 274.
Canon of Scripture, The, 53.
Cappadocian Fathers, The, 116, 126.
Capreolus, 136.
Carlyle, Thomas, 291.
Caspari, Prof., *passim*.
Cassian, 229, 249, 285.
Cassiodorus, 249, 263.
Charlemagne, 177, 186.
Childebert I., King, 230.
Chlodosinda, 159.
Chrysologus, 230, 281.
Chrysostom, S., 111.
Clarke, Dr. S., 96.
Clement of Rome, S., 26 f., 61, 64.

Columban, S., 152 f.
Commentaries on the *Quicunque vult*:
  Bouhier, 164, 170.
  Fortunatus, 160 f., 168, 180 f., 187.
  Oratorian, 165, 170.
  Orleans, 163, 166.
  Paris, 164.
  Rolle of Hampole, 167.
  Stavelot, 163, 167 f.
  Theodulf, 166.
  Troyes, 166 f., 171.
Constans, Emp., 90 f., 203.
Constantine, Copronymus, Emp., 117.
Constantine the Great, Emp., 66, 76.
Constantius, Emp., 91, 100.
Cotton, Bishop, 295.
Councils of Aachen in 809, 118.
  ,, Agde in 506, 278.
  ,, Alexandria in 362, 98–101, 126.
  ,, Antioch in 329, 82.
  ,, Antioch in 341, 83.
  ,, Antioch in 378, 107.
  ,, Aquileia in 382, 206.
  ,, Cæsarea, Forged Acts of, 241.
  ,, Caria in 367, 86.
  ,, Chalcedon in 451, 110–114.
  ,, Constantinople in 381, 107, 109, 121.
  ,, Ephesus in 430, 111.
  ,, Frankfort in 794, 118, 164, 175.
  ,, Friuli in 791, 117.
  ,, Gentilly in 767, 117.
  ,, Hethfield in 680, 117, 159.
  ,, Laodicea in 360, 262.
  ,, Milan, 285.
  ,, Rome in 369, 107.
  ,, Sardica in 344, 90.
  ,, Seleucia in 357, 86.
  ,, Sirmium in 357, 91.
  ,, Toledo in 447, 117.
  ,, Toledo in 589, 114, 117, 119.
  ,, Toledo in 633, 153.
Creeds:
  Antioch, Second Creed of, 83–85, 86, 94.
  Antioch, Third Creed of, 87.
  Antioch, Fourth Creed of, 86, 87–89, 91, 203.
  Antioch in 344, Creed of, 90.
  Antiochenes, Union Creed of the, 139.
  Apostles' Creed, Our, 221–240.
  Apostolic Constitutions, 105.
  Aquileia, 57, 201.
  Ariminum, of Orthodox at, 214 f., 219.
  Athanasian Creed, The, 124–197, 289–295.

Creeds—*contd.*
  Augsburg, Confession of, 155.
  Augustine, 209–213.
  Auscultate expositionem, 179, 243.
  Bacchiarius, 131, 138, 144, 181, 222.
  Bangor Antiphonary, 60, 228 f., 243.
  Beatus, 255.
  Bratke's Berne MS., 63, 241 ff.
  Cæsarius, 224 f., 239.
  Constantinople, 203.
  Constantinople in 525, 114.
  Constantinople in 553, 114.
  Cyprian of Carthage, 48, 209, 283 f.
  Cyprian of Toulon, 225 f.
  Damasus, 130, 153 f., 181, 216, 244–243.
  Dated Creed, 92 ff.
  Didascalia, The, Appendix F.
  Deer, Book of, 63.
  Denebert, 161, 172, 174 ff.
  Dionysius, 46.
  Eastern and Western compared, 70, 287.
  Egyptian Church Order, 69.
  Eligius of Noyon, 227.
  Etherius, 255.
  Eusebius of Cæsarea, 77–80.
  Faustus, 222 ff., 226.
  Fides Romanorum, 129, 161, 168, 177, 215–219.
  Gelasian Sacramentary, 231 f.
  Gregory Thaumaturgus, 72.
  Gregory of Tours, 227.
  Hincmar, 130.
  Ildefonsus, 255.
  Isidore, 154 f.
  Jerusalem, 34, 98, 101–106, 119, 254.
  Leporius, 132 f., 139 ff.
  Lucianic Creed, The, 83, 86, 90.
  Martin of Bracara, 60, 254 f.
  Mesopotamia, 105 f.
  Missale Gallicanum, 221, 229, 234 f., 236, 239 f., 244.
  Mozarabic Liturgy, 214, 255.
  Munich Cod. lat. 14508, 63, 160.
  Nicene Council, 76–80, 99, 104, 110, 119.
  Our Nicene Creed, 7, 98 seq., 102, 103, 110, 203, 286 ff., 288.
  Niceta, 62, 205, 239, 252–255.
  Niké, 94, 203.
  Novatian, 46.
  Pelagius, 138, 139 f., 228.
  Philippopolis in 343, 90.
  Phœbadius of Agen, 129, 205, 214–220.

INDEX

Creeds—*contd.*
  Priscillian, 214.
  Ps.-Augustine, Serm. 238, 62.
  Old Roman Creed, 21, 33, 45, 198.
  Sacramentarium Gallicanum, 60, 221, 229, 234 f., 236, 238 ff.
  Salvianus, 222.
  Cod. Sessorian., 52, 63, 237 ff.
  Sirmium in 351, 90.
  Sirmium in 357, Second Creed of, 214.
  Sirmium in 359, Dated Creed of, 92–94, 95, 203 f.
  Turin, 230.
  Victricius, 214, 218 f.
Cursus Leoninus, 249.
Cyprian of Carthage, S., 22, 48, 123, 209, 220, 248, 262, 283 f.
Cyprian of Toulon, 219, 257, 276.
Cyril of Alexandria, S., 111, 113, 137.
Cyril of Jerusalem, S., 6C–69, 99, 107 f., 110, 113 f., 120, 203 f., 220, 253, 281, 284 f.

DAMASUS, Pope, 107 *seq.*, 113, 143, 252.
Dante, 249.
Delisle, M. L., 173.
Didaché, The, 21, 30.
Didascalia, The, 87, 90, Appendix F.
Dido, 177.
Diodorus, 261.
Diogenes, 112.
Dionysius, 46 ff.
Docetism, 204.
Dracontius, 97.
Duchesne, Abbé, 108, 122, 209, 219.

EGBERT, 286.
Elchasaites, The, 22.
Eligius of Noyon, 188.
Elipandus, 118.
Emerson, Ralph Waldo, 291.
Epiphanius, 45, 87, 92, 102, 104 f., 109 f., 113, 116, 170.
Eucherius, 135, 252.
Eunomius, 113.
Euphronius, 169, 170.
Eusebius of Cæsarea, 75, 82, 86, 170.
Eusebius of Nicomedia, 75, 77, 79 ff., 83.
Eustathius of Antioch, 78, 100.
Eutyches, 113, 140; heresy of, 169, 188.

FAITH, 3.
Faustus, 62, 127, 135, 148 f., 182, 222, 286, 290.
Felix of Urgel, 167 f.
Firmilian, 283.
Flavianus, 109, 261.

Florianus, 160.
Fortunatus, Venantius, 159, 171, 201.
Fulgentius, 212, Appendix C.

GELASIAN Sacramentary, The, 166, 234, 250, 284.
Gennadius, 181, 253, 261, 263 f.
Germanus, 219.
Gibbon, 97.
Gibson, Dr., 274, 277 f.
Gloria in excelsis, The, 265–270, 278.
Gnostics, The, 25, 43.
Goldast, 168 *seq.*
Goulburn, Dean, 293.
Gregory the Great, S., Pope, 119, 231, 277.
Gregory III., Pope, 233, 239.
Gregory Nazianzen, S., 99, 108, 110.
Gregory of Nyssa, S., 75, 99, 108, 110.
Gregory of Tours, 171, 182, 188.
Gwatkin, Prof., 82, 91, 100.

HADRIAN, Pope, 118.
Haito, 176.
Harnack, Prof., 5, 25 f., 32, 43, 109, 121, 128, 173.
Harris, Prof. Rendel, 40.
Harvey, 147.
Haussleiter, Prof., 17 f., 20.
Hermas, 55, 61, 64.
Heurtley, Prof., 211, 213.
Hilary of Arles, 135, 148, 276.
Hilary of Poitiers, S., 83, 86, 92, 99, 116, 121, 125, 127, 129, 134, 143, 259 f., 296.
Hilsey, 184.
Hincmar, 119, 157, 173 ff., 176, 215, 258.
Hippolytus, 59 ff.
Homœanism, 121.
Honoratus, 135, 147 ff., 276.
Honorius of Autun, 183.
Hook, Dean, 291.
Hooker, Richard, 295.
Hort, Prof., 104 ff., 114.
Hosius of Cordova, 75, 78.
Hunter, Sir W., 292.

IGNATIUS, S., 10, 28, 31, 38, 68, 73.
Illingworth, Rev. J. R., 6, 128, 296.
Innocent I., Pope, 130, 253.
Irenæus, S., 17 f., 25, *41–44*, 53, 55, 61 ff., 73, 209, 219, 282.

JEROME, S., 64, 100, 109, 205, 215, 244, 248, 252, 285.
John, Abbot of Biclaro, 115.
John Damascene, 123.
John of Jerusalem, 64.

INDEX

Julian, Emp., 101.
Julius Africanus, 170.
Julius of Rome, 83, 106.
Justinian, Emp., 114 f., 159.
Justin Martyr, 15, 21, 30, *35–40*, 43, 62 f., 65, 282.

KATTENBUSCH, Prof. F., *on Jerusalem Creed*, 68 ; *on Second Creed of Antioch*, 86 ; *on Creed of Constantinople*, 110 *et passim*.
Kingsley, Rev. Charles, 289, 295.
Kunze, Prof., 111.

LAGARDE, 267.
Leidrad, 173 f., 178, 191.
Leo I., Pope, S., 70, 113, 230.
Leo III., Pope, 118 f., 186.
Leodgar, 156.
Leontius, 262.
Lerius, Monastery of, 134, 289.
Libellus de Trinitate, 160.
Liberii Gesta, 161, 215.
Lightfoot, Bishop, 28, 30, 294.
Liturgy of S. James, 272.
Loofs, Prof., 80, 155, 178–181.
Louis II., Emp., 233.
Lucas, Father H., 184.
Lucian, 74, 86 f.
Lucifer of Cagliari, 101.
Lumby, Prof., 172, 213.
Lupus, 135, 219.

MACARIUS, 78.
Macedonius, 107, 112 ; heresy of, 110, 112, 269.
Marcellus, 44 f., 56, 68, 78, 81 f., 86, 90 ff., 199.
Marcianus, 253.
Marcion, 24, 44, 52 ff., 283.
Marcus Aurelius, Emp., 35.
Marcus Eremita, 112.
Mark of Arethusa, 92, 203.
Martin of Bracara, 204.
Maxentius, 143.
Maximus of Geneva, 225, 257.
Maximus the Philosopher, 97.
Maximus of Turin, 205 f., 230.
Meletians in Egypt, The, 81.
Meletius, 101, 108.
Melito, 30.
Miracles, 2.
Missale Gallicanum, 270 ; *vide Creeds*.
Missale Gothicum, 270, 274 ; *vide Creeds*.
Mocquéreau, Dom., 252.
Monarchianism, 58–61, 63.
Monothelitism, 166, 169.
Montanism, 59.
Mora, Albert de (Gregory VIII.), 249.

Morin, Dom. G., *on Cod. Sessor. 52*, 161, 232 ; *on Niceta of Remesiana*, 253 ; *on the authorship of the* " *Te Deum*," 256 seq.

NECTARIUS, 109, 111.
Nestorius, 111, 139 ff.; *heresy of*, 167 f., 169.
Newman, Cardinal J. H., 289.
Niceta of Remesiana, 107, 125, 252 *scq.*, 259 *seq.*, 269, 286.
Nicetas of Aquileia, 254.
Nicetius of Trèves, 159 f., 261.
Nicholas I., Pope, 119, 232 f.
Nilus, 111.
Notker, 163.
Novatian, 47, 60, 62 f., 283.

ODILO, 163.
Odoacer, 232.
Ommanney, Preb., 135, 137, 141, 147, 162, 164, 166 f., 183, 185, 188 f.
Origen, 73, 81, 85 f., 122, 205.
Orosius, 143.

PASTOR, 116.
Patrick, S., 229, 275.
Paul of Samosata, 81, 86.
Paulinus of Antioch, 100 f., 109.
Paulinus of Aquileia, 117 f., 168, 176, 178.
Paulinus of Nola, 130, 252 f., 263.
Paulinus of Tyre, 79.
Peter Fullo, 114.
Pelagius I., Pope, 230.
Pelagius, heretic, 218 f.
Philostorgius, 87.
Photinus, 92.
Photius, 119.
Pirminius, 221, 233 f., 238 f.
Polycarp, 28 f., 41, 61.
Pomerius, 249.
Praxeas, 54, 58 f.
Priscillian, 142–145, 247 f.
Priscillianists, The, 117.
Procession Controversy, The, 115 *seq.*, 169.
Proclus, 111 f.
Prudentius, 258.
Ps.-Gennadius *de Fide*, 160.
Ps.-Ignatius, 267 f.

RABANUS Maurus, 176.
Rade, Dr., 109.
Ratramn, 119, 157, 173.
Reccared, 114 f.
Redditio symboli, 52, 281.
Regino, 183.
Rhythm of *Te Deum* and *Quicunque*, 248–252.

INDEX

Robertson, Dr., 10, 74, 78, 86, 95, 100.
Robinson, Prof. J. A., 40.
Rufinus, 45, 46, 47, 57, 200 f., 204 f., 207 f., 285.

SABELLIUS, 59, 169, 203.
Sacramentarium Gallicanum, 270 ff.; vide Creeds.
Salvianus, 134, 222.
Secundus, 80.
Seeberg, Prof., 43, 128.
Semi-Arians, The, 92, 95, 99 f., 110, 121 ff.
Semi-Pelagianism, 290.
Shelly, Mr. J., 248 ff.
Siricius, Pope, 206.
Sisebut, 260.
Socrates, historian, 86, 112.
Sozomen, 86.
Stephen, Bishop of Rome, 23.
Sulpicius Severus, 95, 252 f.
Swainson, Prof., 113, 135, 175 ff.
Swete, Prof., 27, 63, 204.

TARASIUS, 118.
Terentianus Maurus, 249.
Tertullian, 38, 48–58, 61–65, 73, 127, 282 f.
Theodosius, Emp., 108.
Theodotus, 59.
Theodulf, 163 f., 165 f., 177.
Theological Creeds, Of, 72–74.
Theonas, 80.
Theophronius, 87.

Thompson, Sir E. Maunde, 241, 253.
Timothy, S., 14–17.
Timothy, Bishop of Constantinople, 114.
Traditio symboli, 281.
Trèves Fragment, The, 157–160, 172, 174, 178 f.

ULPHILAS, 107, 125.
Urban II., Pope, 249.
Ursacius, 81.
Ussher, Archbishop, 45, 259.

VALENS, Bishop, 81, 91 f.
Valens, Emp., 95, 101, 107.
Valentinus, 53, 63, 112.
Victor, 59.
Victorius, 241.
Victricius, 116, 130, 146 f., 229.
Vigilius of Thapsus, 69, 157, 215, Appendix B.
Vincentius, 135 f., 137 f., 146 ff., 166, 173, 182, 188, 258.
Voss, 168, 259.

WALAFRID Strabo, 176.
Warren, Rev. F. E., 275, 278.
Waterland, Dr., 145, 149.
Westcott, Bishop, 3, 18, 26.
Wyclif, 184.

ZAHN, Prof. Theod., 7, 9, 12, 17, 30, 54, 56 f., 65, 107, 204, 270.
Zephyrinus, 59, 61.

www.ingramcontent.com/pod-product-compliance
Lightning Source LLC
Chambersburg PA
CBHW021154230426
43667CB00006B/390